CW01151971

OXFORD CLASSICAL MONOGRAPHS

*Published under the supervision of a Committee of the
Faculty of Classics in the University of Oxford*

The aim of the Oxford Classical Monographs series (which replaces the Oxford Classical and Philosophical Monographs) is to publish books based on the best theses on Greek and Latin literature, ancient history, and ancient philosophy examined by the faculty Board of Classics.

Self-Representation and Illusion in Senecan Tragedy

C. A. J. LITTLEWOOD

OXFORD
UNIVERSITY PRESS

OXFORD
UNIVERSITY PRESS

Great Clarendon Street, Oxford OX2 6DP
Oxford University Press is a department of the University of Oxford.
It furthers the University's objective of excellence in research, scholarship,
and education by publishing worldwide in
Oxford New York
Auckland Bangkok Buenos Aires Cape Town Chennai
Dar es Salaam Delhi Hong Kong Istanbul Karachi Kolkata
Kuala Lumpur Madrid Melbourne Mexico City Mumbai Nairobi
São Paulo Shanghai Taipei Tokyo Toronto

Oxford is a registered trade mark of Oxford University Press
in the UK and in certain other countries

Published in the United States
by Oxford University Press Inc., New York

© Cedric Littlewood 2004

The moral rights of the author have been asserted
Database right Oxford University Press (maker)

First published 2004

All rights reserved. No part of this publication may be reproduced,
stored in a retrieval system, or transmitted, in any form or by any means,
without the prior permission in writing of Oxford University Press,
or as expressly permitted by law, or under terms agreed with the appropriate
reprographics rights organization. Enquiries concerning reproduction
outside the scope of the above should be sent to the Rights Department,
Oxford University Press, at the address above

You must not circulate this book in any other binding or cover
and you must impose this same condition on any acquirer

British Library Cataloguing in Publication Data
Data available

Library of Congress Cataloging in Publication Data
Data available

ISBN 0-19-926761-8

1 3 5 7 9 10 8 6 4 2

Kolam Information Services Pvt. Ltd, Pondicherry, India
Printed in Great Britain
on acid-free paper by
Biddles Ltd, King's Lynn.

Acknowledgements

THIS book is a revision of an Oxford doctoral thesis. I would like to thank the British Academy for a research grant, St Hugh's College for a Jubilee Scholarship, and both Queen's and St Hugh's Colleges for giving me a temporary home. I thank also for their support the universities and departments which have employed me: Birmingham, Maynooth, and especially now Victoria. I am grateful for the direction and patience of my advisers and examiners, of the Oxford Classical Monographs Committee, and of Lucy Qureshi and her colleagues at Oxford University Press.

More people than I can acknowledge here have helped me, but I would like to single out the following. Angus Bowie, a graduate adviser and also my undergraduate teacher, first made me feel that I could participate in an academic discussion. Robin Nisbet was my first doctoral supervisor and I would like to thank him for his valuable criticism and most particularly for the kindness with which it was given. Don Fowler was for me an adviser, an examiner, and an enormously busy man who yet tried hard to further my career without much assistance from me. Peta Fowler very kindly allowed me to read some of Don's unpublished work on Seneca and so I continue to benefit from his guidance. Thank you also to Elena Theodorakopoulos, Paul Smith, Ken Dowden, and Matthew Fox in Birmingham for their advice and encouragement. I have been fortunate in Victoria to have John Fitch, author of the forthcoming new Loeb edition of the tragedies, as a colleague. I am particularly grateful that he has allowed me to use his excellent and soon-to-be-published translations throughout this book. Honesty compels me to admit that Joy Bithell, Eva Bullard, Richael MacLaverty, and Luke Roman have all helped me at some stage with German or Italian. I would also like to thank my parents, both classicists, both readers of parts of my work and my earliest Latin teachers. Michael Comber first taught me Senecan tragedy when I was an undergraduate, inspired me to write a thesis on the subject, supervised most of the doctorate and all of this book, and still teaches me now. I'm not sure why he should want what he has been forced to read all too often, but this book is dedicated to him nevertheless.

C. A. J. L.

Contents

1. Introduction ... 1
2. The Broken World ... 15
   1. Stoicism and the Locus of Moral Conflict ... 18
   2. Vice and Virtue in a Broken World ... 25
   3. Irony and Lies ... 36
   4. Stichomythia and Paradox ... 40
   5. Ambiguity and Alienation ... 47
   6. The Dramatic World ... 57
   7. Conflicting Perspectives ... 70
   8. Dramatic Reality and Conflicting Perspectives in *Troades* ... 90
3. Images of a Flawed Technical Genesis ... 103
   1. *Hercules Furens* ... 107
   2. *Thyestes* ... 127
   3. *Medea* ... 148
4. Meta-Theatre and Self-Consciousness ... 172
   1. Viewing, Acting, Power ... 175
   2. Viewing, Gender, Power ... 194
   3. Models of Audience Response ... 209
   4. The Development of a Sadistic Spectatorship ... 215
   5. Modelling an Ambivalent Spectatorship ... 240
5. *Phaedra*: Intertextuality and Innocence ... 259
   1. Hippolytus' Hunting Song ... 269

References ... 302

Index of Passages ... 315

General Index ... 325

I

Introduction

ALTHOUGH the influence of Senecan tragedy on Renaissance drama assures it a place in the history of Western theatre its own roots and its own traditions are less sure. Fragmentary plays, some material evidence, and the discussions of ancient critics are all that span the centuries from Sophocles to Seneca. Senecan tragedy springs up fully formed and so different from its Attic precursors that modern critics have questioned whether it was or could be staged, whether it is really drama at all. We lack a secure frame of reference, and interpretation of Senecan tragedy varies hugely depending on whether we approach it as a philosopher's poetry, as public theatre, as text to be read in private by a literary and social elite, as Roman imitation of a Greek original, and so on. Genre in particular plays an important role in fixing our frame of reference: as the title of 'drama' is granted and withheld the figure of Euripides and the institution of Attic theatre looms correspondingly larger and smaller in our thoughts.

In this study I speak of actor, audience, and dramatic illusion while myself remaining agnostic on the staging question. However, no critical practice can be truly agnostic and I should state here that the material for my discussion of Seneca's dramatic characters and of his tragic art is almost exclusively literary. Nowhere do I examine, for example, the problems and possibilities of stage production. If I had to say what Senecan tragedy is I would say that it is Neronian literature and hope thereby to emphasize its place in the Roman world and in the corpus of Latin literature. The isolationist Stoic cast of the moralizing is characteristically Neronian, so too the close and frequently destructive engagement with the literary and political rhetoric of Augustus' Golden Age. Lucan, Ovid, Virgil, even Horace have been more important figures for me than any tragedian. It has long since been unacceptable to characterize Seneca simply as an imitator of Euripides and there is no need to fight a battle already won. No one would now deny the centrality of the *Aeneid* in an interpretation of his work. Nevertheless I think that we continue to underestimate how open Senecan tragedy is to the influence of non-dramatic Latin literature and that its generic identity as drama narrows our perspective undesirably. The question, 'Is this real drama or just the outward form of it?' continues to inform our reception of his work. Before summarizing the focus and contents of this book I want briefly to revisit the insoluble staging question, partly to illustrate what lines of interpretation are and have been bound up with it, partly to justify my own critical practice.

There is no direct evidence for the contemporary performance of any of Seneca's tragedies.[1] If debate has sometimes polarized into a choice between dramatic production and recitation-drama, this is a false view of a wide range of possibilities. A tragedy could be acted in private aristocratic houses, in the public theatre, in the forum, in a temple, a circus, or even a bath; it could be performed in entirety or in extract; it could be a sung or spoken accompaniment or interlude in a dance; it could be performed at a variety of different civic and religious events or not; it could be recited by one or more performers with or without gestures and/or costume and masks; it could be recited in a public venue or to a group of friends; it could be read aloud or silently by a lone reader.[2] In the absence of any direct evidence opponents of dramatic production have argued against performability. The sacrifice scene in *Oedipus*

[1] I am indebted here to fuller discussions particularly by Fitch (2000), who offers a survey of scholarship and Kelly (1979). Braun (1983) and Sutton (1986) support staged tragedies, Calder (1976) staged tragedies in private houses, Tanner (1985) assigns different roles to different voices, Zwierlein (1966) and Goldberg (2000) argue for recitation. On Senecan and Roman tragedy as a theatrical civic ritual see Tanner (1985), Dupont (1985), Leigh (1996), Wiseman (1998), Beecham (1999).

[2] Private house (Pliny, *Epistles* 8.12), theatre (Horace, *Satires* 1.10.39, *Epistles* 1.19.41–2, Seneca, *Epistles* 80.7), forum (Cicero, *Philippics* 9.16), temple (Horace, *Satires* 1.10.38), circus and bath (Petronius, *Satyricon* 91–2). Among the best known evidence for Imperial tragedy and its reception is Suetonius' statement (*Nero* 21) that Nero recited tragedies, complete with masks, but taking different parts himself, Tacitus' account (*Dialogus* 3) of the offence Maternus gave with a recitation of his tragedy *Cato*, and Pliny's statement (*Epistles* 7.11–17) that Pomponius Secundus, inverting the usual practice of offering a poem for criticism first to a group of friends before a wider audience, presented his tragedies to the general public and would then make alterations depending on their response. See also Pliny, *Epistles* 9.34. With Senecan tragedy in mind Zwierlein (1966) 161–2 has gathered evidence for the reception of tragedy in Rome. See also Csapo and Slater (1995) 37–8.

(291 ff.) has troubled even defenders of dramatic performance,[3] but without a knowledge of contemporary dramatic conventions we must agree with Walker that 'there really is nothing which can be termed "unstageable" *tout court*, whether on grounds of obscenity, horror or mechanical difficulty'.[4] Tarrant's study of the conventions of Hellenistic and Roman drama makes certain features of Senecan tragedy (notably the behaviour of the chorus) less surprising,[5] but Walker's caution remains salutary. There is also no reason to support one choice against all the others. If Ovid's non-dramatic poetry could be danced and applauded in the theatre (*Fasti* 5.7.25–8), it seems perverse to argue that Senecan tragedy is a literary not a theatrical art form. One could recite the same poem to a single friend or a vast number—and there is a different aesthetic happening in each case, and variation also within the larger audience—but neither mode of reception is canonical. The same holds for Senecan tragedy.[6]

What is at stake here? The distinction between theatrical and literary drama is often read as a distinction between public and private. As declamation can be represented as degenerate oratory, self-absorbed and sterile, robbed of a practical role in public life, so Senecan tragedy can be represented as degenerate drama, lacking either the political and religious significance of Attic tragedy or the freedom of expression of its Republican predecessors.[7] In one variant of the thesis Dupont takes wordless and spectacular pantomime for popular entertainment as paradigmatic of the drama of Imperial Rome.[8] The dumb show figures

---

[3] e.g. Tanner (1985) 1102. Fitch (2000) 11, following his own generally accepted dating scheme for Senecan tragedy (Fitch 1981), speculates that Seneca may have developed from unstaged drama like *Oedipus*—an early play—to full dramatic production in his later plays.

[4] Walker (1969) 186 on Zwierlein. Cf. Zwierlein's dogmatic style, 'Eine solche Szene ist auf der Bühne undenkbar' (1966) 24.

[5] Tarrant (1978). On the chorus see also P. J. Davis (1993).

[6] Kelly (1979) 43 imagines the tragedian writing in expectation of various modes of production. Peta Fowler kindly allowed me to read some of Don Fowler's unpublished work on 'Reading and other forms of reception' in which he addresses the case of Senecan tragedy specifically—I am particularly delighted to have been introduced to Berger (1989) against 'New Histrionicism' (xv).

[7] For the contrast between Imperial oppression and Republican and Attic liberty (or licence) in ancient literary criticism see e.g. Horace, *Satires* 1.4.1–7; Tacitus, *Dialogus* 36–40; Longinus 44.1–11.

[8] Dupont (1985) 389–91 and *passim*. On mime and pantomime at Rome see also Csapo and Slater (1995) 369–89.

and indicates political dissent silenced in the realm of the actor-king. Serious tragedy, the rarefied preserve of a literary and political elite now diminished by the new autocracy, is relegated to the closet of 'drama for reading'. Seneca's tragedies, if produced theatrically, represent a new direction in Imperial drama and bridge the divide between serious and trivial, elite and popular, literary and wordless. But self-consciously they commemorate the new order of things: at the end of *Troades* Greeks and Trojans lose their national distinctions to become a uniform and passive audience, mere spectators of public reality. So too all the emperor's subjects...[9] More recently Goldberg is committed to a politicized distinction between the literary and the spectacular: to perform literate Senecan tragedy in public would have been 'not just redundant but antithetical to its social and aesthetic ends'.[10]

The simple distinction between art for the stage and art for reading is suspect. Not only could the same work of art be presented in different forms but there are many more than two choices of form. Further, the idea that theatregoers could be innocent of literate culture is a nonsense.[11] The literate cannot conveniently forget the *Aeneid* when watching or staging a wordless pantomime of Aeneas' wanderings and the illiterate are indirectly affected by the written text. Those who never read the text and never heard it recited are not miraculously insulated from the interpretations of literate directors and spectators, and from anything touched by those interpretations. Images of Trojan princes in the forum of Augustus and the *Aeneid* are not independent reflections of some pre-existing Julio-Claudian propaganda but two of the elements which constitute it; they are in contact with each other.[12] Performance and reading, Fowler argues, must be seen 'not as polar opposites but as each implicated in the other'.

An argument for a complex dynamic must be advanced also with reference to Seneca's models. The presumption that because

---

[9] Dupont (1985) 461–2 on *Troades* and more generally 419–20 and 434 ff.
[10] Goldberg (2000) 226 (quotation) and 223–7.
[11] Fowler (unpublished) argues the point more fully and with reference also to Greek and Renaissance drama.
[12] This is an argument from coherence of texts (literary and other) and ideologies. There is also an argument from incoherence, strangeness, or 'ungrammaticality' (in the extended sense). Cf. Riffaterre (1980) 136 on the situation of those who, because of a barrier of era, culture, or social class, are unfamiliar with the relevant intertexts. Though they respond differently from those who recognize

Senecan tragedy is drama it looks back primarily within the boundaries of genre to Greek tragedy has been taken to extremes. Attempts have been made for example to reconstruct Euripides' lost Καλυπτόμενος from Seneca's *Phaedra* by comparing it with the surviving Hippolytus play: deviations mark the influence of the lost play. Such 'terrorisme philhellène' as Dupont termed it has been derided more widely[13] but a presumption of Greek influence continues to appear in more measured form. In the most recent book on Senecan tragedy Boyle lists eighteen texts, eleven of them Roman, rewritten in *Troades* but sees no role for the Roman texts beyond a historico-cultural colouring.[14] *Oedipus*, the next study, fares similarly. In Boyle's own words, 'The Sophoclean focus on Oedipus' identity, on the search for and the revelation of truth, and...concern with plot development and the creation of dramatic suspense are removed from Seneca's play' (p. 92), 'The next two acts [2 and 3] completely change the inherited script' (p. 94), 'The final acts rewrite the Sophoclean ending' (p. 95), 'There were many dramatisations of the Oedipus saga between Sophocles and Seneca' (p. 96). In what sense then is Seneca a 'Greek tragedian reconstituted for Rome' (p. 92)?[15] In the introduction to his study of *Phaedra*[16] Segal stresses the differences between Seneca's play and Euripides' (and Athenian tragedy more generally) and emphasizes its community with Ovid, Tacitus' history, and Rome. Although the only points of contact between the Greek and the Roman tragedy seem to be 'the basic plots' (p. 5) and 'the basic situation' (p. 9), Seneca's parricide is still the killing of Euripides: 'The ghost of Euripides haunts every line' (p. 203).

---

the intertexts, nevertheless, '[the "ungrammaticalities"] function as buoys marking the positions of sunken meaning'. If Dido, a woman, killed herself on stage *with a sword*, a cultural ungrammaticality would be recognized (if imperfectly interpreted) by those who had never read Virgil's *Aeneid* and/or Sophocles' *Ajax*.

[13] Dupont (1985) 135, Barrett (1964) 16–17, Coffey (1963) 310–11 on Zintzen (1960): 'it is difficult to divine the real purpose of this book...The work is...of remote utility'. Zwierlein (1987) finds the influence even of Sophocles in this play. Steiner's (1975) 454 view, 'Seneca's tragedies...are modulations on Euripides' is more representative.

[14] (1997) 89–91.

[15] Cf. Herington's (1966) judgements (with which I largely agree) on this play and more generally on the relationship between Greek and Roman tragedy, 446–7.

[16] Segal (1986) 3–17.

In some cases we can see Seneca apparently reading Euripides through Latin poetry. Angry Juno at the opening of *Hercules Furens* owes something to Ovid, but something also to Juno's summoning of Allecto in *Aeneid* 7. This in turn is modelled on Hera's summoning of Lyssa in Euripides' *Hercules Furens*.[17] That Seneca should adapt the Virgilian characters for a Hercules tragedy suggests a recognition of Euripides in the background. The same scene in *Aeneid* 7 inspires also Furia's summoning of Tantalus at the beginning of *Thyestes*. In this tragedy, particularly in the light of later allusions to the *Aeneid* in the description of Atreus' palace, one may reasonably argue that Seneca engages with Euripides more indirectly. The threat Juno's and Dido's madness poses to Jupiter's destiny for the Roman people informs Seneca's presentation of the tragic. He revisits Greek tragedy not directly but as it is mediated by Virgil.[18] Atreus' revenge is modelled on the tragic myth of Procne from *Metamorphoses* 6 and as a result of this mediation Seneca's treatment of tragic irony in the play (a basic feature of the myth and the genre) shows the mark of Ovid's pathological verbal playfulness. In the fifth chapter of this study I argue that Phaedra's erotic pursuit of Hippolytus, though ultimately inherited from Euripides' play, is informed more immediately by the erotic pursuits of Roman elegy which themselves have their roots in this particular tragedy. For a 'super-reader'[19] who sees the totality of the intertextual web and the totality of a work's literary history Euripides *is* an ever-present ghost, but only one of many. As any commentary shows, Senecan tragedy is stitched together from lines of Virgil and Ovid: this is its primary material. To look past Latin literature's reception of Greek tragedy to first origins is a mistake.

Tragedy is not and never was isolated from non-dramatic poetry. Horace advises an aspiring tragedian to put Homer into dramatic form (*rectius Iliacum carmen deducis in actus* (*Ars Poetica* 129)) and it would be a bold critic who argued that this represents

---

[17] See e.g. Wigodsky (1972) 93–4.

[18] So Most (1992) 393: 'he [Seneca] seems incapable of reading the Greek text except through the medium of the Latin poem'. Note, however, the phrase 'seems incapable'.

[19] The term is appropriated from Riffaterre (1966) 214–15, for whom it is a totalizing interpretative mechanism which incorporates the readings of all cultures, eras, and aesthetics.

a major departure from the practice of Aeschylus. The study of Roman tragedy, fragmentary before Seneca, presumes and depends on its influence on more complete non-dramatic texts, both prose and poetry.[20] In a memorable image of bees distilling honey from the nectar of various flowers (*Epistles* 84.3 f.) Seneca shows his enthusiasm for eclectic imitation and his tragedy shows the allusive quality distinctive of other Latin poetry.[21] Genre is constructed as much as revealed by such literary imitation: the moral darkness of tragic inspiration in Seneca is in part a creation of the *Aeneid*'s opposition of tragedy to epic and its representation of Roman destiny as the goal of an epic narrative. The erotic sufferings of Medea, Phaedra, or Juno show not simply Euripidean models but the partial, selective reading of his tragedy by the post-Euripidean tradition. When *Phaedra* revisits *Heroides* 4, Seneca does not so much re-appropriate tragic Euripides as absorb an elegiac reading of tragedy. To trace the ancestry of Senecan tragedy is to cross and re-cross generic boundaries.

I am primarily concerned in this book with the representation of Seneca's dramatic characters in the overtly artificial environment of his tragedies. By allusions to other literary texts, by self-referential theatrical scenes, and by other devices, Senecan tragedy continually reminds its readers of the fictive quality of its dramatic reality. In some respects the characters share the feeling that their lives are roles, their actions a scripted or a staged spectacle. The moral voice of the characters and of the tragedies as a whole is coloured by this sensibility.

[20] See Wiseman (1998) on the presence of tragedy in Livy and Ovid. Reconstruction of lost tragedies from tragic episodes is inevitably speculative—intertextuality as the sound of one hand clapping—but the less ambitious argument, that e.g. historical episodes can be written as tragic, is significant in showing the dramatic genre as part of a wider body of literature.

[21] Cf. also Seneca, *Epistles* 79.6–7 on a poet reworking a familiar subject: *parata verba invenit, quae aliter instructa novam faciem habent. Nec illis manus inicit tamquam alienis. Sunt enim publica.* Pound (1960) 25–8 argues that it is in a consciousness of the habitual context of words that Catullus, Propertius, and Ovid represent an advance over their Greek predecessors. I would prefer the less elegant distinction between Hellenistic and pre-Hellenistic but with this qualification I accept the point. For Fantham (1978) 110–11 Seneca views imitation as a more positive and active practice than do other critics of the 1st cent. AD. Against Quintilian 10.2.11 see, however, Longinus 13.4 for a defence of such literary borrowing. For tragedy as imitative see e.g. the Elder Seneca, *Suasoriae* 3.7. More generally on the theory of imitation in Latin literary criticism see Russell (1979*a*).

Chapter 2, 'The Broken World', discusses the moral and physical disorder of the dramas. Atreus' determination to surpass all conventional standards of wickedness (*Thyestes* 267–86) and his banishment of the gods and the sun (*Thyestes* 885–92) are typical of Senecan tragedy. I am interested here in the ambiguities of self-representation in a world in which no order is sure or lasting, a world without moral necessity. This subject I approach from both a philosophical and a literary perspective. Stoicism, particularly Seneca's Stoicism, offers a rhetoric of self-sufficiency which flourishes in a broken world. By insisting that true goods exist only in the disposition of one's soul and by dismissing the external world as illusory Stoicism promises the power to function as a moral agent in the most chaotic and hostile environment. This determined self-sufficiency, this willingness to abandon the shared, public world as a source of moral authority is, however, problematic. The Stoic sage's rejection of conventional moral order can resemble the autonomy of a tyrant: both seek to be absolute rulers of a world they construct and sustain for themselves. Austerity can be misrepresented as cruelty, martyrdom as madness, self-sufficiency as an inhuman alienation. Particularly in the bare paradoxes exchanged as *sententiae* it becomes difficult to distinguish between the polar opposites of vice and virtue. Ambiguity of this kind Seneca confronts in his prose works where it is charged that Stoic rationality is madness and Stoic invulnerability achieved through a mere play on words. A similar ambiguity can be seen in the dramatic works where maddened protagonists speak Stoically. Medea, for example, tells Jason that Fortune has always been beneath her (*Fortuna semper omnis infra me stetit* (*Medea* 520)). If Medea's words can be interpreted as a kind of sacrilege, a clear misappropriation of the language of Stoic virtue, the defiance of Megara, modelled on her husband's ambivalent virtue, is not so easily explained away. More important than the judgement that one character is a martyr, another a maniac is the fragility of Stoic self-representation. The Stoic sage may be invulnerable in his isolation but his image is not.

The literary perspective takes as its starting point the artificiality of Senecan tragedy, specifically the way in which we are constantly made aware that the dramatic worlds, events, and people are literary constructs. Not only is the poetry highly allusive but the dramatic characters commonly show an awareness of their own tragic myths. Medea strives to fulfil a role she already knows (*Medea* 171, 910). This prescripted necessity can be seen as providing a sense of order otherwise absent in a chaotic world. The gods who should defend Medea's rights are nowhere in evidence; Jason concludes the play with the words that there are no gods (*Medea* 1027). And yet, even if there is no sure moral authority ordering the world, we know—as in some strange sense Medea herself knows—that Medea will win her vengeance because that is how the story is written. Rather differently in *Hercules Furens* the tyrant Lycus advises Megara not to judge his accession to the throne: it is the victors who write the histories (*Hercules Furens* 406–10). Whether it is the literary past determining the present or the present constructing its past history, necessity and moral order return to the world of Senecan tragedy only as fabrications.

The artificiality of Seneca's dramatic worlds plays well with the philosopher's insistence that the external world is an illusion. The stage is used repeatedly in Seneca's philosophical prose as a metaphor for the unreality of existence outside the confines of the philosopher's mind. Certainly *Troades* explores these themes. In this tragedy the inevitability of dramatic events is particularly strong: Achilles' ghost rises from the grave and the crimes of the past, the deaths of Hector and Iphigenia, are re-enacted in different bodies. In seeming defiance of these events the Epicurean second ode dismisses ghosts as empty words and a *fabula* (story/play) like a bad dream (*Troades* 404–5). We may say that the ghost is dramatically real (it shakes the earth and sacred Mount Ida (171–7)) and a true expression of the power of Greeks over the land they have conquered. At the same time, however, it is just the creature of a *fabula*. The Epicurean ode breaks both dramatic illusion and dramatic necessity. Achilles' vengeance is irresistible in the staged reality which is *Troades* yet no more than a malignant fiction to those who refuse to countenance that illusion. Whether in this play or in the more problematic cases of *Hercules Furens*, *Medea*, and *Thyestes* Seneca's artificial style, his presentation of reality and necessity as constructions, poses distinctive moral challenges for his heroes.

The second chapter speaks very much to the melodramatic aspect of Senecan tragedy, its enthusiasm for exaggerated postures and moral extremes. The confusions of vice and virtue, of tyrants and sages, of maniacs and martyrs, of passion and reason are confusions of polarities. However problematic it may be, the moral vision is still black and white. In the third chapter I look for richer images of tragic madness, in particular through Seneca's recurrent allusions to the myth of Phaethon and to the myths of post-Golden Age criminality. Through allusion these myths frame and inform the passions of the tragic protagonists. Seneca's most important source for these paired myths is Ovid's *Metamorphoses*. The destruction of the world at the end of the Golden Age is echoed by the destruction which follows Phaethon's chariot ride. In both myths divine government is challenged, but the deliberate criminality which marks the decline of the Ages differs from the charioteer's fatal aspiration to divinity. These myths of the criminal genesis of human art have a different tone and of this opposition (pre-made in Ovid's placement of the myths at the beginning of the first and second books of his epic) Seneca creates genuinely ambivalent heroes. Is *Hercules Furens* the tragedy of a failed Olympian or of an anti-Olympian consumed by chthonic passions? The myths of Phaethon and of the more obviously impious revolts against Olympian order frame the myths of Hercules and of Medea as contrasting images and interpretations of their tragic madness.

These opposed framing myths offer contrasting images of the tragic madness not only of dramatic characters but also of the poetry itself. The anger of the Fury is familiar as an icon of the boundless, destructive energy of epic and tragedy. Seneca, Lucan, and Statius all look to Virgil's Juno and Allecto to inspire self-consciously criminal poetry. Atreus, melodramatic villain and architect of *Thyestes*, is possessed by just this figure. He plots a vengeance which will surpass the limits of both moral and literary tradition. With the Fury as Muse the poetics of revolutionary excess are characterized as unequivocally impious. The Fury is not, however, the only meta-literary icon. In ancient literary criticism the charioteer also figures the inspired poet. Balancing various passages in which the poet conjures up Furies for his audience, Longinus imagines the soul of Euripides climbing into the chariot of Phaethon to share the danger. 'Had it not been up among those heavenly bodies and moved in their courses he could never have visualized such things.' Phaethon and the Fury, the failed Olympian and the chthonic power, offer contrasting images of the madness both of the dramatic heroes and of the poetic art itself. With these opposed myths of criminal genesis Seneca balances the traditional representation of his characters and his art as melodramatically black with an image of flawed sublimity.

Chapter 4 is a discussion of theatrical scenes and images of viewing in Senecan tragedy. In drama (whether actual or virtual) the experiences of inscribed viewers are fruitful material for the discussion of a theatrical self-consciousness. Seneca's tragic spectacle suggests a variety of responses from revulsion to sadistic pleasure. *Phoenissae* offers a normative perspective on criminal horror: as Oedipus waits in a cave on Mt Cithaeron to see his sons' civil war the very landscape is described as a spectator weeping and crying out. The hollowed-out cave is an image of his broken eyes and tragic spectatorship here is consistently represented as a damaging experience. It is an experience which Seneca's vengeful protagonists inflict on their victims. Medea and Atreus expect and depend on this normal human reaction: when their victims, Jason and Thyestes, unwittingly expose their frailties they fabricate a suitable revenge whose fruition is coextensive with the unfolding of the tragedy. Much of the warped pleasure Medea and Atreus take in the spectacle of horror is at one degree removed. Not the sight of the tragic acts themselves but the pain of the helpless spectator-victims delights them. Medea insists that Jason be forced to watch the murder of one of his children (*Medea* 992–4) and Atreus wishes that the gods themselves be dragged back to watch what they flee (*Thyestes* 893–5). The distinction between tragedian and victims is reinforced also by irony. At the end of the tragedies the victims discover what has been plotted, but for the greater part of the drama their understanding is limited. They are the victims not only of Seneca's irony, but also of the protagonists'. Even as Jason and Thyestes betray themselves from their own mouths Medea and Atreus display a mastery of wit and language which is proof against any argument from their interlocutors. The rhetorical glamour for which Seneca is variously loved and despised is not the common possession of all his dramatic characters but is an attribute primarily of the powerful characters and an element of their power. The victim who cannot participate effectively in speech is reduced to a passive body.

Commonly the relationship between the controlling gaze and the manipulated body is gendered. Thyestes' banquet is explicitly modelled on the banquet of Tereus, which itself restages and avenges the rape of Philomela. In a reversal of roles the rapist Tereus is transformed into a victim of irony and a helpless visual object. Thyestes is not a rapist but has threatened Atreus' political and domestic authority by seducing his wife Aerope. Atreus fears Thyestes as a rival for the throne of Argos and as perhaps also the father of Agamemnon and Menelaus. At the banquet Thyestes is, like Tereus and Philomela before him, reduced to a helpless visual object. Furthermore the upheaval in his stomach suggests an ugly mimicry of childbirth. Seeing Thyestes like this Atreus is reassured as to the paternity of his children (*Thyestes* 1098–9). Nothing parallels the undercurrent of sexual violence in *Thyestes*, but in both *Troades* and *Medea* a clear contrast is drawn between the domestic world of the victims and the political power of their tormentors. Not only do Ulysses and Medea (more of a man than Jason) both exploit their victims' attachment to their children, but they stage and observe the pain which comes from this vulnerability. Like Atreus, Medea associates political and sexual power and in this tragedy also there are echoes of Procne and the reversal of Tereus' rape, in Medea's revenge. Medea claims her virginity restored by Jason's defeat and the pleasure she takes from his pain is coloured by the pleasure of erotic domination.

Pain and a sadistic, voyeuristic pleasure compete as models for the response of the actual audience sitting in the theatre or reading the play. This audience would seem to find a more obvious pattern in the spectator-victims than in the protagonists who direct the dramatic events—it cannot after all intervene in the action. Particularly with tragic irony, however, the audience resembles more closely an Atreus or a Medea. The significance of their words, though hidden from the other dramatic characters is appreciated and understood by the audience and arguably in this phenomenon we may observe the modelling of a sadistic spectatorship. Seneca admits variation in a reader's response to images of crime and madness (*De Ira* 2.36.1–3): some are revolted, some take perverse pleasure, and the images themselves cannot enforce any particular response. In *Agamemnon* and *Thyestes*, however, narratives of horror follow a similar trajectory from fearful paralysis to active pleasure. This final image of savage viewing contrasts with the

Introduction

normative images of vulnerable tragic viewing in *Phoenissae* and elsewhere. Of all the tragedies *Troades* offers the most developed study of tragic spectatorship. Even before the closing *mise en abyme* a form of catharsis is examined in Andromache's pain. She encourages the messenger to recount the death of Astyanax saying that grief finds consolation in its expression (1065–7). Earlier Ulysses gave her pause for lamentation only to find that far from being assuaged or resolved her pain grew and set itself no limit (*Troades* 784–6, 812–13). Thus despite her words one approaches the theatrical deaths at the close with the experience of a grief which feeds on the visualization. The deaths of Astyanax and Polyxena are observed by an audience of both Greeks and Trojans whose responses range from pity and fear to vengeful pleasure. The frenzy of Andromache's excessive grief contrasts with the resolve of the victims who gladly leave this theatre behind. As interesting as the plurality of audience responses offered is the triviality of the tragic spectators. Though the victims' resolve is morally admirable it is not clear that this is what the spectators admire as they turn tearfully and eagerly from one death to another. There is a particular contrast between the ugly images of a shattered city and of Hecuba herself offered as a moral spectacle at the beginning of the tragedy and the aesthetically beautiful visions of *mors immatura* at the close. The young Trojans act out their contempt for a servile life, but the response of an explicitly trivial audience to their affecting display is morally more ambiguous.

The final chapter is a study of a single play, *Phaedra*, and explores the importance of intertextuality in Seneca's dramatic characterization. In particular I am concerned to show dramatic roles and self-identity defined and controlled by the influence of earlier texts. Seneca's Phaedra represents herself as condemned to suffer the experience of other Cretan princesses and this curse is doubly realized. Not only are there parallels between her fate and that of her mother and sister, but her laments echo those of Ovid's Phaedra (*Heroides* 4) and Iphis (*Metamorphoses* 9). The past repeats itself through verbal reminiscence. If Phaedra cannot avert this repetition of the past she does at least recognize what is happening. Hippolytus by contrast is innocent of Phaedra's desires: he does not feel them, nor does he recognize them. The intertextual dimension to irony in Senecan tragedy I have mentioned earlier in Chapters 2 and 4. Though in many ways Phaedra is unlike Medea or Atreus she shares with these powerful characters an understanding which looks beyond the dramatic illusion. Phaedra's recognition of the origins of her passion is associated with literary memories of the texts which define her role in the tragedy. In a similar way Atreus' adoption of Procne's revenge as a suitable model manifests itself through the literary influence on Seneca's text of Ovid's narrative of the myth of Procne. At the banquet scene and elsewhere Atreus mocks his victim with double-meanings intelligible only to himself and the audience (for example, the promise that Thyestes will never be parted from his children (*Thyestes* 998)). In Phaedra a similar kind of double meaning is generated also through intertextual means. Innocent Hippolytus is contaminated by allusions to particular erotic narratives and by elegiac topoi. Phaedra's willingness to run over icy mountains (608 f.) is both an imitation of Hippolytus' chastity and a stock element in the elegiac lover's *servitium amoris*. The gesture has two radically different meanings. The attempts to love Hippolytus in the elegiac register have their origin in the comparable attempts of Ovid's Phaedra in *Heroides* 4. An audience familiar with this text and with elegy more widely can read Phaedra's hidden desire as Hippolytus cannot. His sexual innocence is figured as unfamiliarity with elegiac convention. His astonishment that he has seemed easy material (*materia facilis* 685–6) for Phaedra's desire is shared by no reader of Roman elegy: there can be little material more easily eroticized than the hunter. With an irony less sadistic than that of *Thyestes* but equally destructive the literate, experienced audience disfigures Hippolytus' innocent self-representation. The curse of Venus on Phaedra and Hippolytus, the law of Nature which governs their dramatic world, operates here as the fictive necessity created by the influence of past texts.

2
The Broken World

MEDEA famously ends with the line, *testare nullos esse, qua veheris, deos* (bear witness where you ride that there are no gods *Medea* 1027). Having seen Medea's evil unchallenged and unpunished Jason denies a guiding moral principle in the universe. *Thyestes*, like *Agamemnon*, perhaps looks at its close beyond the scope of the tragedy to future vengeance in the house of Pelops,[1] but otherwise Atreus' vengeance, like Medea's, is a victory over the traditional forces of moral order. Both set themselves up as gods:

> Medea superest: hic mare et terras vides
> ferrumque et ignes et deos et fulmina.
> *(Medea* 166–7)

(Medea remains: here you see sea and land, steel and fire and gods and thunderbolts)

> Aequalis astris gradior et cunctos super
> altum superbo vertice attigens polum.
> . . . .
> dimitto superos.
> *(Thyestes* 885–6, 888)

(Peer of the stars I stride, out-topping all, my proud head reaching to the lofty sky . . . I discharge the gods)

This magnification of the stature of the protagonists is in part a matter of style. In Senecan tragedy human criminality is translated to the cosmos and the plays end with an 'explosion of evil'.[2] There is of course also a moral dimension. If the dramatic world reflects the passion of a character and the evil of the tragic act, then it does not surely function as an external framework to contain

---
[1] Thyestes' curse *vindices aderunt dei; his puniendum vota te tradunt mea* (1110–11) will, creatively interpreted, come true. This would fit well with the opening of the tragedy and Furia's promise of crime without end (*semper oriatur novum* 30). Cassandra's closing prophecy for Clytemnestra in *Agamemnon*, *Veniet et vobis furor* (1012), needs less interpretation.
[2] I borrow the phrase from Herington (1966) 449.

them. Far from being contained Medea stands alone as a universe in herself and the battle for right and wrong in this drama is a battle also of conflicting worlds. The disruption of the physical universe in *Thyestes* is matched by a disruption of its moral rhetoric as the very standards of right and wrong are broken.

The moral rhetoric of Seneca's tragedies is broadly Stoic: the stylized conflicts between freedom and slavery, tyrants and their victims, reason and passion, life and death are as clear in *Troades* as in Cicero's *Paradoxa Stoicorum*. Appropriately therefore the dislocation of the physical and moral universe of the tragedies has often been discussed from a Stoic perspective. Many scholars have argued that Seneca's tragedies, because they appear to defy divine providence, are un-Stoic or anti-Stoic.[3] Whether the tragedies are pro- or anti-Stoic they are informed by Stoicism. I argue below that the absence of a controlling order in the world speaks particularly to the concerns of Seneca's isolationist brand of Stoicism which urges disengagement and withdrawal from an irredeemably corrupt world. Some passages in the tragedies accommodate a Stoic interpretation along these lines, most notably the martyrdom of Astyanax and Polyxena in *Troades*. More commonly a 'straight' Stoic reading of this kind is problematic.

Medea rebukes Jason for his weakness, saying that Fortune has always been beneath her. In this way the tragic Fury talks like a Stoic *sapiens*. Perhaps her tone is mocking, but the charge that Stoic indifference is a kind of madness is one which Seneca feels obliged to confront in his moral works. In *Hercules Furens* Megara models her defiance of the tyrant Lycus on her husband's virtue, but elsewhere in the drama Hercules' virtue is shown to resemble both his own madness and that of Juno. Characteristic Stoic postures and *sententiae* cannot be taken as secure marks of virtue. In a broken world, a world without a controlling, authoritative order, such uncertainty remains unresolved.

A major issue for the interpretation of Seneca's tragedy (as of Lucan's epic) is the vulnerability of Stoic virtue to mispresentation. Tragic crime (or civil war) and the pointed declamatory style produce a paradoxical chaos in which right is confused with wrong and moral values almost flippantly inverted. Here I argue that

---

[3] See e.g. Dingel (1974) 99 f., Curley (1986) 168 f., and for an overview Motto and Clark (1988) 43–65.

Seneca's isolationist philosophy is predisposed to such confusion. Stoic criticism, which finds its characteristic form in paradox and negation and depends on an individual's will to defy public, conventional values, echoes the absolute autonomy of a tyrant. The confrontation of sage and tyrant, the true and false king, is exploited to rhetorical effect in the philosophical tradition. In Seneca's tragedies, in worlds which conspicuously lack a unifying principle of moral order and in which the heroism of a Hercules or a Medea is variously interpreted, this paradoxical resemblance of opposites is less easily controlled.

The order of the physical world is commonly interpreted as an interpretative authority. If Atreus cannot be stopped, he can at least be marked as criminal by the inversion of the natural order. Figuratively also systems of physical imagery (fire, flood, and the like) appear to function as an objective commentary on the tragic acts and characters. In each case passions are externalized into the physical context. Here again, however, Seneca favours ambiguity. As the disorder of a single soul becomes the common reality of all, its origin is obscured. It is possible to track the image of fire from the passions of Deïanira's soul via the poisoned robe to Hercules' funeral pyre, but it is also possible to interpret Hercules' burning agony as the product of his own life, as Alcmena in fact does (*Hercules Oetaeus* 1396–8). The physical context does not so much resolve as reiterate the ambiguities of heroic *virtus*. A Medea's mocking use of Stoic cliché also finds its parallels in the physical context. Hybristic Ajax is described defying a storm in terms suggestive of a Stoic's defiance of Fortune; Oedipus resolves to withdraw from the political world into the sanctuary of a private hell with a mad rationality which hovers awkwardly between vice and virtue.

Senecan tragedy constantly draws attention to its literary and dramatic nature. In doing so it reminds the reader that the world it represents, its events and its laws, are constructions. This artificial style is appropriate to worlds in which the antagonists strive to enforce different realities upon each other. A successful tyrant acts outside the laws of conventional morality and forces his subjects to live the consequent paradoxes: *quod nolunt velint* (they must want what they do not want *Thyestes* 212). History itself is something fashioned by the victor: *quaeritur belli exitus, | non causa* (The question about war is its outcome, not its cause *Hercules Furens*

407–8). The power of the tyrant to fabricate his own reality, his own necessity, mirrors that of the *sapiens* who insists on the illusory nature of public reality and defines his own private reality in opposition to it. The point is commonly expressed in Seneca's moral works through theatrical metaphor: the goods and powers of this world are no more real or necessary than the props and roles of the dramatic stage. This aspect of the broken world, the world as *fabula*, is explored most fully in *Troades*.

1. STOICISM AND THE LOCUS OF MORAL CONFLICT

The dissolution so characteristic of Seneca's tragic worlds is not in itself un-Stoic. No Stoic said that divine providence prevented human evil: God's hand is visible in everything *except* the actions of the wicked.[4] Stoicism had two methods of reconciling human freedom to choose evil with divine providence. One was to argue that passion and evil are essentially unstable. Grown sufficiently corrupt, the entire world is cleansed by fire or flood, a new beginning is made and the order of the universe is preserved. The other method was to argue that only the moral disposition of the soul was truly significant and that even in a fallen world and in the midst of suffering our moral disposition remains within our power. In Seneca's time cataclysm and ekpyrosis were myths rather than literal beliefs[5] but still had figurative value. In *Epistles* 9 Seneca argues that virtue is sufficient for a happy life (*se contentus est sapiens ad beate vivendum* 9.13) and likens the life of the *sapiens*, who through confinement or shipwreck has lost his world and his people, to that of Jupiter at the end of the world:

'Qualis est Iovis, cum resoluto mundo et dis in unum confusis paulisper cessante natura adquiescit sibi cogitationibus suis traditus. Tale quiddam sapiens facit; in se reconditur, secum est' (*Epistles* 9.16)

(It is like that of Jupiter, who, amid the dissolution of the world, when the gods are confounded together and Nature rests for a space from her work, can retire into himself and give himself over to his own thoughts. The sage does something similar; he retreats into himself and lives with himself)

Thus both the order of the universe and its microcosmic image, the soul of the wise man, are proof against evil.

---

[4] See e.g. Cleanthes, *Hymn to Zeus* 15–17 (*SVF* 1.537).
[5] See Fantham (1982) 266–7.

Like Jupiter at the end of the world the wise man escapes from the violence and confusion which surrounds him by a shift of perspective: he turns away from the external world, withdraws into himself and lives in the world of his own mind. The story of Stilbo, the primary hero of *Epistles* 9, illustrates the point well:

hic enim capta patria, amissis liberis, amissa uxore cum ex incendio publico solus et tamen beatus exiret, interroganti Demetrio, cui cognomen ab exitio urbium Poliorcetes fuit, numquid perdidisset, 'Omnia', inquit, 'bona mea mecum sunt.' Ecce vir fortis ac strenuus! Ipsam hostis sui victoriam vicit. (*Epistles* 9.18–19)

(For this man, after his country was captured and his children and his wife lost, as he emerged from the general desolation alone and yet happy, spoke as follows to Demetrius, called Sacker of Cities because of the destruction he brought upon them, in answer to the question whether he had lost anything, 'I have all my goods with me.' There is a brave and vigorous man! He was victorious over the very victory of his enemy.)

State and family, the traditional domains of human existence, are not essential to Stilbo; he walks out of the conflagration of the public world secure in his Stoic isolation. Although Demetrius and Stilbo live in different worlds, when they meet they fight for the same language. The result of this collision of worlds or perspectives is paradox. Stilbo's defiance is marked by his echoes of the tyrant's military power: he conquered his enemy's conquest and in doing so revealed himself a brave and energetic man. *Strenuus* is not the most natural word for Stilbo's display of Stoic resolve but it is a pointed challenge to a man whose very name commemorates his military victories.

Though easily accommodated in the declamatory rhetoric of Imperial Rome, paradox, inversion, and aggressive extremism always were distinctive features of Stoic argument. Zeno, not Seneca, wrote that 'general culture was useless... All those who are not virtuous are hostile and enemies and slaves and alien to each other, parents to children and brothers to brothers, relatives to relatives... only virtuous men are citizens and friends and relatives and free men so that in the eyes of the Stoics, parents and children are enemies, since they are not wise'.[6] The isolation of Zeno's Stoics in a useless general culture is intensified in Seneca's moral writings where he calls insistently for withdrawal

---

[6] Diogenes Laertius 7.32–3.

into the sanctuary of the individual soul: *recede in te ipsum quantum potes* (Withdraw into yourself as far as you can *Epistles* 7.8), *undique nos reducamus* (On every front let us retreat into ourselves *Epistles* 14.10). Just as suicide, the ultimate retirement, is justifiable only when a moral life is no longer possible, so the isolation of a Stilbo is undesirable, even unnatural.[7]

However, Stoicism distinguishes itself from other philosophies, notably Epicureanism, by parading its ability to function unaffected by even the most extreme circumstances. Epicurus stresses the importance of friendship to the wise man; Seneca likens the friendless man to a maimed body but insists that this trunk is no less content than the whole: *et erit inminuto corpore et amputato tam laetus quam integro fuit* (he will be as happy in his impaired and maimed body as he was when it was whole *Epistles* 9.4). Epicurus contrasts a society of friends with association with the many;[8] while Seneca approves the words, he recasts the opposition as one between the many and the self: *Ecquid habeas cur placeas tibi, si is es, quem intellegant multi? Introrsus bona tua spectent* (Do you have any reason to be pleased with yourself if you are the kind of person whom the many understand? Let your good qualities face inward *Epistles* 7.12).

Seneca's Stoicism is habitually conducted *in extremis* and in isolation. To some extent this is his own style. Panaetius and Posidonius had justified the Roman empire Stoically as an expression of the natural order of things.[9] Commenting on the dominance of Stoicism in Augustus' regime and the following two centuries Griffin writes that 'to many Romans, Stoicism as a moral philosophy seemed like a rationalization of... Rome's own traditional ideals'.[10] Cicero and Quintilian praised the Romans for practising philosophy in the course of public life rather than discussing abstract subjects in seclusion in the Greek manner.[11] Yet in the age of Nero the Stoicism of Seneca, Lucan, and Persius

---

[7] On suicide see *Epistles* 78.2 and M. T. Griffin (1976) 372–88. On isolation see *Epistles* 9.14–17.

[8] *Egregie hoc tertium Epicurus, cum uni ex consortibus studiorum suorum scriberet: 'Haec,' inquit, 'ego non multis, sed tibi; satis enim magnum alter alteri theatrum sumus.'* (*Epistles* 7.11).

[9] Erskine (1990) 199–204.

[10] M. T. Griffin (1989) 8. See more generally 5–11.

[11] Cicero, *De Oratore* 2.22, Quintilian 12.2.30, and M. T. Griffin (1989) 11–37. See also Cicero's out-reaching vision of human life in *De Finibus* 3.16 f.

The Broken World 21

is determinedly isolationist.[12] There is no real incoherence here: in Lucan's epic Stoic Cato commits himself to traditional Roman ideals which flourish under the Republic. When this context of ethical life is destroyed he becomes an isolated figure.[13] Certainly Stoicism could be adapted to serve the purposes of different individuals and groups, but the extremism and the confrontational stance which Seneca and his contemporaries adopt is not grafted onto the philosophy but constructed from it.[14]

However unnatural a corrupted world may be, it is the habitual environment of a *sapiens* in Stoic and particularly Senecan-Stoic writing. It is not a desirable environment in which to live, though one's virtue may be strengthened by the challenge, but it is an ideal context in which to display the power of the philosophy and to mark its difference from its rivals.[15] Seneca encourages Lucilius to temper his spirit by fighting with Fortune as if in a boxing match:

ille, qui sanguinem suum vidit, cuius dentes crepuere sub pugno, ille, qui subplantatus adversarium toto tulit corpore nec proiecit animum proiectus, qui quotiens cecidit, contumacior resurrexit, cum magna spe descendit ad pugnam. (*Epistles* 13.2–3)

---

[12] M. T. Griffin (1989) 20–1 on the suggestion that under Nero Stoicism was seen as isolationist and politically subversive. Sullivan (1985) 115–52 on the same theme distinguishes sharply between the Stoicism of Seneca and that of the more revolutionary Lucan. Rudich (1993) 163–4 too argues that Stoic rhetoric both served and opposed the Neronian regime. In *Epistles* 73 Seneca argues that philosophers, far from being opposed on principle to terrestrial authority, welcome it if it grants them the leisure to pursue their philosophical pursuits. Virgil, *Eclogues* 1.6–7 is quoted with approval: *O Meliboee, deus nobis haec otia fecit. | namque erit ille mihi semper deus.* The philosophers are thus defended from the charge of being politically subversive but at the same time they are relegated to the seclusion which Cicero and Quintilian deplored in the Greeks. For Persius' isolation see e.g. *Satires* 1.1–7, 1.119–23, 4.51–2.

[13] Cato explicitly rejects a life of philosophical *otium*, preferring to die with the Republic (Lucan, *B.C.* 2.286 f.). Whether the Republic was worth fighting for and whether Cato acted correctly was one form in which the larger question of Stoic isolationism and political involvement was discussed. See George (1991) especially 243–5. On the iconic status of Cato in Roman Stoicism see Sullivan (1985) 117–20 and M. T. Griffin (1989) 10. On the motivation of Stoic dissenters like Thrasea Paetus as conservative Roman rather than revolutionary philosophical see M. T. Griffin (1989) 33.

[14] The proudly ugly images of Stoic defiance recall perhaps also the influence of Cynicism's abrasive physicality and its opposition to civic values. On Stoics and Cynics see Diogenes Laertius 7.121, Rist (1969) 54–80, and Long (1974) 109–11.

[15] On this as the basis for Seneca's fascination with violence see Pratt (1948) 10.

(He who has seen his own blood, whose teeth have cracked under the fist, he who has been tripped and with his whole body felt the force of his adversary's charge, but did not cast down his spirit, who whenever he fell arose more defiant, goes down to fight with great confidence.)

At the end of this episode he changes tack and argues that in general Fortune is not so terrifying an adversary; often one's fears do not come true. Commenting on his change of tack Seneca says:

Non loquor tecum Stoica lingua, sed hac submissiore. Nos enim dicimus omnia ista, quae gemitus mugitusque exprimunt, levia esse et contemnenda. (*Epistles* 13.4)

(I am not speaking to you in Stoic language, but in this milder tone. For we [Stoics] say that everything which provokes cries and groans is trivial and to be despised.)

Stoic moralism returns to screams and groans, blood and violence because it is here that defiance and self-sufficiency are most in evidence. Anyone can live a life which Fortune accommodates, but only the wise man can make a world for himself and be sure to live in it untroubled. Jason and Thyestes, who suffer extravagantly and see the criminal agents of their suffering raised to the level of gods, are challenged in such a way. Jason sees Medea unpunished and a path to heaven opening for her.[16] In Atreus' victory Thyestes sees the day driven back, the gods shamed and crime without limit.[17] Neither victim acquits himself Stoically and this is particularly true of Thyestes. Atreus assured his servant that Thyestes would yield to a combination of hardship and the *vetus regni furor* (old passion for power *Thyestes* 302) and enter the royal palace. Thyestes, speaking Stoically, recognizes the false lustre of royal power,[18] contrasts it unfavourably with the true power of self-sufficiency,[19] but then fails to follow his own warning and enters the palace. Medea accuses Jason of desiring royal power, probably unfairly, but he certainly fears it.[20] At the

---

[16] *patuit in caelum via* (*Medea* 1022).
[17] *Hoc est deos quod puduit, hoc egit diem | aversum in ortus* (*Thyestes* 1035–6), *sceleris est aliquis modus* (ibid. 1051).
[18] *clarus hic regni nitor | fulgore non est quod oculos falso auferat* (*Thyestes* 414–15).
[19] TANTALUS. *pater, potes regnare.* THYESTES. *Cum possim mori.* | TANTALUS. *Summa est potestas*—THYESTES. *Nulla si cupias nihil* (*Thyestes* 442–3).
[20] *Hinc rex et illinc*— (*Medea* 516), *Et quis resistet, gemina si bella ingruant, | Creo atque Acastus arma si iungant sua?* (525–6), JASON. *Alta extimesco sceptra.* MEDEA. *Ne cupias vide* (529). On this agon and the characterization of Jason see below, pp. 37–40.

end of the tragedy in the burning ruins of Corinth he looks hopelessly for the gods to guarantee moral order. How different from Stilbo standing in the burning ruins of his city, having lost his wife and children: *'Omnia', inquit, 'bona mea mecum sunt'* ('I have all my goods with me,' he said).

Parallel to the collapse of the framework of the physical universe in Senecan tragedy is a collapse of moral standards. No judge intervenes to punish Atreus and Medea, and in this sense their deeds challenge what is acceptable, but in addition their deeds threaten the very limits of criminality. Tantalus anticipates a crime which will make him an innocent by comparison, Medea embraces infanticide as a crime beside which her past murders will seem piety.[21] Differently Atreus claims that whatever wrong he does to his wicked brother will be a right: *Fas est in illo quidquid in fratre est nefas* (All that is wrong in dealing with a brother is right in dealing with him *Thyestes* 220). Where the fabric of the world and its moral rhetoric unravel we look for the soul of the *sapiens* to be a source of order and stability. Thyestes and Jason surrender to their misfortunes and in doing so fall short of the Stoic ideal, but it is clearly Stoic (not Epicurean, Aristotelian, or other) virtue which they fail to attain. Their isolation amidst unspeakable horrors calls for a Stoic response and their failure to give it is marked as a Stoic failure. Thyestes submits to his son's desire to enter Atreus' royal palace with an inappropriate echo of a Stoic's submission to Fate: *ego vos sequor, non duco* (I am following you, not leading *Thyestes* 489).[22] Medea plays the Stoic to Jason's cowardice:

JASON.   Cedo defessus malis.
   et ipsa casus saepe iam expertos time.
MEDEA. Fortuna semper omnis infra me stetit.   (*Medea* 518–20)

(JASON. I give up, worn out by troubles. Even you should fear the odds of chance, which you have tested many times. MEDEA. I have always risen above Fortune in every form.)

Oedipus is similarly rebuked by Jocasta for the prologue he delivers to his play. The plague has confused age and sex in a

---

[21] *iam nostra subit | e stirpe turba quae suum vincat genus | ac me innocentem faciat et inausa audeat* (*Thyestes* 18–20); *quidquid admissum est adhuc | pietas vocetur* (*Medea* 904–5).

[22] Cf. *ira qua ducis sequor* (*Medea* 953), words which Medea utters at the apparition of the *antiqua Erinys*.

common funeral pyre,[23] heaven has the face of hell,[24] the boundary between the upper and lower worlds is broken and the waters of the Styx are mixed with Thebes' 'Sidonian' river.[25] This confusion of course mirrors Oedipus' criminal confusion of the royal family:

> sperare poteras sceleribus tantis dari
> regnum salubre? fecimus caelum nocens.
> (*Oedipus* 35–6)

(Could you expect that a healthy kingdom would be accorded to such crimes? I have made the heavens baneful.)

Jocasta sees Oedipus paralysed by despair at the sufferings of his kingdom and says:

> regium hoc ipsum reor:
> adversa capere, quoque sit dubius magis
> status et cadentis imperi moles labet,
> hoc stare certo pressius fortem gradu:
> haud est virile terga Fortunae dare.
> (*Oedipus* 82–6)

(The quality of a king lies, I think, in the very ability to take on adversities. The more unsure his situation, the more the balance of supreme power tilts toward falling, so much more firmly should he stand, resolute and unbudging. It is not manly to retreat before Fortune.)

Jocasta's rebuke, even more than Medea's, is Stoic. If Oedipus were a true king, not merely king of Thebes, he would not crumble as his empire falls. Oedipus fails because he loses himself in a world which he cannot control, the external world governed by Fortune. We might contrast his behaviour with that of the Roman Stoic icon Cato. In an unstable Libyan desert which reduces a myth of Rome's greatest law-maker to the operation of blind chance[26] and whose very boundary is a confusion of land and water,[27] Cato refuses to consult an oracle because he already

---

[23] *sed omnis aetas pariter et sexus ruit, | iuvenesque senibus iungit et gnatis patres | funesta pestis, una fax thalamos cremat* (*Oedipus* 53–5).

[24] *obtexit arces caelitum ac summas domos | inferna acies* (*Oedipus* 48–9).

[25] *Rupere Erebi claustra profundi | turba sororum face Tartarea | Phlegethonque sua motam ripa | miscuit undis Styga Sidoniis* (*Oedipus* 160–3).

[26] Lucan suggests that the *ancile* Numa received from heaven was in reality the work of a Libyan whirlwind (*B.C.* 9.474–80).

[27] On the Syrtes as neither land nor water see Lucan, *B.C.* 9.303–4. On Africa in general as having no fixed framework Lucan, *B.C.* 9.467 f.

knows everything necessary for a virtuous life:[28] *Scimus, et hoc nobis non altius inseret Hammon* (We know, and Hammon will not root this more deeply in us, Lucan, *B.C.* 9.572).

The plague in Thebes, the civil war in Libya, the crimes of Argos or Corinth are all relevantly similar scenes. The cosmos and the moral order it represents dissolve in the face of evil, and in their dissolution reflect its image on the grand stage. With the possible exception of *Troades* Senecan tragedy does not portray Stoic heroes, but it does place its victims in this familiar environment of Stoic heroes and it does suggest the Stoic fortitude which they might display.

2. VICE AND VIRTUE IN A BROKEN WORLD

The previous section opened with images of vice, Atreus and Medea, and ended with an image of virtue, Cato. Atreus and Medea defied the moral and physical framework of the world to become their own gods. Cato achieves the same thing at the oracle of Hammon:

> ille deo plenus, tacita quem mente gerebat,
> effudit dignas adytis pectore voces
>   (Lucan, *B.C.* 9.564–5)

(He, full of the god whom he carried in his secret thoughts, poured out worthy speech from the temple of his heart.)

There is nothing vainglorious in Cato's characterization: Stoicism promises divinity if not immortality.[29] Though at opposite ends of the moral spectrum an Atreus and a Cato resemble each other inasmuch as both are omnipotent rulers of their chosen realm. Stoicism promises freedom defined as 'the authority to act on one's own' and the *sapiens* therefore is naturally parallel to and opposed to the tyrant, the autocrat who is supremely powerful and supremely free in the terrestrial world.[30] Whether or not there

---

[28] On the knowledge of the wise man see Kerferd (1978) especially 129–30 on Seneca *Epistles* 88 and its proud independence: 'He goes on (88.28) to say that philosophy is entirely independent of the special sciences—"Philosophy asks no favours from any other source—it builds everything on its own soil."'

[29] *Hoc enim est, quod mihi philosophia promittit, ut parem deo faciat* (Seneca, *Epistles* 48.11). See also *Epistles* 41.1–4 (where also the Stoic needs no temple) and 73.11–16.

[30] Diogenes Laertius 7.122.

was historically a Stoic opposition to the emperor in Seneca's Rome, a political faction based on allegiance to a philosophical school, Stoic moralism is structurally suited to such a rivalry. The strength of a tyrant and the strength of a sage are revealed in autonomy, the ability to write one's own laws independently of external influences. The aggression of Stoicism, its isolationism, and its delight in paradox strain moral rhetoric in a manner which is disturbing when it suggests its unacceptable political analogue. We have already seen Zeno's transformation of society into a civil war which ranks parents against children, brothers against brothers, relatives against relatives.

Lucan's *Bellum Civile* opposes a tyrant, Caesar, to a Stoic hero, Cato. A number of scholars have suggested that this opposition is compromised by uncomfortable similarities between what we would like to believe are polar opposites.[31] We would like to be assured, for example, that the spectacle of death which Scaeva offers Caesar (*B.C.* 6.138–262) is different from the spectacle of death which Cato's unhappy soldiers offer their leader (*B.C.* 9.734–889), or that Cato as he marches through the desert is an Alexander refashioned in Stoic form not just another Alexander.[32] Arguably, however, this moral security is not to be found in the chaotic environment, both physical and rhetorical,[33] of civil war. Hershkowitz concludes her discussion of Lucan, 'Cato, the last Republican wise man, should be sane, but in the slip-slidin'-away world of the *Bellum Civile*, even the wise man is mad'.[34] An aspect of this 'slip-sliding' is a shift of signification: 'Caesar effects the slippage of *furor* into *virtus*; and Cato effects the slippage of *virtus* into *furor*'.[35] This moral confusion of crime and virtue, promised in the epic's second line (*iusque datum sceleri canimus*, and legality conferred on crime we sing) is part of a wider phenomenon of rhetorical

---

[31] Johnson (1987) 35–66 undermined Cato's *aristeia* by representing his austerity as excessive, ludicrous, and destructive, but for the uncomfortable identification of *furor* and *virtus* see Leigh (1997) 158–84, 265–91 and Hershkowitz (1998) 231–48.

[32] On Cato's trials in the desert as the heroism of a Stoic Alexander see Viarre (1982), though she does not question the integrity of his victory. On Stoic treatment of Alexander more generally see Frears (1974).

[33] The emphasis on chaos of both world and word is due in no small degree to the influence of Henderson (1988) and subsequently Masters (1992).

[34] Hershkowitz (1998) 246.

[35] Hershkowitz (1998) 245.

damage.[36] Chaotic language mimics the chaos of civil war and thus taints its user: 'to destroy normative syntax is in some measure... to show oneself as corrupted by chaos as the world one describes'.[37]

Where Bartsch and Hershkowitz emphasize more the destabilizing, corrupting impact of Lucan's *Civil War* on rhetoric, Leigh in his discussion of spectacle and viewing in the epic exposes the instability of a rhetoric already ripe for the deconstruction which it duly receives in Lucan's epic. To some extent this distinction is a matter of presentation. In the case of Cato's virtue, however, I do think that the Stoic sage is predisposed to find himself in a Lucanian epic. Not only does he thrive on a tyrant's persecution, but his rejection of a public ethic and a public world for a private realm over which he has absolute power creates an image of the very world he opposes. This is not to say that sage and tyrant are therefore equivalent: Cato is not an Atreus or a Caesar and there are ways of distinguishing them. Nevertheless the Stoic sage's autocratic pose is I think dangerous because it is easily usurped. We have already seen Medea play the Stoic to Jason: *Fortuna semper omnis infra me stetit* (I have always risen above Fortune in every form *Medea* 520).

Before turning to Seneca let us briefly compare Caesar and Cato as they embark on civil war. Before the battle of Pharsalus Caesar reminds his troops that they are fighting not only for victory but for moral justification: *haec acies victum factura nocentem est* (This battle will make the conquered guilty *B.C.* 7.260). Caesar is a moral relativist:

> Si pro me patriam ferro flammisque petistis,
> nunc pugnate truces gladio exsolvite culpam:
> nulla manus, belli mutato iudice, pura est.
> (*B.C.* 7.261–3)

(If in my defence you have attacked your native land with fire and sword, now fight fiercely and expiate your crime with the sword: no hand is pure when the judge of the war is changed.)

That his soldiers should purify themselves of guilt through the shedding of blood is paradoxical and the linguistic strain reflects

---

[36] Cf. above, pp. 23–4, on confusion in Oedipus' Thebes. Note also the resemblance between Henderson (1988) on Lucan, *Bellum Civile*, and Henderson (1991) on Statius, *Thebaid*.

[37] Bartsch (1997) 25.

the moral instability of a world in conflict. For Caesar moral value is not an absolute but something to be fashioned by the victor when the war is won. Earlier in the epic Stoic Cato committed himself to the criminal war in equally awkward language:

> at illi
> arcano sacras reddit Cato pectore voces:
> 'Summum, Brute, nefas civilia bella fatemur;
> sed quo fata trahunt, virtus secura sequetur.
> crimen erit superis et me fecisse nocentem.'
> (*B.C.* 2.284–8)

(But Cato returned a sacred utterance from the sanctuary of his heart: 'I admit that civil war is the ultimate crime, Brutus. But where the fates drag her, virtue will follow secure. It will be a reproach to the gods that they have made even me guilty.')

Cato will be simultaneously guilty and secure in his moral integrity, depending on who constructs his position. It would be a mistake to insist on a single interpretation of tension in the epic's moral rhetoric. Cato's reluctance can and should be contrasted with Caesar's willingness to entrust himself to the shifting moral landscape of civil war. Caesar's character is such that one may reasonably observe a cynical wit in his paradoxes, while Cato's character, and the tone of the rest of his speech, will not allow any such levity in what is the death of a world.[38] Caesar not Cato initiates the civil war[39] and one may read in the paradoxes of Cato's speech the confusion of the world which Caesar has made. Nevertheless there is a certain irony that the icon of the Republic is philosophically inclined to respond to the threat of tyranny and Imperial gods with his own autarchy, his own divinity.[40]

The tyrants of Senecan tragedy insist as Caesar does that moral value is fashioned by the victor against the will of his subjects or opponents. As such it is an expression of his power:

> Maximum hoc regni bonum est,
> quod facta domini cogitur populus sui
> tam ferre quam laudare
> (*Thyestes* 205–7)

[38] See especially 2.297–303 and 7.617–46.
[39] Cf. from the description of the battle of Pharsalus: *Civilia bella | una acies patitur, gerit altera* (*B.C.* 7.501–2).
[40] *Bella pares superis facient civilia divos* (Lucan, *B.C.* 7.457); cf. *Hoc enim est, quod mihi philosophia promittit, ut parem deo faciat* (Seneca, *Epistles* 48.11). On the irony of a Republic defended by an *unus homo* see Hardie (1993) 10–11.

The Broken World

(This is the greatest value of kingship: that the people are compelled to praise as well as endure their master's actions.)

> Laus vera et humili saepe contingit viro,
> non nisi potenti falsa. quod nolunt velint.
> *(Thyestes* 211–12)

(Sincere praise often comes even to a lowly man; false praise comes only to the mighty. They must want what they do not want!)

The subject of *Thyestes* is the *vetus regni furor* (the old passion for power 302) and Atreus' conception of kingship is informed by his rage for revenge. The open-ended *qua iuvat reges eant* (kings should go where they please 218) reflects the indefinite, *Fas est in illo quidquid in fratre est nefas* (All that is wrong in dealing with a brother is right in dealing with him 220). Atreus only secures his power by exceeding all moral limits in the revenge he takes on Thyestes. Through his self-conscious criminality, he reassures himself of his power and his claim to the throne. The unpunished outrage inflicted on man, gods, and the ritual which connects them is a testament to his authority. The madness of Atreus' tyranny is visible not only in the confusion of moral rhetoric but in the physical universe: as the day is driven back the chorus anticipates another giant rebellion and the collapse of the world into chaos (789–884). In a metaphor which recalls the criminal feast Atreus drives himself to fill the empty space left by the departing gods: *perge dum caelum vacat* (892).[41] We recall Tantalus' boast in the prologue:

> regione quidquid impia cessat loci
> complebo—numquam stante Pelopea domo
> Minos vacabit.
> *(Thyestes* 21–3)

(Any space unused in the quarter of unnatural crimes I shall fill up; while the House of Pelops stands, Minos will never be empty-handed.)

Atreus' usurpation of divine power is the victory of *furor*. It is revealed as such by echoes of the criminal banquet and by the instability characteristic of a world out of joint. Atreus' madness, reflected in this broken world, is, however, motivated by a desire to achieve a final victory. He remembers a recent past in which blood and power were uncertain and he wandered, paradoxically, as an exile in his own kingdom: *per regna trepidus exul erravi mea* (Throughout my own realm I have wandered

---

[41] The line also echoes 890–1: *pergam et implebo patrem | funere suorum.*

fearfully in exile 237). The crime which exceeds all limits and banishes the gods will, Atreus hopes, put him beyond the wheel of Fortune and impose closure on the struggle for power in the house of Pelops. The chorus (336–403) offers an alternative model of kingship and a Stoic resolution to the woes of the royal house. Uncertain power is contrasted with the sweet satisfaction of the simple life:

> Stet quicumque volet potens
> aulae culmine lubrico:
> me dulcis saturet quies.   (*Thyestes* 391–3)

(He who wishes may stand in power on a palace's slippery peak: let sweet repose sate me.)

The true king desires and fears nothing, sees all things beneath him (*infra se videt omnia* (366)) and confers his kingdom on himself: *hoc regnum sibi quisque dat* (390). Such a king is clearly an image of and an alternative to Atreus who, having transcended the physical and moral limits of the world, is also a self-sufficient source of his own power and also sees everything beneath him:[42]

> Aequalis astris gradior et cunctos super
> altum superbo vertice attingens polum
>   (*Thyestes* 885–6)

(Peer of the stars I stride, out-topping all, my proud head reaching to the lofty sky)

It is certainly possible to argue that the distinction the second chorus makes between tyrant and sage, between true and false kingship holds good even in Atreus' victory: the satisfaction his ultimate revenge gives him is fleeting indeed (889–91, 1065–8). All I wish to claim here is that the tragedies rehearse the familiar Stoic opposition between tyrant and sage in a potentially unsettling way. Perhaps the cliché that political power is unstable and therefore inferior to self-control breaks down with the order of everything else in so total a victory as Atreus'. If so his self-sufficiency is a mocking echo of that of the sage.

---

[42] Cf. also the description of the royal palace: *aequale monti crescit atque urbem premit* (643) and *Medea* 518–20 discussed above. Moral argument by paradox and redefinition (especially of power and kingship) is both Stoic and Senecan. See Seidensticker (1969) 42–4. On Atreus as an inversion of the Stoic sage see Knoche (1941) 66–76.

In *Hercules Furens*, morally a more complex play than *Thyestes*, the distinction between virtue and vice is more fragile. For Lycus, as for Atreus and Caesar, the victors write the history:

> sed ille regno pro suo, nos improba
> cupidine acti? quaeritur belli exitus,
> non causa. sed nunc pereat omnis memoria:
> cum victor arma posuit, et victum decet
> deponere odia.
> (*Hercules Furens* 406–10)

(But was he fighting for his kingdom, while I was driven by shameless ambition? The question about war is its outcome, not its cause. But now let the past be completely forgotten; when the victor lays down arms, the vanquished should also lay aside hatred.)

It is appropriate (*decet*) that the vanquished lay aside their hatred, and with it their every memory, for the victor initiates a new order. Even more revolutionary, Lycus makes a virtue of his isolation as a usurper. He is to be admired because he does not need the external support of social and familial honours:[43]

> nobiles non sunt mihi
> avi nec altis inclitum titulis genus,
> sed clara virtus: qui genus iactat suum,
> aliena laudat.
> (*Hercules Furens* 338–41)

(I do not have noble ancestors, nor a family distinguished by lofty titles, but glorious valour. A man who boasts of his family is praising others' achievements.)

Lycus is a less confident figure than Atreus. He does deliver a *sententia* claiming the essential quality of kingship to be the power to impose oneself on an unwilling people (*ars prima regni est posse invidiam pati* (353)) and he does aspire to the stereotypically tyrannical power of giving or withholding death from his helpless subjects, as they least desire it.[44] But for expediency's sake he

---

[43] Tyrannical though Lycus is, his boasts are very much those of any *novus homo*. See Cicero on Cato the Censor and the contrast between *virtus* and *genus* (*In Verrem* 2.5.180). Like Cicero and Cato, Lycus turns out not to be a real revolutionary (see below). So Astin (1978) 68 on Cato: 'the aim was acceptance into the governing class, not a general assault on it'.

[44] *Qui morte cunctos luere supplicium iubet | nescit tyrannus esse: diversa inroga; | miserum veta perire, felicem iube* (*Hercules Furens* 511–13). Cf. *perimat*

prefers to accept Theban society and legitimate himself by marrying Megara (341–7). Rather than rely on his own revolutionary *clara virtus* (340) he prefers to acquire her royal *clarum nomen* (359–60). Though Lycus is a less extreme and therefore less convincing autocrat than Atreus he is significant as a parallel for Hercules. Amphitryon views Lycus' *clara virtus* as a simple lie, as a mark of a chaotic world:

> prosperum ac felix scelus
> virtus vocatur; sontibus parent boni,
> ius est in armis, opprimit leges timor
> (*Hercules Furens* 251–3)

(Crime which prospers and flourishes is given the name of valour; good people take orders from the wicked; might is right, and the laws are stifled by fear.)

Yet Hercules' virtue, which Amphitryon opposes to Lycus' false virtue, is not itself free from contradiction. Amphitryon describes Hercules' hands as *ad omne clarum facinus audaces* (dauntless in every deed of renown 247). *Audax* and especially *facinus* often have criminal associations, rendering Herculean *virtus* problematic even in the mouth of its staunchest defender. Lycus I represented as a half-hearted autocrat because he needs to bolster his revolutionary *virtus* with that of the establishment. Hercules, as represented by Amphitryon, is liable to the same charge of inconsistency. Amphitryon contemptuously rejects the authority of a mere exile but trusts in a slave's power to overthrow a king:

> tremitis ignavum exulem
> suis carentem finibus, nostris gravem.
> qui scelera terra quique persequitur mari
> ac saeva iusta sceptra confregit manu
> nunc servit absens fertque quae fieri vetat,
> tenetque Thebas exul Herculeas Lycus.
> (*Hercules Furens* 269–74)

(You tremble before an unknown exile, shut out of his own state and oppressive to ours. The one who hounds crimes by land and sea, and smashed cruel sceptres with righteous force, is now far away in

---

tyrannus lenis; in regno meo | *mors impetratur* (*Thyestes* 247–8); AEGISTHUS. *rudis est tyrannus morte qui poenam exigit.* | ELECTRA. *Mortem aliquid ultra est?* AEGISTHUS. *Vita, si cupias mori* (*Agamemnon* 995–6).

servitude and endures what he forbids elsewhere, while the exile Lycus holds the Thebes of Hercules.)

The awkwardness in Amphitryon's position, that he wants to praise both the established order in Thebes and the self-justifying, revolutionary *virtus* of Hercules, recalls the paradoxes of Juno's prologue. Juno, displaced from Olympus, plays an anti-Olympian role by summoning Furies yet at the same time presents herself as the defender of heaven against Hercules' assault. Hercules' final labour is at once a liberating victory over the tyranny of Death and a rehearsal for the overthrow of his celestial brother.[45] As Lycus himself suggests, Jupiter is a model for the terrestrial king—*Quod Iovi hoc regi licet* (What Jove is allowed, a king is allowed 489)—and the struggle for moral ascendancy in Thebes mirrors the grander struggle in the heavens.

Hercules' *virtus* and particularly his final deeds, his victory over death and his apotheosis, are related to the *virtus* of a Stoic sage through a long allegorizing tradition.[46] In Seneca's tragedy (as in Euripides') Lycus, the tyrant, argues that Hercules' virtue is not what his defenders claim. Here, however, the brittle exchanges of paradox and antithesis suggest now Stoic defiance now the chaos of a broken world. Hercules' moral ambivalence is constructed partly through the unwelcome resemblance between tyrant and sage. Megara rejects Lycus' proposal of marriage even when threatened with death. Lycus is astonished that a husband buried in Hell can inspire such loyalty. Megara replies with paradoxes: *Inferna tetigit, posset ut supera assequi* (He visited the underworld to gain the upper world 423) and *Nullo premetur onere, qui caelum tulit* (No burden will crush the one who carried the heavens 425). These paradoxes of Hercules' place in the physical world inspire Megara to a version of a famous Stoic paradox, *Cogi qui potest nescit mori* (One who can be forced does not know how to die 426).

The effect is to give a Stoic cast to the earlier paradoxes of Hercules' labours. It is Hercules who inspires Megara to Stoic defiance and it is natural to read that Stoicism back into his life, even into the more troubling aspects of his heroism. Lycus

---

[45] On this and the resemblance between Juno and Hercules, *furor* and *virtus*, in the prologue see below, pp. 72–3, 114–19.
[46] See *SVF* 3.84.2–7, Seneca, *De Beneficiis* 1.13.3, 4.8.1, *De Tranquillitate Animi* 16.4, Galinsky (1972) 56, 127–8, 147–9, 167–8, and Tietze (1991).

expresses his astonishment once again, this time that Megara prefers death over life and a slave over a king. She replies, *Quot iste famulus tradidit reges neci!* (How many kings that 'slave' has delivered to death! 431), and proceeds to define virtue as endurance of authority, *Imperia dura tolle: quid virtus erit?* (Take away harsh commands: what will valour be? 433). In language reminiscent of the Roman Stoic theodicy of *Georgics* 1[47] Megara argues that the world has been ordered to reward hardness: *Non est ad astra mollis e terris via* (The path from earth to the stars is not a smooth one 437). Yet this same woman, like an Atreus or a Medea, elsewhere looks also to the powers of the underworld and a long tradition of Theban crime. At 495 ff. she looks for inspiration in the weddings of Oedipus and of the Danaids and promises Lycus *explebo nefas* (I shall complete the crime 500).[48] In her first speech to Lycus she rehearses Thebes' tradition of evil closing symbolically with serpentine (Fury-like)[49] Cadmus who drags the long marks of his body behind him *(longas reliquit corporis tracti notas* (394)). Cadmus' line awaits Lycus if he decides to rule in her kingdom:

> haec te manent exempla: dominare ut libet,
> dum solita regni fata te nostri vocent.
> *(Hercules Furens* 395–6)

(These precedents await you. Play the despot as you will, as long as the usual fate of our kingship beckons you.)

It is difficult to dissent from Lycus' diagnosis of this warped pride in a criminal tradition:[50] *Agedum efferatas rabida voces amove* (Come now! Drop this wild and frenzied talk 397).

Amphitryon succeeds Megara as Lycus' interlocutor at line 439. This second part of the agon is concerned particularly with the boundary between human and divine. Lycus plays conservative to Amphitryon's revolutionary: Lycus is unwilling to admit that mortals can become gods, that gods can have been slaves or exiles;

---

[47] Through the use of competing literary models Virgil withholds from the *Georgics* a uniform view of the order of the world: see e.g. Gale (2000) 58–67. The providential father and his determination that the farmers should be hardened by toil have a Roman Stoic cast: see e.g. Wilkinson (1969) 137–41. On Seneca's *Hercules Furens* and the *Georgics* see Fitch (1987) 159–60.

[48] For parallelism with *Medea* 748 ff. and 13 ff. in content and phrasing see Fitch (1987) 246.

[49] On snakes and Furies see Bartsch (1997) 32–4.

[50] Cf. e.g. Atreus, Phaedra, Medea; and Fitch (1987) 226.

Amphitryon advances Bacchus and Apollo as counter-examples (447–58). In the light of his earlier remarks it is ironic that Amphitryon should defend the social mobility of exiles against Lycus. Amphitryon begins his defence of Hercules on sure ground. He speaks of his deeds against the giants at the battle of Phlegra, spattered with impious blood (*post Phlegram impio | sparsam cruore* (444–5)).[51] By the end of the agon, however, Jupiter himself appears as an example of a god who suffered hardships:

> quid? qui gubernat astra, qui nubes quatit,
> non latuit infans rupis exesae specu?
> (*Hercules Furens* 459–60)

(Did he who governs the stars and shakes the clouds not lie concealed as an infant in a cave of a hollow cliff?)

What Amphitryon does not mention is that this infancy in the cave under Mt Ida[52] was a necessary concealment if Jupiter was to survive to adulthood and overthrow his father's kingdom. What Amphitryon suppresses, Hercules later reveals in his madness:

> vincla Saturno exuam
> contraque patris impii regnum impotens
> avum resolvam; bella Titanes parent,
> me duce furentes.
> (*Hercules Furens* 965–8)

(I shall strip off Saturn's chains, and against my unnatural father's unbridled rule I shall loose my grandfather. Let the Titans in rage prepare war under my leadership.)

The compromised opposition between *furor* and *virtus* is the most important dynamic in this tragedy and I will return to it later. My point here is that we approach the paradoxes, the revolutionary nature of Herculean *virtus* through Megara's Stoic defiance of the tyrant. We are encouraged to see her obduracy as the image of his. In the agon between Amphitryon and Lycus the tyrant becomes the speaker for the establishment and Amphitryon allows even Olympian order to be subsumed in a cyclical struggle of power. It is difficult to resist the conclusion that moral ascendance is the victor's prize, and this relativism is damaging not only

---

[51] On the battle between Olympians and giants as the battle of law against chaos see Hardie (1986) 90–7 and 154–6 on the erosion of the distinction between them.
[52] So in fact MS E: *ideae* for *exese* (A).

to Hercules but also to the Stoic rhetoric on which he trades. Without a secure means of distinguishing between independence and tyranny, between an autonomous, self-sufficient rhetoric and simple arrogance, the paradoxes of Stoic defiance can appear nothing more than posturing.

3. IRONY AND LIES

Various characters in the tragedies deliberately misrepresent themselves. Atreus deceives Thyestes with a show of brotherly love, Medea persuades Creon that she is less lethal than she is. In such situations there is no dangerous collapse of vice into virtue; the characters are lying and it is easy for us to distinguish the truth from the lie.[53] Verbal irony, where a single phrase has two levels of significance, is more problematic. At the feast Atreus reassures Thyestes with the words *ora quae exoptas dabo | totumque turba iam sua implebo patrem* (I shall show you shortly the faces you long for, and fill the father full with his own dear throng *Thyestes* 978–9). There are two clearly distinguishable interpretations of the sentence and Atreus' word-play does not suggest a moral equivalence of cannibalism with parental love. Atreus alludes to the murder and Thyestes is reassured, but not by the allusion. That said, Atreus' doublespeak is threatening for the same reason as his claim to divinity. As the divine superstructure ceases to be a restraining, controlling force but becomes a locus of conflict when Atreus himself attains divinity, so common human rhetoric becomes a locus of conflict as Atreus draws a private, criminal significance from the words he apparently shares with Thyestes.[54]

The moral confusion of this tragedy is not that of *Hercules Furens*. Juno's anger and Hercules' madness are genuinely ambiguous as Atreus' revenge is not: Atreus may present the tragedy as a crime which Thyestes brings on himself through his mad desire for royal power (302), but by his own proud admission Thyestes' desires are also his own.[55] Just as no power intervenes to protect the rituals of divine sacrifice, no power intervenes to

---

[53] On such a distinction see Clark and Csapo (1991) 112–19.
[54] Cf. Meltzer (1988), who argues 311 ff. that Atreus' black humour, which transgresses the boundaries of natural and appropriate meaning, is an expression of his power.
[55] See *Thyestes* 271–2 and 1104–10.

protect the rituals of moral rhetoric from Atreus' perversion. That Tantalus and Thyestes surrender to madness in language which recalls a sage's obedience to fate is an outrage.[56] It is of great moral significance that no corrective power intervenes to punish this sacrilege, to restore the ritual, the cliché. The foundations of moral order are questioned, its structures corrupted, yet at no point do we ask, as we do in *Hercules Furens*, 'Is this an act of *furor* or *virtus*?'

Thyestes is Seneca's most influential revenge-drama and also the most extreme in its moral darkness. The more ambiguous portrayal of revenge in *Hercules Furens* is in fact more representative. Here and in *Medea* revenge is an alloy of moral sensitivity and savagery. The revenging tragic Fury, whose role Medea assumes, combines just such qualities in Aeschylus. However, in the *Aeneid* and the tradition of Latin literature the Fury tends towards deliberate criminality.[57] The tension between Olympian and pre-Olympian powers in the *Oresteia* is heightened in Virgil and Seneca by Stoicism's rigid opposition of reason to passion, order to disorder.[58] Reconciling the most beautiful Olympian to the dog-like Furies is less of a challenge than accommodating them in a moral system which describes anger as 'the most disgusting and insane emotion of all'.[59] The collision between Stoicism and the more acceptable face of Fury of Attic tragedy is pointed in *Medea* where a morally ambivalent avenger who explicitly assumes the role of Fury speaks as a Stoic. Medea's apparently Stoic pronouncements should be seen in the wider context of the Roman-Stoic cast of the moralizing in the tragedy. The power of kings is again a significant element. Medea's agon with Jason is dominated by his failure to resist the threats and charms of royal power. His decision to approach her anger with prayers is characteristic; he approaches Creon in the same way:

constituit animus precibus iratam aggredi (*Medea* 444)

(My mind is resolved to tackle the angry woman with an appeal).

---

[56] *Thyestes* 100 and 489. See Tarrant (1985) 160 on this line and the use of *sequor* in a moral context.

[57] On the Furies of Latin literature, their Greek predecessors, and Seneca's *Medea* see Hershkowitz (1998) 48 ff. and below, Ch. 3.

[58] On Stoicism and revenge see Burnett (1998) 7–10.

[59] *affectum...maxime ex omnibus taetrum ac rabidum* (Seneca, *De Ira* 1.1).

Compare:

> Perimere cum te vellet infestus Creo,
> lacrimis meis evictus exilium dedit.   (*Medea* 490–1)

(When Creon in rancour wanted to destroy you, my tears prevailed on him to grant you exile.)

> gravis ira regum est semper   (*Medea* 494)

(the anger of kings is always harsh).

Jason sees himself trapped between angry royal powers. Here and elsewhere Medea confirms his perception with her willingness to compete with Creon and Acastus as a royal power in her own right. In argument with Jason Medea promises to bury any opposition beneath the waves:

> His adice Colchos, adice et Aeeten ducem,
> Scythas Pelasgis iunge: demersos dabo.
>   (*Medea* 527–8)

(Add the Colchians, add Aeetes to lead them, combine the Scythians with the Pelasgians: I shall bury them.)

To the nurse's warning, *Rex est timendus* (A king must be feared), she replies, *Rex meus fuerat pater* (My father was a king 168). The royal power she has defied she inherits at the end of the tragedy: she celebrates her victory with the words, *iam iam recepi sceptra* (Now in this moment I have recovered my sceptre 982), *rediere regna* (My realm is restored 984). Seen in this light Medea is another Atreus, another tyrant.

Jason's failure to resist tyrants is un-Stoic and Medea exposes this weakness by presenting herself as a Stoic: *Fortuna semper omnis infra me stetit* (I have always risen above Fortune in every form 520), *Contemnere animus regias, ut scis, opes | potest soletque* (My mind has the power and habit, as you know, of disdaining the wealth of kings 540–1). When he says he is ashamed to have received his life from Medea she replies, *Retinenda non est cuius acceptae pudet* (One need not hold onto a life one is ashamed of receiving 505). Suicide is the Stoic's final victory over the tyrant and again Jason shows himself both weak and un-Stoic. Medea's position in this argument is less clear. There is an explicit contrast between Jason's fear and her defiance of kings and Fortune, and one does not have to look too far to support an implicit contrast between the two characters in line 505:

> Nunc summe toto Iuppiter caelo tona
> . . . . . .
> quisquis e nobis cadet
> nocens peribit, non potest in nos tuum
> errare fulmen.
> *(Medea* 531, 535–7)[60]

(Now, highest Jupiter, thunder across the whole sky...whichever of us falls, the guilty will die; against us your thunderbolt can make no error.)

Medea's Stoicism, in so far as it pertains to her, is, however, in bad faith. Fortune, kings, and wealth are beneath her not because she is a *sapiens* but because she is a supreme tyrant. Her use of Stoic rhetoric is similar to that in *Thyestes*: the victim's weakness is exposed and simultaneously Stoicism itself is mocked by the impropriety, the sacrilege, of passion usurping reason's rhetoric.

In her agon with Creon Medea's reflections on the transience of royal power sound like Hecuba's[61] but because we know she is deliberately misrepresenting herself there is nothing problematic in her words. Creon enters as the king Jason fears and Medea, for her own un-Stoic reasons, plays the martyr to his tyrant. She heralds his entry, *ipse est Pelasgo tumidus imperio Creo* (It is himself, swollen with Pelasgian power: Creon 178), and he takes his cue: *regium imperium pati | aliquando discat* (She must finally learn to endure a king's authority 189–90), *aequum atque iniquum regis imperium feras* (You must endure a king's command, just or unjust 195). She responds with, *iniqua numquam regna perpetuo manent* (Unjust kingship never remains unbroken 196), and opens her formal speech with personal reflections on royal power:

> Difficile quam sit animum ab ira flectere
> iam concitatum quamque regale hoc putet
> sceptris superbas quisquis admovit manus,
> qua coepit ire, regia didici mea. *(Medea* 203–6)

(How difficult it is to turn a mind from anger once it is aroused, and how kingly it appears, to one who has laid his proud hands on the sceptre, to continue a course once begun, I learned in my own royal home)

> rapida fortuna ac levis
> praecepsque regno eripuit, exilio dedit.
> *(Medea* 219–20)

---

[60] Cf. also NURSE. *Moriere.* MEDEA. *Cupio (Medea* 170).
[61] *Medea* 219–20, quoted below. Cf. *Quicumque regno fidit et magna potens | dominatur aula nec leves metuit deos |...me videat et te, Troia (Troades* 1–2, 4).

(Fortune, so swift and fickle and precipitate, snatched me from my kingdom, and delivered me to exile)

Creon assures her that he is not a man to wield the sceptre with violence (*non esse me qui sceptra violentus geram* 252) and Medea is allowed her day in Corinth. Creon, like Thyestes, is doomed by his lack of rigour. Thyestes, though succumbing to the lures of empire, is pleased to be reconciled with Atreus; Creon, though willing to uphold an obviously unjust argument,[62] is reluctant to reject a suppliant. Had they acted either morally (Thyestes does not enter the palace, Creon leaves Jason to Medea) or tyrannically (Thyestes and Creon try to exterminate Atreus and Medea), they would not have been such easy victims. The mixed moral virtue of the victim is a classic part of the tragic effect—thus far Seneca is a good Aristotelian[63]—but less Aristotelian is the suggestion that the essential virtues in these tragedies are rigour, strength, power, lack of moderation. The suggestion that if you push vice and virtue far enough they meet is present in the structure of the tragedy. The agons with Jason and with Creon are parallel. Both are concerned with the same subject, the guilt of Jason and Medea, and in both Medea uses Stoic rhetoric to make trial of her opponent. Jason rejects Stoicism, Creon rejects tyranny, and both are thereby doomed. Medea speaking Stoically, the Devil quoting Scripture, is certainly ironic, but it is not necessarily a very dangerous irony. More serious is the suggestion that there is a real resemblance between Stoicism and tyranny, virtue and vice. Seen in the wider context of the parallel agons Medea's Stoic posturing before Jason (*Fortuna semper omnis infra me stetit* (I have always risen above Fortune in every form 520)) is a significant misrepresentation.

4. STICHOMYTHIA AND PARADOX

Medea moralizes most conspicuously in argument with the Nurse, who alone of the Corinthians is on Medea's side and trusted with

[62] His judgement on Jason is given at lines 263–5: *nullus innocuum cruor | contaminavit, afuit ferro manus | proculque vestro purus a coetu stetit.* The weak part of the argument, that Jason has not associated with Medea, has pride of place at the end of the sentence (and in fact the section). Zwierlein (1986*b*) begins a new paragraph with the next line: *Tu, tu malorum machinatrix facinorum* (266).

[63] Aristotle, *Poetics* 1453^{a}7–12.

her plans for vengeance. Misrepresentation is not necessary here as it is in the agons with Creon and Jason. Much of Medea's conversation is conducted in stichomythia, a form of dialogue which in Senecan tragedy is rich in *sententiae*, pointed antitheses, and other forms of verbal artifice. T. S. Eliot, in his introduction to Thomas Newton's translation of the tragedies, commented that 'in the plays of Seneca the drama is all in the word, and the drama has no reality behind it. His characters all seem to speak with the same voice, and at the top of it; they recite in turn.'[64] In *Troades*, for example, Pyrrhus and Agamemnon exchange the clichés of popular morality and its tyrannical inversions less in dialogue than in simple contraposture:

PYRRHUS.	Lex nulla capto parcit aut poenam impedit.
AGAMEMNON.	Quod non vetat lex, hoc vetat fieri pudor.
PYRRHUS.	Quodcumque libuit facere victori licet.
AGAMEMNON.	Minimum decet libere cui multum licet.

(*Troades* 333–6)

(PYRRHUS. No law spares a prisoner, or forbids reprisal. AGAMEMNON. What law does not forbid, a sense of restraint forbids. PYRRHUS. The victor has a right to do whatever he pleases. AGAMEMNON. He who has much right should please himself least.)

Generalities are commonly blended with particular references:

PYRRHUS.	Est regis alti spiritum regi dare.
AGAMEMNON.	Cur dextra regi spiritum eripuit tua?
PYRRHUS.	Mortem misericors saepe pro vita dabit.
AGAMEMNON.	Et nunc misericors virginem busto petis?
PYRRHUS.	Iamne immolari virgines credis nefas?
AGAMEMNON.	Praeferre patriam liberis regem decet.

(*Troades* 327–32)

(PYRRHUS. It is the act of a great king to grant life to a king. AGAMEMNON. Why then did *your* hand deprive the king of life? PYRRHUS. Often a compassionate man will grant death rather than life. AGAMEMNON. And now as a compassionate man you seek a virgin for the tomb? PYRRHUS. So nowadays you consider sacrifice of virgins a crime? AGAMEMNON. To put fatherland before children befits a king.)

Stunt rhetoric of this kind is a familiar feature of declamation, Ovid, Seneca, Lucan. At its best the essentials of the argument are

[64] Eliot (1927) ix.

condensed and enlivened by the verbal ingenuity. Sometimes one feels that the dialogue merely degenerates into a clever game.[65] In the passage above we might single out line 329 as particularly weak: it is hard to believe that Pyrrhus believes that Priam's death was a mercy-killing and by line 333 he has changed his position completely. The rhetoric, it seems, has strayed from the realities of the case. Pyrrhus' line (329) signifies little but his continued intransigence. For Pyrrhus, the disputant, as for us, the readers of the tragedy, the form is more important than the content: he has made a paradox to answer Agamemnon's accusation, delivered his line and not surrendered. Eliot's impression of characters reciting in turn, divorced from each other and from the world of the drama is offered as an aesthetic judgement. However, in another essay he argues that Seneca's characters speak less to communicate than to assert before an audience, 'I am myself alone'. This is not just a matter of style but, like the characters' obsessive self-dramatization, a reflection of Stoic individualism.[66] The distinctive combination of self-assertion and isolationism is evident also in the unreal dialogue of Seneca's stichomythia. Here also declamatory style suits the ethical context.

Stichomythic exchanges are an ideal form for the refusal to communicate. Phaedra resists Theseus' questions, until he threatens to torture the nurse, with stichomythia:

THESEUS. Effare: fido pectore arcana occulam.
PHAEDRA. Alium silere quod voles, primus sile.
THESEUS. Leti facultas nulla continget tibi.
PHAEDRA. Mori volenti desse mors numquam potest.
THESEUS. Quod sit luendum morte delictum indica.
PHAEDRA. Quod vivo.
THESEUS.   Lacrimae nonne te nostrae movent?
PHAEDRA. Mors optima est perire lacrimandum suis.
THESEUS. Silere pergit.
                       (*Phaedra* 875–82)

(THESEUS. Speak out: I shall hide your secret in my faithful heart. PHAEDRA. If you want another to keep a secret, first keep it yourself. THESEUS. You will be given no opportunity for death. PHAEDRA. If someone wants to die, death is always in reach. THESEUS. Let me know the offence that needs to be punished by death. PHAEDRA. The fact that I live. THESEUS. Do my tears not move you? PHAEDRA. To die

[65] So Hadas (1939) 226.   [66] Eliot (1964) 38–43

mourned by loved ones is the best of deaths. THESEUS. She continues to keep silence.)

For Theseus this exchange of one-liners is an obdurate silence. Inversion, negation, and paradox are colourless modes of communication. Theseus' words and opinions return contradicted or twisted and he feels, quite rightly, that he has heard nothing but defiance. Compare this exchange of half-liners from *Thyestes*:

TANTALUS. pater, potes regnare.
THYESTES.   Cum possim mori.
TANTALUS. Summa est potestas—
THYESTES.   Nulla, si cupias nihil.
                                (*Thyestes* 442–3)

(TANTALUS. Father, you can be king! THYESTES. Yes, since I can die. TANTALUS. The highest power is—THYESTES. No power, if you want nothing.)

Thyestes continues with a 25-line speech on the evils of wealth and power and thus gives some colour to vice if not to virtue.[67] The point of the comparison between Thyestes and Phaedra, however, is that the passionate woman and the Stoic speak similarly. Phaedra's *libido moriendi* is distinguishable from a Stoic's rational suicide,[68] lonely despair from a philosopher's retirement from life, but not in these clipped phrases alone. Stoic Thyestes sees no role for himself in the world of wealth and political power and his two half-lines of extinction and nothingness communicate the extremism of his dissent. Tantalus' words break up on his father's paradoxes and negations in a dialogue whose fractured form echoes the violence and the absolute rejection which is Thyestes' moral response.

Seneca's Stoicism, as I remarked before, is isolationist because it is habitually conducted *in extremis*. In a hopelessly corrupted world there is no context for worthwhile activity; the only valuable act is a refusal to participate. Paradox, inversion, and negation, all kinds of rhetorical damage, reflect at a formal level not only rejection but also disengagement. Thyestes does not want to be

[67] Even so his description is very general. The only particulars are the names of the Getae and the Parthians, who belong more properly to the Roman world. Jupiter is mentioned in line 463 and the palace on the peak of the mountain recalls Atreus' (455 cf. 642–3) but these are both symbolic figures.
[68] On the distinction see Seneca, *Epistles* 78.1 f.

accommodated in the world of princes any more than Phaedra wishes to share her thoughts with Theseus. The brittleness and artificiality of some of Seneca's stichomythic exchanges give the impression of rhetoric losing touch with reality. This form accommodates the crisis of absolute alienation. Isolationist Stoicism, by abandoning the world, the shared locus of human activity and human meaning, has abandoned any conceptual space for self-definition. The virtuous self which survives the loss of a world is, for all its violent display, essentially colourless. It may sketch the world it rejects, it may warp and damage the rhetoric of general culture (as Zeno made a civil war of life in the *polis*), it may define itself through grand antitheses (life and death, freedom and slavery, virtue and vice), but ultimately it lacks its own material for self-construction. Stoic isolationism is a life which has peeled away from reality into a self-supported exercise.

Formalism has its limits. We can and should distinguish between the disputants in the stichomythic exchanges: Pyrrhus probably didn't have a convincing excuse for his murder of Priam; Phaedra's situation has become impossible through circumstance—Hippolytus has rejected her as he might not have done, Theseus has returned as he might very well not have done; Stoic Thyestes is ideologically committed to the impossibility of life at Argos and the preferability of life among the mute beasts. Nevertheless the formal parallelism between the speech of these different characters is significant. With the rejection of the world and its rhetoric of self-definition very little is left to the Stoic soul but the will to defy. This naked exercise of will or power is dangerous for its resemblance to the self-sufficiency of the tyrant. In the stichomythic exchanges we see not only the proximity of vice and virtue, but the failure of rhetoric to discriminate. In Medea's argument with the nurse we see not only the unwelcome conjunction of *furor* and *virtus*, but a significant triviality. Moral rhetoric loses its grip and Stoicism is implicated in the failure.

NUTRIX. Siste furialem impetum,
   alumna: vix te tacita defendit quies
MEDEA. Fortuna fortes metuit, ignavos premit.
NUTRIX. Tunc est probanda, si locum virtus habet.
MEDEA. Numquam potest non esse virtuti locus.
NUTRIX. Spes nulla rebus monstrat adflictis viam.
MEDEA. Qui nil potest sperare, desperet nihil.

NUTRIX. Abiere Colchi, coniugis nulla est fides
nihilque superest opibus e tantis tibi.
MEDEA. Medea superest: hic mare et terras vides
ferrum et ignes et deos et fulmina.
NUTRIX. Rex est timendus.
MEDEA. Rex meus fuerat pater.
NUTRIX. Non metuis arma?
MEDEA. Sint licet terra edita.
NUTRIX. Moriere.
MEDEA. Cupio.
NUTRIX. Profuge.
MEDEA. Paenituit fugae.
NUTRIX. Medea.
MEDEA. Fiam.
NUTRIX. Mater es.
MEDEA. Cui sim vide.
. . . .
NUTRIX. Compesce verba, parce iam, demens, minis
animosque minue: tempori aptari decet.
MEDEA. Fortuna opes auferre, non animum potest.
(*Medea* 157–71, 174–6)

(NURSE. Control your impulsive rage, my child; even silence and stillness can hardly protect you. MEDEA. Fortune fears the brave, but crushes cowards. NURSE. Courage is praiseworthy when it is in place. MEDEA. It can never happen that courage is out of place. NURSE. No hope points a way for our battered fortunes. MEDEA. One who can feel no hope need feel no despair. NURSE. Colchis is lost, there is no loyalty in your husband, and nothing remains of your great wealth. MEDEA. Medea remains: here you see sea and land, steel and fire and gods and thunderbolts. NURSE. A king must be feared. MEDEA. My father was a king. NURSE. You do not fear arms? MEDEA. Not even if sprung from the earth. NURSE. You will die. MEDEA. I desire it. NURSE. Escape! MEDEA. I regret escaping. NURSE. Medea— MEDEA. I shall become her. NURSE. You are a mother MEDEA. You see by whom... NURSE. Control your words, give up your threats now, crazy woman, subdue your proud spirit; it is right to adapt to circumstances. MEDEA. Fortune can take away my wealth, but not my spirit.)

At the heart of this scene is Medea's famous claim to be a world in herself (166–7). Through her magical arts she has the power to control sea and earth. The form of her reply is dictated by the nurse's previous challenge: *Mare et terras* etc. caps *Colchi, coniugis, fides*, etc. and Medea carries her point. Whatever she means, she says, 'I survive, and in me you see all the world'. She demonstrates her self-sufficiency also in her consciousness of her own myth at line 171: NURSE. *Medea.* MEDEA. *Fiam.* There are hints of Medea's metadramatic power in her manipulation of Creon in the following scene (discussed above). He assumes and discards the costume of a tyrant as she prompts. Creon, like Thyestes, can be interpreted psychologically as a weak, inconsistent character. Both can be interpreted differently as prisoners of a criminal myth. The very awkwardness of their shifts of character bears witness to the inexorable power of the protagonists. Creon and Thyestes are the plastic creatures they are less because it is psychologically convincing than because the vengeance of Medea and Atreus has the authority of an established myth.[69] The dramatic illusion is shaken, the world broken, at line 171 because Medea implies a knowledge of the course of the tragedy. The Nurse speaks of Medea as a person, Medea of herself as a myth already written. There is parallelism between this assertion of power and the claim in lines 166–7. As Medea steps out of the dramatic illusion her name becomes a shorthand for the destiny of that world. What is—earth and sea, gods and thunderbolts—and what will be in this tragedy is all contained in Medea's name. Costa valuably quotes Corneille's imitation of lines 166–7:[70]

NÉRINE. Dans un si grand revers que vous reste-t-il?
MÉDÉE.   Moi,
   Moi, dis-je, et c'est assez.
                            (Corneille, *Médée* 320–1)

Discarding Seneca's 'earth and sea' Corneille writes more purely than the original. Medea answers the question and closes the line with a single word. 'What remains to you?' 'I'.

Medea's Stoic responses earlier in the scene depend on a similar self-sufficiency. The Nurse argues that there is a time and a place for virtue, Medea that there is always a place for virtue; that is, that it is not dependent on circumstances (160–1). Medea paradoxically agrees that in her situation 'no hope shows a path', that is that her resolve is proof against any event (162–3). At the end of

---

[69] On fabricated, literary necessity see further below in Sections 5 and 8. Medea's self-sufficiency, like Atreus' is apparent also in the private significance she finds in the shared activity of communication: only the audience understands the word 'Medea' as she does.

[70] Costa (1973) 87.

the scene the Nurse again asks Medea to subordinate her spirit to her situation (*animosque minue: tempori aptari decet* (175)); she is mad (*demens*) to defy the Corinthians. This draws the Stoic response, *Fortuna opes auferre, non animum potest* (Fortune can take away my wealth, but not my spirit 176), just as the earlier plea, *Siste furialem impetum* (Control your impulsive rage 157), was answered with, *Fortuna fortes metuit, ignavos premit* (Fortune fears the brave, but crushes cowards 159). The scene is thus framed with an impossible juxtaposition of opposites, *furor* and *virtus*. Defying not only circumstance but even the context of moral placement Medea survives.[71]

5. AMBIGUITY AND ALIENATION

Megara's devotion to Hercules could be constructed as a passionate death-wish or Stoic resolution. Medea's determined criminality is an obstacle to an ambiguity of this kind: though she has a sense of moral order, as she argues with the nurse she has already delivered two long speeches urging herself to surpass the crimes of the past. Medea's ambiguity is the ambiguity of incoherence. In her first speech she calls first on the Olympians and then, with a paradox to mark the awkwardness of this combination, on the chthonic powers.[72] This is appropriate for a character who combines deliberate evil with a role as the avenger of the broken convenants of both marriage and Nature. For Atreus, Thyestes' crime is significant only as an offence against him rather than as a wrong in some more objective sense. In the act in *Thyestes* (176–335) parallel to Medea's conversation with her Nurse Atreus makes no use of Stoic rhetoric: he represents himself to his follower as a supreme tyrant and moralizes only in inverted form.[73] One approach to the Stoic moralism in Medea's dialogue with the Nurse is to see it as another manifestation of the paradox of the Fury, the disorderly servant of order. Read this way Medea's

---

[71] On the unreal, inhuman quality of Medea's *sententiae* and her stichomythic exchanges with the Nurse see Henry and Walker (1967) 176.

[72] *quosque Medeae* magis | *fas est precari: noctis aeternae chaos,* | *aversa superis regna manesque impios* (*Medea* 8–10). On the opening scene, Medea's characterization, and the subject of this tragedy see below, pp. 148–53.

[73] e.g. *Laus vera et humili saepe contingit viro,* | *non nisi potenti falsa* (*Thyestes* 211–12).

speech is a stylized representation of an unresolved tension in her characterization.

Medea's deliberate misrepresentation of herself in the agon with Jason sits awkwardly with this approach. Her words to Jason, *Contemnere animus regias, ut scis, opes | potest soletque* (My mind has the power and habit, as you know, of disdaining the wealth of kings 540-1), are a tyrant's misuse of Stoic rhetoric rather than the voice of her better nature. If this is accepted then it is doubly difficult to take her words to the Nurse, *Fortuna opes auferre, non animum potest* (Fortune can take away my wealth, but not my spirit 176) at face value. Read this way Medea's apparent Stoicism in the stichomythia is a sign that the world of *Medea*, no less than the world of *Thyestes*, is unhinged. *Furor* speaking as *virtus* is one of many outrages in the tragedy, and it bears witness to the totality of passion's victory. There is much to recommend this approach. Both tragedies repeatedly represent Natural order as confounded; the physico-ethical framework of the world as dissolved. We return to the model of the 'slip-slidin' world'. It should be stressed, however, that the resemblance between Stoic and tyrant is not entirely a confusing effect created by the broken world, but a potential for confusion realized in it. Stoic and tyrant are both distinguished by their autonomy, their ability to assert themselves in defiance of whatever rhetoric and reality circumstance has ratified. The rhetorics of Stoicism and of tyranny are both distinguished by paradox, inversion, and negation. Thus there is also a more narrowly formal resemblance. Stichomythia, where this stylized speech is particularly prominent in the tragedies, accommodates the isolation of a Stoic or a tyrant, the disengagement of a frivolous disputant or of a passionate suicide. In each case the brittleness[74] of the speech is a mark of the speaker's alienation from the world. In *Medea* 157f. Stoic rhetoric is perceived as madness, and juxtaposed with the crimes of Medea's past.[75] Taken with Medea's calculated posturing elsewhere, the effect is a staging of the fragility of Stoic self-representation.[76] Nothing

---

[74] Note the images of dissolution and fragmentation in Quintilian's discussion of *sententiae* 8.5.27-30.
[75] *Forsan inveniam moras* (173) clearly alludes to the murder of Absyrtus. So Costa (1973) 88.
[76] Foley (1989) 63-4 finds Seneca's Medea an uninteresting vision of the subjugation of reason by passion. Certainly her presentation is more heavily mor-

can touch the *sapiens* in his philosophical retirement, but the representation of this victory is not equally inviolable.

The suggestion that the *sapiens* resembles his passionate opposite is one which Seneca addresses. *'Quid ergo' inquit, 'fortis inminentia mala non timebit? Istuc dementis alienatique, non fortis est'* ('What then', he asks, 'will the brave man not fear the evils hanging over him? That would be the condition of a madman, a lunatic, rather than of a brave man' *Epistles* 85.24). To this Aristotelian interlocutor Seneca replies in orthodox fashion: *Verum est, quod dicis, si mala sunt; sed si scit mala illa non esse et unam tantum turpitudinem malum iudicat*...(What you say is true if they are evils; but if he knows that they are not evils and believes that the only evil is baseness...85.25). These dangers are morally indifferent and the *sapiens* will avoid them because they are not preferable: *non timebit illa, sed vitabit* (he will not fear them though he will avoid them 85.26). Of course it is in the wise man's contempt for such things that he is recognizable as *fortis* and immediately Seneca is back in the familiar territory: *Describe captivitatem, verbera, catenas, egestatem et membrorum lacerationes*...(Paint a picture of slavery, whips, chains, hunger and the mutilation of limbs 85.27). The wise man is accused of madness again in *De Constantia*, and importantly here the frustrated interlocutor claims that the Stoic invulnerability is achieved through nothing more than a play on words: Stoicism offers, for example, an escape from slavery by redefining slavery, by changing the names of things (*mutatis rerum nominibus* (*De Constantia* 3.2)).[77] The idiolect of a Stoic's alienation and the idiolect of a maniac's nonsense do resemble each other and a *sententia* which presumes an utterly hostile environment is not an adequate basis for discrimination: *Fortuna fortes metuit, ignavos premit* (Fortune fears the brave, but crushes cowards *Medea* 159).

The exchange of *sententiae* where Medea replies Stoically to her nurse is disturbing also because of its impersonal abstraction. It is probably anachronistic to observe a further distancing effect in

---

alized and more abstract and certainly she is more inhuman a character, but she is far from being a passive, mythological dummy dressed in passion's costume. Most self-conscious of all Seneca's characters she reasons her way through the disintegration of a world and its moral order.

[77] On this passage see Hershkowitz (1998) 245, who compares also Horace, *Odes* 2.2.19–21 ([*Virtus*] *populumque falsis | dedocet uti | vocibus*).

Medea's avoidance of the feminine gender (*Qui nil potest sperare* (One who can feel no hope need feel no despair 163)),[78] but certainly there is nothing in lines 159–63 to associate them with this tragedy and this speaker rather than any other. When the nurse breaks the pattern in line 164 by referring to the Colchians and the dishonoured marriage Medea still contrives an impersonal effect by referring to herself in the third person: *Medea superest* (166). *Fiam* (I shall become her 171) functions similarly as the metadramatic resonance makes Medea's role strangely external to Medea herself. There is a speaker determined to become Medea, who therefore is not yet Medea. In the strangeness of Medea's metadramatic self-consciousness and in the distancing effect of her moral generalizations we have a strong sense of a role being fashioned for Medea to play rather than of life being lived. There is something unreal about both a pre-written life and a life constructed from abstractions.

Abel's approach to Brechtian alienation from Shakespearean metadrama is an instructive comparison.[79] Brecht insisted that actors and spectators alike distance themselves from the acts represented on stage in order to reflect on the events more responsibly. These words in approval of Chinese acting may be taken as representative, 'The efforts in question were directed to playing in such a way that the audience was hindered from simply identifying with the characters in the play. Acceptance or rejection of their actions and utterances was meant to take place on a conscious plane, instead of, as hitherto, in the audience's subconscious.'[80] Elsewhere, 'By means of a certain interchangeability of circumstances and occurrences the spectator must be given the possibility (and duty) of assembling, experimenting and abstracting.'[81] Such a critical perspective is, by design, dispassionate: an assembly of experiments and abstractions does not inspire sympathy. In the loss of necessity in Brecht's theatre, assent withheld from an objective order which might frame and limit the dramatizing powers of the characters and spectators, Abel sees unreality: 'But if one does not see any inner necessity in the lives of people, will not their lives appear dreamlike?... [Brecht's perspective] is precisely the kind of thinking that can never assert the reality of any

---

[78] Cf. *Mors optima est perire* lacrimandum *suis* (*Phaedra* 881).
[79] Abel (1963) 105–7.   [80] Brecht (1964) 91.   [81] Brecht (1964) 60.

person not oneself. Life, in a way, had to be a dream for Brecht, given his extreme devaluation of individual feelings.'[82] The liberty of the individual soul and other bourgeois myths,[83] though they have real potency, are ultimately fictions which masquerade as necessity. These fictions, of (false) necessity, make illusions of the bodies they control. And with this Brecht is inscribed in a tradition which looks back, ultimately, to the bad dreams which constitute the reality of Hamlet or Macbeth. The comparison with Seneca should not be pushed too far: the disgust of Hamlet and Macbeth[84] at finding themselves actors in bad plays has more in common with Brechtian disdain and ridicule than it does with Medea's triumphant apotheosis from the dramatic illusion. However, the emotional coldness of a scripted world, a world whose vital forces are postures and whose players therefore cannot be lamented or loved with a whole heart, remains a common element.

Medea's disengagement is felt most keenly because of the contradictory elements in her dialogue, the Stoic moralizing and the criminality of the Medea myth. A morality play conducted exclusively in symbols, abstractions, and generic figures offers a form of necessity in the coherence of its own moral rhetoric. *Medea*, by offering incompatible necessities and by representing both, determinedly, as roles or postures is not such a play. The false form of necessity is created also in the first act of *Phaedra*. Phaedra recognizes 'a certain interchangeability of circumstances', the curse on all Cretan princesses, and surrenders to the role of distanced spectator of her own life.[85] At a formal level in two substantial speeches given over to self-description (*Phaedra* 85–128, 177–94) there are only two first-person active verbs, and both of these are verbs of observation: *agnosco* (113) and *scio* (177). Her nurse

---

[82] Abel (1963) 106.
[83] See e.g. Althusser (1976) 133–9 on modes of reading history, on the idealist category of the Subject, and the opposing perspective of dialectical materialism.
[84] Cf. Ferrucci (1980) 140–8, for whom the guilt which Macbeth and his wife feel is inappropriate in a dramatic reality which is itself deceptive and evil. Malcolm and Macduff fare better in such a world essentially because they are more at ease with a conception of their moral characters as mere personas. The fictive quality of moral necessity in the world does not trouble them.
[85] Cf. Mr Gradgrind's criminal son: 'If a thunderbolt had fallen on me,' said the father, 'it would not have shocked me less than this!' 'I don't see why,' grumbled the son. 'So many people are employed in situations of trust; so many people, out of so many, will be dishonest. I have heard you talk, a hundred times, of its being a law. How can *I* help laws?' Dickens, *Hard Times*, book 3, ch. 7.

argues that the curse is a construction, a necessity which Phaedra has fabricated:

> Deum esse amorem turpis et vitio favens
> finxit libido, quoque liberior foret
> titulum furori numinis falsi addidit.
> *(Phaedra* 195–7)

(The story that love is a god was invented by base lust, in the interests of its own depravity; to have greater scope, it gave its mad passion the pretext of a false divinity)

Shortly afterwards Phaedra engages in some brief exchanges with the nurse which combine the elevation of her passion to a dramatic necessity with the breakdown of communication into a playful triviality:

NUTRIX. Ferus est.
PHAEDRA. Amore didicimus vinci feros.
. . . .
NUTRIX. Patris memento.
PHAEDRA. Meminimus matris simul.
NUTRIX. Genus omne profugit.
PHAEDRA. Paelicis careo metu. *(Phaedra* 240, 242–3)

(NURSE. He is wild. PHAEDRA. I have learnt that wild things are overcome by love. NURSE. Remember your father! PHAEDRA. I remember my mother as well. NURSE. He shuns our whole kind. PHAEDRA. I have no fear of a rival.)

Phaedra represents Pasiphaë's crime as a lesson she has learned, as one of life's truths. Her assurance of Hippolytus' fidelity is a piece of tortured logic which would be a joke in another context,[86] but fits well with the superficiality of *patris* answered with *matris*. The triviality of Phaedra's speech about her own life is a sign of its unreality and of her alienation from herself as she surrenders to the family myth. What is morally unproblematic in *Phaedra* is problematic in *Medea*, where Stoic disengagement is presented in parallel with a surrender to a criminal narrative already written.[87]

Anger, the greatest of the passions, is distinguished by its carelessness of the self; it rages with a desire that is utterly inhuman,

---

[86] Cf. Andromache on Astyanax's death in *Troades*, p. 249 below.
[87] Medea's myth is not, strictly speaking, a family myth like Phaedra's but there is a sense in which she inherits her own past. She looks to match and surpass what she did as a *virgo* and her past crimes provide the inspiration for her future.

careless of itself so long as it damages the other (*minime humana furens cupiditate, dum alteri noceat sui neglegens* (Seneca, *De Ira* 1.1)). Its lack of self-control is evident in its contempt for both decorum and necessity (*aeque enim impotens sui est, decori oblita, necessitudinum immemor* (*De Ira* 1.2)). Again, *in extremis* the common structures through which we live and are defined, the necessities, must be rejected by a Stoic. The loss of the self which Seneca sees as characteristic here of passion is also characteristic of the social ruin which a Stoic will accept in a corrupt world. Medea reflects Stoically in generalizations which exclude the particulars, the necessities, of her own situation and this alienated posture is characteristic of opposing poles of the ethical spectrum. In one of the suicide epistles Seneca tells the story of a meeting between emperor[88] and slave:

C. Caesar, cum illum transeuntem per Latinam viam unus ex custodiarum agmine demissa usque in pectus vetere barba rogaret mortem: 'nunc enim,' inquit, 'vivis?' Hoc istis respondendum est, quibus succursura mors est: mori times; nunc enim vivis? (*Epistles* 77.18)

(C. Caesar was passing along the Via Latina when a man stepped out from the ranks of prisoners, his grey beard hanging down even to his breast, and begged for death: 'What!' said Caesar, 'are you alive now?' That is the answer which should be given to men to whom death would come as a relief: you are afraid to die; what! are you alive now?)

The Stoic philosopher takes up the tyrant's words and repeats them as his own. The slave symbolizes someone enslaved by fear and desire for the gifts of Fortune; the tyrant symbolizes the Stoic. Striking to a modern reader is the inhumanity of the advice. In the closing section of the epistle even the contented interlocutor is obliged to face mortality. Seneca argues in the metaphor of the stage:

Quomodo fabula, sic vita non quam diu, sed quam bene acta sit, refert. Nihil ad rem pertinet, quo loco desinas. (*Epistles* 77.20)

(It is with life as it is with a play: it matters not how long the act is spun out, but how good the acting is. It makes no difference at what point you stop.)

---

[88] The emperor's name is uncertain. *C.* (i.e. *Caius*) is the reading of Bentley and the OCT; MSS V and Q suggest *t* and *tullius* respectively.

The advice to the happy man and to the metaphorical slave depend on the same point, that there is nothing real in this world. What matters is the quality of the acting, the moral disposition of the soul as it makes its choices in a staged reality. The world is an illusion not a necessity because it holds nothing of true value; it has value only indirectly (and this is not true value) as the context in which the soul expresses its disposition. The absolutism of this ethic is evident also in the confrontation between the emperor and the slave. The emperor is supremely powerful in his world, the prisoner completely inactive; the subject of their conversation, life and death, is equally polarized and is articulated through paradox. The slave, inasmuch as he is attached to an illusory world of moral indifferents, is himself a shadow and valueless. The moral indifference of the external world and its slave is expressed here in a tyrant's/Stoic's indifference to his suffering.[89] The slave does not, figuratively speaking, share a world with the Stoic or the tyrant, and from this alienation comes both the cruelty and the triviality of the exchange.

Epistle 77 is a particularly savage (and fine) letter. The anecdote of emperor and slave is parallel to the story of a Spartan boy who chose suicide over a degrading and servile life. Turning back to his addressee Seneca writes of a self-imposed slavery, *Infelix, servis hominibus, servis rebus, servis vitae. Nam vita, si moriendi virtus abest, servitus est* (Unhappy fellow, you are a slave to men, a slave to business, a slave to life. For life, if you lack the courage to die, is slavery *Epistles* 77.15). The letter progresses to the emperor and the slave via an attack on luxury in which the unfortunate addressee is effectively condemned to death for a worthless existence:

Quid est aliud, quod tibi eripi doleas? Amicos? Quis enim tibi potest amicus esse? Patriam? Tanti enim illam putas, ut tardius cenes? Solem? Quem, si posses, extingueres. Quid enim unquam fecisti luce dignum? (*Epistles* 77.17)

(What else is there which you would regret to have taken from you? Friends? But who can be a friend to you? Country? What? Do you think enough of your country to be late to dinner? The sun? You would extinguish it if you could. For what have you ever done that was fit to be seen in the light?)

---

[89] Cf. Bartsch (1997) 42–3, who argues that Stoic contempt for the body colludes with the pleasures of those who enjoy seeing it mutilated.

The Broken World 55

From this, easily, to the tyrant's contemptuous, *nunc enim vivis?* (are you alive now?). This section of the letter is unusual in its presentation of isolation. Here a man is isolated by his own vice from potential friends, where normally in the *Epistles* we find a man isolated from friends by their vice.[90] The tone is accordingly different and this leads to the surprising repetition and endorsement of a tyrant's words. However, the moral principle which makes such an endorsement possible is perfectly conventional. One of the crucial distinctions between vices and virtues is that vices are rooted in an external world over which we have no power (*non erunt in nostra potestate. Quare? Quia extra nos sunt, quibus inritantur Epistles* 85.11).

The identification of tyrant and all-powerful Stoic is controlled in *Epistle* 77 by the surrounding argument. In *Medea* no framing narrative controls such an identification;[91] there is no power in the tragedy higher than Medea herself. Standing outside family, country, gods, and dramatic illusion she resists moral definition. I do not wish to argue here that this marginalized figure belongs to another world, that her resistance to moral definition is an expression of 'otherness' of this kind, that the world of *Medea* is fragmented in the sense that it presents a conflict of incompatible, but individually coherent, realities. I am arguing here for a vision of Medea not as an irruption from beyond, but as a fracture internal to the rhetoric of virtue itself. This is Stoicism deconstructed, not the dualism of a Freudian or Nietzschean interpretation.[92] Stoicism, and particularly Seneca's Stoicism, is prone to surrender the public world as corrupt and to withdraw into the

---

[90] See especially *Epistle* 7.

[91] The myth of *Argo*'s voyage and the breaking of Nature's covenants, the *foedera mundi* (335), frames the myth of Jason's breach of the oath of marriage. Far from controlling the myth of domestic disorder the macrocosmic analogue echoes its confusions: Medea is both a manifestation of outraged Nature and a technological, Argonautic criminal. On this see below, pp. 151–68.

[92] For Freud and Senecan scholarship see Ch. 4, n. 9. I cannot offer a doctrinaire Nietzschean scholar of Senecan tragedy, but it seems to me that there should be one. Dionysus would have to be rewritten as a Fury but the displacement of the Olympians in *Thyestes*, and in *Medea* the vengeance of primal Nature and an indomitable will rooted in chaos (see *Medea* 8–9), these elements are surely some encouragement. See also Curley (1986) 166 and Hershkowitz (1998) 245–6 on Lucan, 'And we find ourselves once more in the Nietzschean world: "Once you had passions and called them evil. But now you have only virtues: they grew out of your passions. At last your passions have become virtues and all your devils angels." (Nietzsche, *Thus Spoke Zarathustra*, i).'

sanctuary of a realm over which one exercises complete power. Stripped of a context in this way the Stoic self retains very little definition despite its assertions of self-sufficiency. It delights physically in torment and death, verbally in paradoxes and negations, for these are the means through which it expresses its contempt for the world and its detachment. The Stoic is not insane (as one of Seneca's interlocutors suggested) nor a tyrant, but without a world in which to express its virtuous dispositions in the conventional and preferable manner the maimed self which survives speaks with the inhumanity of a maniac or a tyrant. Medea is no more Stoic in her dialogue with Jason or the nurse than Caligula is with the slave, but she sounds Stoic.

Seneca writes that particular vices are corruptions of particular natural, virtuous dispositions, and therefore that vices, though unequivocally vices, are the marks of a better nature.[93] Even in dissolution and failure we can see the image of what might have been. In *Hercules Furens* and even in *Medea* (as I shall argue in the following chapter) this sense of loss is an important element in an interpretation of the confused boundaries of vice and virtue. In *Thyestes* the paradox is emotionally colder: Atreus as a sacrilegious priest and an anti-God suggests piety and divinity through sacrilege. The echoes of Stoic obedience and Stoic self-sufficiency in this tragedy operate in precisely the same way: sacrilege requires a mocking resemblance. Medea's manipulation of Stoic rhetoric is no less deliberate. In this respect as in many others she resembles Atreus. The failure of moral order in these tragedies reflects the extraordinary power of its criminal protagonists, but ironically Stoic rhetoric concedes this power through the very means by which it empowers its adherents. In the moral nihilism of *Thyestes* this irony is grimly amusing. In *Medea*, a play dominated by an ambivalent myth of human aspirations to divinity, the tone is less clear. The juxtaposition of calculated evil with failed magnificence, nihilism with tragedy, is typically Senecan. In so far as Stoicism is implicated in the fragmentation of the world in

---

[93] This is not, as it might appear, a Peripatetic argument. These vices are irrational perversions of natural dispositions not virtues possessed in an exaggerated or inadequate degree. *Non ideo vitia non sunt, si naturae melioris indicia sunt* (Seneca, *De Ira* 2.15.3). It may be argued on the basis of this passage and elsewhere that by 'nature' Seneca understood 'one's own personal nature'—so Asmis (1990).

Senecan drama perhaps we should observe not only anti-Stoicism but the makings of a Stoic tragedy.

6. THE DRAMATIC WORLD

In the previous sections I discussed the erosion of a distinction between vice and Stoic virtue. Central to this discussion was the absence of necessity in the dramatic world. This absence of necessity I approached in three related ways. Seneca's isolationist Stoicism, determined to present a soul defined from within and in defiance of a hostile public reality, does not look to the dramatic world to be the framework of its existence. This unnecessary external world is rejected as a framework because of its instability: Fortune is chaotic. The rejection of the world as morally unnecessary reflects the absence of a parallel physical necessity in the external world. The cosmos as a whole is a coherent system: one event follows another in accordance with fixed and eternal laws, hence the moral prescription, 'Live in accordance with Nature.'[94] This inexorable sequence of events in accordance with stable laws is necessity expressed physically. Although the disorder of Fortune, and of evil, is ultimately incorporated within an orderly system, the perspective from within the system sees only the chaos of its immediate context: the citizens of tragic Thebes or Argos see flux not necessity. Finally, metatheatrical consciousness undermines necessity in both these physical and moral senses, but in a different way. The representation of life as a role, as something fabricated, draws attention to the possibility of it being fabricated otherwise. Existence is no longer a given, a common necessity, but something to be asserted and fashioned. Not only the individual but his/her reality is a matter of perspective. This autonomy of the metadramatic character plays interestingly with the autonomy, the private perspective, of the Stoic.

A distinctive feature of Senecan tragedy, in comparison with Greek, is its description of the landscape.[95] What is an unavoidable part of the myths of *Oedipus* or *Thyestes* is embraced also in

---

[94] Diogenes Laertius 7.85–9.
[95] The terms 'landscape' and 'world' I will use broadly to include all the objects which constitute the physical context of the tragedies. In this extended sense Medea's poisoned gifts are as much part of the landscape as Atreus' palace or the celestial bodies.

the other plays: the disordered world is an image of the tragic crime. This is most striking in *Medea* where the heroine's vengeance on Jason is simultaneously vengeance on the Argonauts who disturbed the world's divine laws. When Medea performs her magic rite to poison gifts for Creusa most of her incantation concerns the disruption of Nature (740–842); when the gift is delivered not just Creusa but Corinth bursts into flame (888–90). The disordered landscape, commonly read as a challenge to moral order in the tragic world, can paradoxically also be read as an affirmation of moral order. The reflection which the tragic act casts in the surrounding landscape can be interpreted as an unambiguous and, crucially, objective test of its moral value. Thus even as Atreus' act shatters the limits of crime and banishes the gods it indicates its moral ugliness. This observation is not as trivial as it sounds. In ancient literary criticism one of the great threats of mimetic art is that its audience will assimilate itself to the model represented, that, in this case, the audience will be infected by Atreus' passion.[96] A human audience cannot identify with a disordered cosmos. Therefore the descriptions of the landscape, as an objective, dispassionate index, reflect but control the reception of the tragic crimes.[97] Some scholars, looking to the physicality of Stoic ethics and the doctrine of cosmic sympathy, have seen Seneca's tragic worlds as Stoic worlds. Like the ever-expanding ripples on a pond, crime in the soul spreads to the body to the landscape and finally to the wider cosmos.[98] Most have approached Seneca's tragic landscape in a more narrowly literary fashion: the landscape reflects the dramatic characters in a figurative rather than Stoically real fashion. By this approach the landscape is usually figurative and real at the same time: Phaedra's

---

[96] Nussbaum (1982) 86 distinguishes two strands in Plato's attack on mimetic poetry: 'its failure to embody a systematic understanding' and 'its unhealthy relationship with the irrational'. The poetic passion of an Atreus is dangerous not just as a bad example but as a bad example which is created, presented, and received in a magical, charming, or overpowering form which obstructs the systematic analysis necessary to recognize it as a bad example. Rather than analysing the mimesis the reader/audience uncritically echoes it.

[97] Tietze (1988), invoking Brecht's epic theatre, makes this argument.

[98] The world as dynamic continuum (expressed here in the simile of a fluid) is an important concept here. See Rosenmeyer (1989), Reinhardt (1926) 111 ff., Sambursky (1959) 1–20, 41–4. The tragedies' Stoic concern with the Law of Nature, Fiore (1975) 5 argues, is the chief reason for their popularity and influence in 17th-cent. Spain.

The Broken World

incarceration in the royal palace is simultaneously an independently real event, a real cause, and a figurative representation of her sexual repression.[99] The important point here—and it makes no difference which of the two approaches, Stoically real or figurative landscape, is adopted—is the return of an external necessity even in the dissolution of the world. The landscape functions as an objective ethico-physical context for human action; even as it collapses into disorder it interprets tragic events coherently.

One objection to this restoration of necessity is that the representation of a disordered landscape indicates no more than a world in crisis. It is clear, for example, that the post-Golden Age world of *Medea* is unstable and that Medea and the Argonauts are both involved in this instability, but there is not the discrimination here for an interpretation of the tragedy. Representations of cosmic disorder restate and amplify the crisis but they do not interpret further. This is essentially the same phenomenon we have seen at a rhetorical level: there is a formal resemblance between the tortured language of Cato and Caesar in Lucan's *Bellum Civile* because linguistic strain, like cosmic disorder, indicates no more than crisis. Representations of the physical or rhetorical structure of the world as unstable, abnormal, inverted are often spectacular but they are not capable of fine discrimination. Figurative interpretations of the landscape which look for more than harmony or its absence tend to be more productive because they allow one to track the progression and the source of evil more precisely.

In *Medea* the author of *Argo*'s voyage dies as follows:

> ustus accenso Pelias aeno
> arsit angustas vagus inter undas.   (*Medea* 665–6)

(Pelias, boiled in the heated cauldron seethed while wandering in narrow waters)

The manner of his death recalls the greater voyage which is also the reason for his death: Nature takes vengeance on those who transgressed her laws. The combination of flames and water characterizes not only this particular crime but, symbolically, Medea's passion more generally. This ode begins (579–90) by comparing

---

[99] On Phaedra see Segal (1986) 29–37. More generally on a compatibilist approach to the literary landscape see Lapidge (1979) 359.

the anger of a discarded wife to the violence of flame and raging water. Medea herself made the same comparison (406–14). The imagery of fire and flood performs a structural and a moralizing function: the water-fed fire which engulfs the fragile isthmus at the end of the play (885–90 cf. 35–6) is not merely caused by Medea but *is* her anger, externalized in physical form. Passion as elemental imbalance is a commonplace of both philosophical and literary traditions;[100] the violence of fire and/or water recurs as a major figurative system in all of Seneca's tragedies.[101] The effect is simplifying and reductive: the final scene of the tragedy is an image of Medea's soul and easily interpreted through a familiar tradition.

Medea's passion is communicated directly and simply, through the same imagery, from her soul to the landscape via the gifts which hold the hidden seeds of fire.[102] The reductive effect is particularly apparent in tragedies with unforeseen events. At the level of dramatic action Phaedra is indirectly responsible for Hippolytus' death. Symbolically the monster which kills him recalls Pasiphaë's bull and the minotaur (1170–3, 1039 cf. 116).[103] Phaedra represented her desire in the same terms (112–18)[104] and figuratively therefore Hippolytus is killed directly by Phaedra's passion. His lost struggle to control his horses, expressed in the image of a sailor lost at sea, recalls specifically an earlier description in the same image of Phaedra's surrender to her passion (1072–5 cf. 181–3).[105] Deïanira's killing of Hercules in

[100] On Stoicism particularly and elemental imbalance see e.g. Seneca, *De Ira* 2.19.1–5, Virgil, *Georgics* 1.231–7, Mynors (1990) 54–5 ad loc., and Ross (1987) 45–62.

[101] See Pratt (1963) 205–9 and *passim*. For Pratt the elemental imagery is part of 'the Stoic orientation of the dramas' (205). On the similar representation even of different passions (e.g. anger and desire) see Regenbogen (1961) 434.

[102] For a collection of inanimate objects in Senecan tragedy having human characteristics, see Liebermann (1974) 111 ff. Cf. Benjamin (1977) 133 on Calderón: 'And the mysterious externality of this dramatist does not consist so much in the way the stage-property constantly comes to the fore in the twists of the dramas of fate, but in the precision with which the passions themselves take on the nature of stage properties. In a drama of jealousy the dagger becomes identical with the passions which guide it.'

[103] For these points in greater detail see Segal (1986) 74–6. Cf. also Orlando (1978) 30 on Racine's use of the same symbolic system.

[104] See also the Nurse's words, *natura totiens legibus cedet suis, | quotiens amabit Cressa?* (176–7).

[105] So Henry and Walker (1966) 226 f. Cf. Clytemnestra's similar surrender, *Agamemnon* 138 ff.

The Broken World 61

Hercules Oetaeus is handled similarly.[106] Like Juno in *Hercules Furens*,[107] Deïanira intends to confront Hercules with another labour, a monster born of her hatred:

> commoda effigiem mihi
> parem dolori: non capit pectus minas.
>
> . . . . . .
>
> quid rogas Ditem mala?
> omnes in isto pectore invenies feras
> quas timeat; odiis accipe hoc telum tuis.
> (*Hercules Oetaeus* 265–6, 268–70)[108]

(Give me a form to match my pain: my heart cannot contain its threats... Why ask Dis for evil? You will find all the monsters to terrify him in that heart of yours. Take this as the weapon of your hate)

At the level of dramatic action she kills Hercules accidentally by sending him a robe as a love-charm. The robe was given to her by Nessus, who was born where Medea's baleful herbs grow (493 cf. 465–6), and whom she encountered in the world of Hercules' labours (495–500). Nessus tried to abduct her, was shot by Hercules, mutilated himself and urged her to smear his blood on a garment for a love-charm. Deïanira describes the *amoris pignus Herculei* (the pledge of Hercules' love 490) to the nurse as if she knew it was destructive: they term it variously *malum* (evil 491, 566), *tabes* (gore 520, 528), *virus* (poison 536, 565), *pestis* (plague 566), *vis dira* (evil force 568). It is also to be Hercules' last labour: *Amorque summus fiet Alcidae labor* (474). The burning poison and the pyre which raises Hercules to heaven (*in astra tollunt* 1638) are ultimately caused by the flames of Deïanira's passion and the imagery makes the connection immediate:

---

[106] Defenders of the authenticity of this play include Rozelaar (1985) and Nisbet (1987) 250. For the opposing view see Friedrich (1972) and Zwierlein (1986*a*) 313 ff. My own position is, 'in respect of this use of imagery *Hercules Oetaeus* might as well be by Seneca'.

[107] Deïanira takes Juno as her model: *incogitata, infanda, Iunonem doce | quid odia valeant: nescit irasci satis* (297–8). For Juno's anger as the source of Hercules' labours and finally becoming his latest labour see *Hercules Furens* 83–5, 96–9, 107–9.

[108] Cf. a similar reductive tone in *Thyestes*: TANTALUS. *Me pati poenas decet, | non esse poenam. mittor ut dirus vapor...* (86–7); ATTENDANT. *Quonam ergo telo tantus utetur dolor?* | ATREUS. *Ipso Thyeste* (258–9). The mechanisms and instruments of the tragic crime are the characters themselves.

DEÏANIRA. est aliquid hydra peius: iratae dolor
nuptae. quis ignis tantus in caelum furit
ardentis Aetnae?
(Hercules Oetaeus 284–6)

(There something worse than the hydra: the pain of an angry wife. What fire of burning Aetna rages so strong against heaven?)

NUTRIX. Quid ipsa flammas pascis et vastum foves
ultra dolorem?
(Hercules Oetaeus 351–2)

(Why do you yourself feed the flames and further cherish a great pain?)

The poison in Hercules' body (*pestis* 1249) is Deïanira herself (*pestem* 851) expressed in the medium of the robe (*pestem* 566). When Alcmena sees Hercules' agony she misrecognizes it, significantly, as the psychological *furor* of the other play:

dolor iste furor est: Herculem solus domat.
Removete quaeso tela et infestas, precor,
rapite hinc sagittas: igne suffuso genae
scelus minantur.
(Hercules Oetaeus (1407, 1404–6)[109]

(The pain is madness: it alone masters Hercules. Please remove his weapons and I beg you take his deadly arrows from here: the fire running through his cheeks threatens evil)

What we see on the stage are passions in physical form. Through familiar patterns of imagery sequences of actions are reduced to successive representations of the same passion. The source of the tragic crisis can be traced to a character, here Deïanira, and the very conventionality of the generic representations of passion simplifies moral interpretation. Necessity returns in the coherence of familiar systems of imagery, whether or not underpinned by Stoic beliefs in the law of Nature and the interrelatedness of the cosmos.

It is characteristic of Seneca's tragic practice that the externalizing of passion into the dramatic landscape does not restore necessity in the manner that I have just sketched above. Rather, the morally weighted descriptions of landscape are implicated in the

---

[109] The crowd draws the same conclusion, *vulgus antiquam putat | rabiem redisse* (806–7).

The Broken World

same contradictions which confuse the more transparent rhetoric of vice and virtue. In *Agamemnon* Clytemnestra describes the disorder of her soul in conventional, but particularly detailed imagery:

> Maiora cruciant quam ut moras possim pati;
> flammae medullas et cor exurunt meum;
> mixtus dolori subdidit stimulos timor;
> invidia pulsat pectus, hinc animum iugo
> premit cupido turpis et vinci vetat;
> et inter istas mentis obsessae faces
> fessus quidem et deiectus et pessumdatus
> pudor rebellat. fluctibus variis agor,
> ut, cum hinc profundum ventus, hinc aestus rapit,
> incerta dubitat unda cui cedat malo.
> proinde omisi regimen e manibus meis:
> quocumque me ira, quo dolor, quo spes feret,
> hoc ire pergam; fluctibus dedimus ratem.
> ubi animus errat, optimum est casum sequi.
> (*Agamemnon* 131–44)

(My torments are too great for me to endure delays. Flames are burning my heart and bones; mixed with my pain, fear goads me on; jealousy pounds in my breast, and again rank lust oppresses my spirit and will not be controlled. And amid these fires besetting my mind, though weary and defeated and ruined, shame fights back. I am driven by conflicting waves, as when wind and tide pull the sea each way, and the waters hesitate, uncertain which scourge to yield to. So I have dropped the rudder from my hands. Wherever anger, pain, hope carry me, there I shall proceed; I have given up the boat to the waves. When one's spirit is astray, it is best to follow chance.)

In the first section *pudor*, the better part of Clytemnestra's self, refuses to be enslaved by the flames of passion. In the second, Clytemnestra surrenders utterly to external forces: she changes from being driven by waves (138) to actually becoming a wave (140). In a phrase with clear philosophical overtones[110] she gives up the rudder/direction of her soul. Both sections begin with the physical metaphors and progress to psychological interpretation. The analysis (Clytemnestra's and my own) seems laboured and unnecessary, but it is important to see how emphatically the imagery is interpreted. The surrender of the *regimen* (141) is

[110] Tarrant (1976) 202 quotes philosophical parallels from Seneca (*Epistles* 94.67, *De Ira* 3.25.4) and Lucretius (3.95) but is less convinced by his own point.

recast in psychological terms (142–3) and the same progression is then repeated as *ratis* (*ratem* 143) is glossed as *animus* (144). *Fluctibus dedimus ratem* (143) echoes the similarly placed *fluctibus variis agor* (138) which opened the section. The word *ratis* even sounds like *ratio*.[111]

The dramatic reality of *Agamemnon* is made up of flames, boats, and waves. Clytemnestra's passion springs in part from the sacrifice of Iphigenia. Later in the same conversation with the nurse she remembers the torches of her daughter's marriage (*memini faces* 158) and the nurse describes the sacrifice thus:

> Redemit illa classis immotae moras
> et maria pigro fixa languore impulit.
> (*Agamemnon* 160–1)

(She remedied the delays of the motionless fleet, and mobilised seas fixed in sluggish idleness)

It is a major theme of this tragedy that the history of Agamemnon's house is a criminal repetition.[112] In the drama itself 'no character dominates even two consecutive acts' yet despite this changing cast of characters and particulars the same theme endures and the same generic events recur.[113] This repetition is expressed in part through a common imagery. The criminal sacrifice of Iphigenia is repeated as it is revenged in Clytemnestra's anger. It inspires the 'fires of a mind besieged' (136) in 'the torments too great to allow delay' (132) and most obviously in the rousing of the calm sea. The act in which Clytemnestra so carefully explains that fire and water represent the tides of passion is introduced by an ode on the fragility of royal power which ends with the statement that it is safer not to sail on the open sea but to steer a course nearer shore (103–7). Thyestes' ghost promised that the palace would 'swim' in blood (*Iam iam natabit sanguine alterno*

---

[111] Cf. Cicero, *Tusculans* 1.30.73: *tamquam in rate in mari immenso nostra vehitur ratio*.

[112] Cassandra, for example, returns to consciousness (*recipit diem* 788) and sees Agamemnon's palace as another Troy. Agamemnon disagrees (*hic Troia non est* 795) and is proved wrong. On repetition in this tragedy and more generally see Schiesaro (1997*a*) 77, 85 and *passim*.

[113] Quotation from Tarrant (1976) 3. Arguably the thematic unity is made all the more prominent by the generic quality, the lack of individuality, of the various characters. So Seidensticker (1969) 119f. Cf. also Vitse (1988) 359–60 on this same quality in 17th cent. Spanish theatre.

domus 44) and when Agamemnon dies he does so in watery fashion:

> cupit fluentes undique et caecos sinus
> dissicere et hostem quaerit implicitus suum.
> (*Agamemnon* 895–6)

([The king] tries to part the blinding folds that pour around him, and searches for his enemy while ensnared)

The third act is dominated by a description of the storm which wrecked Agamemnon's fleet (421–578). What is in one sense dramatically unimportant—it has no bearing on Clytemnestra's revenge—is an extravagant development of the figurative language which imposes thematic unity on the tragedy. Though the storm is a conventional subject, Tarrant in his overview isolates four models as particularly influential (Virgil, *Aeneid* 1.81 f., 3.192 f.; Ovid, *Metamorphoses* 11.474 f., *Tristia* 1.2 f.) of which the storm from *Metamorphoses* 11 features most prominently in the subsequent commentary.[114] The allusions to the storm which took faithful Alcyone's husband from her are surely ironic in a tragedy where the storm is a figurative expression of Clytemnestra's passion for revenge.

Like Homer's Odysseus (*Odyssey* 5.360 f.) and Virgil's Aeneas (*Aeneid* 1.94 f.) before them Seneca's despairing Greeks envy those who died at Troy, all that is except the lesser Ajax: *solus invictus malis* | *luctatur Aiax* (Ajax alone was still struggling, unconquered by disaster 532–3). What Tarrant finds puzzling (the other Greeks are not in fact all dead)[115] is resolved by a psychological interpretation: Ajax alone is unconquered *in spirit*. The psychological interpretation, apart from resolving the awkwardness, is consistent with the figurative use of the storm for an upheaval of the soul. Ajax is to be contrasted not only with the Greeks but also Clytemnestra who surrendered to the storm. Unlike Clytemnestra he struggles to control his boat (533–4 cf. 138–44) but with her second cast Pallas transfixes him with a

[114] More precisely, the storm of *Metamorphoses* 11 is most influential on the storm itself in Seneca's description. As the focus turns from the weather to the sailors Seneca turns naturally for his model from Ovid's storm to the Trojan material of the *Aeneid*. On the dominant influence of *Met.* 11 up to this point see Jakobi (1988) 145–8 in conjunction with Tarrant (1976) 248–85.

[115] Tarrant (1976) 275, comparing the account in Quintus Smyrnaeus, suggests that *solus* means 'alone of his crew'.

thunderbolt. Though pierced by fire and carried off by it nevertheless he resists:

> transit Aiacem et ratem
> ratisque partem secum et Aiacem tulit.
> nil ille motus, ardua ut cautes, salo
> ambustus extat, dirimit insanum mare
> (*Agamemnon* 537–40)

(It passed through Ajax and his ship, and carried away part of the ship and Ajax himself. Unshaken, like a lofty crag, he stood out though scorched from the saltwater, sundered the maddened sea.)

The image of a rock unmoved by the raging sea which surrounds it, while literally appropriate to Ajax, is a common figure for resistance. King Latinus, beset by his subjects' mad desire for Juno's quasi-civil war, resists for five lines (*ille velut pelago rupes immota resistit...* (he resisted like a rock unmoved by the sea *Aeneid* 7.586 f.)) before surrendering in the appropriate metaphor: '*frangimur heu fatis,*' inquit, '*ferimurque procella*' ('alas,' he said, 'we are broken by fate and carried off by the storm' 594). What is restricted to figurative language here is dramatically real in the world of Seneca's *Agamemnon*.[116] Again the potential awkwardness of an over-literal reading (Ajax is carried off, but moved in no respect?) emphasizes the figurative and psychological. Transfixed by fire and immersed in the insanity of the sea he resists:

> superasse saevum pelagus atque ignes iuvat,
> vicisse caelum Palladem fulmen mare.
> (*Agamemnon* 545–6)

(I glory in having overcome flood and fire, in having conquered heaven, Pallas, lightning, sea)

The real awkwardness of this scene is that his defiance is clearly defined as *furor* (*furibundum* 544, *furens* 557). The intransigent Greek hero cannot be accommodated in the broadly Stoic context of Roman epic or tragedy with its rigid opposition of *ratio* to *furor*.

---

[116] Although this figurative storm in *Aeneid* 7 is parallel to the 'real' storm in *Aeneid* 1 I still think it is reasonable to represent the world of Senecan tragedy as more determinedly symbolic than that of Virgilian epic, but it is not an important point. Compare also Latinus' surrender of the metaphorical reins of state with Hippolytus' battle with the reins of his chariot in the symbolic landscape of Phaedra's passion (*Phaedra* 1072–7).

Although Ajax is destroyed by an angry god in Greek and Roman myths alike, the moral context of Greek epic and tragedy is sufficiently flexible to concede a certain fatal greatness to its heroes in a way that the Roman-Stoic context is not. As Seneca's heroes strive to surpass what is conventional, natural, and familiar they trespass against the pattern of moral rightness in the world.[117]

The disjunction between Greek and Roman has the potential to be morally problematic and Seneca realizes it. Pallas' thunderbolt is the greatest of various weapons; it caps 'whatever Pallas can do with aegis and Gorgon's madness' (*quidquid...| aegide et furore Gorgoneo potest* 529–30).[118] The hendiadys here exposes the *furor* of divine anger more nakedly. The speech as a whole recalls the storm of *Aeneid* 1, and with it the familiar tensions of Juno's un-Olympian (or all-too-Olympian) anger. Juno's storm was brought to an end by Neptune and the same god intervenes here:

> plura cum auderet furens,
> tridente rupem subrupit pulsam pater
> Neptunus imis exerens undis caput
> solvitque montem; quem cadens secum tulit
> terraque et igne victus et pelago iacet.
> (*Agamemnon* 552–6)

(As he dared say more in rage, father Neptune raised his head from the depths of the waves, struck and dislodged the rock with his trident, and toppled the crag. He carried it with him in his fall, and lies conquered by earth and fire and sea.)

Particularly if Neptune's appearance here is inspired by that in the *Aeneid*, as Tarrant suggests,[119] the difference between the two episodes is striking: Seneca's Neptune brings calm and resolution

---

[117] Seidensticker (1985) 131 contrasts the self-assertiveness of the Greek tragic hero with the self-consciously criminal transgression of the Senecan hero. Cf. also Zintzen (1972) 207–9 on Senecan tragedy as a critique of the Greek tragic hero. Knox (1964) 36–8 argues that it is essential for the Sophoclean hero to be able to define himself outside the boundaries which define others: 'This uniqueness, this sharply differentiated individuality, is something of which the Sophoclean heroes are fully aware, indeed they insist on it' (38).

[118] There is a problem in the text here: *haut* for *aut* in lines 529–30 is one emendation (Miller); *nunc* for *aut* in line 531 another (Castiglioni). See Tarrant (1976) 275–6. Whether or not Pallas actually tries alternative weapons before resolving on the thunderbolt, it is the last and greatest of the selection.

[119] Tarrant (1976) 280 on line 554: 'Probably inspired by Virg. *Aen* 1.127 *[Neptunus] summa prospiciens placidum caput extulit undis*'. See also *sensit Neptunus et imis | stagna refusa vadis* (*Aen.* 1.125–6).

by burying the hero in the flame and sea he had hitherto resisted. Poetic memory does not make Ajax Aeneas any more than Juno's memory achieves the reverse;[120] it merely brings the earlier myth to mind. Hubristic Ajax is punished on his own particular merits and the divine anger of Pallas should be interpreted accordingly. Nevertheless, in Clytemnestra's laborious analysis of her passions in the independently familiar imagery of flame and flood we have what appears to be an abstract schema for interpretation which suggests a contradictory reading. Add the opposition of *furor* to *furor* (Ajax's to Pallas'), the approbation implicit in *solus invictus*... (532), and the schema, destabilized, amplifies and feeds off the contradictions of the *Aeneid*. The final effect is similar to that created by the misuse of Stoic rhetoric in *Thyestes* or *Medea*: it is not sensible to argue that Ajax is virtuous because he succeeds where Clytemnestra fails or that Medea is Stoic because she speaks like one. It does seem sensible to argue that Seneca damages a framing, controlling rhetoric by misusing or inverting it. My point here is that the necessity of world order, even interpreted as the internal coherence of a system of physical imagery, is fractured in Seneca's dramatic reality.

More commonly, as in the two Hercules plays, this confusion is rooted in a more central opposition of perspectives: Hercules' ambivalent *virtus* is the primary focus of *Hercules Furens* and *Hercules Oetaeus*. Descriptions of the physical world do not resolve rival constructions of Herculean *virtus* but are incorporated into them. In *Hercules Oetaeus* the burning passion which destroys the hero can be constructed as Deïanira's but it can also be constructed as Hercules' own. Jealous of Iole she represents Hercules' labours as a sequence of rapes:

> errat per orbem, non ut aequetur Iovi
> nec ut per urbes magnus Argolicas eat:
> quod amet requirit, virginum thalamos petit.
> si qua est negata, rapitur; in populos furit,
> nuptas ruinis quaerit et vitium impotens
> virtus vocatur.
>
> (*Hercules Oetaeus* 417–22)

(he wanders over the earth not in order to rival Jupiter or to walk as a great man through the cities of Greece. He looks for someone to love, girls'

---

[120] Juno takes Pallas' victory as her model (*Aeneid* 1.39–49).

The Broken World

bedrooms he seeks. If any is denied him he takes her by force; he rages against the nations, looks for brides in the ruins and uncontrolled vice is called virtue)

When Deïnaira's poison takes effect Hercules tears his own limbs apart (825–7) as also the abductor Nessus did (521–2). When Deïanira hears a description of Hercules' agony she calls on Jupiter and other powers to destroy her in a chaos of fire and broken rock (842–4); Hercules makes a similar request for himself (1290–1336). Here parallel descriptions can as easily problematize as simplify an interpretation. Hercules' self-mutilation, physical and mental agony are clear signs of madness, but this tragedy by suggesting that his *virtus* is flawed or false suggests also the possibility that his agony may be his own, not simply an imposition of Deïanira's. A similar argument can be advanced in *Hercules Furens*.[121] If the dramatic world is a medium in which souls collide directly through imagery rather than through the apparatus of actions and objects, cause and effect, it is difficult to define the boundaries of the different souls.

Most commentators on *Phaedra* see the tragedy as the product of the *furor* of both Hippolytus and Phaedra. The hunter, Hippolytus, becomes prey and one can argue that the irony is significant, that the violence which destroys him at the end of the tragedy is recognizable as Hippolytus' own.[122] If the argument is transposed to *Hercules Oetaeus*, the agony of Nessus which Hercules recalls in his own death becomes a reflection of Hercules' characteristic activity, his violent labours. Hercules describes his pain metaphorically through the monsters of his labours (1359 ff.) and Alcmena, who (mis)recognized his madness as that of the earlier tragedy, (mis)recognizes this agony again as not Deïanira's poison but a product of his own life:

> Non virus artus, nate, femineum coquit,
> sed dura series operis et longus tibi
> pavit cruentos forsitan morbos labor.
> (*Hercules Oetaeus* 1396–8)

(Son, it is no woman's poison which cooks your limbs, but the hard chain of labour and long toil perhaps has nurtured some bloody disease in you)

---

[121] See below, pp.114–19, and above, pp. 32–6.   [122] So Leeman (1976) 203–4.

Add to this Deïanira's characterization of the labours as passionate conquests and the parallelism between Nessus and Hercules as abductors and the reductive imagery of passion no longer tracks crime securely. Hercules' body is a site on which his own passions or Deïanira's (or both) may be externalized in a generic rhetoric appropriate to either.

In Segal's interpretation of *Phaedra* the monstrous bull represents both Phaedra's passion and 'a monstrous projection of his own [Hippolytus'] violent hatred of a part of himself'.[123] The bull reminds Hippolytus of Theseus and the minotaur:

> haud frangit animus vanus hic terror meum:
> nam mihi paternus vincere est tauros labor.
> (*Phaedra* 1066–7)

(This empty terror does not break my spirit, for conquering bulls is a task I inherit from my father.)

For Segal Hippolytus fights not only with Phaedra's passion but with his own repressed fears and desires. In the lines quoted he rivals his father as Phaedra hoped he would (see especially 646 ff.); the conflict with the bull is as much a representation of his subconscious as it is of Phaedra's passion. Instead of a formal agon between Theseus and Hippolytus, Seneca creates a landscape in which Phaedra's desire and Hippolytus' subconscious discourse with his parental figures meet, 'the point of precarious, unstable juncture between her fantasies and his terrors'.[124] The 'unstable juncture' in the significance of the bull and the irony (i.e. two distinct levels of meaning) in lines 1066–7 have important implications for the interpretation of more than this tragedy. Who creates dramatic reality? With whose eyes do we see it? For Segal here the landscape is formed from a collision of Phaedra's fantasies and Hippolytus' terrors; it represents less an objective reality than an unstable juncture of perspectives.

7. CONFLICTING PERSPECTIVES

The monstrous bull in Segal's *Phaedra*, like the imagery of burning passion in *Hercules Oetaeus*, can be interpreted as the reflection or creation of different souls. The different constructions of

---

[123] Segal (1986) 75.
[124] Segal (1986) 75. See also 129, 176–9, and *passim*.

the symbolic landscape, the collision of perspectives, is ultimately unproblematic in Segal's *Phaedra*, where the tragedy is the creation of both central characters. Rather than interacting in the conventional sense in a shared dramatic world Phaedra and Hippolytus interact through the juncture of distinct perspectives. In the Hercules plays, where commentators have been more inclined to look for an opposition between vice and virtue, the conflict of perspectives is more problematic. It matters very much whether the madness of Juno and Deïanira cooperates with the madness of Herculean *virtus* or corrupts it into vice by misrepresentation. What Segal reads in *Phaedra*, though his interpretation is not so moralistic, is essentially a cooperation of vices. A recurrent theme in my discussion has been an uncomfortable erosion of distinctions between moral opposites. As important for me as the fact that the violent passions of Hippolytus and Phaedra combine to tragic consequence is the fact that Phaedra's erotic hunt simultaneously mimics and deforms what for Hippolytus is a gesture of chastity.

Paradoxical misrepresentation of this kind is a familiar and significant technique: Junonian *furor* misrepresents Herculean *virtus*, Medea speaks like a Stoic, Cato can be read as a Caesar. Misrepresentation is no simple thing, but common to interpretation of all the various pairs I have mentioned is the theme of compromised self-definition. Characters and ideals come to resemble the enemies from which they struggle to distinguish themselves. Because descriptions of the landscape are morally significant, dramatic reality is itself a locus of this conflict of character-construction. Segal's argument that the landscape of Senecan tragedy is a place where perspectives collide is, I think, a very valuable one, though commonly that collision is more agonistic than he allows.[125]

In the passages discussed above single events, postures, and figures have suggested differing, often opposing, interpretations. Descriptions of dramatic reality are implicated in a wider confusion of moral rhetoric. Senecan tragedy is not, however, uniformly

---

[125] This difference is a reflection of Segal's psychoanalytic approach and his subordination of this form of agon to a more fundamental one. For him the primary conflict of this myth—whether told by Euripides, Seneca, or Racine—is less a conflict between characters than 'between the irrational power of sexual drives and society's insistence that those drives be sublimated' (1986) 59.

confused in this sense. Often distinctions between speakers are expressed by a pairing of contrasting descriptions of the same object. *Medea* begins with opposing claims to legitimacy: Medea and chorus look for Lucina's blessing (1–2, 61–2) on the old and new marriage respectively. The conflict of intention is expressed in part through ambiguity, an unstable juncture of meanings. The chorus plans to sacrifice to Lucina:

> Lucinam nivei femina corporis
> intemptata iugo placet   (*Medea* 61–2)

(Lucina must be appeased by a female of snow-white body, untried by the yoke).

By *femina* it means a cow, to contrast with the bull (*taurus*) to be sacrificed to Jupiter in the previous lines (59–60), but after Medea's veiled threats of human sacrifice (37–40) the phrasing is ill-omened. Medea in her prayers represents Sun and Moon as personally connected with her: the Sun is her grandfather (28–9) and the Moon, invoked as Hecate triformis (7), goddess of witchcraft, is the patron of her profession.[126] The chorus prays that Creusa will conquer other wives just as the Sun and Moon outshine the stars (89–98):

> Sic, sic, caelicolae, precor,
> vincat femina coniuges   (*Medea* 89–90)

(Just so, I pray the heavens, as a woman may she outdo wives).

What elsewhere would be merely a conventional part of the wedding song[127] has particular point here because the chorus represents Creusa as the very bodies which Medea had assumed as her own. The rivalry for divine favour is conducted in part through rival constructions of the bodies which give order to the world, and in this way dramatic reality forms part of the rhetoric of conflict.

The struggle between Medea and the chorus's favourite is morally less significant than the more oblique conflict which begins *Hercules Furens*. Whereas Medea and Creusa seek precisely the same prize, Juno and the chorus have different goals and values and this difference is apparent in their different visions of the

---

[126] See Costa (1973) 62–3 on Hecate. Invoked after the Sun (5) and described as giving light (*praebens...iubar* 6), Hecate here is clearly 'addressed in her guise as Luna'.

[127] See Costa (1973) 78.

landscape. Juno laments her displacement by Jupiter's loves; the chorus sings of the virtues of the simple life. Juno breaks off her lament and the chorus begins its song with references to the coming of the dawn, but this motion of the celestial bodies has different significance for the different characters. Juno views the sky as a battleground; she herself is driven out of heaven by the creation of new constellations: *tellus colenda est, paelices caelum tenent* (I must dwell on earth; whores inhabit the skies 5). In an endless process deities who were once usurpers are themselves upstaged in turn: Apollo at whose birth the floating earth was forced to stand still (*mobilis tellus stetit* 15) is himself forced to halt his chariot when the world loses a night at Hercules' conception (24–6). Juno fears that victory and apotheosis for Hercules will bring an end to the established order of things and that he will rule in an empty world:

> iter ruina quaeret et vacuo volet
> regnare mundo
> (*Hercules Furens* 67–8)

(he will forge a path by destruction, and he will want to rule in an empty sky).

To combat him she is prepared, ironically, to be equally ruthless and destructive: in capturing Cerberus Hercules broke the threshold of infernal Jupiter (47) and Juno is prepared to follow in his footsteps in bringing back whatever is left:

> educam et imo Ditis e regno extraham
> quidquid relictum est
> (*Hercules Furens* 95–6)

(I shall bring forth all that remain, and fetch them from the depths of Dis' kingdom).

In the self-defeating logic of anger she calls for the Furies to attack her first so that she may be inspired with the madness which will bar Hercules from heaven. She vows not to surrender as Apollo did but to fight *aeterna bella* to keep Hercules in his place (27–9). She does not properly comprehend either that she is equally as damaging of Olympian order as Hercules is or that her struggle is a single episode in a larger process, that Olympian Apollo was once the offspring of a hated *paelex*.

Juno's speech ends with the coming of the day and her determination to set wars in motion:

> Movenda iam sunt bella: clarescit dies
> ortuque Titan lucidus croceo subit.
> *(Hercules Furens* 123–4)

(Now let warfare begin: the daylight grows stronger, and radiant Titan rises in saffron-coloured dawn.)

The chorus responds to both elements with an extended representation of the celestial bodies as armies. The first words, describing the scattered stars (*Iam rara micant sidera* 125), recall the campfires of the Rutulian army (*lumina rara micant* Virgil, *Aeneid* 9.189).[128] In what follows the military aspect of the movement of the constellations is communicated not through allusion but through metaphor:

> Iam rara micant sidera prono
> languida mundo, nox victa vagos
> contrahit ignes luce renata,
> cogit nitidum Phosphoros agmen.
> *(Hercules Furens* 125–8)

(Now scattered and weak are the stars shining in the sinking heavens. Vanquished night gathers her straggling fires now the light is reborn; the Dawnstar shepherds the glittering throng)

In this context of warfare in the heavens perhaps even the phrase *prono...mundo* suggests a defeated adversary. Phoebus' sister flees, only to return (136), as the rays of the new day illuminate the violent metamorphoses of heroic and divine life: the Sun looks out over Mt Oeta where Hercules' mortal body will be burned away, and over the hills around Thebes where one of the new gods bloodily asserted his divinity:[129]

> iam Cadmeis incluta Bacchis
> aspersa die dumeta rubent
> *(Hercules Furens* 134–5)

(now the thickets made famous by Cadmean Bacchants grow red, spattered with daylight).

The opening part of the song, picking up the opening of Juno's prologue (4–5), ends with the complaints of the Thracian *paelex* (149) as one voice in the dawn chorus. The wars in the heavens are

---

[128] So Fitch (1987) 163. See also 164 on the military metaphors which follow.
[129] Juno mentions Bacchus and Thebes in her lament at 16–21 and compares him favourably with Hercules at line 66.

far from the experience of the humble chorus, which is happy to let others strive for a place among the stars (192–201). Where Juno sees a personal history and a personal affront behind almost every constellation the chorus in its first description sees a more remote battle between night and day. These grand struggles frame the chorus's simpler existence and from this more distanced perspective the vicious circularity which undermines Juno's vengeance suggests instead a higher harmony. The continual warfare of gods and heroes is juxtaposed with the rhythms of pastoral life: from the day's youth (137–40) the chorus moves to a greater cycle of life with a description of young animals (141–5).[130] Though the red light on Mt Cithaeron recalls the violent struggle between Dionysus and Pentheus it is also the familiar, even clichéd, sign of another dawn.[131] In the same way the violent crises of Juno's political world are absorbed into the familiar cycles of the rustics' stable existence. The chorus's repetition of material from Juno's prologue and the two descriptions of the motions of the celestial bodies concentrate attention on the differences between them. The chorus distinguishes itself from Juno by the world it perceives and the life it chooses for itself.

Hercules Furens and *Medea* begin with contrasting views of the world and the forces which order it. Seneca is more concerned with the contrast of perspectives than with the coherence of dramatic reality. In *Hercules Furens*, for example, Juno states in the prologue that she has seen Hercules' triumph over the underworld (50–63), while the following chorus clearly believes that he has merely hastened his death by crossing the Styx prematurely (183–7). One expects Juno to be better informed than mortals, but she adds the detail that he has led Cerberus in triumph through the cities of Greece and caused the Sun to recoil in fear (59–61). Cosmic disruption of this kind would be visible the world over, yet the chorus is unaware of it. Similarly, Furia ends the first act of *Thyestes* with a description of Hell coming to Argos: in the

---

[130] It might be argued further that the following description of the sailor entrusting himself to the winds suggests the world's youth and a still greater cycle: 'the invention of navigation was traditionally one sign of the end of the Golden Age'. See Costa (1973) 99 on *Medea* 301 ff. and Smith (1913) 245–7 on Tibullus 1.3.37 ff.
[131] On the double associations of *rubere* with blood and dawn light see Fitch (1987) 167.

image of the receding waters of his infernal punishment, Tantalus' spirit causes the sea and rivers of Greece to dry up (*Thyestes* 105–19). The nobles of Argos fear the familiar ancient thirst (119), yet in the following song a chorus of Argive citizens is unaware of any such disaster and names many of the places just affected by Tantalus' touch.[132] Corinth is described conventionally as dividing the seas when in Furia's speech it is now so far from the sea that it can barely hear it (125 cf. 111–14); the Alpheus, only recently dried up (115–16), is once again a clear, cold river (130–1).

Advancing many similar examples from *Thyestes* and *Hercules Furens* Shelton argues that Seneca disrupts the linear progression of time in order to represent the same event from different perspectives. Juno's prologue is a representation in a divine, supernatural mode, of human megalomania. The temporal awkwardness of her speech sets it apart from the subsequent tragedy as an authoritative commentary: 'the dramatist's skillful manipulation of time, and consequent preparation of two points of perspective, have given us superior knowledge of the thoughts in Hercules' mind'.[133] The ghost of Tantalus, likewise, is to be read as Atreus' lust represented in the supernatural mode. This is very much Owen's response to the apparition of Achilles' ghost in *Troades*. For example, Talthybius reports that Achilles' ghost demands vengeance (*Troades* 164–202), yet in the scene immediately following Pyrrhus and Agamemnon argue about what Achilles might have wished (203–359). This agon is resolved by Calchas' ruling, made without reference to any supernatural apparitions (360–70). Then the chorus wonders whether there is life after death (371–408). Owen concludes, 'we the audience have been interrupted in the middle of a flow of events, moved from the religio-philosophic plane to that of cold policy, and back again'.[134] As in the disruptions of *Thyestes* and *Hercules Furens*, events on different planes or in different modes reiterate and reinforce each

---

[132] Though there is nothing in the chorus's language to fix its status definitively, it is natural to presume that these are Argives praying for their own city (so Tarrant (1985) 106). On the difficulties of identifying the chorus in Senecan tragedy see Tarrant (1976) 181 and Littlewood (1995) 327. On the chorus's repetition of the places just listed by Furia see Hine (1981) 270–1.

[133] Shelton (1975) 265.

[134] Owen (1970) 122. See further discussion below, Sect. 8.

other. Seneca's technique can, however, also serve to contrast different versions of reality. Whether or not Juno's world-view is an authoritative vision of Hercules' mind, it differs markedly from the world-view expressed in the following ode. In this play particularly the selection of one world in preference to another is an important way in which moral choices are made.

The jarring effect of temporal confusions of the kind Shelton discusses, where incompatible realities apparently coexist, focuses attention on these critical choices: an agon is created through the juxtaposition of distinct worlds. In *Hercules Furens* the moral choice which the hero faces at the end of the tragedy—whether to commit suicide or to accept the rehabilitation which Amphitryon and Theseus offer—is expressed in part as a choice between different landscapes. The opposition between the political and the simple life, sketched in the tragedy's opening prologue and song recurs at the end of the play where Hercules, if he is to recover from his madness, is obliged to retire from the grand stage he walked in his earlier life. The contrasting worlds or lives at the end of this play are not dramatically problematic as are the contrasting visions of Argos at the opening of *Thyestes* where Furia and the chorus, apparently simultaneously, see the same landscape as a desert and as an idyll. Yet Hercules' despair when he discovers his crime is expressed in the earth-shattering rhetoric of his madness. In this way his resistance to Amphitryon's pleas for sanity echoes the preceding scene where Amphitryon tried in vain to recall his son from a nightmare reality which he alone could see.

Lucretius famously said that the torments of Hell are illusory but exist allegorically in the lives of those who cannot control their desires (3.978 ff.).[135] Mortals who misguidedly believe in punishment after death are pressed down by fear of the gods; they bring into being the non-existent rock suspended over Tantalus' head. Mythological tragedy accepts such ghosts and demons as Epicurean philosophy does not, but by juxtaposing contrasting realities in the same drama Seneca hints at the same subjectivism as Lucretius: the maddened visions of Juno and Hercules are realities which misguided souls make for themselves. Lucretius' catalogue of allegorical torments begins with a fear of divine punishment and

---

[135] On parallelism between this passage of Lucretius and Seneca, *Ad. Marciam* 19.4–5 see Manning (1981) 111.

moves to other moral failures: Sisyphus, for example, symbolizes the pursuer of political power (3.995–1003). The argument moves easily from an empty fear (*metus... inanis* 982) of a non-existent Hell to a desire for power which is empty (*imperium quod inane est* 998). Metaphorically speaking the rods and the axes of Rome are as illusory as the apparatus of Acheron: distinctions between what does and does not matter look back, in typically Lucretian fashion, to the physical rhetoric of substance and void.[136] In a similar way mad Hercules' vision of things which literally do not exist looks back to the moral delusion in the perspective of his alter ego. The *falsum caelum* (954) of Hercules' violent insanity echoes and comments on the morally flawed vision of Juno which opens the tragedy[137] and anticipates also the madness of his grief.

When Hercules discovers his crime he calls for Jupiter's anger to shake the heavens and for himself to suffer the punishment of Prometheus (1202 ff.). Tantalus in *Thyestes* claimed with a certain twisted pride that his descendants, daring things yet undared, would fill up Minos' realm: *numquam stante Pelopea domo | Minos vacabit* (*Thyestes* 22–3). Here Hercules looks to fill the mountains of the Caucasus with his agony:

> cur Promethei vacant
> scopuli? vacat cur vertice immenso feras
> volucresque pascens Caucasi abruptum latus
> nudumque silvis?
> (*Hercules Furens* 1207–10)[138]

(Why are Prometheus' cliffs empty? The sheer flank of Caucasus, bare of trees, which feeds wild beasts and birds on its vast heights—why is it empty?)

His second imagined punishment is to chain the Symplegades with his body as they rush together to drive the intervening sea

---

[136] On the physicality of Lucretius' philosophical poetry see West (1969) e.g. 98–9 on *inanis, casum,* and *cassa* in the description of the rock hanging over Tantalus (Lucretius, 3.980–3) and more generally Kenney (1971) 222 ff.

[137] *quo, nate, vultus hic et huc acres refers | acieque falsum turbida caelum vides?* (953–4). The continuity between Hercules sane and Hercules mad and the parallelism between the prologue and the mad-scene are excellently discussed in Fitch's introduction to his commentary (1987) 21–33.

[138] Zwierlein's OCT reads *paretur* in line 1208 from MS b in place of *vacat cur*, Leo's correction of *vagetur* (which makes no sense) from MS E. I follow Fitch (1987) 428 here, who argues persuasively against the blandness of *paretur* and shows a close parallel at *Phaedra* 174: *cur monstra cessant? aula cur fratris vacat?*

up into the sky (1210–15). From this he moves to the image of a funeral pyre built up with a forest piled together (*nemore congesto* 1216). Not only are these again monumental images of agony, but they recall the first onset of Hercules' madness. Earth cannot hold him (*non capit terra Herculem* 960), rocks and woods are heaped up to pave his way to Olympus:

> saxa cum silvis feram
> rapiamque dextra plena Centauris iuga.
> iam monte gemino limitem ad superos agam
> (*Hercules Furens* 968–70)

(I shall carry rocks and trees, and grasp ridges full of Centaurs in my right hand. With a pair of mountains I shall now construct a pathway to the world above).

In the pain of recognition Hercules' *furor* is, as Juno intended, now turned against himself,[139] but it is recognizably the same kind of madness which afflicted him when he saw phantasms. Amphitryon saw *furor* in Hercules' attack on his children (991) and *furor* again in his grief:

> Nondum tumultum pectus attonito carens
> mutavit iras, quodque habet proprium furor,
> in se ipse saevit.
> (*Hercules Furens* 1219–21)

(His heart is not yet free of frenzied turmoil; his anger has shifted, and he turns his fury on himself—the hallmark of mad rage.)

Furthermore, Amphitryon is unwilling to outlive Hercules and thus Hercules' intended suicide threatens his father's life as the previous madness killed Megara and the children: HERCULES. *morte sanandum est scelus.* | AMPHITRYON. *Perimes parentem?* (the healing of the crime must be by death. | You will kill your father? 1262–3).

Amphitryon begs Hercules to show himself the clemency which he denied to others[140] (1265–7) and to end his passion: *nunc magna tibi | virtute agendum est: Herculem irasci veta* (now you

---

[139] Juno summons, among others, *in se semper armatus Furor* (98). Cf. Amphitryon's description of Hercules quoted from 1220–1.

[140] On the importance of *clementia* and Hercules' lack of it in this play see Rose (1979–80) 141. Cf. Lawall (1983) 25, who quotes *De Clementia* 2.7.1 and *Epistles* 20.2 supporting Hercules' stance: 'Hercules has no choice in the matter. He must punish now as he has punished in the past. His integrity is at stake.'

must act with great valour. Do not let Hercules give way to anger (1276–7). Hercules will not drive his father to suicide by his own self-destruction (1314–17), but his madness does not disappear. In his final speech Hercules again ranges unsatisfied to the limits of the world:

> Quem locum profugus petam?
> ubi me recondam quave tellure obruar?
> quis Tanais aut quis Nilus aut quis Persica
> violentus unda Tigris aut Rhenus ferox
> Tagusve Hibera turbidus gaza fluens
> abluere dextram poterit? Arctoum licet
> Maeotis in me gelida transfundat mare
> et tota Tethys per meas currat manus,
> haerebit altum facinus.
> *(Hercules Furens* 1321–9)

(What place shall I seek out in exile? Where shall I hide myself, in what land be buried in oblivion? What Tanais or what Nile or what Persian Tigris with its violent waters or fierce Rhine or Tagus, turbid with Spanish treasure, can wash my right hand clean? Though chill Maeotis should pour its northern seas over me and all the Ocean stream across my hands, the deed will stay deeply ingrained.)

The violence and the expanse of Hercules' geography recall the aggression of his labours and the global conflict of his madness even as he surrenders the heroic life for domestic piety. Hercules' desire for purification in these running waters is juxtaposed with the different resolution which Amphitryon offers through his acceptance of his son's bloodstained hands:

> Hanc manum amplector libens,
> hac nisus ibo, pectori hanc aegro admovens
> pellam dolores.
> *(Hercules Furens* 1319–21)

(But I grasp this hand gladly, I shall lean on it to walk, and clasp it to my troubled breast to banish my griefs.)

The humbler, domestic world of Amphitryon's love is contrasted with the grander scope of Hercules' heroic passions. Landscape is an important element in the representation of Hercules' choice, his selection of one sphere of existence for another. The madness episode where Hercules sees an illusory reality is merely the most forceful formulation in this play of a dramatic technique familiar in

Senecan tragedy, the juxtaposition of contrasting worlds. If Juno's vision of conflict in the heavens inspires the tragedy and sets in motion a fatal critique of Herculean *virtus*, the chorus's and Amphitryon's vision of a simpler life offers closure and an uncomplicated exit from the grand stage and from its fatal ambiguity. Read in these terms, *Hercules Furens* offers its own clearly defined resolution to the more familiar moral chaos of Senecan tragedy.[141]

The theme of retirement from the hazards of a grand, public life is familiar not only from Seneca's own moral works but from a wide range of poets and philosophers. The first ode of *Hercules Furens*, in praise of the simple life, takes an ode from Euripides' *Phaethon* as its primary model and renews it smoothly and comfortably with allusions to the Epicurean *ataraxia* of Horace, *Odes* 1.1 and Virgil's *Georgics*.[142] In returning to this very conventional praise of retirement and simplicity at the end of the tragedy Seneca thus suggests a secure resolution of the drama. Hercules is encouraged to redefine his *virtus* (see especially 1276-7 quoted above) and in so doing to renounce the landscape which we associate with his labours and with his aspirations to divine power. In *Agamemnon* the presentation of Ajax in the storm seemed calculated to disrupt a reassuringly systematic imagery of passion, just as Medea's misuse of Stoic self-sufficiency seemed calculated to undermine virtue's self-representation. The close of Seneca's *Oedipus*, when compared to the close of *Hercules Furens*, appears subversive in a similarly calculated manner: it misuses, or uses problematically, the conventional theme of retirement from the grand stage.

Oedipus opens with a description of the plague delivered not by the people of Thebes but by the hero. More than a simple mark of divine displeasure the plague reflects Oedipus' crime in its family confusion: young and old, fathers and sons are mingled on the same pyre (54-5).[143] Though he does not read the signs so precisely

---

[141] Zintzen (1972) 207-9 argues that Hercules deviates from Stoic virtue and that Seneca's tragedy, in part through its close relationship with Euripides', stages the inadequacy of the heroism of Attic tragedy: the δυσδαίμων of Euripides is transformed into the morally simpler *nocens* in Seneca's tragedy.

[142] This ode I discuss in detail below, p. 107-12. See also Fitch (1987) 158 ff. I agree with his summation of the second half of the ode, 'This section is best described as using conventional themes with Horatian-Epicurean overtones', though I would argue for a Stoic tone in the Virgilian *labor...durus* of line 137.

[143] Cf. Usher (1969) 28-30 and Hornblower (1991) 316-18 on Thucydides' narrative of the plague in Athens. As in Seneca's tragedy the effects of the plague

Oedipus recognizes his guilt (*fecimus caelum nocens* (I have made the heavens baneful 36), *sperne letali manu | contacta regna* (Spurn the kingdom infected by your deadly hand 77–8)). With the secret all but revealed in the prologue, the focus of the drama is as much on Oedipus' response as on the crime itself and the city's suffering.[144] The plague spares Oedipus alone (*mihi parcit uni* 31) yet his despair resembles that of the infected. He returns to the theme of his nightmare life in death at the conclusion of the prologue:

> Adfusus aris supplices tendo manus
> matura poscens fata, praecurram ut prior
> patriam ruentem neve post omnis cadam
> fiamque regni funus extremum mei.
> o saeva nimium numina, o fatum grave!
> negatur uni nempe in hoc populo mihi
> mors tam parata?
>
> (*Oedipus* 71–7)

(Prostrate at the altar, stretching out hands in supplication, I demand an early fate, so as to anticipate my fatherland's collapse, not fall after everyone and become the last death in my own kingdom. The gods are too cruel, fate too harsh! Is death, then, though so readily available, denied me alone out of the whole nation?)

Jocasta's condemnation of his reaction as unkingly (*regium hoc ipsum reor: | adversa capere* (The quality of a king lies, I think, in the very ability to take on adversities 82–3)) separates Oedipus' prologue from a parallel description in the first ode (110–201). This ode also ends with a prayer for death (*prostrata iacet turba per aras | oratque mori* (Crowds lie prostrate among the altars and pray to die 197–8)) but here the citizens are driven to despair by the physical symptoms of the plague (*O dira novi facies leti | gravior leto* (O strange and dreadful form of death more grievous than death itself! 180–1)).

Jocasta's Stoic demand that Oedipus stand firm (*stare certo... gradu* 85) while his empire slips and falls (*cadentis imperi moles*

---

parallel the moral degeneracy of its cause (the plague arises because of the decision to go to war and in its effects resembles the moral degeneracy which attended and caused such a decision).

[144] For a similar emphasis on the centrality of the hero's response to the trials of Fortuna see Schetter (1972) 424. Oedipus names Fortuna as the villain in his opening speech (*imperia sic excelsa Fortunae obiacent* 11), a view with which Henry and Walker (1983) 136–8 concur.

labet 84) is phrased in language appropriate to the plague. Plague victims, even doctors, fall to the ground (*cadunt medentes* 70) and this fall is the will of Fortune. Seneca plays on the double sense of bodies falling and events befalling:

> quin luctu in ipso luctus exoritur novus,
> suaeque circa funus exequiae cadunt.   (*Oedipus* 62–3)

(Even in the midst of grief new grief arises, and mourners fall around the corpse they are following)

Here their own funeral befalls the mourners, and at the same time the mourners fall.[145] In these lines the distinction between the physical and psychological effect of the plague is blurred. 'But in their very grief' (or 'an event which inspires grief') 'a new grief (or "an event which inspires grief") arises. While they are engaged in a funeral (or "around a corpse") their own funeral procession (be)falls.' In Seneca's symbolic landscape the healers betrayed by physical frailty, the citizens unable to master their pain, and Oedipus surrendering to Fortune's horrors all fall in the same way. As empire and citizens collapse and events (be)fall Oedipus' spirit does likewise:

> Horrore quatior, fata quo vergant timens,
> trepidumque gemino pectus affectu labat
>   (*Oedipus* 206–7)

(I am trembling with fear, apprehensive about fate's direction. My anxious heart wavers between two feelings)

Oedipus' nightmare is the creation simultaneously of his actions and his moral cowardice. When Creon enters the stage the chorus, which like Oedipus has just described Thebes' suffering,[146] wonders whether its sickened soul sees reality or a hallucination: *adestne...Creon | an aeger animus falsa pro veris videt?* (203–4). Creon is of course as objectively real as the plague, but in an environment which the victims produce in part through their own despair the reference to the visions of a sick mind is particularly effective. As in *Hercules Furens* the rhetoric of truth and

---

[145] For Töchterle (1994) 187, as for Fitch, this second sense is the primary one: '*exequiae*...meint hier die Menschen, die den Leichenzug bilden'.

[146] The chorus speaks of dying in the first person (*interimus* 124), but most of its speech is delivered from the perspective of an observer. The crowd which prays for death at the altars (196 ff.) is described in the third person.

illusion functions both literally and figuratively in a moral sense. Like Hercules' madness the plague is an external curse (whether Juno's or Fortune's) which befalls its victim, yet at the same time it is the victim's choice and responsibility; Hercules and Oedipus in their different ways make what is morally insignificant real.

This early presentation of the plague affects our interpretation of Oedipus' resolution of the tragedy. His first intention, to dare something worthy of his crimes (*nunc aliquid aude sceleribus dignum tuis* 879), is typical of the passionate protagonist. Medea likewise looks to her past crimes for inspiration: *scelera te hortentur tua* (*Medea* 129). He ends his speech with the black humour of an Atreus, *gratare matri liberis auctam domum* (congratulate your mother on enhancing our house with children! 881).[147] Typically again—and here Thyestes and Hercules are the most obvious parallels—he calls for the earth to open up in response to his crime.[148] The messenger's speech which describes his deed (915–79) presents it in a more ambiguous light. Oedipus grasps the fate from which he earlier recoiled and passes judgement on himself:

> Praedicta postquam fata et infandum genus
> deprendit ac se scelere convictum Oedipus
> damnavit ipse...
>
> (*Oedipus* 915–17)

(After Oedipus had grasped the fate foretold for him and his unspeakable parentage, and condemned himself as one convicted of crime...)

Oedipus is likened to a raging Libyan lion (*qualis per arva Libycus insanit leo* 919), he rages in anger (*ira furit* 957), and even after blinding himself does not stop scratching at the empty sockets: *saevitque frustra plusque quam satis est furit* (he is pointlessly savage and rages excessively 970). Yet this savagery is the result of a closely reasoned, legalistic argument. Oedipus talks determinedly of paying his debts[149] and selects his punishment as a private

---

[147] Cf. e.g. the words which accompany Atreus' revelation of the heads of Thyestes' children: *Iam accipe hos potius libens | diu expetitos: nulla per fratrem est mora; | fruere, osculare, divide amplexus tribus* (*Thyestes* 1021–3).

[148] *Dehisce, tellus...*(*Oedipus* 868); cf. *Sustines tantum nefas | gestare, Tellus?* (*Thyestes* 1006–7) and *Hercules Furens* 1277–94.

[149] *Solvendo non es* (942), a financial metaphor to express Oedipus' inability to make restitution, is particularly striking, though Töchterle's recent commentary (1994) 593 favours the reading of MS w: *solvenda non est illa, quae leges ratas |*

The Broken World

death by which he may be decently separated from living mother and dead father:

> quaeratur via
> qua nec sepultis mixtus et vivis tamen
> exemptus erres
> (*Oedipus* 949–51)

(Search for a way to wander without mixing with the dead, and yet removed from the living).

Calculating madness is characteristic of Seneca's protagonists— Medea and Atreus proceed to their revenge only after careful analysis of past crimes and of the wrongs they themselves have suffered—and Poe argues rightly against Schetter that the emphasis on Oedipus' rational calculation is no index of virtue.[150] Where Oedipus differs from Atreus is his insistence on the justice of his act:[151]

> parcite en patriae, precor:
> iam iusta feci, debitas poenas tuli;
> inventa thalamis digna nox tandem meis
> (*Oedipus* 975–7)

('Look, spare my fatherland, I pray you: I have done justice, have taken the penalty owed. At last I have found a night suited to my marriage-chamber.')

Atreus described his revenge on Thyestes as right only in the context of a general confusion of right and wrong (*Fas est in illo quidquid in fratre est nefas* (All that is wrong in dealing with a brother is right in dealing with him *Thyestes* 220)). Oedipus' desire that his country be spared is morally natural and in this context the

---

Natura in uno vertit Oedipoda (942–3). Financial metaphors are extremely common in Seneca's moral epistles, see e.g. *Epistles* 7.10 on the value of his moral advice and *Epistles* 25.3, *expecto* cum magno fenore *vitia reditura, quae nunc scio cessare, non deesse.* Inpendam *huic rei dies et utrum possit aliquid agi an non possit experiar.*

[150] Poe (1983) 153–4 on Schetter (1972) 424ff. On the theme of reasoned passion Poe refers also to Wanke (1964). Her concern is determinedly stylistic— and not at first glance therefore very helpful for moral interpretation—but her insistence that the combination of verbal ingenuity and an arousal of emotion is very familiar (1964: 149–50) arguably makes Oedipus' paradoxically rational passion less problematic. Cf. also Tarrant (1985) 241 on brittle sophistry in *Thyestes* 1098–9 and *Medea* 982–4: 'It is in passages like these, with their unsettling mixture of logic and sheer delusion, that Seneca's understanding of madness is most clearly revealed.'

[151] See also *iusta persolvi patri* (998).

reference to 'a night worthy of his marriage' is therefore not so obviously warped as the phrase it recalls, *nunc aliquid aude sceleribus dignum tuis* (now show some daring worthy of your crimes 879). In his final speech in the tragedy Oedipus again speaks of the city that will be saved by his self-imposed exile (1052–61).

Arguments for Oedipus as Stoic martyr tend to be strained: *superavi fata impia* (1046), for example, in context clearly means, 'in driving my mother to suicide I have surpassed my impious destiny' not 'I have defeated my destiny'.[152] The theatrical martyrdom of some of Seneca's icons seems far from the rigid calm more expected of Stoic self-possession, and one cannot proceed as if this is unproblematic to the conclusion that Seneca's Stoicism finds its true voice in a passionate heroism and in extravagant expressions of agony.[153] Oedipus' moral instincts are not as simply inverted as Atreus' and his belief that further contact with his mother is wrong is quite sane: *congredi fas amplius | haut est nefandos* (1014–15). Poe' solution to this ambiguous virtue is to blame fate: 'We should bear in mind that this is a universe which has contrived moral perversions... As a perversion Oedipus elects the only course possible—to act in accordance with nature's perversity'.[154] Oedipus cannot choose good instead of evil because he is part of a guilty universe. Even the punishment he selects is informed by a distorted natural law: the novelty of his punishment reflects the novelty of the birth which nature gave him:

> illa quae leges ratas
> Natura in uno vertit Oedipoda, novos
> commenta partus, supplicis eadem meis
> novetur.
>
> (*Oedipus* 942–5)

---

[152] See Schetter (1972) 432–3. Töchterle (1994) 634, discussing also the similar possible interpretations of *victor* in 974, rejects Schetter's approach (though not by name).

[153] Schetter (1972) 426–8, for whom Oedipus' self-mutilation is of a kind with that of Mucius Scaevola, is again the target here. On the problematic violence of Stoic martyrdom see above, pp. 20–2.

[154] Poe (1983) 155 and 156. See also Dingel (1974) 72–3, who argues that the problem of fated evil is Stoically unsolvable and (78) sees a clear conflict between the unhappy traditional myths of Thebes and Stoic philosophy. Cf. Aggeler (1970) 511 on Marston, *Antonio's Revenge*: 'Pandulpho is rejecting a belief that underlies all of Stoic moral doctrine, the belief in the rationality of nature... He sees only chaos in nature and therefore, like his Machiavellian antagonist, "no reason to be reasonable" (1.ii.227).'

(Nature, who alters her fixed laws in regard to Oedipus alone, by inventing unheard-of procreation, must change yet again to provide my punishment.)

The moral awkwardness that Oedipus, like a good Stoic, acts in accordance with Nature even to the last is reinforced by the chorus's very conventional ode 980–97 on the necessity of yielding to Fate. Oedipus' manic rationality differs markedly from the carefree acceptance advocated by the chorus:[155]

> Fatis agimur: cedite fatis;
> non sollicitae possunt curae
> mutare rati stamina fusi   (*Oedipus* 980–2)

(We are driven by fate, and must yield to fate. No anxious fretting can alter the threads from that commanding spindle.)

Nevertheless in an important respect the chorus's words echo Oedipus' contorted calculations and in concluding that Oedipus echoes Nature's perversity Poe recognizes that Schetter's representation of Oedipus as a Stoic hero 'is perhaps not entirely wrong'.[156] The function of the chorus here is to suggest what cannot be, that Oedipus' savagery is virtue.

If patterning himself after Nature forms part of Oedipus' quasi-virtuous intention, another part is his determined withdrawal from contact with his parents and with Thebes. After the final ode Oedipus enters the stage closely followed by Jocasta. Oedipus' tragedy is over—*peractum est* (998)—and he considers himself forgiven:

> quis deus tandem mihi
> placatus atra nube perfundit caput?
> quis scelera donat?   (*Oedipus* 999–1001)

(What god, kindly disposed to me at last, has poured a cloud of blackness over my head? Who pardons my crimes?)

Jocasta by contrast rushes around the stage like a Maenad, her physical instability reflected in her indecision: *dubitat afflictum alloqui, | cupit, pavetque* (She hesitates to speak to the ruined man, desires yet fears to do so 1007–8). Where Oedipus' blinding suggested now a moral resolution, now an insane impulse to

---

[155] On the contrast between Stoic equanimity, even joy, in hardship and Oedipus' rage see Töchterle (1994) 609.

[156] Poe (1983) 155.

surpass his criminal fate, Jocasta's suicide is unquestionably driven by the latter desire:

> Agedum, commoda matri manum,
> si parricida es. restat hoc operi ultimum.
> *(Oedipus* 1032–3)

(Come now, lend your hand's service to your mother, if you are a parricide: this task remains to complete your work.)

Oedipus does not participate as Jocasta wishes, but clearly the suicide by her son's sword is both punishment and repetition of her crime:[157]

> hunc, dextra, hunc pete
> uterum capacem, qui virum et gnatos tulit.
> *(Oedipus* 1038–9)

(Strike this, my hand, this capacious womb, which bore husband and children.)

The contrast between Jocasta's state of mind and Oedipus' is reinforced by Oedipus' pathetic admission that he has in fact driven his mother to suicide (*matrem peremi* 1045) and done involuntarily what she asked and what he was unwilling to do a moment ago. Speaking of the plague Oedipus shows himself very different from the man lost in contemplation of disaster at the opening of the tragedy. Oedipus ended his first speech urging himself to flee the corruption he brings with him:

> linque lacrimas, funera,
> tabifica caeli vitia quae tecum invehis   *(Oedipus* 78–9)

(leave behind the tears, the deaths, the corruptive maladies in the sky which you brought with you).

Even to his own ears the prayer is hopeless and Oedipus closes with the self-mocking suggestion that he flee to his parents: *profuge iamdudum ocius—* | *vel ad parentes* (Quickly, make your belated escape—even to your parents! 80–1). At the end of the tragedy he does depart the kingdom and drags its vices with him: *mortifera mecum vitia terrarum extraho* (I am drawing with me the deadly maladies of the land 1058). The uprooting of the land's

---

[157] See Fantham (1983) 69, Töchterle (1994) 630. Cf. Seneca, *Phaedra* 713–14 and (Jocasta to Eteocles) Statius, *Thebaid* 11.338–9 and 342: *prius haec tamen arma necesse est* | *experiare domi*... | ...*perque uterum sonipes hic matris agendus.*

The Broken World

vices is a powerful image as Oedipus internalizes the corruption which currently taints the Theban landscape. The personified demons of Destiny (*Fata*), Plague (*Macies, Pestis*), and Pain (*Dolor*) Oedipus takes with him with emphatic self-assertion: *mecum, ite, mecum* (1061). Whatever construction is put upon this ending, Oedipus is clearly not the helpless figure he was at the end of his first speech (1–81).[158]

In an optimistic interpretation Oedipus accepts the violence of fate, draws it into himself, and leaves a gentler sky behind him (*mitior caeli status | post terga sequitur* 1055). In support of such an interpretation one would point to his words in his first speech where he criticized the man who rejoices in royal power: *Quisquamne regno gaudet? o fallax bonum* (Does anyone take joy in kingship? So deceptive a good 6). Here at the end of the tragedy, while displaying sane moral responses in his pity for his fellow citizens, Oedipus resolves the plague by walking out of his kingdom. Salvation through retirement into a more private life is familiar, as I said, not only from the moralists but also from the close of *Hercules Furens*.[159] Against this interpretation one might argue that in uprooting the corruption Oedipus is not so much resolving and internalizing it as taking it elsewhere. Furthermore, his final words, *ducibus his uti libet* (I rejoice to have such guides as these 1061), are suspicious not least because they echo the words with which the chorus cues his entrance in this last act:

> Sonuere fores atque ipse suum
> duce non ullo molitur iter
> luminibus orbus.   (*Oedipus* 995–7)

(A sound from the doors: he makes his own way with none to guide him, laboriously, bereft of the light.)

The resolution of Oedipus' subsequent speech (*peractum est* 998) is thus introduced by the statement that he himself makes his own journey without any guide. By the end of the tragedy he has surpassed the crimes to which he had resigned himself and gives himself up to the leadership of madness, surrendering his earlier

---

[158] On the parallelism between the prologue and the final scene of the tragedy see Schetter (1972) 434–5.

[159] For a Stoic interpretation of this last scene and comparison with the close of *Hercules Furens* see Henry and Walker (1983) 136.

self-determination.[160] Oedipus cannot, I feel, be made to play the role of Stoic sage, but Poe was right at the last to sympathize with Schetter: it is central to the effect of the final scenes of the tragedy that Oedipus mimics Stoic resolution. As Medea elsewhere masks her implacable anger as the serenity of a sage Oedipus here retires from the grand stage not into a moralist's self-knowledge, but a private Hell.

8. DRAMATIC REALITY AND CONFLICTING PERSPECTIVES IN *TROADES*

Troades begins at Troy's end and relives its death; painful repetition is a dominant motif.[161] The Trojan women introduce themselves in a familiar role as the singers of ten unbroken years of pain:

> Non rude vulgus lacrimisque novum
>   lugere iubes:
> hoc continuis egimus annis...
>
>   .   .   .   .   .   .
>
> non indociles lugere sumus.
>   (*Troades* 67–9, 82)

(This is no untrained crowd, new to tears, that you bid lament: we have done this for years unbroken... we are not unschooled in mourning)

From Hecuba's opening words Troy is presented as an image of doomed mortality. Through practical argument and symbolic gesture alike Astyanax is condemned to death by his ancestry. Odysseus insists that Astyanax die to free the Greeks from the fear of later retribution (736–8) and Andromache herself, well aware of the irony of her action, commits the last living traces of Hector to the grave in a futile attempt to save his life (476–88).

---

[160] On the allusion to 998–9 see Töchterle (1994) 640, who rejects the possibility of a positive Stoic interpretation. Henry and Walker (1983) 139 n. 10 argue that *libet* (1061) cannot be intended ironically, but it is not clear to me that Oedipus speaks in a single tone throughout the final act. For warped pleasure in crime cf. e.g. *Medea* 911–14: *iuvat, iuvat rapuisse fraternum caput, | artus iuvat secuisse....|...iuvat in exitium senis | armasse natas*.

[161] See Boyle (1994). On linear progression defeated and the importance of the cyclical form of Ovid's *Metamorphoses* see especially Schiesaro (1997*a*) and Williams (1978) 248.

The drama of a death already told,[162] an existence already ended is essentially static. It is surely not a coincidence that temporal incoherencies of the kind evident also in *Thyestes* and *Hercules Furens* are most prominent in *Troades*.

In *Thyestes* the Fury sees later events before they happen (*Thyestes* 59 ff.); the chorus sings of a cool, pure landscape which we have just seen contaminated by the burning heat of Tantalid passion (122–35 cf. 106–21).[163] In *Troades* a messenger's report that Achilles' ghost demands vengeance (168–202) is ignored in the subsequent scene as the drama works towards an identical resolution through an agon between Agamemnon and Pyrrhus (203–352). Though the agon itself is inconclusive, Agamemnon ends by promising to consult Calchas. The prophet replies, *Dant fata Danais quo solent pretio viam* (Fate grants the Danaans passage at the customary price 360) and the matter is solved. Rather than condemning the agon for ignoring the apparition or the prophecy for making the preceding scenes redundant, a sympathetic reader observes the same event represented sequentially in different modes. Achilles' ghost is to be read as the supernatural image of the *fervor paternus* (inherited ardour 251–2) which Agamemnon sees in Pyrrhus' speech. In his landmark article on the play Owen (1970) analyses the disjointed structure of the tragedy in such terms.[164]

Repetition in *Troades* is commonly a restrictive force. Boyle in his commentary valuably emphasizes the impotence of those who struggle against the determinism of both history and literary tradition.[165] The absence of any single dominant figure in this drama, as in *Agamemnon*, again expresses the subordination of individual self-determination to the generic event and the prescribed form.[166] At the same time repetition is an opportunity for the creation of a different perspective. Though Pyrrhus speaks on behalf of his father, though Agamemnon recognizes Achilles' spirit (and the quarrel of the *Iliad*) in his words, and though both apparition and agon ensure the sacrifice of the same Trojan

---

[162] See e.g. M. Wilson (1983) 36, 'The Trojan Women is not so much a play about the aftermath of war but is itself the last phase of the war recreated on stage'.
[163] For discussion of this passage see above, pp. 75–6.
[164] See also Lawall (1982) on the doubling of characters and events.
[165] Boyle (1994) 26–7.
[166] See Boyle (1994) 31 and n. 113 above on Agamemnon.

blood, the scenes are not to be interpreted as tautologous. The difference of mode which Owen observed, a movement 'from the religio-philosophic plane to that of cold policy'[167] is a significant one. Imperial power is typically justified by its representation as divine will, but this is an act of representation not the recognition of an essential reality.[168] Here the god-like authority of Achilles' uninterrupted demand is to be contrasted with the agonistic recollection of phrases and events from the *Iliad* which culminates in Agamemnon's submission to the crimes of the past.

Agamemnon begins the agon a wiser man than the Homeric king who quarrelled with Achilles. Fantham rightly comments on his reference to the quarrel (*spiritus quondam truces | minasque tumidi lentus Aeacidae tuli* (Once I calmly tolerated the harsh arrogance and threats of proud Aeacides 252-3)), 'This represents Agamemnon's behaviour in the quarrel of Briseis in a most un-Homeric light'.[169] Despite this promising beginning Agamemnon is drawn into a recreation of the quarrel with Achilles. Pyrrhus' demand for a murderous union is a 'perverse repetition'[170] of the Homeric quarrel over Briseis. Pyrrhus alludes contemptuously to the Homeric ἄναξ ἀνδρῶν in his description of Agamemnon as *regum tyranne* (303) and reiterates Achilles' criticisms of Agamemnon's arrogation of supreme authority.[171] Significantly Agamemnon responds for the most part by attacking Achilles, not Pyrrhus himself: he complains, for example, that Achilles played his lyre while the ships burned (318-21) and made truce with Priam while Greeks and Trojans were still at war (325-6). Agamemnon's opposition to Pyrrhus fails ultimately because of his earlier toleration of the sacrifice of Iphigenia. Ominously he refers the decision to Calchas, *cuius ingenti mihi | mercede constant ora* (whose pronouncements cost me an enormous price 357-8). The crumbling of his moral position is expressed through the trajectory of his speech in which he moves from an un-Homeric endurance of Achilles' insults through a repetition of Homeric material to a submission to the old, familiar destiny.[172]

---

[167] Owen (1970) 122.
[168] Cf. Livy, *Pref.* 7 on Rome tracing its ancestry to Mars: *tam et hoc gentes humanae patiantur aequo animo quam imperium patiuntur*.
[169] Fantham (1982) 249.   [170] So M. Wilson (1983) 34.
[171] See Fantham (1982) 254-5 on *Troades* 301 ff. and *Iliad* 1.225-8, 287-8.
[172] Fantham (1982) 259-60 and Boyle (1994) 170 both comment on the Stoic quality of Agamemnon's submission to fate. The providential nature of this destiny

The agon and the messenger speech offer complementary images of the constraints of the past upon the present. The juxtaposition of different perspectives is achieved at the expense of dramatic unity and a linear progression through the tragedy. More than *Thyestes*, where temporal incoherencies and repeated visions of the same crime also obstruct a linear progression through the tragedy, *Troades* draws attention to its disjunction. Andromache dreams that she sees Hector's ghost (438 ff.) and later imagines that she sees him when the Greeks cannot:

> arma concussit manu,
> iaculatur ignes—cernitis, Danai, Hectorem?
> an sola video?
> (*Troades* 683–5)

(He brandished his weapons in his hands, he is hurling firebrands! Can you perceive Hector, you Danaans? Or do I alone see him?)

The reality of the supernatural apparition is questioned directly here and implicitly by the ode which precedes the dream (371–408), where the survival of the soul after death is denied. The easy literary transition from one mode of representation to another, from supernatural to political, is complicated when the nature of dramatic reality is a subject of argument. The awkwardness that Agamemnon and Pyrrhus are not aware of Achilles' ghost cannot simply be explained in terms of dramatic stylization when the drama demands that we question whether or not ghosts exist. In addition to representing the same force of necessity in different modes *Troades* represents images of reality which are clearly not to be reconciled with each other.

Andromache's delusion that Hector's ghost has appeared to defend their child is similar to the delusion of the hero of *Hercules Furens*.[173] Both Andromache and Hercules are mad—they see

---

is far from clear and Agamemnon's submission is accordingly ambiguous for this reason also. This scene may usefully be grouped with other scenes troubling for their apparent Stoic cast. See above on *Medea* 953 and *Thyestes* 100 and 489. On the moral threat of Homeric repetition cf. Lyne (1987) 107–13 and Putnam (1995) 253–4 on the Iliadic *Aeneid* and its close. Hardie (1997) 142–4 makes the important point that the end of the *Aeneid* is not simply Iliadic and un-Roman but lacks also the ritual closure of either Homeric epic. Nevertheless the opposition of Iliadic/Greek to Roman remains significant.

[173] I refer to Seneca's *Hercules Furens* but Fantham (1982) 306 notes also the influence of Euripides' *Hercules Furens* 494–5 in which Megara calls for the ghost

what no one else sees—but their hallucinatory visions reflect their character. Madness returns Hercules to the world of his labours and Andromache to a time when Troy and Hector stood, to Iliadic glories. As surely as Hercules is defined by the violent conquests of his past so Andromache is defined by her love for a city and a man which no longer exist. In *Hercules Furens* the representation of the hero's madness as a hallucination has a moral implication. When Hercules resists the simple life offered by Amphitryon he takes refuge in the extravagant violence of the heroic life and in the landscapes of his labours. The continuity between this world and the world of the hallucination suggests that the heroic life is a form of madness and that its values are illusory. Emphasizing physical rather than moral power Owen writes of *Troades* that 'our ghosts manifest ourselves'. Hector's ghost, insubstantial and invisible to all but Andromache, manifests Trojan impotence; the weakness of this 'para-ghost' is to be contrasted with the vital force of dead Achilles.[174] With this analysis we return to an interpretation based on modes of representation: Andromache's frailty has its supernatural analogue in Hector's ineffective ghost. Yet at the same time the distinction between life and death, reality and dream, is important in an interpretation of the tragedy. It is significant that the Trojan reality through which Andromache and her fellow-captives define themselves endures now only as dust, smoke, and shadow. The ghosts and dreams of *Troades* are to be interpreted paradoxically both as manifestations of reality and as its false images. The effect is a blurring of the distinction between the real and the unreal.

The second ode of *Troades*, which formally questions the reality of existence beyond the grave, begins as follows:

> Verum est an timidos fabula decipit
> umbras corporibus vivere conditis?   (*Troades* 371–2)

(Is it true, or a tale to deceive the fainthearted, that spirits live on after bodies are buried?)

The tone of this chorus is Lucretian. The conclusion that death is 'atomic' (*individua* 401), the representation of infernal punish-

---

of Hercules to appear as a shade or a dream. Death and delusion are thus foreshadowed.

[174] Quotations from Owen (1970) 126.

ments as the empty torments of the fearful (402–6), the image of the soul as dissipating smoke (392–6) are all familiar.[175] As we have said, this Epicurean posture cannot be reconciled with the beliefs expressed by the chorus elsewhere (67–163) or with the apparition of Achilles' ghost. The ode anticipates the emptiness of Andromache's dream-Hector in the following scene and her later hallucination, but jars with the mythological assumptions of the rest of the tragedy. Fantham's conclusion that 'this ode is not spoken by the Trojan women but from outside the dramatic action' finds support in Boyle's observation that the references to a *fabula* which begin and end the song have a metadramatic resonance:[176]

> rumores vacui verbaque inania
> et par sollicito fabula somnio   (*Troades* 404–5)

(hollow rumours, empty words, a tale akin to a troubled dream.)

Fabula can mean 'play' or 'dramatic plot' as well as the more general 'story'.[177] The chorus's rejection of mythological terrors is easily accommodated if directed towards the stage as a rejection of 'empty words and a play like a bad dream'.

Troades is exposed as mere theatre, reality as representation. By breaking the dramatic illusion in this way, the chorus liberates the Trojan victims from the paralysis of necessity. Certainly the historical and literary forces which demand the sacrifice of another Iphigenia cannot be averted: Polyxena will die in accordance with the script. But this recognition that destiny is only an act, and therefore in some sense unreal, is a familiar feature of the *consolatio*:

---

[175] See Cicero, *Tusculans* 1.42, Lucretius 3.978–1023 and 3.455–6.

[176] Fantham (1982) 263, Boyle (1994) 173 and 34–7 on theatrical self-consciousness generally in the tragedy. How Boyle would interpret the metatheatrical force of this line particularly is not clear to me.

[177] See e.g. the theatrical metaphors in Livy 3.10.10: *Tribuni coram in foro personare, fabulam compositam Volsci belli, Hernicos ad partes paratos*. In ancient literary criticism all poetry is a lie. Aristotle's criterion of 'the plausible' (τὸ εἰκός, discussed *Poetics* 1454^{b}6, 1460^{a}11–17) is clearly advanced in opposition to a Platonic rhetoric of truth and falsehood, but Aristotle himself speaks of Homer teaching the poets 'to lie as is necessary' (ψευδῆ λέγειν ὡς δεῖ *Poetics* 1460^{a}18). Tragedy, with its impostors (actors) and fantastic events, is not only a lie but does not even resemble truth (Ps.-Cicero, *Ad Herrenium* 1.13, Quintilian 2.4.2). Cicero writes (*De Oratore* 2.193), *quid potest esse tam fictum quam versus, quam scaena, quam fabulae?* Obviously one can communicate moral truth through falsehood (see e.g. Plutarch, *De Poetis Audendis* 19e–20c and Seneca, *De Beneficiis* 7.13.1), but the critical rhetoric of falsehood governs the use of the stage as a moral metaphor.

Quicquid est hoc, Marcia, quod circa nos ex adventicio fulget, liberi, honores, opes ampla atria et exclusorum clientium turba referta vestibula, clarum nomen, nobilis aut formosa coniunx ceteraque ex incerta et mobili sorte pendentia alieni commodatique apparatus sunt; nihil horum dono datur. Conlaticiis et ad dominos redituris instrumentis scaena adornatur. (Ad *Marciam* 10.1)

(All these fortuitous things, Marcia, that glitter about us—children, honours, wealth, spacious halls, and vestibules packed with a throng of unadmitted clients, a famous name, a high-born or beautiful wife, and all else that depends upon uncertain and fickle chance—these are not our own but borrowed trappings; not one of them is given to us outright. The properties that adorn life's stage have been lent, and must go back to their owners.)

Whatever is conferred upon us fortuitously is not truly ours, and its passing cannot therefore truly be regretted. The stage as a metaphor for illusory goods recurs elsewhere in Seneca's prose:

Nemo ex istis quos purpuratos vides, felix est, non magis quam ex illis, quibus sceptrum et chlamydem in scaena fabulae adsignant; cum praesente populo lati incesserunt et coturnati; simul exierunt, excalceantur et ad staturam suam redeunt...

Hoc laboramus errore, sic nobis imponitur, quod neminem aestimamus eo, quod est, sed adicimus illi et ea, quibus adornatus est.

(*Epistles* 76.31–2)

(None of those whom you behold clad in purple is happy, any more than one of those actors upon whom the play bestows a sceptre and a cloak while on the stage; they strut their hour before a crowded house, with swelling port and buskined foot; but when once they make their exit the foot-gear is removed and they return to their own stature.

This is the error under which we labour: by this we are burdened: we value no man at what he is, but add to the man himself the trappings in which he is dressed up.)

Saepius hoc exemplo mihi utendum est, nec enim ullo efficacius exprimitur hic humanae vitae mimus, qui nobis partes, quas male agamus, adsignat. Ille qui in scaena latus incedit et haec resupinus dicit, 'En impero Argis (etc.)', servus est... Ille qui superbus atque inpotens et fiducia virium tumidus ait, 'Quod nisi quieris, Menelae, hac dextra occides', diurnum accipit, in centunculo dormit. Idem de istis licet omnibus dicas, quos supra capita hominum supraque turbam delicatos lectica suspendit; omnium istorum personata felicitas est. Contemnes illos, si despoliaveris. (*Epistles* 80.7–8)

(I often feel called upon to use the following illustration, and it seems to me that none expresses more effectively this drama of human life, wherein we are assigned the parts which we are to play so badly. Yonder is the man who stalks upon the stage with swelling port and head thrown back, and says, 'Lo I am he whom Argos hails as lord (etc.)', He is a slave... who proud and wayward and puffed up by confidence in his power declaims, 'Peace, Menelaus, or this hand shall slay thee', takes a handout and sleeps on rags. You may speak in the same way about all these dandies whom you see riding in litters above the heads of men and above the crowd; in every case their happiness is put on like the actor's mask. Tear it off and you will despise them.)

The posturing of tragic drama[178] figures the unreality of wealth and social status. In each case the representation of reality as theatrical artifice is a judgement on the illusory value of the goods which Fortune has to give.

Troades is only a myth and the necessity of Troy's doom binds only those who choose to inhabit this dramatic illusion. Andromache, awake or asleep, sees Hector's ghost because she is unable to relinquish his image, Astyanax (*hos vultus meus | habebat Hector* (This countenance my Hector had 464–5)). In her dream, itself a memory of *Aeneid* 2.268 f., she recalls Hector as he once was (444–7) and sees the marks of more recent defeat (*squalida obtectus coma* (masked by filthy hair 450)). She will be forced to see, at least in her mind's eye, the familiar features broken a third time when Astyanax falls from the wall (*sic quoque est similis patri* (Even in this he is like his father 1117)). She cannot follow her husband as she would like (418), because she cannot abandon Astyanax, and she cannot abandon Astyanax because he is Hector's image: *[testor] non aliud, Hector, in meo nato mihi | placere, quam te* (I love nothing else, Hector, in my son but you 646–7). This cruel irony is in part of her own making: the fall of Troy is Fortune's work, but it is her devotion to Hector which denies her release. By this passion for a ghost she is confined to a living death.

The moral choice which lies at the centre of this tragedy, whether or not to live a life in the dull repeated rhythms of Trojan death, encourages paradox. The Trojans whose laments begin the tragedy

---

[178] It is significant that the posturing actor is slave. Suspicion of acting as an unnatural deception (see e.g. Seneca, *Epistles* 11.7, Quintilian 6.2.26) is echoed in Roman social reality, where actors were marginalized figures with restricted civic rights. See Edwards (1993) 123–30 and Csapo and Slater (1995) 275–85.

retain their community with their dead city by covering themselves in its ashes. Andromache, herself only half alive (*torpens malis rigensque sine sensu fero* (I endure without feeling, dazed and numbed by adversity 417)), entrusts her son to the grave. The dissipating smoke which the chorus described as an image of the soul disintegrating at death (392–6) is recalled by the ugly column of smoke rising from Troy. This image of extinction is the sign by which the Trojans recognize their home (1053–5) and, scattered across the sea, endure the living death of cultural dissolution.[179] To be contrasted with these representations of a life resembling death are the representations of death as free and vital. The Trojan women envy the freedom of lucky Priam, who has taken his kingdom with him: *Felix Priamus dicimus omnes: | secum excedens sua regna tulit* ('Blest is Priam', we all say: in departing he has taken his kingdom with him 156–7). Andromache likewise sends her son to die with the words, *i, vade liber, liberos Troas vide* (Your Troy awaits you: go in freedom, go to see free Trojans 791).

The hope of Troy reborn in Elysium is questioned not only by the power of Achilles' ghost and the weakness and absence of Hector's but also by the Epicurean ode on the extinction of the soul at death. However, as Polyxena and Astyanax accept the death decreed for them they exhibit an energy and freedom unmatched by any of the Trojan survivors. When the sacrificial marriage is revealed Polyxena hears the news joyfully and willingly puts on the garments of royal dignity: *cultus decoros regiae vestis petit* (She welcomes being finely adorned in royal clothes 946). Hecuba, like Andromache outliving Hector (416–17), subsides into the stupefaction of grief: *at misera luctu mater audito stupet; | labefacta mens succubuit* (But her unhappy mother is stunned to hear of this grief; her weakened mind has given way 949–50). The paradox is prepared by Andromache's anger earlier: *Hoc derat unum Phrygibus eversis malum: | gaudere* (For the ruined Phrygians this was the one woe missing—to rejoice 888–9). Lit by the torch of Troy's flames only a perverse marriage[180] is appropriate:

---

[179] So Fantham (1982) 365, Boyle (1994) 21.
[180] On *thalamis...novis* (900) as a novel kind of marriage see Boyle (1994) 212. Andromache does not control the irony of the phrase quite as Medea does at 743 in her play (Boyle's favoured parallel), but it is clearly the same irony present in both cases.

The Broken World

> thalamis Troia praelucet novis.
> celebrate Pyrrhi, Troades, conubia;
> celebrate digne. planctus et gemitus sonet.
>   (*Troades* 900–2)

(Troy lights the way for this strange wedding. Celebrate the nuptials of Pyrrhus, you Trojan women, celebrate them worthily—with sounds of blows and groaning.)

In celebrating her death like a marriage Polyxena echoes Andromache's paradoxical demand that the marriage be celebrated as a death. Not only is death preferable to life in this world but it is more life-like.

The behaviour of the audience at the deaths of Astyanax and Polyxena is varied and ambiguous,[181] but the contrast between Hecuba's passivity and Polyxena's animation here recurs also in her final scene. She walks in front of Pyrrhus to a death she has accepted and the sympathetic crowd, like Hecuba, is stunned (*stupet omne vulgus* 1143); they tremble as their victim does not: *omnium mentes tremunt* (1147). Astyanax likewise moves his audience while remaining steadfast himself:[182]

> ferox superbe moverat vulgum ac duces
> ipsumque Ulixem. non flet e turba omnium
> qui fletur.
>   (*Troades* 1098–1100)

(He moved the people and their leaders and Ulysses himself. Of the whole crowd, he did not weep who was wept for.)

He walks eagerly to death (*nec gradu segni* 1090) and jumps down from the wall of his own accord (*sponte desiluit sua* 1102), while his spectators offer a lesser echo, swaying on their high vantage points: *et tota populo silva suspenso tremit* (1083).[183] Though a victim of his father's name, Trojan destiny, and the spectacle staged by the Greeks, Astyanax finds a heroic freedom in being less affected than his viewers by his last act. The contrast between an audience, moved by events by happening to someone else, and the central actors unmoved by their departure from a mere *fabula*, is pointed.[184]

---

[181] Discussed below, pp. 245–58.
[182] Cf. of Polyxena, *hos movet formae decus* (1144).
[183] On the Greeks following Astyanax's course in this way cf. M. Wilson (1983) 54–5.
[184] Cf. Dollimore (1984) 29–40 on Marston's use in his drama of images of the stage to express the unreality (in Stoic terms) of life.

The inscribed audience in the final act of *Troades* comprises both Greeks and Trojans. Both sides are moved by the deaths and Greek tears surpass Trojan at Polyxena's death (1160–1). The community of their response is anticipated by Hecuba's prologue and her representation of the death of Troy as exemplary. Agamemnon likewise begins his agon with Pyrrhus with general reflections on youth's lack of self-control and the instability of violent empire. Troy's destruction leads him to reflect on his own kingdom:

> Troia nos tumidos facit
> nimium ac feroces? stamus hoc Danai loco
> unde illa cecidit. fateor, aliquando impotens
> regno ac superbus altius memet tuli.
> sed fregit illos spiritus haec quae dare
> potuissent aliis causa, fortunae favor.
>
> (*Troades* 264–9)

(Does Troy make us too arrogant and self-assured? We Danaans stand in the very place from which she fell. I admit, at one time I was unrestrained and proud in government, bearing myself too high; but that arrogance was broken by the very cause that could have produced it in others, Fortune's favour.)

Not only are the Trojans doomed to extinction through the reiteration of the forms of Troy's death, but the Greeks too play their part in the cycle of the rise and fall of nations. Astyanax's death ends the threat of another Hector (550–1, 737–8) but the play will close with the ships setting sail for disasters known at least to the audience. Many will die in a storm and particular dooms await Agamemnon and Ulysses.[185] At the close Hecuba asks:

> Ubi hanc anilis expuam leti moram?
> natam an nepotem, coniugem an patriam fleam?
> an omnia an me?
>
> (*Troades* 1169–71)

(Where shall I spew out this obstacle to an old woman's death? Shall I weep for daughter or grandchild, husband or country? For my whole world, or for myself?)

---

[185] The description of a storm at sea (1029–41) in the final chorus is an obvious piece of foreshadowing. Hecuba promises Ulysses that her evil destiny will dog him too (993–8), though the audience's familiarity with the myth is perhaps foreshadowing enough. Note also the ironic, *Ite, ite, Danai, petite iam tuti domos* (1165). See Boyle (1994) 24–5.

The Broken World 101

By 'my whole world' she means the Trojan world, but the indefinite phrasing and our memory that the Greeks stand now where Troy once did, encourages us to think in more general terms. The death of Trojan Polyxena is an echo of the death of Greek Iphigenia as Ulysses reminds Andromache:

> neve crudelem putes,
> quod sorte iussus Hectoris natum petam;
> petissem Oresten. patere quod victor tulit.
> (*Troades* 553–5)

(And do not think me cruel because the lot ordered me to demand Hector's son: I would have demanded Orestes. Endure what the victor bore.)

The *fabula* of *Troades* is a single episode in a longer cyclical history of the rise and fall of empires. Within this episode Greek supremacy is total. Myths of supernatural power have real force; a dead Greek hero is more active and powerful than any of the living Trojans, let alone the dead. Though the second chorus rejects belief in an afterlife, Achilles' epiphany remains real; supernatural power is a true mode of the extent of Greek domination. In the world of *Troades* the antithesis between Greek and Trojan is more significant than that between the living and the dead. This displacement of the most fundamental boundary of human reality by a Greek fabrication is a sign of their power.

For the brief moment which is the tragedy of *Troades* the repetition of past events coincides with Greek desires: Astyanax dies his father's death, reiterating and reinforcing the Greek victory. Greek imperial destiny is manifest in the structure of reality and in the inexorable, prescribed narratives of Trojan doom. However, in the wider context the rhythms and ironies of cyclical myth are controlled not by the Greeks but by a power which preys without discrimination on all the human actors. The death of Iphigenia is echoed by the death of Polyxena without reference to a distinction between Greek and Trojan. In this mythological world what is probable and necessary is dictated less by mundane laws of cause and effect than by more poetic laws of echoing episodes and images.[186] This artificiality, this fictive quality of dramatic reality, confers a peculiar power on the Greeks while

---

[186] Lawall (1982) 250 argues that 'the perspective of the audience/reader is distanced by the very structure of the play' and that this artifice has a deliberate

their goals coincide with those of poetic necessity: reality appears a Greek fabrication. Without such a coincidence reality appears merely as the fabrication or drama of Fortune, and it is from this fiction or *fabula* that Epicurean extinction offers a release.

That life is a drama, illusory, a construction rather than an ultimate necessity, is a common consolation. The overtly poetic principle of necessity which dominates *Troades* and the disjointed, plastic nature of its dramatic reality expose it as a fiction. The play represents imperial fictions operating above the laws of reality, supernaturally. Even as it celebrates the power to enforce such constructions, it reveals it as transient. Hecuba's lesson, that the most powerful empire is unstable, is communicated not only through the vision of Troy's defeat but through the form of an incoherent and agonistic dramatic reality. Necessity exists only intermittently as it can be enforced or in an overtly artificial, literary form which marks the world as a poetic construct. Commonly the loss of necessity in Senecan tragedy and the profusion of paradoxes mark the dissolution of a controlling interpretative framework. Here, drawing on the familiar representation of the external world as mere theatre, Seneca disrupts the dramatic illusion of *Troades* to point its fictive quality. More surely than in *Hercules Furens*, he turns at the end of *Troades* to escape from the theatre; extinction alone offers closure to the shifting values, the ambiguities and paradoxes characteristic of Seneca's staged reality.

point: 'The fragmentation of our attention distances us to a point from which we may view the play as the tragedy of a whole society or world (including Trojans and Greeks alike) or of mankind itself'.

3
Images of a Flawed Technical Genesis

PERHAPS the most striking example of literary self-consciousness in Senecan tragedy is Medea's exotic sense of her own myth and name.[1] 'I shall become Medea' she promises the Nurse (171). The dramatic illusion is broken as the heroine appears to conceive of herself both as a person and as a literary construct. Through her dual perspective the text acquires a figurative self-consciousness, patterned on the self-consciousness of a dramatic character. Literary self-consciousness need not be figured in so personal a form; it need not take its pattern so directly from the representation of a psyche. Reference to other texts through verbal reminiscence, whether observed by a dramatic character or not, draws attention to the construction of the poem. Here also the work, in some less personal sense, can be said to expose the mechanism of its production and thus to reflect on itself.[2] The difficulty with the less direct, less personal sense of self-consciousness is that it may be extended to exclude very little. Every work of literature encourages and obstructs different analyses of itself, and if any and all its features are taken as marks of the text 'reading itself', then reflexivity becomes so pervasive as to render meaningless terms like 'self-referential' and 'self-conscious'. If the terms are to be used productively there must be a distinction between an object and its reflection; literary self-consciousness is dependent on the separation of these two elements and the creation of two levels of significance.[3]

[1] *Medea* 166, 171, 1021–2. See also Rosenmeyer (1989) 52, Hershkowitz (1998) 61 on the gallery of past literary images from which Medea fashions her role, and Pöschl (1978) 75, Fitch and McElduff (2002) 18–19 on the centrality in the masked genre of issues of self-construction. Cf. Richardson (1977) 437 on Propertius 4.4.43–4: 'This couplet, in which Tarpeia seems to see herself as a subject for legend and literature, has a strong neoteric ring.'
[2] Cf. Conte's impersonal metaphor of 'poetic grids', personal metaphor of 'memory', and his survey of the field: Conte (1986) 23–39.
[3] Hamon (1977) 284 raises a further theoretical problem for the definition of metalinguistic operations, 'A la limite, la tautologie... est-elle un appareil métalinguistique?' but for the practice of literary criticism this is a less significant concern.

One means of constructing the desired separation is by setting the central myth which the tragedy presents in a wider context. Medea's personal vengeance on Jason for his abandonment of her is set in the wider context of vengeance for an Argonautic voyage which the chorus sees as an affront to the natural order of the world. The framing myth, the Argonautic voyage, is a myth of technology, the end of divine supervision and the end of the Golden Age. This general theme, whether it appears as the *Argo's* voyage, or as Phaethon's chariot ride, or simply as the end of the Golden Age, is recurrent in Senecan tragedy. *Hercules Furens* begins with fear and anger at the mortal assault on heaven and remembers Phaethon from Euripides and Ovid. Furia, the inspiration of *Thyestes*, recalls the criminality of the end of the Golden Age and sends Tantalus to infect Argos; he scorches the earth as Phaethon did. Hippolytus in *Phaedra* tries to escape criminal desire in the sanctuary of the Golden Age.[4] The image of the frame is inexact in *Medea* and *Phaedra*, where the personal myths of the protagonists are more closely interwoven, but in *Hercules Furens* and *Thyestes* the myths of humanity's freedom from divine supervision appear at the opening of the tragedies and again to introduce their culmination—Hercules' madness and Thyestes' banquet. In this way the structure of the drama presents them as a reflection and an interpretation of tragic criminality. Crucially, these myths of flawed genesis do not simply reiterate each other: Phaethon's hubris is to be distinguished from the deliberate criminality in Ovid's account of the decline of the Ages. These myths thus offer contrasting reflections of the tragic acts which they frame.

The opposing figures of the charioteer and of the Fury, criminal madness personified, are also familiar and contrasting symbols of poetic inspiration. In this way the framing myths interpret not only Hercules' madness or Jason's breach of faith but the animating passions of the tragedy itself. Medea's strange awareness of her

---

If an object is identical with its reflection there is practically no material for discussion. Less extremely some paraphrases do not appear significantly different from their object and will likely be discarded by a commentator not because they fail to satisfy the criteria of a metalinguistic operation but because they are unproductive.

[4] All these passages and characters are discussed in greater detail below except Hippolytus, who is the subject of Ch. 5.

own myth and her role as a witch who forms the world with her magical song encourage a meta-literary interpretation. The figure of the witch and the seer are familiar 'poet-surrogates' in a tradition which depends ultimately on a similarity between the arts of magician, divinely inspired speaker, and poet. Characterized now as Phaethon's relative now as Nature's Fury, Seneca's Medea offers contrasting images of Seneca's tragic art, conflicting 'autobiographies of the work'.[5] As there are recurrent systems of imagery in Seneca's tragedies[6] so there are recurrent mythological figures from the Underworld and from the end of the Golden Age. These figures form a significant part of the language of Senecan tragedy's self-consciousness.

Medea and Atreus, Seneca's most powerful and most self-conscious protagonists, are both concerned to conquer the past. Atreus' desire to exact a revenge more terrible than has ever been seen is persistently unsatisfied. Even as his victim is affirming that it is a crime without parallel Atreus imagines how it might have been enacted better (*Thyestes* 1047–68). Other myths are material to be rivalled and surpassed, and often a myth is recalled for comparison by allusion to a specific version. Atreus' decision to imitate and surpass the revenge of Procne (*Thyestes* 272–9) parallels Seneca's decision to imitate Ovid's version of the myth in the *Metamorphoses*. Characters like Atreus view their actions in the context of a wider mythological tradition, and their struggles to establish a place in that tradition is productively read as images of the genesis of Senecan tragedy.

Similar contrasts appear here as in the more abstract self-consciousness created by the myths of Phaethon's chariot ride and the end of the Golden Age. The desire to surpass what is established is criminal and paradoxically a successful innovation is in some sense worse than the model it conquers. This dark, Bloomian tone is characteristic of the self-consciousness of Silver Latin literature of other genres, particularly epic, but it is not the only image which Seneca's tragedy offers of its poetic genesis. Phaethon is over-bold in transgressing human boundaries, but not deliberately criminal: flawed and fatal aspirations to sublimity are not to be glossed simply as rebellion against an established

---

[5] A reference to Ferrucci (1980) quoted from Segal (1983) 241.
[6] For a survey see Pratt (1963).

order, whether cosmic, poetic, or political. If Medea, modelled on Virgil's Dido and Juno, suggests an inversion of the *Aeneid* by giving victory to Virgil's losers, the celebration of empire with all limits removed (364–79) surpasses rather than inverts Jupiter's famous prophecy for the Roman people.[7] Criminality is complex, as it must be if the characterization of literary invention as criminal is to be critically productive.[8]

By his use of opposing images of poetic inspiration and by engaging differently with past texts, Seneca offers contrasting representations of the genesis of his poetry and a plural self-consciousness. Central to his tragic vision is an opposition of the deliberate criminality of a Fury and the flawed magnificence of a Phaethon. The tragedies are not all of a type: we have already seen how the nihilistic confusion of right and wrong in *Thyestes* differs from the genuine ambivalence of heroic virtue represented in *Hercules Furens*. Similarly the opposition of images of poetic genesis is collapsed in *Thyestes* as it is not in *Hercules Furens* or *Medea*, and the single-minded inversion of Augustan texts (and their ideological freight) in *Thyestes* is relieved in *Hercules Furens* and *Medea* by more ambivalent forms of literary emulation. The varied effects collectively termed literary self-consciousness are not of course authoritative interpretations of the tragedies of which they themselves are part. Framing myths of creation, poet-surrogates, intertextual dynamics are no more and no less than images of the process of literary construction.

---

[7] These passages are discussed in Sect. 3 of this chapter. In the second Argonautic Ode in *Medea* the chorus marks its shift from the world of *Argo*'s voyage to a world with Roman boundaries with the words *Nunc iam* (*Medea* 364). One may confidently argue here that the chorus has broken the dramatic illusion and that the text therefore has a distinct reflexive structure. The anachronism is signalled, the myth not merely Roman but self-consciously so.

[8] As the figure of the Fury has been the dominant icon of Senecan tragedy (see e.g. Rosenmeyer (1989) 3), so, and with equally good reason, calculated inversion and negation have featured prominently in interpretation of Seneca's tragic poetics. These are not, however, their only modes, and their moral voice is accordingly complex. Particularly in totalizing interpretations where it is argued that *all* poetic creativity is essentially criminal it is important to insist on discrimination within the term if it is to remain useful. On Seneca see Schiesaro (1997a), who, though he certainly does not argue so crudely (see the conclusion 99 ff.), does bring the issue into view (94–5). On a different Neronian author cf. Hooley (1997) 26–63 on Persius' adoption of the persona of Horace's 'mad poet', especially 60–1.

1. HERCULES FURENS

Hercules Furens is a tragedy of power. Hercules returns victorious over the tyranny of death to discover that Lycus has taken advantage of his absence to seize power in Thebes. He kills Lycus, but even as he makes sacrifice to Jupiter he is driven mad by Juno, who fears his inexorable march to the heavens. Juno's motives are most clearly given in her opening monologue (1–124). In an angry lament modelled in part on Ovid's Juno in *Metamorphoses* 2.508 f.[9] she complains that heaven is full of Jupiter's mistresses and that her own position is undermined. Again Ovidian is her admission that her attempts to destroy Hercules have not only failed but have increased his glory and proved his paternity (*dum nimis saeva impero, | patrem probavi, gloriae feci locum* 35–6).[10] Her concern with Hercules' paternity is as much political as personal: *caelo timendum est, regna ne summa occupet | qui vicit ima—sceptra praeripiet patri* (It is heaven we must fear for—that after conquering the lowest realm he may seize the highest. He will usurp his father's sceptre! 64–5). The ode (125–201) following and contrasting with her monologue offers a more stable image both of the celestial bodies, and of human life: humble rustics do not live the dangerous lives of semi-divine heroes. It opens with a clear allusion to dawn on the day of Phaethon's fatal ride in Ovid *Metamorphoses*,[11] and for half its length is closely modelled on the parodos of Euripides' *Phaethon*.[12] Phaethon is not a tyrant and he does not aspire to political power, but particularly to Juno's perception his similarity to Hercules is not difficult to see.[13] In the

---

[9] There are many models here. See Fitch (1987) 116–17 for an overview.

[10] Cf. Ovid, *Metamorphoses* 2.518–22.

[11] *cogit nitidum Phosphorus agmen* (*H. F.* 128), cf. *diffugiunt stellae, quarum agmina cogit cogit | Lucifer* (*Met.* 2.114–15). The following lines of Ovid's account (*Met.* 2.116–17) are reworked by Seneca (*H. F.* 135–6). For both parallels see Fitch (1987) 159, 168, and Jakobi (1988) 7.

[12] The fisherman (155–8) does not appear in Euripides' list of natural phenomena and daily tasks, but it is in the extended moralizing conclusion to the list where Seneca departs significantly from Euripides (159–201; cf. Euripides, *Phaethon*, 87–90). All references to *Phaethon* are to Diggle (1970). He comments authoritatively 96, 'That the one ode was written with full knowledge of the other is beyond dispute.' Whether Seneca had read all of Euripides' tragedy or just this ode is another question and one which cannot be argued by reference to Seneca's *Hercules Furens*. See Fitch (1987) 158 and, for an overview of the Phaethon myth in Greek and Latin literature, Diggle (1970) 4–32.

[13] So P. J. Davis (1993) 133–5.

conclusion to the non-Euripidean part of the ode the chorus neatly creates a political Phaethon with reference to a Roman triumph:

> Alium multis gloria terris
> tradat et omnes fama per urbes
> garrula laudet *caeloque parem*
> *tollat et astris*;
> *alius curru sublimis eat:*
> me mea tellus lare secreto
> tuto tegat.   (192–7)

(Another may be carried to many countries by Renown; garrulous Rumour may praise him through every city, and raise him equal with the starry heavens; another may ride high in a chariot. For me, let my own land hide me in a safe and secluded home.)

In both Euripides' and Ovid's accounts Phaethon's chariot-ride is a disastrous assertion of his divine paternity. Ovid's Clymene ends the first book of the *Metamorphoses* by sending her son across Ethiopia to the house of the Sun to have his paternity confirmed (1.760–79). The fatal gift is itself the proof (2.40–8). Euripides' myth is complicated by a marriage, but otherwise, as far as the fragmentary text allows one to say with certainty, it introduces its tragedy in a similar way: Clymene, in Ethiopia, sends Phaethon to the Sun to receive the gift which is the proof.[14] Immediately after describing her failure to suppress Hercules' paternity and glory (35–6 above) Seneca's Juno continues:

> qua Sol reducens quaque deponens diem
> binos propinqua tinguit Aethiopas face,
> indomita virtus colitur et toto deus
> narratur orbe.   (37–40)

(Where the Sun restores the day and relinquishes it, blackening both Ethiop tribes with the closeness of its torch, *his* indomitable valour is revered, and throughout the whole world he is storied as a god.)

It seems unlikely that Ethiopians are included here, in connection with Hercules' divine paternity, except to anticipate the identification of Hercules with Phaethon.[15] The consequences of

---

[14] On the very fragmentary lines 8–44 and for reconstruction see Diggle (1970) 83 ff.

[15] Cf. Fitch (1987) 133, for whom this is merely a variant in the frequent expressions of Hercules' universal fame. Fitch (1987) 161 and n. 36, when indicating precise connections between Juno's monologue and the subsequent odes, makes

Phaethon's assertion of his identity, in Ovid if not in Euripides,[16] are more than personal: the world is threatened with total destruction when his chariot careers off course. In the *Metamorphoses* this episode parallels the great flood which Jupiter sends in response to the criminality which follows the degeneration from the Golden Age. The broad thematic similarity is pointed by structural parallelism and verbal reminiscence.[17] The world cannot be created anew at the beginning of book 2 as it is at the beginning of book 1, so instead there is a representation of the cosmos on the doors of the palace of the Sun (2.1-18). Phaethon's failed and destructive attempt to assume a divine role and to direct the course of the day is parallel to the more gradual development of human technology and human criminality which follow the Golden Age. Ovid is not the only writer to have made the association: Hyginus records that Jupiter destroyed Phaethon not with a thunderbolt but with a flood as an excuse for punishing the rest of humanity.[18]

The reckless Phaethon is not criminal in the same way that the inhabitants of the Bronze and Iron Ages are,[19] but myths of human progress are ambivalent; the awkwardness which Ovid expresses by inexact parallelism is a central feature of the genre. Phaethon's epitaph offers a sympathetic view of flawed magnificence:

> Hic situs est Phaethon currus auriga paterni
> quem si non tenuit magnis tamen excidit ausis
> (*Met.* 2.326-7)

---

the crucial point that it is a familiar feature of Seneca's dramatic practice to follow a monologue with an ode which is parallel and opposed: 'This technique of ironic recall is used to greater effect in the opening odes of *Med.* and *Thy.*'

[16] The death of Euripides' Phaethon is recounted in a messenger speech (168-77), but these few lines are insufficient evidence. See Diggle (1970) 41 ff. and in more detail 134-8.

[17] See e.g. the description of the horses leaving their proper course: *exspatiantur equi* (2.202). The verb *exspatior* is used by Ovid elsewhere only of the rivers bursting out onto the land in the flood: *exspatiata ruunt per apertos flumina campos* (1.285).

[18] Hyginus, *Fabulae* 152A. Diggle (1970) 21 argues that this passage must be an interpolation. Quite apart from the problem of a sinister Jupiter who requires a false pretext to destroy humanity, the conjunction of fire and flood seems awkward. However, fire and flood, ekpyrosis and cataclysm, are functionally equivalent (see e.g. Seneca, *Naturales Quaestiones* 3.28.7-29.3) and, whether interpolated or not, this passage is significant for its association of myths.

[19] See *Met.* 1.125-50, which concludes, *victa iacet pietas, et virgo caede madentis | ultima caelestum terras Astraea reliquit.*

(Here lies Phaethon who drove his father's chariot. If he could not retain it he nevertheless surpassed what he greatly dared.)

In Ovid's account Phaethon does not reply to his father's warnings. In *De Providentia* Seneca quotes ten lines of Apollo's warning from *Met.* 2 (63–9 and 79–81) and supplies not only his own commentary[20] but also a reply for Phaethon:

'Placet', inquit, 'via; escendo. Est tanti per ista ire casuro... Iunge datos currus! His quibus deterreri me putas incitor. Libet illic stare ubi ipse Sol trepidat.' Humilis et inertis est tuta sectari; per alta virtus it.[21]

(*De Prov.* 5.10–11)

('I like the path,' he said, 'I will ride. Though I fall it is worth so much to travel through such places... Harness the chariot you have given me! I am roused by the very things which you think frighten me. I take pleasure in standing where the Sun himself trembles.' It is for the lowly and the feeble to follow the safe path; virtue walks the heights.)

That Seneca chose to read Phaethon in this way here is not an argument to impose the same reading blindly on Phaethon and Hercules in a tragedy which itself has some effect on the reception of its central character.[22] It is sufficient to say here that a reader's ambivalent expectations of Phaethon and the myths of the Fall frame the representation of Hercules' problematic *virtus* in the tragedy. The Stoic use of Hercules as a symbol of the heroic *sapiens* sits awkwardly with this tragic representation of a hero apparently consumed by *furor*. This ambivalence is reflected in the ambivalence of the framing myths of Phaethon and of the end of the Golden Age.

Immediately before Hercules goes mad he offers a prayer to Jupiter. This is a prayer for peace which recalls the first ode of the tragedy and reinforces its Virgilian tone. One of the features of

---

[20] Cf. Bömer (1969) 256 on philosophical readings of these lines of Ovid particularly *Met.* 2.63 f.

[21] Cf. *Hercules Furens* 201: *alte virtus animosa cadit*. The fatal chariot ride appears also in *Phaedra*. Skovgaard-Hansen (1968) 110–11 contrasts Hippolytus' inflexibility unfavourably with the natural adaptation of Phoebe and Phoebus. In this passage of *De Providentia* Phaethon's determination to walk where the Sun trembles is interpreted as heroism and virtue. *Constantia* and living in accordance with Nature are both Stoic virtues and the Phaethon myth is open to different constructions.

[22] Cf. Marti's (1945) interpretation of *Hercules Furens* as allegorical teaching 223–5. In reading Seneca's tragedies as drama rather than 'philosophy on stage' Regenbogen (1961) marks a new beginning in Senecan studies.

that ode which distinguishes it from its Euripidean model is the comparative hardship of the life of Seneca's simple rustics: *labor exoritur durus et omnis | agitat curas aperitque domos* (Hard Toil arises, bestirs every care and opens every home. 137–8). As Fitch notes, 'In Roman poetry such a note is associated particularly with Vergil's *Georgics*, and indeed the phrase with which Seneca introduces it, *labor durus* (hard toil), occurs there twice (2.412, 4.114).'[23] In the prayer to Jupiter Amphitryon advises Hercules to ask for an end to his labours: *Finiat genitor tuus | opta labores, detur aliquando otium | quiesque fessis* (Ask that your father end your toils, that peace and rest be granted at last to our weary spirits 924–6). Hercules duly contrasts the warfare of his past with the more wholesome *ruris...labor* (toil of the countryside 930) of the *Georgics*[24] and the first ode:

> ferrum omne teneat ruris innocui labor
> ensesque lateant   (930–1)

(may iron be used only in the harmless toil of the countryside, and may swords be hidden away).

The description which follows makes it clear that a world in which weapons are hidden will be a second Golden Age:[25]

> nulla tempestas fretum
> violenta turbet, nullus irato Iove
> exiliat ignis, nullus hiberna nive
> nutritus agros amnis eversos trahat.
> venena cessent, nulla nocituro gravis
> suco tumescat herba. non saevi ac truces
> regnent tyranni.   (931–7)

(May no violent storm disturb the seas, may no fire streak down from angry Jove, may no river fed with winter snows ravage the uptorn fields. May poisons disappear, and may no deadly herb swell with harmful juices. May no fierce and cruel tyrants reign.)

This is a resolutely political Golden Age: it will come to pass when wars cease and it will be distinguished by the absence both of an

---

[23] Fitch (1987) 159–60. On the importance of Virgil see also P. J. Davis (1993) 127–9.
[24] Cf. in sentiment Virgil, *Georgics* 1.501 ff. and Putnam (1979) 71–81: 'war, especially civil antagonism, is a corrupt version of man's enmity with nature' (71).
[25] On the traditional elements of the Golden Age and this passage in particular see Fitch (1987) 361.

angry Jupiter and of terrestrial tyrants. The absence of poison is an unusual detail which surely recalls the Golden Age of Virgil, *Eclogues* 4 (*occidet et serpens et fallax herba veneni | occidet* (the serpent will perish and the deceitful poison-herb will perish 24–5)), which again is explicitly political. Hercules' prayer for a Golden Age contrasts not only with his past labours but with the madness which befalls him even as he is praying. In this respect it is parallel to the earlier ode which contrasts with its preceding monologue, where Juno gives her account of Hercules' labours (40–63) and drives herself mad (100–12). The Euripidean ode on which Seneca's ode is modelled must surely have performed a similar function in contrasting the idyllic life of its humble shepherds and sailors with the fatal glory of Phaethon.

Hercules begins his prayer for a Golden Age with the words, *ipse concipiam preces | Iove meque dignas* (*I* shall pronounce prayers that are worthy of Jove and of myself 926–7). These words recall the description of Ovid's Jupiter before the flood: *ingentes animo et dignas Iove concipit iras* (he conceived in his heart huge anger worthy of Jupiter *Met.* 1.166).[26] This allusion is ominous and undermines Hercules' hope for a Golden Age without an angry Jupiter (932–3). There is conspicuous irony in Hercules speaking for his father Jupiter without any sense either of the doom about to befall him or of the resonance of the words he has chosen. Thematically, his mistaken confidence in speaking for Jupiter fits in well with the myth of the hero who believes he can drive his father's chariot. At the same time there is a poignancy in the dissimilarity between the myth of Phaethon and the myth of the flood. Hercules may overreach himself in speaking for Jupiter and in challenging the earth to provide him with new evils to conquer, but he is not unequivocally criminal like the people of the Iron Age or of the Giants' rebellion, a race to be wiped out by the flood (*Met.* 1.141–62). These contradictory characterizations are present in the description of Hercules' madness. He looks for a labour worthy of himself (*dignus Alcide labor* 957) and finds it not in the Golden Age but in the leadership of the Titans against his father (965–73). Though he is thus deserving of precisely the extinction which his allusion threatened, at another point he recalls Phaethon more closely. In the unnaturally dark sky he

[26] So Fitch (1987) 362, Jakobi (1988) 13.

Images of a Flawed Technical Genesis

sees his first labour, the Nemean lion, not contributing to celestial harmony but seething with anger:

> primus en noster labor
> caeli refulget parte non minima leo
> iraque totus fervet et morsus parat.
> iam rapiet aliquod sidus.   (944–7)

(Look, my first labour, the Lion, shines in a large segment of the sky, burns all over with anger and prepares to bite. Soon he will pounce on some constellation.)

The lion-skin is one of Hercules' most distinctive features and this savage lion symbolizes Hercules himself, but the figure of the threatening constellation is modelled on Ovid's Scorpio who so terrifies Phaethon that he loses the reins of his chariot (*Met.* 2.195–200).[27] When Hercules recovers consciousness after the crime he asks where in the world he is:

> ubi sum? sub ortu solis, an sub cardine
> glacialis ursae? numquid Hesperii maris
> extrema tellus hunc dat Oceano modum?
> quas trahimus auras?   (1139–42)

(Where am I? Beneath the sun's rising, or beneath the turning point of the icy Bear? Can this be the limit set to Ocean's waters by the farthest land on the western sea? What air do I breathe?)

These words have particular relevance because they come not only from the great world-traveller, but from the figure who in his madness has just raged through the globe and beyond. The phrase *quas trahimus auras?* is a striking figure of speech and paralleled before Seneca only by Ovid's description of Phaethon:[28] *ferventes auras velut e fornace profunda | ore trahit* (the air he breathes is like the hot air of a deep furnace *Met.* 2.229–30).

---

[27] So Fitch (1987) 365.
[28] On the world-traveller see Fitch (1987) 414–15, who also notes the echo of Ovid's Phaethon but emphasizes a vaguer parallel with Euripides' *Hercules Furens* (1092–3) and reads no significance into the Ovidian reminiscence. On the relationship between madness and walking the grand stage see especially the final act of the tragedy: Amphitryon and Theseus urge Hercules to control himself (*Herculem irasci veta* 1277) and to live for his father alone. Hercules' resistance to their entreaties is represented in part by his refusal to abandon the grand perspective as, for example, he calls for *all* the woods of Pindus and Cithaeron and ultimately the whole vault of heaven to crush him (1285–94).

Ovid marks the differences between the myth of Phaethon and the degeneration into criminality which follows the end of the Golden Age by presenting them in parallel in his narrative. Seneca creates a single, ambivalent hero by characterizing him as a figure from these dissimilar but related myths. Interpretation of this tragedy hinges on the origin and the nature of its criminal madness: it may be seen as an extension of Hercules' *virtus* or an alien state of mind imposed upon him by a vengeful Juno.[29] To some extent the nature of tragic madness is bound up with its origin: Hercules tends toward the Phaethonic madness of overreaching and breaking boundaries, while Juno's madness is more deliberately anarchic and evil. However, Seneca is at pains to confuse Juno with Hercules, by making them imitate each other, and thereby obstructs any simple identification of the tragic madness. The interest of the tragedy lies in the interweaving of two different characterizations of criminal madness. These alternatives are proposed by the pairing of the tragedy's first ode, which suggests Phaethon is an important model, with the preceding monologue, where Juno's summoning of *Scelus*, *Impietas*, and *Furor* from the underworld (89–99) is a naked expression of criminality.

Juno's complaint that Jupiter's mistresses and their children have usurped her place is graphically expressed as they take possession of parts of the sky:

> Soror Tonantis (hoc enim solum mihi)
> nomen relictum est) semper alienum Iovem
> ac templa summi vidua deserui aetheris
> locumque caelo pulsa paelicibus dedi;
> tellus colenda est, paelices caelum tenent.   (1–5)

(*Sister* of the Thunder God: this is the only title left me. Wife no more, I have abandoned ever-unfaithful Jove and the precincts of high heaven; driven from the skies, I have given up my place to his whores. I must dwell on earth; whores inhabit the skies.)

Hercules develops this usurpation of her power further by transforming even her anger into his own glory:

---

[29] For a representative of each view see Shelton (1978) and Lawall (1983) respectively. For an overview with full bibliography see Fitch (1987) 21–44, especially 21–33.

superat et crescit malis
iraque nostra fruitur; in laudes suas
mea vertit odia: dum nimis saeva impero,
patrem probavi, gloriae feci locum   (33–6)

(*He* prevails and grows greater through hardships, thrives on my anger, turns my hatred to his own glory. By imposing such cruel commands, I have proved his parentage and given scope to his reputation.)

The helplessness of Juno in this transformation is only part of its significance. Hercules' *virtus* and *gloria* are not just dependent on Juno's anger but created from it: Hercules is armed with her hatred which the hostile earth casts in monstrous physical form: *armatus venit leone et hydra* (he comes armed with lion and hydra 45–6). The final labour of Juno (or her representative Eurystheus)[30] is that Hercules descend to the underworld to bring back Cerberus. Juno introduces this labour with the words, *Nec satis terrae patent: | effregit ecce limen inferni Iovis* (Even the earth is not room enough. See, he has broken through the gates of nether Jove 46–7). The earth has birthed a sequence of horrors, but in this final case it must open even further. Hercules, the transgressor of boundaries, forces a passage to the underworld. The first part of the description places the labour in the tradition of the earth giving birth to Juno's monstrous hatred; the second part rephrases the same act in characteristically Herculean terms. Cerberus, the end of the labour, is a memorial simultaneously of Juno's *ira* and Hercules' *virtus*.

Juno models her criminal vengeance on his labour:

quaeris Alcidae parem?
nemo est nisi ipse: bella iam secum gerat.
Adsint ab imo Tartari fundo excitae
Eumenides, ignem flammeae spargant comae,
viperea saevae verbera incutiant manus.
i nunc, superbe, caelitum sedes pete,
humana temne. iam Styga et manes, ferox,
fugisse credis? hic tibi ostendam inferos.
revocabo in alta conditam caligine,
ultra nocentum exilia, discordem deam
quam munit ingens montis oppositu specus;

---

[30] Note that the description of Eurystheus at 78, *ipse imperando fessus Eurystheus vacet* echoes the description of Juno at 40–2, *monstra iam desunt mihi | minorque labor est Herculi iussa exsequi, | quam mihi iubere.*

> educam et imo Ditis e regno extraham
> quidquid relictum est: veniet invisum Scelus
> suumque lambens sanguinem Impietas ferox
> Errorque et in se semper armatus Furor—
> hoc hoc ministro noster utatur dolor.   (84–99)

(Do you need a match for Alcides? There is none but himself. Now he must war with himself. The Eumenides must be summoned here from the lowest depths of Tartarus, their burning hair must scatter fire, their cruel hands brandish snaky whips. Go ahead, proud man, aspire to the gods' abodes, despise human status! You think you have now escaped the Stygian world and its merciless spirits? *Here* I will show you infernal powers. I shall call up one buried in deep darkness, beyond the sinners' banishment, the goddess Discord, immured by the vast flank of a mountain blocking her escape. I shall bring forth all that remain, and fetch them from the depths of Dis' kingdom: hateful Crime shall come, and savage Disloyalty, lapping its own blood, and Confusion, and mad Rage, always armed against itself—yes, *this* must be the agent of my resentment.)

By imitating Hercules and leading or dragging up from the kingdom of Dis whatever he has left, Juno will force him to revisit the ghosts he thinks he has escaped. Her call to civil war,[31] *bella iam secum gerat* (now he must war with himself), is realized in the figure of *in se semper armatus Furor* (Rage, always armed against itself): Hercules will come to resemble her Fury. Already her anger, in threatening to tear him apart with its bare hands, imitates him:[32] *Perge, ira, perge et...manibus ipsa dilacera tuis* (Onward, my anger, onward and...tear him apart with your own hands 75–6). Finally, she says that if Hercules is to rage then she must do so first:

> ut possit animum captus Alcides agi,
> magno furore percitus, nobis prius
> insaniendum est: Iuno, cur nondum furis?   (107–9)

(So that Hercules can be hounded, deranged and enraged, you must first feel madness.—Juno, why are *you* not yet raging?)

---

[31] Juno's anger, her eternal wars, and her invocation of the Fury are modelled on the speeches of Virgil's Juno at the beginning of books 1 and 7 of the *Aeneid*. See Fitch (1987) 116–17, 131–2, 146–53, Lawall (1983) 6–8, and Schiesaro (1994). Virgil's Allecto is invoked to inspire a quasi-civil war between two peoples who will later be a single nation. The phrase *Alcidae parem* suggests perhaps a gladiatorial pair. On Lucan's use of this motif for the corrupt spectacle of civil war see Ahl (1976) 86–7, developed further by Masters (1992) 44 and *passim*.

[32] Juno, Ἥρα in Greek, is anger (*ira*) personified. On the prominence of Hercules' powerful hands in this tragedy see Fitch (1987) 157 on line 122.

Images of a Flawed Technical Genesis 117

In this tragedy Herculean *virtus* (115) is an imitation of and a model for the *scelus* which Juno intends (121). Juno and Hercules are inseparable from each other. The very complaints of Seneca's Juno mingle the complaints of Ovid's Juno with the boasts of Ovid's Hercules on Mount Oeta.[33] Fitch notes at line 105 an ambiguity created through Juno's Virgilian model: Juno's command, *concutite pectus*, echoing the Virgilian *concute pectus* (*Aen.* 7.338), is generally taken as an order to strike Hercules' breast, 'but in Vergil the *pectus* is Allecto's own'.[34] The phrase is located between the command to exact punishment from Hercules (104) and to turn on Juno herself (107–9) and is, I would argue, ambiguous by design. Throughout this monologue Seneca offers two competing models: in the first, Juno imposes criminality on Hercules; in the second, a composite Hercules-Juno figure destroys itself. In the opening of *Thyestes* Fury drives Tantalus against his will to infect his house *with himself* (*Thyestes* 83–9). Though there are important differences between Tantalus and Hercules and between the opening scenes of these two tragedies, in both Seneca questions the relationship between an infernal criminality and a different vice which is both its extension and its victim.

When Hercules descends into madness there is no explicit divine intervention.[35] One may argue as reasonably that the Furies he sees (982–6) just before he kills his children are a manifestation of his madness as that they are its cause. The madness begins abruptly after a boast which recalls Juno's description of her frustration in the prologue (30–3):

> si quod etiamnum est scelus
> latura tellus, properet, et si quod parat
> monstrum, meum sit   (937–9)

---

[33] Seneca, *H. F.* 33 f. cf. *Met.* 2.508 f. and Seneca, *H. F.* 40–2, 78 cf. *Met.* 9.198 f. See Fitch (1987) 117 for the first, dominant model and Jakobi (1988) 6 for the second.

[34] Fitch (1987) 153. The allusion is supported by further parallelism: *acrior mentem excoquat* (*H. F.* 105); cf. *femineae ardentem curaeque iraeque coquebant* (*Aen.* 7.345). Fitch does not leave an unresolved ambiguity but concludes that *concutite pectus* 'indicates that the Furies must first madden themselves'. He translates, 'Rouse your hearts'.

[35] This is not itself proof that the madness originates in Hercules. After the event Hercules does not contradict Amphitryon's view that he was merely Juno's instrument: AMPHITRYON. *Hoc Iuno telum manibus emisit tuis* | HERCULES. *Hoc nunc ego utar* (1297–8).

(If the earth is even now to produce some wickedness, let it come quickly; if she is furnishing some monster, let it be mine.)

Not only does he bring crime on himself in these words but he can also be interpreted as appropriating the monstrous hatred of Juno and the earth. This interpretation is supported by further associations with Juno. The first sign of his madness is his perception of the day withdrawing (939–43) to leave a dark sky against which a now threatening Leo, his first labour, is clearly visible. The sun traditionally recoils from a crime it does not wish to expose or to witness. In this tragedy it did so when Hercules brought Cerberus up from the Underworld: *viso labentem Cerbero vidi diem | pavidumque Solem* (I saw the daylight faltering at the sight of Cerberus, and the Sun afraid 60–1). Thus the onset of Juno's infernal madness recalls his own final labour. A curious feature of Hercules' vision is that he first wishes to lead a rebellion of Giants against Olympus (965 ff.) and in his next speech fears their uprising (976 ff.). His shifting position to this potent symbol of a threat to cosmic order perhaps exposes an ambivalence in Herculean *virtus*,[36] but it also recalls Juno's changing alignment. In the *Aeneid* she is an Olympian who appears to obstruct Olympian purposes by summoning forces of darkness and disorder only to be recognized as truly Olympian for her relentless anger.[37] Similarly here Seneca's Juno summons infernal and chthonic powers against Jupiter's favourite. Like her Virgilian counterpart she shows reckless disregard for the order of the universe:

> Titanas ausos rumpere imperium Iovis
> emitte, Siculi verticis laxa specum,
> tellus gigante Doris excusso tremens
> supposita monstri colla terrifici levet,
> sublimis alias Luna concipiat feras.   (79–83)

(Release the Titans who dared disrupt Jove's sway; open the cavern in the Sicilian peak, and let the Dorian land, which trembles whenever the giant struggles, free the pinioned neck of that horrific monster, let the moon on high conceive other wild beasts)

---

[36] Lawall (1983) 14 and Fitch (1987) 369 see his willingness to fight on the side of the giants as a perversion of the *virtus* which he displayed fighting against them earlier (79–84).

[37] *es germana Iovis Saturnique altera proles, | irarum tantos volvis sub pectore fluctus* (*Aeneid* 12.830–1).

In general sentiment and in the precise detail of a monster lifting up its neck against the constraints imposed upon it, this passage jars with Juno's characterization only ten lines earlier of Hercules as Atlas and herself as a defender of Olympus:

> robore experto tumet,
> et posse caelum viribus vinci suis
> didicit ferendo; subdidit mundo caput
> mediusque collo sedit Herculeo polus
> nec flexit umeros molis immensae labor;
> immota cervix sidera et caelum tulit
> et me prementem: quaerit ad superos viam (68–74)

(Swollen with confidence in his well-tested might, he has learnt through bearing the heavens that his strength can conquer them. When he bent his head to support the sky, the toil of that immense weight did not bow his shoulders; no, the firmament rested more securely on Hercules' neck. Without budging, his back supported the stars and heavens—and my pressure. Yes, he is seeking a path to the gods.)

My aim here is to determine not who is at fault in the tragedy but what kind of fault is represented. In the parallel scenes of the genesis of the crime, the madness of Juno (1–124) and the madness of Hercules (939–86), the text suggests two broad characterizations of tragic madness and excludes neither.

The criminality of Juno's invocation of *Scelus* is of a kind with Hercules' leadership of a gigantomachy which is also a civil war (965–7). Hercules' desire to speak and act for his divine father is a mad presumption which is differently criminal. Framing and interpreting these characterizations are the myths of Phaethon and of the end of the Golden Age. In Ovid's narrative of the degeneration at the end of the Golden Age, the description of the Iron Age is followed by the gigantomachy and a short-lived, wicked race created from their blood (*Met.* 2.151–62). In response to this the Saturnian father conceives the anger worthy of Jupiter to which Seneca's Hercules unwittingly alludes even as he is praying for a Golden Age.[38] In a few lines Hercules will imagine that he is leading a gigantomachy against his father. The criminality of Hercules here is secure in a rigid set of binary oppositions: chthonic forces make war on Olympian; chaos on order; madness on reason. Hercules' divine paternity serves only to make this war

---

[38] *Met.* 1.166; cf. *Hercules Furens* 926–7.

which is already unequivocally criminal also civil. By contrast, the models of Euripides' and Ovid's Phaethon suggest the different criminality of a hero more than human but less than divine.

The madness of Juno and Hercules is the animating principle of the tragedy and to that extent an image of the nature of the genesis of the drama, with Juno as tragedian.[39] In her monologue she plots the events which will follow while simultaneously reminding the reader of the literary nature of her creation through marked allusions and, in her invocation of Fury, the more abstract figure of the inspired poet. That Juno finds her inspiration in Hell and that Hercules, mad, is presented as a giant fighting a civil war, coincides with the deliberate, self-conscious criminality which is a distinctive voice of post-Virgilian Roman epic.[40] This aspect is certainly present: the tragedy's concern with tyranny, its recollections of Virgil's Juno, and Hercules' Oedipal assault on his father, all speak with this voice, which represents Silver Latin as an *inmedicabile corpus* asserting itself through the destruction of its Golden parent.[41] But this is not the only voice of Seneca's *Hercules Furens*. The myth of Phaethon, anticipated by Juno's reference to the Ethiopians (36–40) and introduced by the first ode, suggests a different interpretation of Hercules and also of the tragedy's madness. The myth of Phaethon frames and reflects the myth of Hercules. Introduced in opposition to the metadramatic monologue of Juno it contributes its myth of flawed magnificence to the self-consciousness of the tragedy.

The course of a chariot is a familiar metaphor for the course of a poem. It can be developed: at the end of *Georgics* 1 Virgil likens the wreck of the world he has just recounted to a chariot careering out of control, and at the beginning of book 3 imagines himself in a triumphal chariot commemorating the military victories of Caesar.[42] The description of a literary chariot which most closely

---

[39] See e.g. Schiesaro (1997b) 92: 'Medea is similar to other central characters in Senecan plays: Juno in *Hercules Furens*, or Atreus in *Thyestes*. All appear on stage debating aloud their revengeful plots and voicing their tormenting doubts and emotions of creation.'

[40] See especially Hardie (1986) 85–156.

[41] On the Oedipal characterization see Bloom (1973) 19 ff. *Inmedicabile corpus* is Jupiter's description of the fallen world (Ovid, *Met.* 1.190).

[42] Virgil, *Georgics* 1.511–14, 3.16–18. In this second passage the Pindaric ancestry of the poetic chariot is particularly dominant (see e.g. *Ol.* 9.81, *Pyth.* 10.65).

corresponds to the myth of Phaethon is the myth of irrational inspiration described in Plato's *Phaedrus* (245a). In both myths the charioteer struggles to control winged horses in order to break free from the earth into the realm of the divine. Seneca quotes (in Latin translation) from this passage of Plato and paraphrases at greater length in *De Tranquillitate Animi* 17.10–11. The section ends:

desciscat oportet a solito et efferatur et mordeat frenos et rectorem rapiat suum eoque ferat, quo per se timuisset escendere. (*De Tranq.* 17.11)

(it [the mind] must forsake the common track and be driven to frenzy and champ the bit and run away with its rider and rush to a height that it would have feared to climb for itself.)

In his discussion of this passage Schiesaro notes that, 'although Seneca is not engaged here in an explicit declaration of poetics but is addressing most directly the issue of philosophical reflection, the presence of the Platonic quotation and the term *cecinit* ('chants', 17.11) suggests that the same state of enthusiastic lack of control lies behind artistic creation and philosophical excitement'.[43] As he also says, quite rightly, the primary obstacle in making use of this passage for an interpretation of Senecan tragedy is that because it represents horror and crime it cannot be construed as sublime. Longinus, author of *On the Sublime*, argues that 'strong and inspired emotion' (τὸ σφοδρὸν καὶ ἐνθουσιαστικὸν πάθος) is a source of sublimity, but restricts the emotions which achieve this effect: καὶ γὰρ πάθη τινὰ διεστῶτα ὕψους καὶ ταπεινὰ εὑρίσκεται, καθάπερ οἶκτοι λῦπαι φόβοι (Some emotions such as pity, grief, and fear, are found divorced from sublimity and with low effect 8.2). But he has no hesitation in saying that 'nothing is so productive of grandeur as noble emotion in the right place' (οὐδὲν οὕτως ὡς τὸ γενναῖον πάθος, ἔνθα χρή, μεγαλήγορον 8.4). Elsewhere he prefers *Iliad* 13.18 ff. to *Iliad* 21.388 ff. because in the first passage divinity is represented as 'genuinely unsoiled and great and pure' (ἄχραντόν τι καὶ μέγα...

---

[43] Schiesaro (1997*b*) 98–9. See also Mazzoli (1991) 192 ff. on this passage and its parallelism with the thought of Longinus. De Lacy (1948) 271 is right to read Stoic approval of the power of poetry in Cleanthes, *SVF* 1.109 and Seneca, *Epistles* 108.10 as approval of grand poetry for a divine not hellish theme. Cf. Persius' desire to celebrate Cornutus' Stoic teaching in the language of high poetry: *hic ego centenas ausim deposcere voces...* (*Satires* 5.26).

ὡς ἀληθῶς καὶ ἄκρατον 9.8), but in the second the gods fight with each other which is 'blasphemous and indecent' (ἄθεα καὶ οὐ σῴζοντα τὸ πρέπον 9.7).

Tragedy, the art of pity and fear, let alone Senecan tragedy with its self-conscious villainy, would seem to have difficulty satisfying the moral criteria of true grandeur.[44] In offering 'moral protreptic in the guise of literary criticism' in this way[45] Longinus, like other ancient literary critics including Seneca himself,[46] runs the risk of simply collapsing aesthetics into ethics. Longinus does not exclude tragedy from his study. The first examples in his discussion of *phantasia*, 'when, through enthusiasm and emotion, you seem to see what you are saying and bring it visually before your audience' (ὅταν ἅ λέγεις ὑπ' ἐνθουσιασμοῦ καὶ πάθους βλέπειν δοκῇς καὶ ὑπ' ὄψιν τιθῇς τοῖς ἀκούουσιν 15.1–2), are descriptions of the Furies from Euripides' *Orestes* and *Iphigenia in Tauris* (15.2).[47] These satisfy the criterion of *phantasia*: ὁ ποιητὴς αὐτὸς εἶδεν Ἐρινύας· ὃ δ' ἐφαντάσθη, μικροῦ δεῖν θεάσασθαι καὶ τοὺς ἀκούοντας ἠνάγκασεν (The poet himself saw the Erinyes, and has as good as made his audience see what he visualized). The second examples are from Euripides' *Phaethon*, probably from the messenger speech in which the fatal chariot ride is described.[48] Longinus comments:

ἆρ' οὐκ ἂν εἴποις, ὅτι ἡ ψυχὴ τοῦ γράφοντος συνεπιβαίνει τοῦ ἅρματος καὶ συγκινδυνεύουσα τοῖς ἵπποις συνεπτέρωται; οὐ γὰρ ἄν, εἰ μὴ τοῖς οὐρανίοις ἐκείνοις ἔργοις ἰσοδρομοῦσα ἐφέρετο, τοιαῦτ' ἄν ποτε ἐφαντάσθη. (15.4)

(May one not say that the writer's soul has mounted the chariot, has taken wing with the horses and shares the danger? Had it not been up among

---

[44] Aristotle, *Poetics* 1452ᵃ on pity and fear as tragic emotions. Michel (1969) 255–6 sees in Medea's passion the superhuman greatness of soul which produces sublimity in poetry. In *Epistles* 41.6 Seneca does indeed admire the ferocity of a lion in its natural state, but to read Medea or Atreus as magnificent beasts of this kind is to pass over the rationality which distinguishes human nature and the self-conscious criminality of these characters.
[45] Russell (1981) 85.
[46] So Maguinness (1956) 83.
[47] Cf. Quintilian 11.2.26 ff. and Leigh's (1997) survey 6–40, especially 13–15, on 'visualization' in ancient literary criticism. As Leigh (1997) 14 rightly argues, Longinus does not observe his own distinction between a rhetorical *phantasia* which produces vividness (ἐνάργεια) and a poetic *phantasia*, morally less attractive and producing shock (ἔκπληξις) in its listeners.
[48] So Diggle (1970) 41 ff.

those heavenly bodies and moved in their courses, he could never have visualized such things.)

Longinus' metaphor of Euripides' soul climbing into the winged chariot conveys the essential point, that Euripides seems to see what he describes, but also recalls the famous Platonic description of poetic inspiration; the myth of Phaethon not only exemplifies but figures poetic magnificence.[49] Although Longinus' work cannot be dated securely, the subject of the final chapter (44), political slavery and literary decline, is a strong reason to argue that it is a product of the first century AD.[50] So, a literary critic who in all likelihood was broadly contemporary with Seneca, interpreted the myth of Phaethon as Plato's metaphor of poetic inspiration.

The other tragic passages which Longinus quotes in this section can also be interpreted as figuring as much as exemplifying the impact of poetry. The Fury, his first example, is a familiar metaliterary figure in Roman epic, Senecan and to a lesser degree Greek tragedy.[51] Next follows the description of Phaethon, which is in turn followed[52] by quotation from Aeschylus, where the Seven, dipping their hands in blood, swear an oath by more Fury figures (15.5):[53]

ἄνδρες γὰρ ἑπτὰ θούριοι λοχαγέται,
ταυροσφαγοῦντες εἰς μελάνδετον σάκος,
καὶ θιγγάνοντες χερσὶ ταυρείου φόνου,

---

[49] Cf. the divine aspirations of a later poet in Milton's invocation of the Muse in *Paradise Lost* 7.12 f. 'Up led by thee | Into the heav'n of heav'ns I have presumed, | An earthly guest, and drawn empyreal air, | Thy temp'ring; with like safety guided down, | Return me to my native element, | Lest from this flying steed unreined (as once | Bellerophon, though from a lower clime) | Dismounted, on th' Aleian field I fall, | Erroneous there to wander and forlorn.'

[50] So Russell (1964) xxv, Michel (1969) 246.

[51] For Greek tragedy see Belfiore (1992) 28 f. on Aeschylus, *Eumenides*.

[52] I omit the words of Euripides' Cassandra (15.4) because we do not know the full quotation and therefore the significance of ἀλλ', ὦ φίλιπποι Τρῶες (But, O Trojans, lovers of horses). See Russell (1964) 124. Certainly Cassandra, as prophetess, is a good candidate for a poet-surrogate and Seneca arguably uses her as a self-conscious voice of *Agamemnon*. See Curley (1986) 206–7 and Schiesaro (1997a) 85–6), but there is no point in pursuing these arguments here while Longinus' quotation from Euripides remains so completely opaque.

[53] In Roman literature little distinction is made between true Furies and Fury-like figures. See e.g. Fitch (1987) 148 on the *discordem deam* of *Hercules Furens* 93. On blood, passion, and poetic 'otherness' see Schiesaro (1997b) 95–7 and Padel (1992) 162 f. and *passim*.

Ἄρην Ἐνυὼ καὶ φιλαίματον Φόβον
ὡρκωμότησαν

(Aeschylus, *Septem* 42–6)

Seven men of war, commanders of companies,
killing a bull into a black-bound shield,
dipping their hands in the bull's blood,
took oath by Ares, by Enyo, by bloodthirsty Terror

The final quotations before Longinus returns again to the Furies of *Orestes* are of Pentheus' palace and Mount Cithaeron succumbing to the frenzy of the god of tragedy (15.6):[54]

ἐνθουσιᾷ δὴ δῶμα, βακχεύει στέγη   (Aeschylus)[55]

the palace was possessed, the house went bacchanal.

πᾶν δὲ συνεβάκχευ' ὄρος.   (Euripides, *Bacchae* 726)

the whole mountain went bacchanal with them.

These passages, like the others, are selected as examples of *phantasia* because they represent a mechanism of poetic excitement. Longinus' assertion in connection with the Euripidean Furies that 'the poet...has as good as made his audience see what he imagined' needs no further explanation: the means by which this is achieved is apparent in the example itself. The example of Phaethon is distinguished from the example of the Furies. Euripides, though pre-eminent in generating the emotions of madness and desire, occasionally forces himself, even though it is not in his nature, to create true grandeur. The lines from Phaethon exemplify this true grandeur and Longinus' approval is evident: the quotation is framed by the allusion to Plato and by a quotation which casts Euripides as Achilles (15.3).[56] The passage wins his approval because it affords a cosmic vision which transcends the pettiness of human society. Elsewhere he writes:

οὐδέ γε τὸ ὑφ' ἡμῶν τουτὶ φλογίον ἀνακαιόμενον, ἐπεὶ καθαρὸν σῴζει τὸ φέγγος, ἐκπληττόμεθα τῶν οὐρανίων μᾶλλον, καίτοι πολλάκις ἐπισκοτουμένων, οὐδὲ τῶν τῆς Αἴτνης κρατήρων ἀξιοθαυμαστότερον

---

[54] Cf. the literary-critical term which Longinus records that Theodorus coined for *phantasia* which fails: παρένθυρσον (the 'pseudo-bacchanalian' 3.5). In this circumstance the audience feels nothing.

[55] Russell (1964) 124, 'probably from Ἡδωνοί, the first play of the trilogy... which told the story of the Thracian king Lycurgus'.

[56] *Iliad* 20.170.

Images of a Flawed Technical Genesis 125

νομίζομεν, ἧς αἱ ἀναχοαὶ πέτρους τε ἐκ βυθοῦ καὶ ὅλους ὄχθους ἀναφέρουσι καὶ ποταμοὺς ἐνίοτε τοῦ γηγενοῦς ἐκείνου καὶ αὐτομάτου προχέουσι πυρός...

Οὐκοῦν ἐπί γε τῶν ἐν λόγοις μεγαλοφυῶν... προσήκει συνθεωρεῖν αὐτόθεν, ὅτι τοῦ ἀναμαρτήτου πολὺ ἀφεστῶτες οἱ τηλικοῦτοι ὅμως παντὸς εἰσὶν ἐπάνω τοῦ θνητοῦ καὶ τὰ μὲν ἄλλα τοὺς χρωμένους ἀνθρώπους ἐλέγχει, τὸ δ᾽ ὕψος ἐγγὺς αἴρει μεγαλοφροσύνης θεοῦ καὶ τὸ μὲν ἄπταιστον οὐ ψέγεται, τὸ μέγα δὲ καὶ θαυμάζεται. (35.4–36.2)

(Nor do we feel so much awe before the little flame we kindle, because it keeps its light clear and pure, as before the fires of heaven, though they are often obscured. We do not think our flame more worthy of admiration than the craters of Aetna, whose eruptions bring up rocks and whole hills out of the depths, and sometimes pour forth rivers of the earth-born, spontaneous fire...

So when we come to great geniuses in literature... we have to conclude that such men, for all their faults, tower far above mortal stature. Other literary qualities prove their users to be human; sublimity raises us towards the spiritual greatness of god. Freedom from error does indeed save us from blame, but it is only greatness that wins admiration.)

Again here Longinus shifts between flawed magnificence in the universe and in literary composition. The universe, the art of God,[57] is a sublime subject for reflection, literary or otherwise, but Longinus uses it here as an analogy for literary composition. Aetna's fire, a familiar feature of the literary landscape,[58] is used as an analogy for the creative fire of art. As the fires of heaven are flawed by obscurity, so Aetna's fires are flawed by their origin in the earth. The earth-born which it produces are the giants: flawed magnificence in art is figured here, as in Seneca's *Hercules Furens*, through the rebellion against the cosmic order represented by the Olympians. Seneca blends nature, art, and ethics in a similar way in *Epistles* 79. At the beginning of the letter he asks Lucilius, travelling in Sicily, to climb Aetna and describe its natural features (79.2 ff.). He then says that there is no need for him to ask Lucilius for a description as he will surely be unable to resist this literary cliché, a holy place for all poets (*sollemnem omnibus poetis*

---

[57] So Seneca, *Naturales Quaestiones* 1. Pref. 13–17. His contrast between the false glitter of human artifice and the secrets of the universe which the mind learns as it wanders among the stars (*N.Q.* 1. Pref. 7) is very similar in tone to the contrast Longinus draws between the transient goods of human society and true sublimity (*De Sublimitate* 7.1).

[58] For a few examples see Fitch (1987) 154 on *Hercules Furens* 106.

locum, 79.4–5). As a locus of literary activity Aetna is not yet exhausted, however (79.6–7), and Seneca advises him to challenge the mountain in what becomes an ascent of the soul into divine thoughts (*in cogitationes divinas* 79.12). The concerns of the latter part of the letter are narrowly ethical.

The order of the universe is a familiar point of ethical reference, for Stoics and Platonists alike. Ancient literary criticism is not dissociated from ethical criticism, and this is certainly true of the literary criticism of Seneca and Longinus. It is therefore not surprising to find Nature as a vehicle of both philosophical and literary inspiration, and that the critics shift easily in their commentary from one to the other. The most influential metaphor of the flight of the inspired mind is the charioteer of Plato's *Phaedrus*. Longinus quotes from Euripides' *Phaethon* in the context of other tragic figures which are surely to be read with metadramatic force, and his commentary on Phaethon navigating the celestial bodies recalls Plato's charioteer. Of the various representations of poetic inspiration which Longinus gives, *Phaethon* attracts particular approval: in writing these lines Euripides transcended the limitations of his own nature to ride the divine chariot with the tragic hero. The distinction evident in the difference between Longinus' commentary on this passage and his more reserved commentary on the other passages is a distinction which is relevant for an interpretation of the motivating passion of Seneca's *Hercules Furens*. The opposition between the myth of the failed Olympian, and the myths of deliberate post-Golden Age criminality and chthonic rebellion, frames an interpretation of Hercules' madness and the nature of his responsibility for the infanticide.

Through the meta-literary resonance of these myths the motivating passion of the tragedy as an art form is interrogated also. The tragedian is responsible not for madness and infanticide, but for the art of madness and infanticide: Hercules and Juno merely parallel the tragedian. Literary concerns, though bound up with moral concerns, cannot simply be collapsed into them. The same is true of the relationship between literary and historical concerns. In many places this tragedy recalls specifically Roman political power and it is appropriate therefore to read the tragedy as a reflection of Rome, but it is not appropriate to read the trial of Herculean *virtus* as a coded trial of Rome, to strip off its disguise and in this way to collapse art into its historical context.[59] Similarly it is inappropriate to interpret the poetic *virtus* and/or *nefas* of Seneca tragicus as wholly determined by the ambivalent madness of the dramatic character Hercules. The ambivalence of Seneca's poetic inspiration which combines flawed sublimity with criminal horror reflects the ethical ambivalence of Hercules' madness, but it reflects also an ambivalence in ancient literary critical discussion of poetic inspiration. It speaks also in a more modern critical idiom to the poet's ambivalent relationship with his literary father(s): imitator, rival, and destroyer. In the section which precedes his discussion of *phantasia* Longinus characterizes poetic inspiration by literary models specifically in the familiar metaphor of divine possession:

οὕτως ἀπὸ τῆς τῶν ἀρχαίων μεγαλοφυΐας εἰς τὰς τῶν ζηλούντων ἐκείνους ψυχὰς ὡς ἀπὸ ἱερῶν στομίων ἀπόρροιαί τινες φέρονται, ὑφ' ὧν ἐπιπνεόμενοι καὶ οἱ μὴ λίαν φοιβαστικοὶ τῷ ἑτέρων συνενθουσιῶσι μεγέθει. (13.2)

Similarly [like the Pythia], the genius of the ancients acts as a kind of oracular cavern, and effluences flow from it into the minds of their imitators. Even those previously not much inclined to prophesy become inspired and share the enthusiasm which comes from the greatness of others.

This topic, Seneca's relationship with his predecessors, I return to in the following sections. Here I am concerned merely to trace Seneca's use of a particular set of myths to frame and interpret representations of the genesis of tragic inspiration. These form part of the self-consciousness of Senecan tragedy, and are no less valid or important than other modes of self-consciousness simply because they are more abstract. I turn now to *Thyestes* before an extended discussion of *Medea*.

2. *THYESTES*

Hercules Furens opens with a monologue, but one may observe a metaphorical agon over the characterization of poetic inspiration. The opposing myths of Phaethon and of the end of the Golden Age frame and inform this agon. *Thyestes* opens with a true agon,

---

[59] The notorious negative exemplar of this approach to Senecan tragedy is Bishop (1985). See also Calder (1983). More illuminating is this positive example of formal care: '[Seneca rewrites Euripides] to frame the drama with contemporary imperial fictions' (Boyle (1997) 108).

framed and informed by the same myths, though they are used to different effect as the nature of the opening agon differs. Unlike *Hercules Furens*, which Juno sets in motion by summoning infernal madness, *Thyestes* begins with Tantalus, who has been dragged up from hell against his will and without explanation. In an inversion of the usual roles Furia has summoned him to infect his house with criminal madness. Tantalus objects, *Me pati poenas decet, | non esse poenam* (My proper role is to suffer punishments, not to *be* a punishment! 86–7), but to no avail. An ode follows (122–75) which offers a doomed hope that the gods will protect the very landscape Tantalus has just tainted. Then Atreus stirs himself to crime in a scene which is functionally parallel to the first act. He too summons infernal powers[60] but of the two scenes Atreus' is more closely related to the events of the tragedy. Both Atreus and Furia are determined that the crime of this tragedy will surpass all previous crimes. Atreus' primary inspiration is the myth of Tereus and Procne: *animum Daulis inspira parens | sororque; causa est similis* (Breathe your spirit into me, you Daulian mother and sister: our cause is comparable 275–6). Accordingly, this monologue and the crime itself is modelled on the speech and crime of Ovid's Procne in *Metamorphoses* 6.[61] Furia does anticipate Atreus in this respect,[62] but her agon with Tantalus performs a framing function and its representation of the genesis of crime is often more abstract.

As in *Hercules Furens* both the *Aeneid* and the myths of the end of the Golden Age and Phaethon are used to characterize poetic inspiration in the first act of the tragedy. Furia is closely modelled on Juno of *Aeneid* 7, while Tantalus tries unsuccessfully to flee back into the underworld of *Aeneid* 6.[63] As Schiesaro argues, the agon between Furia and Tantalus is a struggle of criminal expres-

---

[60] *Excede, Pietas, si modo in nostra domo | umquam fuisti. dira Furiarum cohors | discorsque Erinys veniat et geminas faces | Megaera quatiens* (249–52).

[61] For an overview and a list of correspondences see Jakobi (1988) 152–67.

[62] She determines that Atreus' crime will take this form—*Thracium fiat nefas | maiore numero* (56–7)—and her description of the house shuddering at Tantalus' touch imitates a similar description from Ovid's account of the Thracian crime. So Tarrant (1985) 103 and Jakobi (1988) 155: *sensit introitus tuos | domus et nefando tota contacta horruit* (*Thy.* 103–4); cf. *ut sensit tetigisse domum Philomela nefandam, | horruit infelix totoque expalluit* (*Met.* 6.601–2).

[63] For Furia as Juno see Tarrant (1985) 85–6 and *passim* and Schiesaro (1994). On the Virgilian nature of the underworld to which Tantalus flees see Tarrant (1985) 99 on *Thyestes* 74–83 and, on the theme more generally, below in Ch. 4, Sect. 4.

Images of a Flawed Technical Genesis 129

sion against repression: Tantalus, if he were allowed to do so, would return to the underworld and prevent the tragedy from happening; he takes no pleasure in Furia's invention.[64] Poetic inspiration is unambiguously evil here, and the relationship between the myths which characterize it—the myth of the end of the Golden Age and the myth of Phaethon—is accordingly different from that in *Hercules Furens*.

Furia's first vision of criminal madness has little specific connection with the tragedy and reworks Ovid's description of the Iron Age.[65] The crime which Atreus will commit will cause the day to recoil in horror and Furia concludes this section of her speech:

> non sit a vestris malis
> immune caelum—cur micant stellae polo
> flammaeque servant debitum mundum decus?
> nox alta fiat, excidat caelo dies.   (48–51)

(And let heaven not be immune to your evil.—Why are the stars glittering in the sky, their fires maintaining their due of glory in the firmament? Let there be another night, let daylight fall from the heavens.)

The damage to heaven anticipates a later event in the tragedy but also corresponds to the gigantomachy which follows the Iron Age in Ovid's account (*Met.* 1.151 f.). Here too earth-born criminality threatens the heavens. Through this parallelism infernal Tantalus is cast as an unwilling giant, an unwilling minister of post-Golden Age evil. In a word which mockingly recalls the obedience of a Stoic *sapiens* to Fate,[66] Tantalus submits to the passions which Furia rouses in him:

> flagrat incensum siti
> cor et perustis flamma visceribus micat.
> *sequor.*
> FURIA. Hunc, hunc furorem divide in totam domum.
>   (98–101)

(My heart is fired and ablaze with thirst, and flames dart through my burnt flesh. I follow! FURIA. Distribute *this* very frenzy throughout the house!)

---

[64] See Schiesaro (1994) 198. On invention see *Thyestes* 4 and 66.
[65] See Tarrant (1985) 93 and Jakobi (1988) 154 on Seneca, *Thyestes* 40–6; cf. Ovid, *Metamorphoses* 1.144–50.
[66] So Schiesaro (1994) 199.

His infection of the royal house begins with the description of the palace itself trembling. Although the words recall Procne's crime, the event has more in common with the phenomena which mark a divine epiphany.[67] His presence scorches the earth in language which recalls Ovid's description of the damage done to the earth by Phaethon's chariot when he lost control of his winged horses.[68] *Hercules Furens*, following a parallelism in the narrative structure of Ovid's *Metamorphoses*, offered Phaethon's reckless daring and the overt criminality of the Iron Age as opposing characterizations of the ambivalent madness animating the drama. The Phaethon which *Thyestes* offers here is a distortion of the traditional figure who, criminally and/or dangerously, assumes a divine role which he is incapable of performing. Tantalus is coerced into playing a divine role against his will, and this 'divine role' is not Olympian order but infernal disorder. In both Euripides' and Ovid's versions of the Phaethon myth, the Sun tries to guide Phaethon's path and thereby offers an image of celestial harmony which Phaethon is unable to reproduce. What distinguishes Phaethon from the giants or the people of the Iron Age is that he aspires to imitate the Olympians whereas they merely strive to displace them. This distinction all but disappears in the first act of *Thyestes*, where the myth of the end of the Golden Age assimilates the myth of Phaethon to itself. As Olympian order and Stoic obedience exist in this drama only in perverted form, so the Olympian aspirations of Phaethon are visible only in a form distorted by Furia's direction. Tantalus attempts to resist the divine role and the Phaethonic journey which Furia forces upon him, but here, as throughout the tragedy, infernal madness cannot be resisted. In the characterization of tragic madness in *Thyestes*, as important as its irresistible power is the way in

---

[67] On the allusion to Procne see n. 62 above. On divine epiphany see Hine (1981) 269.

[68] See Tarrant (1985) 104–5 and Jakobi (1988) 155–6: *ripae vacent* (*Thy.* 108); cf. *ostia septem | pulverulenta vacant* (*Met.* 2.255–6); *Phoronides | latuere venae* (*Thy.* 115–16) cf. *(Nilus) occuluitque caput, quod adhuc latet* (*Met.* 2.255). Tarrant reads lines 116–18 as an allusion to (and inversion of) the beginning of the Soracte Ode (Horace, *Odes* 1.9.1–2), while Jakobi sees these also as echoing Ovid's description of the unnatural effects of Phaethon's chariot ride (*Met.* 2.222–3). I am more persuaded by Tarrant, and am not convinced by Jakobi's further assertion that Seneca's *veterem...Argi sitim* (119), an oblique allusion to the spring of the Amymone and the myth of the Danaids, is motivated by Ovid's simple mention of the name of the stream (*Met.* 2.240).

Images of a Flawed Technical Genesis 131

which it assimilates Olympian order and Olympian aspirations to its own corrupt purposes.

Juno's monologue in *Hercules Furens* obstructs any easy distinction between Junonian *ira* and Herculean *virtus*: She models her summoning of infernal powers on Hercules' final labour and presents herself now as an Olympian resisting an attack from a giant, now as a figure whose anger finds its form in the monstrous earth-born. The opening agon of *Thyestes* also confuses its opposing figures, Furia and Tantalus, but to different effect. Tantalus served his child Pelops to the gods at a banquet. For this he was punished with eternal thirst and hunger in the underworld. He is therefore an appropriate inspiration for the crime of his descendants: Atreus performs the same crime and Thyestes, who cannot restrain his appetites even though he realizes that they cannot be satisfied, is characterized by the same failure of will as Tantalus.[69] In her address to him Furia draws together the roles of both banqueter and viewer:

> epulae instruantur—non novi sceleris
> conviva venies. liberum dedimus diem
> tuamque ad istas solvimus mensas famem.
> ieiunia exple, mixtus in Bacchum cruor
> spectante te potetur.   (62–6)

(Let a banquet be furnished—you will join the diners at a crime familiar to you. We have given you a day of freedom, and released your hunger for this meal: fill up your fasting! Let blood mingled with wine be drunk while you watch.)

In another myth, which Tantalus himself mentions as he tries to obstruct Furia's plan, he is punished for betraying the secrets of the gods:

> ingenti licet
> taxata poena lingua crucietur loquax,
> nec hoc tacebo.   (91–3)

(though I be sentenced to immense punishment and tortured for my talkative tongue, I shall not keep quiet about *this* either)

---

[69] See especially *haec, quamvis avidus nec patiens morae,* | *deceptus totiens tangere neglegit* | *obliquatque oculos oraque comprimit* | *inclusisque famem dentibus alligat.* | *Sed tunc...*(158–62) cf. TANTALUS. *Decipi cautus times?* | THYESTES. *Serum est cavendi tempus in mediis malis.* | *eatur, unum genitor hoc testor tamen:* | *ego vos sequor, non duco* (486–9).

Tantalus is thus ideally suited not only to inspire both roles in this particular tragedy, but also to express them.[70] In his first speech, before he is terrified by Furia, Tantalus appears to be initiating the tragedy on his own. Without waiting to discover who has summoned him or why he promises:

> e stirpe turba quae suum vincat genus
> ac me innocentem faciat et inausa audeat.
> regione quidquid impia cessat loci
> complebo. (19–22)

(Now from my stock there is rising a crew that will outdo their own ancestors, render me innocent and dare the undared. Any space unused in the quarter of unnatural crimes I shall fill up)

The rhetoric of surpassing traditional boundaries and definitions is characteristic of both Furia and Atreus, and his threat to *fill* the underworld foregrounds a major figure of the tragedy.[71] There is nothing in Tantalus on which to found an opposition to Furia and everything to further her purposes. The result of the conflict between Furia and Tantalus is thus inevitable, but more important here is the absence of any alternative characterization of poetic inspiration. The emptiness of Tantalus' opposition, best seen in his recognition that he himself *is* the punishment (86–7), parallels the emptiness of his characterization as Phaethon, when in fact the Phaethon role has been perverted so that it is in no way distinct from the role of the degenerate creatures of the Iron Age. The agon between Furia and Tantalus, like the opposition between the myths of the Fall and of Phaethon, has only the form of a conflict.

In the dramatic illusion and in meta-literary terms there is no opposition to the criminal force which Furia represents. She ends her description, modelled on Ovid's description of Phaethon's chariot-ride, of the scorched earth of Greece as Juno ended her introductory monologue in *Hercules Furens*, with the coming of the dawn:

> *En ipse Titan dubitat* an iubeat sequi
> cogatque habenis ire periturum diem. (120–1)

---

[70] The relevant qualities are part of Tantalus, 'mythical record'. See Schiesaro (1994) 203.
[71] See e.g. Curley (1986) 161 ff. and Poe (1969) 362 respectively.

(See, even the Titan hesitates whether to bid the daylight follow him, and to force it with the reins to come forth to its ruin.)

As Jakobi suggests,[72] *en ipse Titan dubitat* probably recalls the conclusion of the complaint of Ovid's Earth to Jupiter:

> *Atlans en ipse laborat*
> vixque suis umeris candentem sustinet axem.
> si freta, si terrae pereunt, si regia caeli,
> in chaos antiquum confundimur.
> (*Met.* 2.296–9)

(See, Atlas himself struggles and can scarcely hold up the burning sky on his shoulders. If the sea, if the land, if the kingdom of heaven dies we will collapse into primeval chaos.)

The verbal reminiscence in itself is not particularly striking, but it is supported by other parallelism: both phrases conclude the descriptions of the earth which Phaethon (or Tantalus as Phaethon) has damaged. The explicit, imminent annihilation of the world in the *Metamorphoses* interprets the vaguer *periturum diem* in *Thyestes*. The chorus will later sing that the recoiling of the Sun is the beginning of the dissolution of the cosmos, and Atreus will follow the ode with the words, *Aequalis astris gradior et cunctos super | altum superbo vertice attingens polum* (Peer of the stars I stride, outtopping all, my proud head reaching to the lofty sky 885–6). In fact the fabric of the world does not dissolve even though Thyestes ends the play calling for it to do so and for Jupiter to hurl a thunderbolt (1068–96), but the Olympian role in cosmic disorder is a recurrent topic in the tragedy.

The representative of divine order, the Sun, hesitates whether he should order the day to follow (*sequi*) when it is doomed. His hesitation contrasts with the confidence of Furia, who threatens Tantalus with whip-snakes and flames until he submits with the word, *sequor* (100). Thyestes will later echo this fatal submission as, against his better judgement, he enters the royal palace: *ego vos sequor, non duco* (I am following you, not leading 489). In hesitantly echoing Furia the Sun shows his discomfort in imitating her and in expressing Tantalid criminality in the heavens. As becomes clearer later (784 ff.) the Sun's motive in ending the day prematurely is to conceal Atreus' deed in darkness. But as he distorts the

[72] Jakobi (1988) 156.

celestial cycle he resembles Tantalus and Phaethon and, far from obstructing Furia's criminal tragedy, advertises it. The discomfort of the imitation is developed further as the helplessness of the divine charioteer follows the allusions to Phaethon's destruction of the world. Phaethon is a failed Olympian whose imitation of the Sun's orderly path is fatally imperfect. In a reversal of roles the Sun, sensing the criminal taint of Tantalus, hesitates to imitate Phaethon by riding his chariot and thereby bringing a day which is doomed to perish. This ambiguity in the Sun's action, whether curtailing the day will conceal Atreus' crime and repress Furia's tragedy or whether it will in fact promote the crime by reflecting it at a cosmic scale, will recur in the fourth ode and in Thyestes' final speech. Criminal expression will not only be victorious over Olympian obstruction, but will in fact transform it into an advertisement of its own greatness.

Furia's description of the divine charioteer bringing the day to an abrupt end is recalled at the end of the messenger speech (623–788), which as a whole reiterates the agon of the first act. The Messenger begins as a speaker so shocked that he can barely relate the tale (633–8), but 'as he proceeds his control of the narrative becomes more and more overt, reaching at last a witty detachment equal to that of Atreus himself'.[73] The vision of the crime which he relates is a development of the briefer vision which ends Furia's first speech (54 ff.) and the still briefer vision of Atreus (281–2). Of the three characters only Furia, for whom Tantalus plays the role of obstructor, receives the vision with unalloyed pleasure: Atreus and the Messenger have to drive themselves to express it:

ATREUS. tota iam ante oculos meos
　imago caedis errat, ingesta orbitas
　in ora patris—anime, quid rursus times
　et ante rem subsidis? audendum est age.　(281–4)

(ATREUS. Now the whole picture of the slaughter hovers before my eyes—bereavement thrust into the father's face. Why take fright again, my spirit, and slacken before the event? Come, you must be bold.)

Compare:

NUNTIUS. haeret in vultu trucis
　imago facti. ferte me insanae procul,

[73] Tarrant (1985) 193. For an overview of the speech see also 180 and my discussion below, Ch. 4, Sect. 4.

illo, procellae, ferte quo fertur dies
hinc raptus.   (635–8)

(MESSENGER. The picture of that savage deed sticks in my eyes. Bear me far away, you mad cyclones, bear me where the daylight is borne, now stolen from here.)

The experiences of Atreus and the Messenger re-enact the victory of Furia over Tantalus. Tarrant writes of the Messenger, 'Even in the conventional figure of the Messenger, Seneca has dramatized the triumph of evil over all attempts to contain it'.[74] At this last stage of the drama the agon which initiated the tragedy, the conflict between expression and repression, is fought once more. The Messenger resembles Furia nowhere more closely than at the close of his speech:

> in malis unum hoc tuis
> bonum est, Thyestea, quod mala ignoras tua.
> sed et hoc peribit. verterit currus licet
> sibi ipse Titan obvium ducens iter
> tenebrisque facinus obruat taetrum novis
> nox missa ab ortu tempore alieno gravis,
> tamen videndum est. tota patefient mala.   (782–8)

(In your troubles there is this one boon, Thyestes, that you are ignorant of your troubles! But this too will perish. Though the Titan has turned his chariot, tracing a path counter to himself, and though the foul deed is smothered in strange darkness by this oppressive night, released from the East and at an alien time, yet he must see. All his troubles will be revealed.)

A messenger traditionally relates horrors which have just happened but could not be represented on stage. In anticipating the pain of Thyestes' revelation at the conclusion of his story the Messenger becomes the speaker of a second prologue,[75] and his reference to the helplessness of the Sun echoes the end of the first prologue (120–1). Here the motive of the Sun in reversing the course of the day is clarified: it is to conceal the crime. Not only will it be ineffectual, as the Messenger predicts, but in fact it will promote the tragedy which Atreus stages. The Messenger's speech

---

[74] Tarrant (1985) 180.
[75] Atreus responds to this by making a second beginning of his own plans: *bene est, abunde est, iam sat est etiam mihi. | sed cur satis sit? pergam et implebo patrem | funere suorum.* (889–91).

is separated from Atreus' vision of Thyestes at the table by an ode in which the chorus, clearly not privy to the Messenger's speech, speculates on the reasons for the Sun's departure (789–884). The chorus does not know whether Hell has opened up or whether the giants are making war on Olympus (804–12), but is sure that some terrible force has cast down the divine chariot:

> Quid te aetherio pepulit cursu?
> quae causa tuos limite certo
> deiecit equos?   (802–4)

(What has driven you out of your heavenly course? What cause has forced your horses down from their fixed path?)

The ruin of Sun and Moon will be swiftly followed by the ruin of the other gods: *Ibit in unum congesta sinum | turba deorum* (842–3). The effect of the ode is the same as the effect of the Sun's departure: Atreus' crime is inscribed in the fabric of the heavens and Furia's victory is magnified and publicized. After 96 lines of cosmic disorder Atreus' claim, *dimitto superos* (I discharge the gods 888), does not seem simply delusional as it might otherwise have seemed. As in the first prologue the divine charioteer serves Furia's purposes even as he attempts to obstruct them. Olympian order is not merely conquered by Furia but becomes her instrument. Both here and at the end of Furia's prologue (120–1) the Olympian attempt to conceal the crime merely reflects it at a grander level.

The same phenomenon can be seen in the final scene of the tragedy when the crime has been revealed to Thyestes. Briefly and inconsistently Thyestes suggests that the Olympian tactic of repression will be successful (1092–6), but otherwise he calls on the gods to destroy or avenge the world and him (1077–92, 1102, 1110–11). He calls for Jupiter to assert himself not with moderate violence, but with violence suitable for a gigantic crime:

> manuque non qua tecta et immeritas domos
> telo petis minore, sed qua montium
> tergemina moles cecidit et qui montibus
> stabant pares Gigantes, hac arma expedi
> ignesque torque.   (1081–5)

(Not as you strike at innocent homes and buildings with lighter weapons, but as you made the triple mass of mountains fall, along with the Giants who stood tall as mountains: with such force deploy your weapons and launch your fires!)

Images of a Flawed Technical Genesis 137

In his desire that the crime should receive the recognition it deserves, he imitates those whom he wishes to oppose. His speech even begins with an advertisement for Atreus' deed:

> Clausa litoribus vagis
> audite maria, vos quoque audite hoc scelus,
> quocumque, di fugistis, audite inferi,
> audite terrae... (1068–71)

(Seas enclosed by winding shores, listen; listen to this crime too, you gods, wherever you have fled; listen, hell; listen, earth...)

Once again the opponents of Atreus and Furia find themselves in an impossible situation. The attempt to draw a veil over the proceedings, by curtailing the day, has merely drawn attention to the crime and the inability of the Olympians to prevent it. The alternative, which Thyestes suggests here and the chorus feared in the last ode, is a violent reaction which curtails not only the day, but the world. This, however, serves only to magnify the horror. Atreus' response to the chorus, *Aequalis astris gradior* (885), and to Thyestes suggests that he receives these amplified expressions of pain with great satisfaction:

> Nunc meas laudo manus,
> nunc parta vera est palma. perdideram scelus,
> nisi sic doleres. (1096–8)

(Now I commend my hands, now the true palm is won. I would have wasted my crime, if you did not feel pain like this.)

The figure of the charioteer recurs as Atreus celebrates his victory over Thyestes and the helpless Olympians in a metaphor which recalls the criminal victory for which the family is famous. Myrtilus sabotaged the chariot of his master Oenomaus to give Pelops victory and Hippodamia as his prize. Ironically Latin literature persistently identifies Pisa, the site of Pelops' criminal victory, as the site of the Olympic games[76] and in the first ode (122–75) Seneca plays with the ambivalence of the Olympic Games as both a divine festival and a memorial of Tantalid evil. Significantly this ode follows Furia's monologue which ended with the hesitation of the divine charioteer. Like the Phaethon ode in *Hercules Furens* this ode stands in opposition to what

---

[76] Tarrant (1985) 107 quotes Virgil, *Georgics* 3.180–1 and Juvenal 13.99 in addition to other references in Senecan tragedy.

precedes it. While conceding the fatal consequences of heroic endeavour,[77] that ode offers a model of criminal madness which is different from Junonian anger, but here the opposition is as empty as Tantalus' opposition to Furia. The chorus prays for deliverance, but in a way that can only be futile. Its list of places to enjoy divine protection (122–31) overlaps significantly with the list of places which Tantalus has just infected in his Phaethonic course (111–19)[78] and the chorus's call for a god to keep away (*arceat*, 132) a curse which recalls Furia's description of crime[79] is reminiscent of Tantalus' doomed opposition, *stabo et arcebo scelus* (I shall stand and block the crime 95).

The chorus begins with an ill-founded pride:

> Argos de superis si quis Achaicum
> Piseasque domos curribus inclitas... (122–3)

(If any god loves Achaean Argos, or the Pisan district famed for chariots...)

It repeats the theme of Olympic glory (131) and asks for a divinity to prevent the waves of crime which have afflicted the house of Tantalus:

> quem tangit gelido flumine lucidus
> Alpheos, stadio notus Olympico,
> advertat placidum numen et arceat,
> alternae scelerum ne redeant vices. (130–3)

(any touched by the ice-cold current of bright Alpheus, famed for Olympic races: let him bring divine favour to bear, and forbid that a cycle of answering crimes return)

In the subsequent history of Tantalid crime Myrtilus is mentioned as a *deceptor domini* (his master's betrayer 140) who was in turn betrayed. With an aetion of this kind Olympia has little claim on the affections of a divinity, and the chorus's hopes cannot but be vain. Its Olympian sponsorship is compromised as surely as the clear Alpheus with its cold water is consumed by the appetites of Tantalus. The corruption of the Olympic festival is parallel to the corruption of the Sun which concludes the first act. The divine

---

[77] In addition to the general sentiments of the song, note that the dawn reveals the sites of the deaths of Hercules and Pentheus (*Hercules Furens* 133–5).
[78] See Hine (1981) 270–1.
[79] 133–5; cf. 25. So Tarrant (1985) 108.

charioteer, far from representing celestial opposition to Furia, is her imitator and her instrument. Here the Olympic festival is revealed as a commemoration of the very criminality which it is presented as a defence against.

The compromised Olympic festival recurs in the scene where Thyestes, as Tantalus before him, succumbs to his appetites and enters the royal house.[80] Thyestes approaches Argos and recognizes the landmarks familiar from his youth, including the race-track:

> [cerno]
> celebrata iuveni stadia, per quae nobilis
> palmam paterno non semel curru tuli.
> occurret Argos, populus occurret frequens—
> sed nempe et Atreus. (409–12)

([I see] the race-track I frequented in youth, through which I carried the palm in glory more than once on my father's chariot. Argos will come to meet me, the people will come in crowds—yes, but so will Atreus.)

The mention of the chariot of his father, Pelops, is ill-omened. As Thyestes remembers his past victories the audience remembers the destruction of a rival through deception. Thyestes, presumably still remembering the applauding crowds of his athletic past, anticipates the people thronging to celebrate his political return, until the memory of his rival Atreus casts a shadow over the daydream. For the children of Pelops chariot-racing at Olympia is associated with political rivalry. In the first ode of the tragedy this competition, this ritual commemoration of a royal murder, was represented as a Tantalid evil latent in an Olympian festival. Here Thyestes interrupts his list of the monuments of the kingdom of Argos with an aside which seems strangely casual: *et patrios deos | (si sunt tamen di) cerno* (and I see the gods of my fathers (if there really *are* gods); 406–7). Jason, having seen the full horror of Medea's revenge, flings these words at the demonic charioteer, *testare nullos esse qua veheris deos* (bear witness where you ride that there are no gods *Medea* 1027), but the motive for Thyestes' remark is less obvious. It is significant, however, that it appears in the context of a list of the monuments of royal power. Atreus will later set himself against the Olympians explicitly (885 ff.) but this assertion is a development of the representation

[80] See above, p. 131, on the repetition of *sequor* (100 and 489).

of the political power of the Tantalids throughout the drama. One of the emblems of that power and its threat to the Olympians is the chariot-race. Atreus' expression of his victory over Thyestes and the helpless gods at the end of the drama, *nunc parta vera est palma* (now the true palm is won 1097), is the conclusion of a figure which is introduced in the first ode and reiterated in the third act where Thyestes returns to the world of Tantalid power.

The desire of Furia and Atreus to carry out the criminal acts of the tragedy is productively read as a desire to produce a literary crime. Not only do the scenes of demonic possession in the first and second acts suggest the topos of poetic possession, but both characters and crimes are marked by dense allusion as fabrications of a literary tradition. If a meta-literary aspect to the drama is accepted in the scenes of the genesis of the crime, then it is reasonable to wonder if the struggle for the order of the world and more narrowly for the expression or repression of the tragic act throughout the drama also has a meta-literary aspect. To some extent the close relationship between the plans of Atreus and Furia in the opening scenes and the fulfilment of those same plans in the subsequent tragedy makes this inevitable. In *Hercules Furens* the inspiration of the tragic crime in Juno's introductory monologue is not only fulfilled but echoed in the madness of Hercules in the fourth act: the audience sees tragic madness being born twice. This repetition is more marked in *Thyestes*: not only does Atreus' inspiration in the second act reiterate the agon between Furia and Tantalus in the first act, but this sequence is then repeated later in the tragedy where the end of the Messenger's speech echoes the end of Furia's speech (784–8 cf. 120–1) and Atreus again sees the image of the crime before it is represented in tragic action (281–3 cf. 890–919). Whether or not dramatic reality is actually repeated in *Thyestes* such that the same events happen more than once,[81] less controversially the image of tragic crime is born and reborn. Meta-literary interpretation of this tragedy has, reasonably enough, concentrated on Furia and Atreus, the characters who create the tragedy,[82] but the recurrent figure of the chariot-race is also invested with meta-literary significance.

---

[81] So Shelton (1975), who sees a similar repetition of events in *Hercules Furens*. These readings are not without parallel: cf. Owen (1970) on *Troades*.

[82] In addition to Schiesaro (1994) see Boyle (1997) 116f.

Images of a Flawed Technical Genesis 141

I suggested above that Thyestes' aside *si sunt tamen di* (if there really *are* gods 407) should be interpreted in the context of the monuments of royal power which he is describing. Through Pelops' royal murder an Olympian festival and the race-track itself are contaminated, but the threat to the Olympians can be seen more closely in a Horatian reminiscence. Thyestes' sight of the stadium recalls Horace, *Odes* 1.1:

> [cerno]
> celebrata iuveni stadia, per quae nobilis
> palmam paterno non semel curru tuli.
> occurret Argos, populus occurret frequens—
> sed nempe et Atreus. (409–12)

([I see] the race-track I frequented in youth, through which I carried the palm in glory more than once on my father's chariot. Argos will come to meet me, the people will come in crowds—yes, but so will Atreus.)

Compare:

> sunt quos curriculo pulverem Olympico
> collegisse iuvat, metaque fervidis
> evitata rotis palmaque nobilis
> terrarum dominos evehit ad deos;
> hunc, si mobilium turba Quiritium
> certat tergeminis tollere honoribus.
> (Horace, *Odes* 1.1.3–8)

(Some are happy to pick up Olympic dust on their chariot. The limit passed with burning wheels and the noble palm raises these masters of the earth to the gods. This man is happy if the whirling mob of citizens struggles to exalt him with triple honours.)

In *Odes* 1.1 Horace contrasts various pursuits with his own, poetry. Victory at Olympia is the first example. Both the Olympic victor and the poet win a crown and join the ranks of the gods (5–6 cf. 29–30, 36), but the dust and heat of Olympia are implicitly contrasted with the *gelidum nemus* (cool grove 30) of poetic composition. Thyestes' entrance and his allusion to Horace's poem is preceded by an ode (336–403) on the instability of royal power and the preferability of both the true kingship of a virtuous soul (380–90) and the quiet life (391–403), which is also influenced by the same Horatian text.[83] The disapproval of the chorus and of

---
[83] See Nisbet and Hubbard (1970) 6 and Tarrant (1985) 141, 147, and 150. The points of contact between Horace, *Odes* 1.1 and Seneca, *Thyestes* are: 7–10 cf. 350–7 and 409–10; 29 cf. 393; 7 cf. 396.

Horace reinforces the criminality of the Tantalid myth of the father's chariot. Horace follows his description of the Olympic victor with the victor in Roman politics and suggests connections: to describe athletic victors as becoming 'masters of the earth' is an emphatic politicizing of their 'noble' reward, and the favour of the 'mobile Quirites' surely recalls the dangers of the burning wheels. In the less delicate moral environment of Seneca's *Thyestes* only life among wild animals is unpolluted by the struggle for power (412–18), and, as the myth of Pelops' chariot-race shows, Olympic competition is not exempt.

Just as the criticism of political power is more pointed in Seneca's ode than it is in Horace's, so power itself is more extreme. The ideal of power, which terrestrial kings cannot perfectly imitate, can be seen in the sage, *qui tuto positus loco | infra se videt omnia* (one set in a place of safety who sees all things beneath him 365–6). The sons of Pelops are mistaken not in their desire for autarchy, but in their understanding of how it is achieved: *nescitis, cupidi arcium, | regnum quo iaceat loco* (In your greed for strongholds, you mistake the place where kingship lies 342–3).[84] In both Horace's ode and in the myth of Pelops' chariot, chariot-racing is political,[85] but in *Thyestes* power does not admit of a rival and it cannot be a final goal to be one of the divine masters of the earth. Atreus' first words in the final act, *Aequalis astris gradior* (Peer of the stars I stride 885) refer to the disruption recounted in the previous ode, but also recall the claim of the athlete (*palmaque nobilis | terrarum dominos evehit ad deos* (and the noble palm raises these masters of the earth to the gods 5–6) and the poet (*sublimi feriam sidera vertice* (I will strike the stars with my lofty head 36))) in Horace, *Odes* 1.1. The sentiment is not unusual,[86] but the drama encourages one to recall these particular passages through its systematic allusion to this poem and through the myth of Pelops' athletic competition which corrupts and opposes the Olympian festival.

As important as the close relationship between politics and chariot-racing in Horace's ode is the contrast he draws between

---

[84] On similarities between tyrannical and Stoic power see Braden (1970) 39–40 and above, Ch. 2, sect. 2.

[85] Cf. Braden (1970) 31–2 on the world of *Thyestes*: 'there is a certain mad athletic air to the whole environment'.

[86] See Nisbet and Hubbard (1970) 15–16 on Horace, *Odes* 1.1.36.

Images of a Flawed Technical Genesis 143

this kind of activity and his own, writing poetry. In a gesture typical of Roman Alexandrianism he presents himself as turning away from public glory to the secluded world of artistic refinement. By contrast, the desire to reach the stars as a *vates* suggests a sublimity and a political engagement which is very much un-Callimachean.[87]

> me doctarum hederae praemia frontium
> dis miscent superis, me gelidum nemus
> nympharumque leves cum Satyris chori
> secernunt populo...
>
> . . . .
>
> quodsi me lyricis vatibus inseres,
> sublimi feriam sidera vertice.
>
> (*Odes* 1.1.29–32, 35–6)

(The ivy which rewards learned brows joins me to the gods above. The cool grove and the light dances of Nymphs and Satyrs draw me apart from the people... But if you put me in the company of the lyric poets, I will strike the stars with my lofty head.)

The ode as a whole moderates the political aspirations of the *vates* with Callimachean withdrawal, and a delicate balance between seclusion and engagement is constructed.[88] In Seneca's *Thyestes* the art of Furia and Atreus could not be more political. Not only is Atreus' tragedy a means to secure political supremacy, but it is achieved because its unwitting actor does not have the strength of will to resist the allure of the race-track, the adoring crowds, and the trappings of power.[89] Thyestes' fond memories of riding in his father's chariot and Atreus' expression of victory, *nunc parta vera est palma* (now the true palm is won 1097) are both implicitly criticized by the Horatian ode and by the Senecan ode which draws on it. The criticism of Atreus, whose deeds are a work of art, has also an aesthetic dimension. The Horatian statement of poetic triumph is founded, however paradoxically, on the isolation

---

[87] On *vates* and its political connotations in Augustan poetry see Newman (1967) 99–206.

[88] See further Batinski (1991) esp. 369–70 on Bacchus balanced by Apollo, *ingenium* by *ars*, archaic lyric (with political as well as personal concerns) by Callimachean poetry.

[89] SATELLES. *Quonam ergo telo tantus utetur dolor?* | ATREUS. *Ipso Thyeste* (258–9). On Thyestes' guilt see Poe (1969) 362, Curley (1986) 151–3, Boyle (1997) 49–51. Gigon (1938) offers the opposing view, that Thyestes plays the Stoic sage to Atreus' tyrant, but this view has rightly found little favour.

and consequent purity of the poet-priests among whom he wishes to be numbered; the Callimachean seclusion from the crowd is politicized as a renunciation of public glory. Certainly Seneca interpreted Horace's poetic isolation in this way: Horace's opposition between the world of poetry and the world of political glory is recalled in Seneca's opposition between the world of the virtuous plebeian[90] and the corrupt king. The recollection of Horace's literary concerns reinforces the meta-literary aspect of Seneca's tragedy: Atreus the tyrant perverts the ideals of kingship and of an art made pure and divine by its withdrawal from the world.[91]

Throughout the tragedy Tantalid evil contaminates the Olympian powers it opposes. The Olympic festival, an apparent locus of opposition to the criminal politics of the Tantalids, is corrupted by Pelops' chariot race; what appears to be a ritual sacred to Olympian Zeus is in fact a commemoration of political murder. The treatment of poetry is similar. Atreus enacts his crime, the murder and cooking of Thyestes' children, in a grove which is secluded from the crowd:[92]

>   post ista vulgo nota, quae populi colunt,
>   in multa dives spatia discedit domus.
>   Arcana in imo regio secessu iacet,
>   alta vetustum valle compescens nemus
>   penetrale regni   (648–52)

---

[90] This ode combines various alternatives to political kingship: true kingship, which is a Stoic figure (365–8, 388–9), *dulcis...quies* (393) which is more Epicurean, and low social status, which is a familiar tragic topos given a Roman cast here: *plebeius moriar senex* (400).

[91] Cf. Masters (1992) 145 on the confused heaps of massy death which Caesar and the *Civil War* creates as marking 'an epic of bigness, tumidity, anti-Callimachean fatness', 34 on aesthetic disgust in the criminal poem, 25–9 on Lucan's and Caesar's desecration of the grove. See also D. P. Fowler (1995) 253–7 on the implications for the emperor of the politicization of Callimachean aesthetic criticism in Horace's *Odes*.

[92] The sacred grove in *Oedipus* (530–658) is in many ways similar to this one, and it too has been discussed as a reflection of the creation of the tragedy: see Schiesaro (1997*b*) 93–8. For the sublimity (in the poetic sense) of a sacred grove of tall trees see also Michel (1969) 249–50 on *Epistles* 41.3–4. However, the natural grandeur of the grove in *Epistles* 41 is clearly different from the hellish power of the grove in *Thyestes* and the characterization of poetic/tragic madness must also be distinguished accordingly. The political aspect of the grove in *Thyestes* and the warped sophistication of its location beyond what is familiar to the *vulgus* are features peculiar to this grove.

Images of a Flawed Technical Genesis 145

(Behind these public rooms, where whole peoples pay court, the wealthy house goes back a great distance. At the farthest and lowest remove there lies a secret area that confines an age-old woodland in a deep vale—the inner sanctum of the realm.)

The secluded grove is a site of oracular utterance—*hinc auspicari regna Tantalidae solent* ('Tantalid kings regularly inaugurate their reigns here 657)—and Atreus, playing the role of priest, enacts his crime as a careful ritual:

> servatur omnis ordo, ne tantum nefas
> non rite fiat...
> Ipse est sacerdos, ipse funesta prece
> letale carmen ore violento canit.   (689–92)

(Every part of the ritual is kept, to ensure that such an outrage is performed by the rules...He himself is priest, he himself makes sinister prayers and sings the death-chant in a bloodthirsty voice.)

This grove has a pool fed by the Styx (665–7) and other features of the underworld: *nox propria luco est, et superstitio inferum | in luce media regnat* (the grove has a night all its own, and an eerie sense of the underworld reigns in broad daylight 678–9). Like Thebes in the *Thebaid*,[93] this royal palace is in some sense a home for the Fury, and the unnamed god who replies to the Tantalids' questions is surely a personification of the *superstitio inferum*.[94] As in the opening scenes of the tragedy, the 'energy of hell'[95] is a significant power in the genesis of crime. Through this parallelism with the earlier part of the tragedy, but also through the topos of the poet-priest, and words like *carmen* and *cano* which are familiar from a poetic context, Atreus' offence against Olympian order is also an offence against divine poetry.[96] The nature of the offence is to preserve divine and poetic ritual in perverted form. Just as Atreus inspects the children to make sure that they are not

---

[93] Statius, *Thebaid* 100–2.

[94] *et superstitio inferum | in luce media regnat. hinc orantibus | responsa dantur certa, cum ingenti sono | laxantur adyto fata et immugit specus | vocem deo solvente* (678–82).

[95] This is the title of a useful discussion in Hardie (1993) 60–5. See also Curley (1986) 166.

[96] On *vates* and the relationship between poetry and prophecy in Roman literature particularly see O'Higgins (1988) 208–9. To her bibliography should now be added Masters (1992) 142–9, Leigh (1997) 6–40. See also Sect. 3 below on *Medea*.

blemished (694) and takes omens for a future over which he himself has assumed complete control (757–8),[97] so he produces his lethal poem in religious isolation, secluded from the *vulgus*.

The purity of the Horatian grove and its distance from the public world is marked by its otherworldly inhabitants (*nympharumque leves cum Satyris chori* (the light dances of Nymphs and Satyrs 31))) and its strange, foreign vocabulary (e.g. *barbiton* 34).[98] Atreus' grove is nakedly political, set in the heart of the royal palace: *penetrale regni* actually appears in apposition to the key word *nemus* (*nemus | penetrale regni* (a grove—the inner sanctum of the realm 651–2)). Atreus preserves the outward form of piety but assimilates to his corrupt purposes the rituals of art, athletics, and religious observance. Just as Atreus' tyranny is a mirror image of Stoicism's metaphorical autocracy (see Chapter 2, Section 2 above), so his tyrannical and infernal *carmen* recalls in distorted form the Alexandrian disdain for the people and the presentation of poetry as a sacred art. Nailed to the tallest tree of the sacred grove are the memorials of political crime including the famous chariot:

> affixa inhaerent dona: vocales tubae
> fractique currus, spolia Myrtoi maris,
> victaeque falsis axibus pendent rotae
> et omne gentis facinus.   (659–62)

(Here votive gifts are fastened: hanging up are bruiting trumpets and wrecked chariots, spoils from the Myrtoan Sea, wheels defeated because of tampered axles, and all the exploits of the clan.)

Inset in the poetic grove is the memorial of the murder of Oenomaus and evil disguised by the form of Olympian ritual. In the centre of the play the genesis of crime is revisited. Tantalid evil and the inspiration of Furia are a threat to moral order, and the victory of their criminal expression is achieved in the contamination and corruption of the order which they oppose. Throughout

---

[97] At the very least this act is unnecessary: 'he seems to have no serious intention of learning the future but simply to be displaying perverse regard for established form' (Tarrant (1985) 198). I suggest that there is a further irony in his pretending to consult the powers which he is displacing.

[98] See Nisbet and Hubbard (1970) 3. Though the *tibiae* and *barbitos* suggest lyric poetry and hence public panegyric and political involvement (so Batinski (1991) 370), Horace's political rhetoric, invoking archaic Greek poetry as its models, is otherworldly and decently oblique in a way that Seneca's is not. On the Romanness of Atreus' *domus* see below, Ch. 4, pp. 228–30.

the drama oppositions are compromised and resolved by this contamination.

In the first act Furia recalls the deliberate, knowing evil of Ovid's Iron Age. Tantalus opposes her and she drives him to scorch the land of Argos as Phaethon burned the world. Not only is his opposition defeated, but there is a further failure as the myths are harmonized. *Hercules Furens* expresses the ambiguity of tragic madness through the difference between these myths: self-conscious villainy is not the same as failed transcendence. Here infernal Furia mockingly clothes her puppet in the myth of the overreaching, would-be-Olympian. A similar mockery can be seen in Atreus' reverence for religious and poetic ritual. His human sacrifice is as perverted as his poetic seclusion from the people, but both preserve the form of virtue. The same can be said of the Olympic Games, which the chorus presents as a ritual for which Argos should be divinely favoured but which immortalizes the crime of Pelops. As for the Olympians themselves, at the end of the first act their representative, the Sun, hesitates to drive the day onward in a helpless imitation of both Furia and her puppet Phaethon. This anticipates a recurrent feature of the tragedy, that the Olympian attempt to conceal the tragic crime in darkness merely advertises it and celebrates Furia's achievement.

Thyestes defies moral recuperation: not only is the deliberate criminality of Furia and Atreus shocking, but what little opposition is offered is warped and absorbed until it too is an expression of criminality. The myths of poetic production fare similarly. Vatic inspiration exists only in inverted form as a manifestation of infernal power. Alexandrian isolationism and the poetic grove are more subtly compromised and inverted as they are absorbed in Atreus' tyrannical *carmen*. In defiance of the Horatian distinction, poetry and politics are collapsed into a single, criminal art.[99] The corruption of the Horatian ideal of secluded art and the contamination of the Olympic Games by Pelopid crime are framed by the assimilation of the myth of Phaethon to the myth of the Iron Age in the first act. The aspirations of the charioteer to emulate Olympian order are, in poetic terms, aspirations to sublimity and divine

---

[99] Theatre, particularly, is an instrument of power in this tragedy. On the collapse of (political) life into theatre and vice versa in this tragedy see Curley (1986) 181–4.

grandeur. These aspirations are corrupted here as the role becomes an expression of Furia's deliberate criminality.

3. MEDEA

From the first lines of the tragedy Medea parallels her domestic injustice with a greater crime, the *Argo*'s voyage and the end of the Golden Age. The broken oath of the marriage is paralleled by the breach of a greater covenant in the ordering of the world.[100] More directly than in *Hercules Furens* or *Thyestes* the tragic myths of particular royal houses are framed by myths of the criminality of all human civilization and its arts. The myth of Phaethon is invoked here too as a possible paradigm of Argonautic transgression. This tragedy also is inspired and driven by a Fury: Medea assumes the persona in her first speech. Thus Seneca revisits the subject of a flawed or deliberately criminal genesis through his usual opposition of figures. The charioteer and the Fury have a meta-literary resonance which is enhanced in *Medea* by the literary self-consciousness of the heroine. Medea's strange awareness of her own myth, a self-consciousness which threatens the integrity of the dramatic illusion, actualizes the meta-literary potential of the charioteer, the Fury, and that most familiar poet-surrogate, the witch. In this way the meditation on the criminal genesis of human civilization and its arts speaks particularly to the genesis of this literary art.

In the prologue, which reviews the past and establishes the tragic crisis, Medea interweaves domestic and cosmic transgression. The voyage of the *Argo* is significant in its own right not simply as the means by which Jason and Medea met:[101]

> Di coniugales tuque genialis tori,
> Lucina, custos quaeque *domituram freta*
> Tiphyn novam frenare docuisti ratem
> et tu, profundi saeve *dominator maris*... (1–4)

---

[100] See Costa (1973) 70–1. Russell (1979*b*) 107–8 reports the view of Ps.-Dionysius (*Ars Rhetorica* 261.14) that monogamous union was the basis of civilization, and Menander's view that marriage was the foundation not only of human skills but also of stability in the universe.
[101] Cf. Euripides, *Medea* 1–8 and Ennius, *Medea exul* fr. 103 in Jocelyn (1967), discussed 342 ff.

Images of a Flawed Technical Genesis 149

(Gods of marriage! And you, Lucina, keeper of the marriage-bed; and you who taught Tiphys to bridle the novel ship that would tame the seas; and you, ferocious tamer of the deep sea...)

The goddess (Minerva) who taught Tiphys to master the waters and set him in opposition to the divine master of the sea,[102] presides over this myth of Medea as importantly as the gods of marriage. The theme of the human inheritance of divine power is introduced at the opening through the Argonautic myth,[103] but in the subsequent lines it is Medea who gradually assumes divine power. In her invocation of the infernal powers she describes Proserpina as *dominam | fide meliore raptam* (lady stolen like me but shown better loyalty 11–12). After comparing herself to this infernal Juno she revises[104] her marriage as a hellish scene and calls on the Furies to attend her with their torches as they did before and to bring death to the new wife (13–18). When her prayers fall on deaf ears she decides to carry out her own orders: *hoc restat unum, pronubam thalamo feram | ut ipsa pinum* (This alone remains, that I carry the bridesmaid's torch myself into the chamber 37–8).

The delicate hint in the invocation of Lucina (2), properly the goddess of childbirth, as to the mode of Medea's revenge becomes clear later:

> me coniugem opto, quoque non aliud queam
> peius precari, liberos similes patri
> similesque matri—parta iam, parta ultio est:
> peperi. (23–6)

(May he long for me as his wife, and—I can make no worse prayer—for children resembling their father and resembling their mother. My revenge is born, already born: I have given birth.)

Throughout her prologue and in keeping with her development to a superhuman figure Medea develops the infanticide into something more.[105] She continues her plan to be a hellish bridesmaid as follows:

---

[102] The contrast is repeated in the second Argonautic Ode: Tiphys as *dominator profundi* (617) recalls Neptune as *dominus profundi* (597).

[103] On Catullus 64 and the ambivalence of the Argonautic myth see Bramble (1970). On Seneca's treatment see Costa (1973) 62 and Boyle (1997) 126. In Valerius Flaccus there is division among the Olympians: Juno, Jupiter, and Pallas support the voyage, Neptune and his subordinates oppose it (1.211–15, 245–7).

[104] Proserpina, the infernal Juno, balances Lucina of line 2.

[105] Fyfe (1983) 77 amplifies the infanticide neatly to the inversion of a single abstraction, 'a life-process'. The prologue threatens cosmic disorder and also

150 *Images of a Flawed Technical Genesis*

> postque sacrificas preces
> caedam dicatis victimas altaribus.
> Per viscera ipsa quaere supplicio viam,
> si vivis, anime   (38–41)

(and after sacrificial prayers I shall slaughter the victims on a consecrated altar. Through the very guts find a path to punishment, my spirit, if you are alive).

The punishment to be found in the *viscera* will in fact be her children. At the end of the tragedy, having exhausted her material, she echoes her earlier words:

> in matre si quod pignus etiamnunc latet,
> scrutabor ense viscera et ferro extraham   (1012–13)

(If some love-pledge is hiding even now in my mothering body, I shall probe my vitals with the sword, drag it out with steel.)

In context, however, the earlier reference to inspecting entrails is more naturally taken with the sacrificial victims at the marriage. Whether these victims are animals or Jason and Creusa or indeed her own children,[106] Medea's sinister threat suggests taking the omens. One may usefully compare *Thyestes* 757–8 where Atreus, without any practical reason for doing so, reads the fates in the entrails of Thyestes' children. In both places the protagonists' crimes, by association if not logically, are elevated to form part of the pattern of a vengeful universe.

Like Atreus and Juno, Medea drives herself to exceed all past models of criminality. The simplest amplification is the extension of her revenge beyond the human sphere:

> non ibo in hostes? manibus excutiam faces
> caeloque lucem   (27–8)

(Shall I not attack my enemies? I shall dash the bridal torches from their hands, and the light from heaven.)

Destruction in the macrocosm echoes precisely the disruption of Jason's marriage. Less clearly Medea threatens greater crimes now that she has given birth:

---

alludes to the infanticide several times, but the sense of a cosmic infanticide is left very vague.

[106] 'Who or what are the victims?' For a survey of the answers to this question see Costa (1973) 67–8.

> haec virgo feci; gravior exurgat dolor:
> maiora iam me scelera post partus decent. (49–50)

(I did all this as a girl; my bitterness must grow more weighty: greater crimes become me now, after giving birth.)

This is another allusion to the infanticide, but the greater crimes, *tremenda caelo pariter ac terris mala* (evils fearful to heaven and earth alike 46), will cause the universe to tremble in a more immediate sense as Medea draws down a lurid moon on Corinth (787–96) and envelops the city in flames (885–7).

As the active principle of vengeance in the tragedy is Nature's representative, and the text supports an identification of Medea with Nature, her waves of anger are likened to the waves of the Ocean (939–43) and she says of herself, *Medea superest—hic mare et terras vides* (Medea remains: here you see sea and land 166). The second Argonautic ode begins by comparing her passion to elemental violence (579–90) and Medea phrases her anger similarly:

> non rapidus amnis, non procellosum mare
> pontusve coro saevus aut vis ignium
> adiuta flatu possit inhibere impetum
> irasque nostras: sternam et evertam omnia. (411–14)

(No whirling river, no stormy ocean, no sea enraged by northwesters, no force of fire aided by gales, could equal the momentum of my anger. I shall overturn and flatten everything.)

Certainly she embodies natural violence, and in the context of the Argonautic myth binary oppositions beckon invitingly: flawed masculine technology elicits an elemental, feminine response.[107] Medea's Fury persona plays well with this. The Furies historically are chthonic powers, representatives of the old order, and thus appropriate punishers of those who dare to contravene the *foedera mundi* (the covenants of the world 335, 606) and the *ponti iura* (the rights of the deep 614–15) and to write new laws for the winds (*legesque novas scribere ventis* 320).

Unlike Euripides' heroine, Medea has no friends in Corinth apart from the Nurse, and her marginalization is increased further

---

[107] P. J. Davis (1993) 82–3, 93, and Fyfe (1983) *passim*, especially the conclusion, 90–1. Henderson (1983) 99–100 has a usefully condensed list of references out of which to make an argument for Medea's elemental violence.

as the Olympians themselves ignore her prayers and are appropriated by the chorus of hostile Corinthians in the first ode.[108] In this respect Medea resembles Virgil's Dido, who discovers not only that she has been abandoned by Aeneas but that she is an unwelcome digression in Jupiter's world-narrative. The binding force of a marriage which Juno sanctioned[109] evaporates when it becomes clear that the destiny of the world lies elsewhere. Dido's curse, which Medea's monologue recalls,[110] shows human rage escalating to echo the cosmic anger of Juno. If the Euripidean model constructs Medea's otherness through the oppositions of gender and of Greek/barbarian, this Roman antecedent of Seneca's heroine adds a cosmic and imperial dimension.[111] The anger of the earth figures a voice for those dispossessed by the fate of a new world order.

A feature of the avenging Fury is its tendency to re-stage the crime it punishes.[112] The cyclicism of vengeance is pointed by the remembrance and re-enactment of crimes even at the moment of its apparent closure and resolution. In *Thyestes* the madness with which Furia infects the house is the spirit of Tantalus returned to earth and a repetition of the familiar criminal banquet.[113] Atreus and Thyestes, avenger and victim, are blurred into a single figure consumed by an insatiatiable appetite for power. Even the name Tantalus recurs as one of Thyestes' sons bears the ancestral name. In *Hercules Furens* Juno infects Hercules with a fury which is patterned on Herculean virtue. Furies in Latin literature are

---

[108] Cf. Fyfe (1983) 79, 'Ironically the Chorus invokes the same gods as Medea invokes in the prologue to defend her rights.' On Medea's isolation see also Braden (1970) 29–33.

[109] *Aeneid* 4.125–7, 166–70. Note the chthonic presence as the marriage is affirmed: *prima et Tellus et pronuba Iuno* (166).

[110] Dido, as she suggests herself at *Aeneid* 4.600–1, is a parallel for Medea. See Fantham (1975) 6–10. Dido is recalled particularly in the opening monologue (note especially *Medea* 6 ff. and *Aeneid* 4.608 ff.) and in the magic ritual of the fourth act (670–848). See Costa (1973) 63 and 136. For Dido as a dramatic, tragic figure see Lyne (1989) 24–9, Pobjoy (1998), and Wlosok (1976).

[111] Note the explicitly political element in Dido's curse at *Aeneid* 4.625–9. On Juno's anger as the anger of Tanit, goddess of Carthage, see Feeney (1991) 116–17, 130–2.

[112] See famously Aeneas' words *Pallas te hoc vulnere Pallas | immolat et poenam scelerato ex sanguine sumit* (Virgil, *Aen.* 12.948–9). On impersonation and avenging re-embodiment in Roman epic see Hardie (1993) 35–48.

[113] Not only is Tantalus' banquet the inspiration for Atreus', but visions of Atreus' banquet are repeated through the tragedy.

Images of a Flawed Technical Genesis

morally simple inasmuch as they tend to represent chaos, passion, evil in perfect opposition to order, reason, virtue.[114] What distinguishes them primarily from their Aeschylean predecessors is that their thirst for blood is unmitigated by any interest in preserving order: they either have no sense of violence as an instrument of a higher order or promote disorder for its own sake.[115] This is why the presence of *Dirae* at the throne of Jupiter in the *Aeneid* so compromises the moral integrity of Rome's destiny[116] and why the proximity of heroic *virtus* and *furor* is so intolerable in *Hercules Furens*. As Juno simultaneously punishes Hercules' crime and recalls it Medea simultaneously punishes the Argonauts' crime and re-enacts it. When she turns her magical arts against Jason she reflects in amplified form his technological crime.[117] The binary oppositions, in particular that of nature/artifice, are thus not so neatly personified by Medea and the Argonauts. In addition to being the personification of Nature's anger Medea is also an icon of the criminal art which has provoked it.

The ambiguity of Medea's status is developed in the treatment of her role in the Argonautic expedition: she is represented both as a thing discovered and as one of their number who ensures the success of the expedition. The chorus represents her in the first Argonautic Ode as follows:

> Quod fuit huius
> pretium cursus? aurea pellis
> maiusque mari Medea malum,
> merces prima digna carina.   (361–4)

(What was the prize gained by this voyage? The Golden Fleece and Medea, an evil worse than the sea, fit merchandise for the first vessel.)

Here Medea is both a commodity like the golden fleece, a *pretium* or a *merces*, and a natural hazard. In her own view she is a

---

[114] On the philosophical context of the Furies in Roman literature see Gill's introduction 5–15 esp. 13 to Braund and Gill (1997).

[115] For the ambivalence of Aeschylus' Furies compare e.g. *Eumenides* 34–7, 264–6 with *Eumenides* 490–8, 508–15 and see more generally Belfiore (1992) 19 ff.

[116] See Johnson (1976) 130, 'When the *Dira* appears in the poem, both heroes must come to the heart of the poem, to an unknown and terrifying desolation in which their particular virtues are less than useless, and all goodness and all truth are broken and lost.'

[117] This point is well made by Boyle (1997) 126–8 and Segal (1983) 238, 'She [Medea] is identified both with the natural world and the magic arts that exercise dominion'.

participant in the voyage. In her agons with both Creon (190–300) and Jason (447–559) Medea advances the argument familiar from Ovid's treatment in *Heroides* 12 that the Argonauts returned successfully only through her efforts. Medea is the Argonauts' criminal past which Creon and Jason would like to forget,[118] but will not be so easily dismissed. This is expressed most strikingly in Medea's demand for Jason's return: *si placet, damna ream; sed redde crimen* (If you so determine, condemn the accused—but give back her crime 245–6).

Her vengeance is a repetition or a re-staging of crimes which the Argonauts accepted in their pursuit of the golden fleece. The repetition of *scelus* at the close of her first speech, *quae scelere parta est, scelere linquenda est domus* (in crime you gained your home, in crime you must leave it 55), highlights this theme which Medea develops further by describing her past crimes as models for the present:[119] *scelera te hortentur tua | et cuncta redeant* (Your own crimes must urge you on, every one of them must return 129–30). Her vengeance recalls the past in more than just degree (*Si quaeris odio, misera, quem statuas modum, | imitare amorem* (If you wonder, poor wretch, what limit to put on your hatred, copy your love 397–8)). When she kills the first child she is an embodiment of the vengeful spirit of Absyrtus:[120]

> Discedere a me, frater, ultrices deas
> manesque ad imos ire securas iube:
> mihi me relinque et utere hac, frater, manu
> quae strinxit ensem—victima manes tuos
> placamus ista.   (967–71)

(Bid the avenging goddesses draw back from me, brother, and return to the deep shades assured of their purpose. Leave me to myself, and act, brother, through this hand that has drawn the sword. With this sacrifice I placate your shade.)

The crime of reordering nature and ending the Golden Age is conventionally accompanied by social evils like avarice and murder, and Medea's crimes, which the Argonauts accept, are to be interpreted in this tradition. Medea's crimes are notorious (*nota*

---

[118] See especially 262 ff. (Creon) and 498–9 (Jason).
[119] Cf. also *ad omne facinus non rudem dextram afferes* (915).
[120] On the infanticide as an act of atonement or self-punishment for the crimes she committed with the Argonauts see Gill (1997) 218.

fraus, nota est manus (her cunning is well known, so is her handiwork 181)) and the repetition of *fraus* which Creon fears (*Fraudibus tempus petis* (You are seeking time for treachery 290)) should be associated with the *fraus* which did not exist in the Golden Age: *Candida nostri saecula patres | videre procul fraude remota* (Our forefathers saw bright eras with crime and deceit far distant 329–30). Though resembling the Argonauts as a *contriver* of evil deeds (*malorum* machinatrix *facinorum* 266),[121] Medea also embodies Nature. This characterization of Medea as a contriving force of Nature, which commemorates the crime it punishes is well illustrated in her agon with Jason. Here she reworks and inverts the chorus's description of her as a natural hazard and a prize (361–4:

> Est et his maior metus
> Medea... certemus sine,
>   sit pretium Iason.   (516–18)[122]

(There is an even greater threat than these: Medea... let us fight it out, and let Jason be the prize)

The wittiness, the artificiality of Nature's vengeance, is apparent also in the second Argonautic Ode. After comparing Medea's anger to elemental violence (579–90) the chorus recounts the fates of others involved in *Argo*'s voyage, each of whom, except Jason, has already paid the penalty (*exitu diro temerata ponti | iura piavit* (has atoned with a dreadful death for trespass on the rights of the deep 614–15)). This catalogue of deaths is a tapestry of grim allusions to Medea's forthcoming revenge and examples of what can only be described as poetic justice. The elemental forces of fire and flood destroy Pelias in a markedly artificial way: [*ustus accenso Pelias aeno] | arsit angustas vagus inter undas* ([Pelias boiled in the heated cauldron] seethed while wandering in narrow waters 666–7). In a detailed commentary on this ode Henderson

---

[121] The word is paralleled in Senecan tragedy only by *machinator* at *Troades* 750, *o machinator fraudis et scelerum artifex*, where the arch-contriver Ulysses is addressed. See Costa (1973) 96. Petrone (1988) 61 ff. comments on alliteration in Medea's presentation. Through this formal device her name is shown to belong with phrases like *maior metus* (516). See especially *maiusque mari Medea malum, | merces* (363–4). She is named to be the Argonauts' doom.

[122] *Medea* is separated from *certemus* in line 517 of Zwierlein's text by the untranslatable *nos confligere* which he marks as corrupt. The problem remains unresolved (see Costa (1973) 117), and because the offending words have no bearing on my point I have simply omitted them.

comments enthusiastically on the 'intellectual rigour and artistic control' which the poet displays.[123] Importantly, however, it is also the avenging principle of Nature which demonstrates this artistic control, and mocks the aspirations of those who would write a new world order.

The figures of Phaethon and Orpheus also establish a continuity between Medea and the Argonauts. As a failed imitator of Olympian order Phaethon more closely recalls the Argonauts and it is in this spirit that the chorus makes the identification at the beginning of the second Argonautic Ode:[124]

> ausus aeternos agitare currus
> immemor metae iuvenis paternae
> quos polo sparsit furiosus ignes
>   ipse recepit.
> constitit nulli via nota magno:
> vade qua tutum populo priori,
> rumpe nec sacro violente sancta
>   foedera mundi.   (599–606)

(He who dared to drive the eternal chariot, the youth who forgot his father's bounds, after wildly showering fire through the heavens suffered fire himself. The familiar path costs no one dear; walk where people before found safety, and do not violently break the inviolate pacts of the world.)

The first Argonautic Ode recalls Ovid's description of the Golden Age from *Metamorphoses* 1[125] and traces of the familiar contrast between this myth and that of Phaethon's transgression appear. The point I want to make here, however, concerns Medea's role as Phaethon. One of the ingredients in the burning poison which will consume Creusa is living fire from the body of Phaethon, whom she refers to as her relative (*cognato* 827). This can be interpreted as 'poetic justice' of the kind exacted in the

---

[123] Henderson (1983) 106. Note especially the word-play supervening upon the raw forces of Nature: 97 on Medea 583–90 and 109 on Medea 616–51; 'Each of the illustrations of accomplished retribution, Tiphys, Orpheus, Hercules Ancaeus, Meleager, Hylas, has carried a shadow of Medea's criminal dossier—as it will be complete when the play ends.'

[124] See P. J. Davis (1993) 134–5, Fyfe (1983) 89. Jakobi (1988) argues that the word-play at the end of the first stanza recalls Ovid's description of Jupiter's intervention at *Met.* 2.313. Cf. also the description of Tiphys losing control of the *Argo* in the first Argonautic Ode: omnes | labente manu misit habenas (346–7).

[125] See Jakobi (1988) 53: *Medea* 309–11 and 331–4 cf. *Met.* 1.94 f. and 96 f.

Images of a Flawed Technical Genesis 157

second Argonautic Ode: Creusa, like Hylas, Pelias, and many others will recall in the manner of her death the crime for which she dies. At the same time this is Medea's fire, by blood relationship, and the burning of Creusa fulfils the promise of the prologue where Medea, not the Argonauts, assumed the role of divinities. In the great magical ritual of the fourth act Medea recalls magic she has worked in the past and perhaps echoes Ovid's description of Phaethon's disruption of the constellations,[126] but more obviously she ends the tragedy in a winged chariot: *ego inter auras aliti curru vehar* (I shall ride through the air in my winged chariot 1025). Through the double identifications with the figure of Phaethon Medea and the Argonauts resemble each other; through the double identification Medea recalls the crime for which the Argonauts die.

Orpheus is another figure whom Medea recalls in her revenge. Orpheus is one of the Argonauts and contributes to the success of the voyage by surpassing the Sirens' song with his own (355–60). As a magical singer who bends Nature to his will he also resembles the witch Medea; as a poet he suggests more directly than Phaethon a literary dimension to the interpretation of Argonautic art.[127] Orpheus is typically associated with a pastoral tranquillity very different from the cosmic violence of Medea. Where Orpheus softens the rocks with his song (*saxa cantu* mulcet 229) Medea threatens total destruction: *invadam deos | et cuncta quatiam* (I shall attack the gods, and shake the world 424–5). For Segal Medea is an anti-Orpheus figure, opposed to him as black is to white: 'Her power to charm nature by black magic invites comparison with Orpheus' white magic'.[128] That said, Orpheus himself is no simple figure: his role as an Argonaut and his attempt to bring Eurydice back across the ultimate boundary sits awkwardly with the pastoral sympathy which typically characterizes his relationship with

---

[126] See Jakobi (1988) 58: *Medea* 745 and 758 ff. cf. *Met.* 2.240 and 172. Costa (1973) 116 wonders if there is another reminiscence of Ovid's Phaethon narrative, *Met.* 2.99, at *Medea* 492. The chariot is a punishment which appears to be a gift and Medea's exile, she remarks ironically, is a gift which only appears to be a punishment. Paradoxes of this kind are a familiar stylistic feature of both authors and, as Costa notes, the force of the remark is very different in the two passages and I am inclined to discard the parallel.

[127] Note though Nussbaum (1994) 443 and 483 on the meta-literary significance of Medea's appearance in a winged chariot drawn by serpents: an anti-Platonic image of transcendent passion.

[128] Segal (1983) 241.

Nature.[129] As Orpheus and his art are not simple, neither is Medea, his more destructive and violent reflection.

Poetry is traditionally associated with sorcery in ancient literary criticism and it is difficult not to read Medea with and against the poet Orpheus. Poetry leads an audience to assent to its falsehoods by exerting its force beneath the threshold of rationality. It wins listeners over against their will and in its power to charm is like magic.[130] In Orpheus this charming ability can be directed against people, as it is against the Sirens or the powers of the underworld, but as often it is turned on the landscape itself. The traditional power of witches to alter the cycles of nature through magical song is a manifestation of the same ability. Poetry does not simply charm, but fashions its material and creates a world. Magic is thus a fine image for grand poetic projects and sublime art. Tracking the key word *deducere* A. M. Wilson shows how Manilius' play on the two connotations of this word in his prologue are rooted in a poetic tradition and specifically in Virgil's *Eclogues*.[131] Even without the guidance of a poetic tradition and verbal reminiscence the metaphor is quite clear:

> Carmine divinas artes[132] et conscia fati
> sidera diversos hominum variantia casus,
> caelestis rationis opus, deducere mundo
> aggredior primusque novis Heliconia movere
> cantibus...
> (Manilius, *Astronomica* 1.1–5)

---

[129] See e.g. the common lament of Dryads, landscape, and Orpheus at Eurydice's death at Virgil, *Georgics* 4.460–6, of Dryads and landscape at Orpheus' death at Ovid, *Metamorphoses* 11.44–9 and Segal (1983) 230 on Orpheus: 'he points to a poetic vision which mediates two extremes of human nature, the aspiration for a Golden-Age realm of peace and beauty and the knowledge of the dark passions, disobedience to the gods, violations of nature's laws which bring suffering into human life'.

[130] For overviews of modern scholars see De Romilly (1975) and Walsh (1984). For a selection of ancient sources see Plato, *Republic* 601b; Gorgias, *Encomium of Helen* 10; Plutarch, *De Poetis Audendis* 16d; Strabo 1.2. Plotinus, though writing much later argues that magic works through the irrational part of the soul and therefore the wise man is immune to sorcerous influence (*Enneads* 4.4.44). De Lacy (1948) 250, discussing technical terms used by Stoics and others, finds κήλησις used for the influence of words or music, γοητεία for the deceptive influence of the visual (*SVF* 3.98.1–2 and 6 respectively). Schiesaro (1997b) 96 n.11 notes that Horace likens the tragic poet specifically to a magician (*Epistles* 2.1.208–10).

[131] A. M. Wilson (1985).

[132] Cf. also Apuleius' assertion that witchcraft is a divine art (*Apology* 25).

Images of a Flawed Technical Genesis 159

(By the magic of song to draw down from heaven god-given skills and fate's confidants, the stars, which by the operation of divine reason diversify the chequered fortunes of mankind; and to be the first to stir with these new strains the nodding leaf-capped woods of Helicon...)

Manilius presents himself in harmony with the order of the universe, inspired by the very powers which he manipulates: *ad duo templa precor duplici circumdatus aestu | carminis et rerum* (at two shrines I make my prayer, beset with a twofold passion, for my song and for its theme 1.21–2). He gives an unfailingly cheerful account of the growth of human technology despite including many of the traditional elements of post-Golden Age decline which are to be found in the Argonautic Odes of Seneca's *Medea*:

> tumque in desertis habitabat montibus aurum,
> immotusque novos pontus subduxerat orbes,
> nec vitam pelago nec ventis credere vota
> audebant. (1.75–8)

(gold then had its abode in unvisited mountains, and the sea disturbed by none concealed the existence of unsuspected worlds, for man dared not to entrust his life to the deep or his hopes to the winds)

Even the arts of war are airily dismissed as symbiotic with the arts of peace (1.90). Human progress culminates, inevitably, in astronomy but also in prophecy and what is unambiguously witchcraft:

> ne vulgata canam, linguas didicere volucrum,
> consultare fibras et rumpere vocibus angues,
> sollicitare umbras imumque Acheronta movere,
> in noctemque dies, in lucem vertere noctes. (1.91–4)

(Not to tell the commonplace, men learnt to understand the utterance of birds; to divine from the entrails of animals; to burst snakes asunder by incantations; to summon up the dead and rouse the depths of Acheron; to turn day into night and night into the brightness of day.)

What is so familiar to Manilius in the first century AD is to be found in much earlier writers. Just as Manilius elides sorcerous manipulation of Nature with astronomical knowledge, and as the discoveries of Seneca's Tiphys are phrased in prescriptive terms (*legesque novas scribere ventis* (and write new laws for the winds *Medea* 320)), so Empedocles in his Περὶ Φύσεως promises to teach '*pharmaka*... that are a defence for ills and old age and he states that his listener will be able to control the wind and rain and

160   *Images of a Flawed Technical Genesis*

drought, and will even bring the dead back to life'.[133] The ability to describe and predict and therefore harness nature easily slides into control over Nature. There is no moral darkness in Manilius' account of human progress and its crowning glories: magic, astronomy, and, by extension, poetry.[134] Certainly he makes no distinction between Argonautic art and the 'black arts' of a witch, and says that the elements in his catalogue which might appear most suspect—turning night into day and causing snakes to explode with magic words (92–4)—are commonplace.

If Orpheus and Medea, as magicians, are to be associated with the same broad tradition of the development of human arts, the fact remains that Medea is more conspicuously violent and destructive. But more than an anti-Orpheus figure Medea amplifies the tensions and the criminality of the Argonautic artist. The role of Orpheus in *Hercules Furens* is a valuable comparison. The entrance of Hercules at the beginning of the third act (592 f.) is prepared by an ode which contrasts the hero's exploits with those of Orpheus and ends:

> Quae vinci potuit regia carmine,
> haec vinci poterit regia viribus.
> (*Hercules Furens* 590–1)

(The kingdom that could be conquered by song can and will be conquered by force.)

Orpheus' poetry is contrasted with Hercules' violence. The significance of the parallelism is twofold. First, the apparent superiority of Hercules will be reversed as, far from causing the Furies to lament his wife (*deflent Eumenides Threiciam nurum* 577), he kills Megara under their influence. Second, the failure of Orpheus anticipates the failure of Hercules: both will ultimately destroy

---

[133] Lloyd (1979) 34 commenting on Empedocles fr. 111. See also 36, 'Empedocles can be taken as the prime representative of a very different view, according to which the knowledge of nature might be used in some sense to transcend nature herself'. Cf. also Eitrem (1941) 45 on the account of the growth of human civilization in the form of a list of the gifts of Prometheus in Aeschylus, *Prometheus Vinctus* 476–506. If, as he argues, the arts of medicine and prophecy in this list do not constitute magic the passage is more generally relevant as an account of power being criminally wrested from the gods in the development of human knowledge.

[134] Compare these lines, *nec prius imposuit rebus finemque modumque | quam caelum ascendit ratio* (*Astronomica* 1.96–7), to the concluding section of the first Argonautic Ode (*Medea* 364 f.).

Images of a Flawed Technical Genesis 161

their loved ones even as they are saving them.[135] As in *Medea* personal relationships are extended to a global scale. Megara, who corresponds most naturally to Eurydice, calls on Hercules to return from the underworld as the saviour of everything which time has stolen:

> et quidquid avida tot per annorum gradus
> abscondit aetas redde et oblitos sui
> lucisque pavidos ante te populos age.
> (*Hercules Furens* 291–3)

(restore all that greedy time has hidden away through so many passing years, and drive out before you the self-forgetting throngs that fear the light.)

Though Megara mentions herself (298) and singles out her brothers and father from among the dead to be led back to the world above (303–5), she closes her speech in a similarly totalizing vein:

> aut omnis tuo
> defende reditu sospes aut omnes trahe.—
> trahes nec ullus eriget fractos deus.   (306–8)

(Either return safely and defend us all, or drag us all down.—You *will* drag us down, no god will rebuild our broken lives.)

Hercules' violence is recognized by Juno and Megara alike[136] and his failure is the failure of a political Orpheus as it is of a political Phaethon. The tragedy ends with Amphitryon and Theseus urging Hercules to abandon the violence of the grand stage and to live for his father alone (1246–57). In this respect gentler, more private Orpheus is a critical commentary on Herculean *virtus*.[137]

As Orpheus' poetry is contrasted with Hercules' violence so Hercules' pacification of the underworld is to be contrasted with the softness in Orpheus' parallel exploit:[138]

> quodcumque alluitur solum
> longo Tethyos ambitu,
> Alcidae domuit labor.

---

[135] Fitch (1987) 253–4 and Segal (1983) 234–6 also make these points.
[136] See Fitch (1987) 134–5 and 205 respectively on Juno's and Megara's representations of the catabasis.
[137] So Segal (1983) 236.   [138] So Segal (1983) 235.

> Transvectus vada Tartari
> pacatis redit inferis. (886–90)

(Every tract that is washed by Tethys' long circuit has been tamed by Alcides' toil. He crossed the waters of Tartarus, pacified the underworld, and returned.)

Compare:

> Immites potuit flectere cantibus
> Umbrarum dominos et prece supplici
> Orpheus, Eurydicen dum repetit suam.
> quae silvas et aves saxaque traxerat
> ars, quae praebuerat fluminibus moras,
> ad cuius sonitum constiterant ferae,
> mulcet non solitis vocibus inferos (569–75)

(Orpheus could sway the pitiless rulers of the shades with songs and suppliant prayer, when he sought back his Eurydice. The art that had drawn trees, birds and rocks, that had caused rivers to tarry, at whose sound beasts had stood still, soothes the lower world with unwonted song).

There is indeed an important difference in tone, but one might counter by considering the painful violence of the verb *trahere* used of Orpheus' art in 572 throughout the tragedy. Megara prays, *omnes trahe* (drag us all down [to destruction] 307) and, with the recollection of Phaethon's death,[139] there is violence also in Hercules' question, *quas trahimus auras* (What air do I breathe? 1142). There is a comparable ambivalence in Medea's description of Orpheus:

> munus est Orpheus meum,
> qui saxa cantu *mulcet* et silvas *trahit*. (*Medea* 228–9)

(My gift is Orpheus, who charms rocks and draws forests with his song)

In *Hercules Furens* a major difference between Hercules and Orpheus is the political nature of Hercules' ambitions. Hercules aims to dominate the globe, destroys the tyrant Lycus, and fails as in mad fantasy he makes war on the throne of Olympus. Orpheus has no such imperial designs and this also is a feature of his characterization in Seneca's literary past. In the epyllion of *Georgics* 4 Orpheus and his personal, private loss, is the foil to Aristaeus and the

---

[139] Cf. *Met.* 2.229–30 discussed above, p. 113.

Images of a Flawed Technical Genesis 163

political, social success of the ritual which regenerates the bees.[140] More generally, the pastoral register in Roman literature connotes an opposition to or marginalization from the political sphere.[141] Certainly there is violence in Hercules' imperial ambitions but there is also magnificence in a grand Orpheus for whom all of humanity is Eurydice. To a degree Orpheus functions as a corrective to Hercules' shortcomings. At the end of the play Hercules is indeed obliged to abandon tragic madness and the grand stage where it walks, but the aspirations to sublimity which Longinus praised in the figure of Phaethon are echoed by this political Orpheus.

In her play Medea is both contrasted and identified with Orpheus in a manner which develops further her paradoxical characterization as a creature of both Nature and the *Argo*'s voyage. Orpheus has a leading role again in the first Argonautic Ode, where he is presented in parallel with Tiphys and the *Argo* itself:

> Palluit audax Tiphys et omnes
> labente manu misit habenas,
> Orpheus tacuit torpente lyra
> ipsaque vocem perdidit Argo. (346–9)

(Daring Tiphys grew pale, and dropped all the guide-ropes from his unnerved hand; Orpheus fell silent, his lyre dumbfounded, and the *Argo* herself lost her voice.)

A boat's voyage is in itself a familiar metaphor for the progression of a poem.[142] *Habenae* more usually mean 'reins' and the voyage of this boat thus includes and combines also the self-reflexive figures of chariot-riding and song. The following description of the dangers which *Argo* faced begins with the monstrous Scylla, to whom Medea later compares herself (408 ff.), and concludes with Medea herself, a worse evil than the sea. The other danger mentioned is the Sirens:

> Quid cum Ausonium dirae pestes
> voce canora mare mulcerent,
> cum Pieria resonans cithara

---

[140] The opposition has been variously and subtly phrased but it can surely be agreed that the regeneration of the bees is politically charged and that Aristaeus, not Orpheus, achieves it. See e.g. J. Griffin (1985) 163–82, Morgan (1999) 105–38.
[141] On pastoral poetry see below, p. 266.
[142] See e.g. Pindar, *Nem.* 5.51; Propertius 3.3.22; Horace, *Odes* 4.15.3–4.

164   Images of a Flawed Technical Genesis

> Thracius Orpheus
> solitam cantu retinere rates
> paene coegit Sirena sequi?   (355–60)

(What of the time the Ausonian sea was calmed by the melodious voices of those dread dangers, when with answering music from his Pierian lyre Thracian Orpheus almost compelled the Sirens to follow?)

Like Medea and Scylla, the Siren[143] is a female hazard from the sea. The Argonauts triumph over these bestial creatures as Orpheus' voice asserts itself over the monstrous barking of Scylla and the Siren song. The song of *dirae pestes* one would expect to be hellish, but here it softens the sea with melodious voice. The contrast between the melodious voice and the destructive nature of these monsters is the defining characteristic of the Sirens, and Seneca is following Ovid in describing their voice as *canora*.[144] Worthy of note only is that the Natural hazard resembles Orpheus. The general similarity is pointed more closely by Medea's description of Orpheus, *qui saxa cantu* mulcet (who *charms* rocks with his song 229). The Siren, the monster from the sea, is an artist like Orpheus.[145]

In an unwitting allusion to Medea's departure at the end of the tragedy Creon had directly termed her a monster, but one in a chariot:[146]

> Vade veloci via
> monstrumque saevum horribile iamdudum *avehe*.   (190–1)

(Depart with haste, and remove at long last a savage and fearful horror.)

Neatly here and in her alter ego the Siren Medea is represented as a monstrous version of the familiar images of artistic creativity.

---

[143] The singular of 360 may be used collectively (so Costa (1973) 106) but the effect is to create a neater parallel with Medea.

[144] See Ovid, *Ars Amatoria* 3.311.

[145] Biondi (1984) 126 notes the parallelism and that *mulcere* is typical of Orpheus (see Virgil, *Georgics* 4.510), but insists on a black and white distinction between magic and art: *Ma la Sirene mulcent con la magia, Orfeo con l'ars: la suavitas mortifera e malefica delle prime cederà, nella rappresentazione seguente, a quella vitale e benefica del poeta*. On the close association of Fury and Siren in ancient literary criticism see Belfiore (1992) 19 ff.

[146] Of Medea at the end of the tragedy, *qua veheris* 1027. *Avehe* here suggests 'taking away by vehicle or riding animal' rather than simply 'removing'. It is not an odd word for Creon to use but has a resonance because Medea is famous for riding out of Corinth in a chariot drawn by dragons.

Natural vengeance, embodied by Medea, violently surpasses Phaethon, Orpheus, and the Argonauts. Medea's art is not essentially any more destructive than Orpheus' and the Argonauts'. As Orpheus charmed the Siren and traditionally charms animals so Medea charmed the dragon and the fire-breathing bulls and asks for Jason's pity on these grounds, *per victa monstra* (by the monsters I overcame 479). Medea's power over the rhythm of Nature is turned to violence in her ritual, but her magical agriculture and winter harvest (761) is destructive only in that it reorders the world to her own purposes. The confusion of natural law is a crime, but it is a distinctively Argonautic crime. The art of Tiphys, who wrote new laws for the winds (320), and Medea is described in very similar terms:

> Bene dissaepti foedera mundi
> traxit in unum Thessala pinus
> iussitque pati verbera pontum
> partemque metus fieri nostri
> mare sepositum   (335–9)

(The covenants of this well-separated world were dragged together by Thessaly's pinewood boat, which bade the deep suffer lashes, and bade the sea, once alien, become part of our fears.)

Compare:

> pariterque mundus lege confusa aetheris
> et solem et astra vidit et vetitum mare
> tetigistis, ursae.   (757–9)

(With the laws of heaven confounded, the world has seen both sun and stars together, and the Bears have touched the forbidden sea.)

In the second Argonautic Ode the Argonauts atone for trespass on the rights of the deep (*ponti iura* 614–15). The form of their various penalties shows the impotence of their art against the vengeance of Nature.[147] As for Orpheus, 'Orpheus endured sparagmos by the women of Thrace (*sparsus* 630 :: *sparsit* 601): traces again towards poor Absyrtus, strewn piecemeal across the flood by Medea, the crazed Maenad of the play (382 f., 849 f.)...'.[148] Medea will sacrifice her first child to Absyrtus (969–71) and the myth of Orpheus, like that of Meleager and Althaea (644–6), also anticipates the forthcoming infanticide. With the repetition

[147] So Lawall (1979) 425.   [148] Henderson (1983) 104.

typical of a Fury's vengeance Orpheus' death foreshadows a future crime and also recalls the voyage which tolerated murder in its pursuit of gold from abroad.[149] Orpheus conquered the Siren and is conquered in turn by a greater singer.

Atreus in *Thyestes* is determined to surpass his own criminal past and the world's. Medea is similarly concerned to imitate and exceed the crimes of her youth[150] and she parades her wickedness as he does. From this perspective the myth of the monster whose arts surpass the Siren's conqueror suggests an endless narrative of deliberate criminality and successive transgression. Morally simple, Medea recalls Orpheus, Phaethon, and the myths which celebrate human aspirations to divinity only to negate and crush them. These are the 'black arts' of Segal's anti-Orpheus and imitation as mockery. As in *Hercules Furens*, however, the images of boundary-breaking are not uniformly criminal.

The final section of the first Argonautic Ode closes to speak from a present in which any little boat can sail wherever it wants:[151]

> Nunc iam cessit pontus et omnes
> patitur leges: non Palladia compacta manu
> regum referens inclita remos
> quaeritur Argo—
> quaelibet altum cumba pererrat   (364–8)

(These days the sea has yielded, and endures all laws. No need of a boat framed by Pallas, bringing home princely rowers, a famous *Argo*: any little rowboat wanders over the deep.)

The *Argo*'s achievements are surpassed, the heroic voyage now a commonplace. The imperial rhetoric of the sea forced to submit to new laws is developed further in the following lines:

> Terminus omnis motus et urbes
> muros terra posuere nova,

---

[149] Every Argonaut is a *raptor externi...auri* (613) in this ode. On the corruption of the voyage of discovery cf. Seneca, *Naturales Quaestiones* 5.18; Propertius 3.4.5; Horace, *Odes* 3.1.6. Cf. also turning back the sea and the pursuit of luxury in *Thyestes* 459 f. and Walter (1975) 100–2.

[150] See especially 40–55 and 126–34. On the criminal aesthetic of surpassing one's models in Seneca, Lucan, and Statius see Seidensticker (1985) 132.

[151] One may speak bluntly of anachronism here (as Kapnukajas (1930) 121) or of a Roman colouring which speaks more obviously to Seneca's time than to that of the mythological chorus (as Costa (1973) 106 or Hadas (1939) 229). In light of the strain on the dramatic illusion *Nunc iam* (364) is a significant phrase.

Images of a Flawed Technical Genesis 167

> nil qua fuerat sede reliquit
>   pervius orbis:
> Indus gelidum potat Araxen,
> Albin Persae Rhenumque bibunt—
> venient annis saecula seris,
> quibus Oceanus vincula rerum
> laxet et ingens pateat tellus
> Tethysque novos detegat orbes
> nec sit terris ultima Thule.   (369–79)

(All boundaries are removed, and cities have established their walls in new lands. Nothing is left where it once had place by a world opened to access. The Indian drinks the cold Araxes, Persians the Albis and the Rhine. There will come an epoch late in time when Ocean will loosen the bonds of the world and the earth lie open in its vastness, when Tethys will disclose new worlds and Thule not be the farthest of lands.)

As commonly in Senecan tragedy the boundaries of the world are magnified to a Roman imperial scale: the soldiers of Oedipus' Thebes survived Arabs and Parthians and furthest India only to die of the domestic plague (*Oedipus* 110–23), Diana's *regnum* stretches from the frozen Ister to the Sarmatian deserts (*Phaedra* 54–72).[152] For this Argonautic ode on the end of the Golden Age a relevantly similar passage is Tityrus' *adynaton* fron *Eclogues* 1:[153]

> ante pererratis amborum finibus exsul
> aut Ararim Parthus bibet aut Germania Tigrim,
> quam nostro illius labatur pectore vultus.
>   (Virgil, *Eclogues* 1. 61–3)

(Sooner in exile, wandering through each other's land, will Parthian drink the Arar, or Germany the Tigris, than from our memory will his face ever fade.)

The loss of Tityrus' pastoral innocence is evident as his imagination takes on a Roman imperial cast. As Biondi notes,[154] the promise *venient annis saecula seris*... not only resembles but surpasses Jupiter's prophecy for the Romans in *Aeneid* 1.283 f. (*veniet lustris labentibus aetas*... (as the ages slip past a time will come...)). Virgil's vision is of a bounded empire—*imperium Oceano, famam qui terminet astris* (who will bound his empire

---

[152] See Steele (1922) 27–30 and Tarrant (1995) 229 on Seneca's Roman 'sense of the world as a geopolitical entity'.
[153] Biondi (1984) 134 suggests the parallel.   [154] Biondi (1984) 136.

with the Ocean and his fame with the stars *Aeneid* 1.287), Seneca's of a world in which every boundary is removed (*terminus omnis motus* 369, *nec sit terris ultima Thule* 379) and the chains of the universe are loosed (*Oceanus vincula rerum | laxet* 376–7).

The conflict of the *Aeneid* is re-staged as the fury of Juno and Dido, reborn in Medea and now victorious, punishes the imperial Argonauts. This is the familiar, Silver, anti-*Aeneid*, but it is not the only voice. Medea's criminal emulation of the past is balanced by the ambivalence of the Argonauts with whom she is closely associated. They also defy Virgilian restraint and surpass the *Aeneid*'s image of Roman power but in a different spirit. Words failed Orpheus and the *Argo* at the Symplegades (348) but in the imperial present of the ode's final section such terrors do not deter even a rowing boat. Certainly this hubris will be punished and in the manner feared for the empire in Roman moralism and historiography.[155] The globe-conquering enterprise motivated by luxury is vulnerable, and symbolically Creusa is seduced by the lure of gold which destroys all rulers.[156] Medea, a foreign import and a woman, is the agent of destruction. However, even as the tragedy follows this inevitable trajectory of decline and even as the national epic is inverted in Medea's victory, there is celebration of the flawed sublimity of an empire which refuses to observe Virgilian and Augustan boundaries.

As in *Hercules Furens* different perspectives of transgression are offered; the moral darkness of crime surpassing crime is answered by the ambivalent hubris of a political Phaethon. In that tragedy the perspectives collide as Juno finds the inspiration for her madness in an imitation of Herculean *virtus*. In the collision of perspectives the drama asks whether such imitation is a corrosive misrepresentation or a revealing critique. *Medea* avoids a simple opposition between nature and artifice to create a similar collision of perspectives. The figure of Orpheus, mediating the polarities of Golden Age innocence and post-lapsarian transgression, is extravagantly destabilized and surpassed by the fury of Medea and by the

---

[155] See e.g. Livy, *Pref.* 9–12 on Rome's moral collapse through the wealth and luxury which the empire won with its foreign conquests; Sallust, *Jugurtha* 4, 5–9, *Catiline* 5.8–13.5; Juvenal, *Satires* 3.60–184 on foreign cultural invasion and luxury.

[156] CHORUS. *Qua fraude capti?* NUNTIUS. *Qua solent reges capi: | donis* (881–2).

proud arts of an imperial Roman present. Through engagement with the *Aeneid* and through the meta-literary emblems of Phaethon, Orpheus, and the Fury there is also a literary self-consciousness constructed from the opposing visions of Orpheus surpassed. Here and in *Hercules Furens* the poetics of excess and of emulation resist a narrow characterization as criminal. The boundary separating a Fury from a Phaethon or magic from art is fragile and Medea resembles the victims she destroys. The myth of infanticide, whether literal or translated to the cosmic and imperial stage, is essentially self-destructive.

Medea's anger, representing the anger of Nature, is expressed throughout the tragedy as the anger of fire and flood. Seneca's account of the end of the world which closes *Naturales Quaestiones* 3 is an interesting point of comparison for its characterization of Nature. Seneca writes that it is the nature of the sea to purge itself of anything unclean (3.26.7). The appearance of something like excrement (*fimo quiddam simile*) on the shore of Messana lies behind the story that the cattle of the Sun were stabled there. The next example of the sea purging itself is corpses, flotsam, and other remains of shipwrecks cast up on the shore. This reminds Seneca to discuss the cataclysm: *Sed monet me locus ut quaeram, cum fatalis dies diluvii venerit, quemadmodum magna pars terrarum undis obruatur* (But this subject reminds me to wonder, when the fated day of the flood comes, how a great part of the earth will be covered over by water 3.27.1). The drowned bodies and the image of a huge shipwreck are clearly in his mind: when the waves of the flood break city walls he describes the citizens as uncertain whether to complain about a collapse or a shipwreck (*ruinam an naufragium quereretur incertos* 3.27.7). However, the reason for the flood is that humanity needs to be created afresh, and the examples of the sea purging itself of refuse, human and otherwise, are to the point. One might expect the moralist who spent the final two chapters of the first book on comets and rainbows discussing depraved uses of mirrors (1.16–17) to attack at length the vices which made the flood necessary, but there is in fact very little mention of vice.[157]

---

[157] The only people represented are those cut off by the rising waters. They are described as stupefied by the magnitude of the disaster (3.27.11–12).

Seneca quotes several times (3.27.13–14; 3.28.2) from Ovid's description of the cataclysm which follows the degeneration of the Ages in *Metamorphoses* 1 and closes the book with the bleak statement that the innocence of the new world will not last,[158] but offers little detail. The topos of humanity becoming increasingly sophisticated and increasingly corrupt is not entirely avoided: when avarice drives us to dig mines water puts an end to our digging (3.30.3) in a small version of the cataclysm to come. Generally, human degeneration is elevated to more abstract terms as the world is personified in metaphors of decay and senescence. The water-logged earth rots. Like an ulcer it infects any land it touches until the soil sloughs away to expose gaping rock beneath (3.29.6–7). As grey hair is already determined for a child not yet born, so the fate of the world-body was fixed at its birth (3.29.2–3). In a passage with particular resonance for Medea:

Nihil difficile naturae est, utique ubi in finem sui properat... Quam longo tempore opus est ut conceptus ad puerperium perduret infans; quantis laboribus tener educatur; quam diligenti nutrimento obnoxium novissime corpus adolescit! At quam nullo negotio solvitur! Urbes constituit aetas, hora dissolvit; momento fit cinis, diu silva; magna tutela stant ac vigent omnia, cito ac repente dissiliunt. (3.27.2)

(Nothing is difficult for Nature, especially when she hurries to her own destruction... How long a time is needed so that a child, once conceived, may come to be born; what efforts that the tender infant be reared. How with careful feeding the vulnerable body finally grows up! But how with no effort it is all undone! It takes an age to establish cities, an hour to destroy them. A forest grows for a long time, becomes ashes in a moment. Great safeguards may exist and all things may be flourishing, but quickly and suddenly they fall apart.)

Nothing is difficult for Nature when she hurries to her own destruction because the universe is so delicately balanced that any disturbance is fatal (3.27.3; 3.30.5). Humanity and the earth will drown in the flood,[159] and as the waters spread over the globe myths, names, and Nature's own divisions are destroyed:

---

[158] *Cito nequitia subrepit. Virtus difficilis inventu est, rectorem ducemque desiderat; etiam sine magistro vitia discuntur* (N.Q. 3.30.8).

[159] In a line which recalls Lucan's sentiments (*Bellum Civile* 7.617–19) Seneca rebukes Ovid for his childish description of swimming animals (*Met.* 1.304) and says, *Scies quid deceat, si cogitaveris orbem terrarum natare* (3.27.15). For Lucan's use of Ovid's cataclysm see *Bellum Civile* 5.79 ff.

Images of a Flawed Technical Genesis   171

Nihil erunt Adria, nihil Siculi aequoris fauces, nihil Charybdis, nihil Scylla; omnes novum mare fabulas obruet...
 Peribunt tot nomina, Caspium et Rubrum mare, Ambracii et Cretici sinus, Propontis et Pontus; peribit omne discrimen; confundetur quicquid in suas partes natura digessit. (3.29.7–8)

(There will be no Adriatic, no strait of the Sicilian sea, no Charybdis, no Scylla; a new sea will wash away all the myths... So many names will die, the Caspian and the Red Sea, the Ambracian and Cretan Gulf, the Propontis and Pontus; all distinctions will die; whatever Nature separated into its own divisions will be confused)

In these descriptions Nature's anger is explicitly self-destructive (*in finem sui* 3.27.2) and no clear distinction is made between artificial and natural creations. In the first passage her destruction of cities is implicitly likened to the death of a child, and in the second the artificial order of myths (*fabulae*) and names (*nomina*) perishes in a common disaster with the natural order. Sometimes, in keeping with the harsh introductory image of the sea purifying itself of waste, Nature appears as a calculating and alien destroyer:

Ubi non umorem natura disposuit, ut undique nos, cum voluisset, aggredi posset? (3.30.3)
(Where has Nature not put water so that when she wants she can attack us from all sides?)

The waves we see running onto the shore are already practising (*se exercent*) so that when they have to stir themselves to take over the earth it will not seem unfamiliar and difficult (3.30.1–2). But more often it is her child and her own body which die together with the names and the myths.

4
Meta-Theatre and Self-Consciousness

SENECAN tragedy is written as drama. Whether or not the plays were staged they have the literary form of theatrical events. Representations in the tragedies of theatres and spectators are therefore powerful vehicles of self-consciousness inasmuch as they offer images of the production and reception of specifically dramatic literature. In a similar way as the tragic chorus, traditionally as much spectator as actor, offers a model of audience response so representations of spectacles and spectators are formal devices through which actual readers and spectators are made to reflect upon their response to the dramatic events.[1] In discussion of metaphors of tragic madness above I contrasted the complexity of *Hercules Furens* with the more single-minded *Thyestes*. In *Hercules Furens* the myths of the Golden Age and of Phaethon's chariot-ride are presented as rival images of the criminal passion which drives the tragedy. Similar variety is evident in Seneca's representation of spectacles and spectators. Where *Agamemnon* and *Thyestes* show a common trajectory in the development of a sadistic spectatorship, *Troades* apparently reverses this trajectory, as initially savage spectators are moved to tears of pity by the executions of Astyanax and Polyxena. This tragedy differs from *Agamemnon* and *Thyestes* not by exchanging cruelty for pity, a simple reversal, but by representing the experience of viewing as varied. Through complex and contradictory representations of the tragic spectacle *Troades* reflects on the moral impact of violent images.

One of the most dangerous and powerful effects of poetry in ancient literary criticism is its ability to transport the audience into an illusory world where it sympathizes or even identifies with a

---

[1] When a tragic event is narrated—as in a messenger speech—or a theatrical event is inscribed within a drama the chorus typically becomes more spectator than actor and models audience response. See Nuttall (1996) 27 on *Samson Agonistes*.

character. Whether the audience is so transported as to become another person for a few moments, as Plato seems to suggest in the *Ion*, or whether it shares in the suffering of a character without the simultaneous extinction of its own self-identity,[2] the audience is drawn into an illusory world where it responds with an intensity of emotion which would be more appropriate to a real world and to real events. Seneca resists the total assimilation which Plato fears: texts and spectacles produce not passions (*adfectus*) but *principia proludentia adfectibus* (first beginnings, rehearsing for passions *De Ira* 2.2.6), an audience at a gladiatorial show experiences not anger but *quasi ira sicut puerorum* (a quasi-anger like that of children *De Ira* 1.2.5). These proto-passions are nevertheless significant: as he argues in *Epistles* 7, attending the games is not simply a waste of time but actually damaging. The need for some degree of critical detachment by the audience is a common concern in criticism of drama. Whatever Brecht's reservations about the reality of critical detachment in a viewer of classical Greek theatre, Aristotle requires and expects a viewer not to be lost in the dramatic illusion.[3] Nussbaum argues that Stoic acceptance of poetry is dependent on the reader or audience resisting such identification.[4] The inscription of an audience in a drama is a representation of an act of reception and Senecan tragedy offers a variety of different responses to the same events. If the formal structure of Senecan tragedy obstructs simple identification it does not offer any single response as authoritative.

The final act of *Troades* is explicitly likened to a theatrical event and the inscribed audience comprises rival factions, Greeks and Trojans. Astyanax and Polyxena do not die on stage, 'objectively' as it were, but in a speech delivered to Andromache and the Trojan women by a messenger: the inscribed, plural audience is itself framed. There is a resolution of this diffuse, polyphonic

---

[2] Plato, *Ion* 535b1–536d3; cf. Halliwell (1986) 173–8 and 195 on the cognitive aspect of the emotions experienced by an Aristotelian audience.

[3] See e.g. Brecht (1964) 136 ff. arguing that an actor should, by a variety of alienating tactics, not merely disrupt the audience's tendency to assimilate itself to a dramatic character but offer a model of critical practice. For a discussion of Aristotle see Belfiore (1992) 238 ff.

[4] Nussbaum (1993) in fact distinguishes two opposing Stoic views. Seneca, she argues, belongs in the camp of those for whom critical detachment in an audience is an achievable ideal (see esp. 136–49). What is controversial here is not so much the ideal (that the reader/viewer resist identification) as the Stoics' confidence that it could be achieved.

representation: the messenger sides with his Trojan audience, and the Greeks and the Trojans in the inscribed audience end the ritual responding as a single people. This unanimity of response is belied by the ambivalence both of the joy which Andromache and the messenger find in recounting the painful tale, and of the curiously trivial yet undoubtedly tragic sensibilities which inspire the Greek audience to weep for Astyanax's death and then to turn to watch Polyxena's. Despite its apparent resolution into a single voice, *Troades* offers no simple model of the tragic experience.

The opposition most marked in representations of spectating in Senecan tragedy is that between the power of a sadistic voyeur and the impotence of a victim forced to watch.[5] Spectating is not a distinct activity of the audience but an integral part of the dramatic action and part too of the actors' performance. Atreus and Medea particularly are spectators of their own tragedies and insist that their victims be spectators too. Without a spectator to endure the pain or revel in it there is no tragedy, and spectators of whatever kind are participants in the tragic action. The important distinctions are not between spectators and actors but between those whose desires are played out on the tragic stage and those whose eyes and minds are damaged by events which they are powerless to change.

The representation of spectating in Senecan tragedy can be discussed both as an aspect of the tragic action, as an expression of the power or vulnerability of actors and audience, and more narrowly as a model of audience reception. This narrower discussion corresponds more closely to a traditional concern of ancient literary criticism: how (if at all) does mimetic art enforce a particular interpretation of itself on its audience? The models of audience response in Senecan tragedy are not unitary; the metatheatrical consciousness is in dialogue, but we need not assume therefore that the dialogue is entirely open and undirected. First, the activity of the real audience may more closely resemble one group of inscribed viewers than another. This is particularly important in discussion of irony and allusion: when the audience recognizes or participates in the production of a literary effect it has ceased to be an impartial observer. Second, the sequence of

[5] Cf. Barton (1993) 91–8 on 'the paradox of the eye'.

models of audience response constitutes a narrative of reception. There is no common trajectory in the 'reception narratives' of Senecan tragedy and I shall contrast those of *Agammenon* and *Thyestes* with that of *Troades*. Before doing so I want to consider the blurring of the boundary between actor and spectator, the representation of spectating as an integral part of the tragic action and of the construction of power.

1. VIEWING, ACTING, POWER

Seneca's interest in the power of the gaze is not a dramatic or a Roman peculiarity. Atreus' most obvious models are Tereus and Procne of Ovid's *Metamorphoses*, who are not (at least immediately) dramatic figures. From the Greek tragic stage one may usefully compare Pentheus, who views the Bacchants from the safety of a tall tree before becoming the heart of the tragic spectacle.[6] Most memorably the investigating and commanding Oedipus becomes the blind object of his own search. In both cases the reversal in which the investigator becomes the investigated is accompanied by a loss of power. Pentheus and Oedipus, who in the course of their search threaten their opponents with imprisonment and death, end their tragedies as blind, lacerated flesh.[7] The collapse of their royal authority coincides with the discovery that the real controlling powers in their dramas are a Fate which would be cruel if it were comprehensible or a god no less alien and unaccountable. Precisely because the directors of these tragedies are beyond human intelligibility the representation of viewing in the tragedies is more uniform. Although Agave offers her gory trophy for public display she is not permitted to take pleasure in the spectacle for what it is. To see truly is to recognize a script of strange horror, to be overwhelmed and damaged.

In Seneca's version of the Oedipus myth the process of discovery anticipates the violence to the eye which will close the tragedy.

---

[6] For this experience as modelling reader response see Lada (1993) 121–2 on Euripides, *Bacchae* 912–16.

[7] Padel (1992) 63 writes of Sophocles' Oedipus' self-blinding, 'He talks of his act as defense against invasion, against painful emotion and perception which would come at him through his eyes.' Oedipus threatens Creon with death (*Oedipus Tyrannus* 623) and ends the play emphatically as the object of the chorus's gaze (see especially 1297–1306).

Manto, acting for blind Tiresias and ultimately Oedipus, digs through the flesh of a sacrifice to find an unnatural foetus which recoils against the investigators and tries to gore the investigating priests:

> natura versa est; nulla lex utero manet.
> *Scrutemur* unde tantus hic extis rigor.
> quod hoc nefas? conceptus innuptae bovis,
> nec more solito positus alieno in loco,
> implet parentem; membra cum gemitu movet,
> rigore tremulo debiles artus micant;
> infecit atras lividus fibras cruor
> temptantque turpes mobilem trunci gradum,
> et inane surgit corpus ac sacros petit
> cornu ministros; viscera effugiunt manum.
> (*Oedipus* 371–80)

(Nature is inverted, no lawfulness remains in the womb. *I must examine* what causes such stiffness in the innards. What is this monstrosity? A foetus in an unmated heifer! And not positioned as usual, but filling its mother in an unnatural place. It groans as it moves; its weak limbs quiver, stiff and trembling. Livid blood has stained the dark organs; the disfigured torsos make vigorous attempts to walk; one of the gaping bodies rises and attacks the priests with its horns; the entrails escape from my hands.)

When Oedipus hears the final truth he searches more personally, digging through his eyes and into the empty hollows beyond:

> *scrutatur* avidus manibus uncis lumina,
> radice ab ima funditus vulsos simul
> evolvit orbes; haeret in vacuo manus
> et fixa penitus unguibus lacerat cavos
> alte recessus luminum et inanes sinus
> (*Oedipus* 965–9)

(With hooked hands he greedily *probed* his eyes, and from their base, from their very roots he wrenched the eyeballs and let them roll out together. His hands stayed embedded in the cavities, their nails tearing deeply into the hollow recesses of his eyes, those empty sockets).

In this myth where the author of the tragic crime is unknowing and where the minor characters echo his fears and reservations and later suffer with him[8] the representation of viewing varies little: to

---

[8] Seneca's Oedipus is from the start a broken man: *cuncta expavesco meque non credo mihi* (*Oedipus* 27). Creon and Tiresias both fear to pursue the investigation

see and to know the tragic act is not to control it but to recognize the control of another power and to suffer pain in the recognition. If that 'other' is a foundation on which to construct a distinct, non-rational perspective,[9] it is radically different. Certainly it does not share the mundane values or calculations of those who suffer.

The myth of Seneca's other Theban play, *Phoenissae*, depends on the memory of the past: it is presumed (and again this is pointed in Seneca's version of the myth) that the new crime and the experience of viewing it will be modelled on the crime and experience of Oedipus. Oedipus introduces the tragedy of the strife between his sons still haunted by the ghost of Laius:

> sanguineum gerens
> insigne regni Laius rapti furit;
> en ecce, inanes manibus infestis petit
> foditque vultus. nata, genitorem vides?
> ego video.
>
> (*Phoenissae* 40–4)

(Laius rages, bearing the bloodied symbol of his stolen kingship; see, he attacks my empty eyes and claws at them with his malevolent hands. Daughter, can you see my father? I can see him!)

Oedipus spurs his children on to civil war but does not anticipate it with pleasure or represent himself as a voyeuristic participant in the forthcoming crime:

---

and are shocked by its results (351–2, 582 ff.). The chorus sees itself in Oedipus and advises the audience to do likewise: *Fatis agimur: cedite fatis* (980); *quidquid patimur mortale genus, | quidquid facimus venit ex alto* (983–4).

[9] For such an interpretation see Schiesaro (1997*b*) 90–8 on the irrational insights of chthonic poetry in *Oedipus*. 'Poetry invokes the Erinyes, the new Muses of this poetry, but also *the sources of a deeper knowledge*, a knowledge which the proud rationality of Oedipus had not been able to reach' (p. 96, my emphasis). Cf. Griswold (1986) 106 on Plato, *Phaedrus* 246a6–b4, the flight of the inspired mind and revelation beyond *dianoia*. The Furies are central in Schiesaro's dualistic model: as the Furies have their own distinct realm, so they have their own distinct knowledge. Freud is directly influential here: like many Senecan tragedies *The Interpretation of Dreams* makes a beginning in Virgil's Hell: *Flectere si nequeo superos, Acheronta movebo* (*Aeneid* 7.312). See also the title of Schiesaro (1997*a*): 'Intertestualità e i suoi disagi'. Freud is also indirectly influential on Senecan scholarship more widely through Bloom's (1973) Oedipal model of poetic relationships. For a Lacanian interpretation of a Senecan tragedy see Segal (1986). On tragic 'otherness' see also Segal (1982), Zeitlin (1990*a*), and, more generally, Nuttall (1996) 29–55.

178   *Meta-Theatre and Self-Consciousness*

> nemo me ex his *eruat*
> silvis: latebo *rupis exesae cavo*
> aut saepe densa *corpus abstrusum* tegam.
> hinc aucupabor verba rumoris vagi
> et saeva fratrum bella, quod possum, audiam.
> (*Phoenissae* 358–62)

(Let no one[10] root me out of these woods. I shall lurk in the cave of a hollowed cliff, or shelter in hiding behind dense brush. From here I shall catch at the words of straying rumours, and hear as best I can of the brothers' savage warfare.)

Antigone rightly diagnoses Oedipus as consumed by pain rather than calculating malice: *mitte violentum impetum | doloris* (347–8). The hiding place from which he intends to listen to reports of the civil war are images of his past and of his broken eyes. *Abstrusum* is used once elsewhere in the tragedy, where Oedipus describes himself in the womb:[11]

> aliquis intra viscera
> materna letum praecoquis fati tulit:
> sed numquid et peccavit? *abstrusum*, abditum
> dubiumque an essem sceleris infandi reum
> deus egit.
> (*Phoenissae* 249–53)

(Others have suffered premature death in the mother's womb; but did they do wrong as well? Hidden and unknown, my very existence uncertain, I was tried by a god for an unspeakable crime.)

Cavus is used twice of Oedipus' eyes in *Oedipus*, and the word *eruo* is used five times elsewhere in the Theban plays, in each case either of Oedipus' blinding or an act parallel to it.[12] In her first speech in the tragedy Antigone pledges loyalty to Oedipus, prom-

---

[10] Fitch in his forthcoming Loeb reads *eruet* in 358 and translates accordingly.

[11] On repetition figured as incestuous regression and the present's vulnerability to the past in Seneca's *Oedipus* see Schiesaro (1997a) 86–8.

[12] Apart from its appearance at *Phoenissae* 359 to describe Oedipus' hiding place, *cavus* occurs six times in Senecan tragedy, four times in *Oedipus* (283, 569, 968, 972). At line 283 the word is used of the hollow valley in which Laius is murdered, and at line 569 of the hollow valleys in which blind Chaos bursts open when Tiresias calls up the dead. At lines 968 and 972 it refers to Oedipus' eyes. *Eruo* is used of Oedipus' blinding at *Phoenissae* 179, of a removal of his ears to complete his isolation at *Phoenissae* 229, of Tiresias' excavation of the fates at *Oedipus* 297, of an excavation of the truth at *Oedipus* 827, and finally at *Phoenissae* 555 where Jocasta begs Polynices in the presence of Oedipus not to excise his country and its gods.

ising to follow him wherever he goes, but urges him not to give himself up to despair:

> Sed flecte mentem, pectus antiquum advoca
> victasque magno robore aerumnas doma;
> resiste: tantis in malis vinci mori est.
> *(Phoenissae* 77–9)

(But change your thinking, summon up your courage of old, and vanquish your troubles with sturdy resolve. Fight back; amid such evils, to die is a defeat.)

The landscape of his despair, Mt Cithaeron, she describes as a spectator, weeping and crying out:

> hic alta rupes arduo surgit iugo
> *spectatque* longe spatia subiecti maris:
> vis hanc petamus? nudus hic pendet silex,
> hic scissa tellus faucibus ruptis hiat:
> vis hanc petamus? hic rapax torrens cadit
> partesque lapsi montis exesas rotat:
> in hunc ruamus?
> *(Phoenissae* 67–73)

(Here a high crag rises to a lofty peak, looking far out over the reaches of the sea beneath it: do you want us to make for that? Here a bare rock is poised, here the rent earth yawns open in a broken chasm: do you want us to make for that? Here a sweeping torrent falls, and whirls around eroded fragments [literally, 'eaten-out parts'] of a fallen hillside: should we plunge into that?)

This is the landscape which Oedipus recalls as he awaits his sons' civil war (358–62, quoted above). He demands not to be uprooted (*nemo me...eruat* 358) from his hiding place in the socket of the weeping mountain (359 taken with 72). Oedipus introduced himself as still being lacerated by the vengeful nails of his father (40–4, quoted above) and here even as he hopes for the destruction of his children he is reduced by his own characterization to a single suffering eye.

Jocasta tries to avert the tragedy which Oedipus encourages by threatening Polynices with the vision of evil. That Thebes and his family have been forced to see the civil war he has brought against the city is the major part of the crime already enacted: *magna pars sceleris tamen | peracta est: vidit...vidit...vidit...genetrixque vidi: nam pater debet sibi quod ista non spectavit* (542–53). She paints a picture of the sack of Thebes and asks whether he can bear to watch it: *potesne cives leto et exitio datos | videre passim?* (579–80). Polynices remains unwilling to be an exile and Jocasta offers further descriptions of the uncertainty of war and of the bodies that will cover the fields. This can only be the work of *Fors caeca* (blind Chance, 632) and Jocasta aims to avert it by insisting that Polynices put the horrors of war before his mind's eye, *Nunc belli mala | propone* (625–6). Ultimately she will be unsuccessful but at least in what survives of *Phoenissae* tragic spectatorship is consistently represented as an experience of pain. Jocasta's hope that the experience will have an apotropaic effect is different from Oedipus' despairing desire to relive the pain of his past, but neither in this play[13] nor in *Oedipus* do we find calculating enjoyment in the vision of crime.

The protagonists of *Medea* and *Thyestes* perceive their revenge as an amplified reflection of the wrong which they have endured. Their victims and also the guarantors of moral order in the universe are forced to observe the revenge and their own inability to prevent it. The revengers judge themselves by their power to produce these effects and to stage a wrong surpassing that which they have suffered. Heaven and Corinth who have both stood by while Jason deserted Medea will be made to watch a crime that will make them tremble:

> quodcumque vidit Phasis aut Pontus nefas
> videbit Isthmos. effera ignota horrida,
> tremenda caelo pariter ac terris mala
> mens intus agitat.   (*Medea* 44–7)

(Every outrage that Phasis or Pontus saw, the Isthmus will see. Savage, unheard-of, horrible things, evils fearful to heaven and earth alike, my mind stirs up within me.)

The revenger's experience is not the opposite of the victim's: it is not primarily a pleasure in the same spectacle which causes the victim pain but a pleasure in the victim's pain at the spectacle. Though the Messenger in *Thyestes* (627–32) and Jason in *Medea*

---

[13] The play is either a bold experiment in dramatic structure or incomplete. See Tarrant (1978) 229–30, who is happy for the poem to represent a new dramatic subgenre. Eteocles in the last (surviving) section (652 ff.) seems to become a tyrant in the pattern of a Lycus or an Atreus. It is certainly possible if the play is incomplete that he could have delighted in the criminal battle with his brother and perhaps found the opportunity to become his own audience.

(1026–7) can scarcely believe that the horrors which they have seen have occurred in their worlds, the intentions of the revengers are transparent. Not only are the crimes plotted before the audience but more importantly they depend on a conventional human response: Atreus responds to Thyestes' grief, *perdideram scelus, | nisi sic doleres* (I would have wasted my crime, if you did not feel pain like this 1097–8). This sentiment is repeated by Medea:

> derat hoc unum mihi,
> spectator iste. nil adhuc facti reor:
> quidquid sine isto fecimus sceleris perit.   (*Medea* 992–4)

(This was the one thing I lacked, this spectator. I think nothing has been done as yet: such crime as I did without him was lost.)

The essential part of the act of revenge becomes not the crime itself but the spectacle of the victim's recognition. Recognition, reversal, and the pity and fear which these events produce in a spectator are the essence of tragedy.[14] Alienated by both their power and their inhumanity the revengers, the authors of the work, stand apart from their creation to revel in the vision of human nature suffering tragic emotion. The conventional human response upon which the revenger preys appears commonly in the following three forms. In the first the viewer is awestruck by the magnitude of the revenger's deed. In the second the victim is harrowed by a vision which he or she is nevertheless constrained to watch. In the third the victim innocently interprets words and events which have a private significance for the revenger. This last, as we will see, is in fact bound up with viewing: the victim who cannot participate effectively in speech is reduced to a passive body.

For Atreus to take satisfactory revenge on Thyestes he must commit an act which posterity will remember (see 192 ff. quoted below). Both Medea and Atreus see themselves as the rivals not only of their personal enemies but of the figures of their literary/ mythological past. Medea has been abandoned by Jason and by Corinth while Atreus has been robbed of his wife and the talisman of royal power (*Thyestes* 220 ff.). Their desire to reassert themselves in the world of the dramatic illusion is paralleled by a desire to reassert themselves in the broader context of their literary/ mythological tradition. Atreus cannot match Medea's awareness

[14] So Aristotle, *Poetics* 1452^a36–$^b1$.

of her own myth, but nevertheless he views himself as performing for a posterity which is as familiar as he is with the myth of Tereus and Procne.[15] Atreus' revenge on Thyestes will be a victory partly because of the personal suffering he will inflict but partly also because he will have produced a spectacle without rival. His rival for the throne will be able only to acknowledge defeat and to wish that he had devised such a crime:

> Age, anime, fac quod nulla posteritas probet,
> sed nulla taceat. aliquod audendum est nefas
> atrox, cruentum, tale quod frater meus
> suum esse mallet—scelera non ulcisceris,
> nisi vincis. et quid esse tam saevum potest
> quod superet illum?
> (*Thyestes* 192–7)

(Come, my spirit, do what no future age will endorse, but none forget. I must dare some fierce bloody outrage, such as my brother would have wished his own. You do not avenge crimes unless you surpass them.— And what could be cruel enough to outdo him?)

The sense of *vincere* (surpass) shifts as Atreus moves easily from his victory of invention and production (195–6) to a more conventional one in which he breaks Thyestes' spirit (196–7). A similar double-meaning can be observed in Tantalus' words in the prologue: *iam nostra subit | e stirpe turba quae suum vincat genus* (Now from my stock there is rising a crew that will outdo their own ancestors 18–19). The most important audience for the revenger is the victim himself. Medea demands Jason specifically as a spectator (992–4 above) and Atreus similarly is content to let the gods flee the crime as long as Thyestes sees it:

> utinam quidem tenere fugientes deos
> possem, et coactos trahere, ut ultricem dapem
> omnes viderent—quod sat est, videat pater.
> (*Thyestes* 893–5)

(Indeed I wish I could hold the fleeing gods, and drag them all under duress to see this feast of revenge. But it is enough that the father see it.)

---

[15] See especially 272–4 on the cannibal banquet as a crime *immane...| sed occupatum*. On the influence of Ovid's account of Tereus and Procne in *Metamorphoses* 6 see below, Sect. 2.

The first variety of response which the revenger looks for in the audience is a public recognition of the magnitude of the crime. Atreus' and Medea's desire that an unwilling audience attend the crime is again a concern with their own power and status. What distinguishes this second variety of audience response from the first is the manner of its engagement. When posterity or even Thyestes cannot keep silent about Atreus' deed it is in a spirit of wonder or awe at the magnitude of the crime and its author. Here, however, the audience is an unwilling observer of the events unfolding before its eyes. The revenger draws satisfaction from the impotence of audience or actor when compared with the authority of the dramatist. The depth of the revulsion of an audience which can neither halt the events nor leave the scene is a tribute to the power of the dramatist. Atreus' wish to detain the gods follows closely from an assertion of his power:

> Aequalis astris gradior et cunctos super
> altum superbo vertice attingens polum.
> nunc decora regni teneo, nunc solium patris.
> (*Thyestes* 885–7)

(Peer of the stars I stride, out-topping all, my proud head reaching to the lofty sky. *Now* I hold the kingdom's glories, *now* my father's throne.)

Those who might challenge his supremacy,[16] the gods and more importantly Thyestes, are forced to witness a drama which appals them. Further, the pain of this recognition and the horror of the crime is expressed in Thyestes' body. Atreus' power over his actor-audience watches his scripted revenge fulfilled in the passive flesh of his victim.

The inequality in the relationship between dramatist and actor is the source of satisfaction even when apparent only to the former. When Jason reveals his love for his children, Medea withdraws briefly from the dialogue to mark his revelation in an aside, *Sic natos amat? | bene est, tenetur, vulneri patuit locus* (Does he love his sons so much? Good, he is caught! The place to wound him is laid bare 549–50). To oversee and direct the dialogue in this way is itself a mark of power. Jason's failure to hear not only Medea's

---

[16] The people of Mycenae lie in subjection before the palace of Pelops: *In arce summa Pelopiae pars est domus | conversa ad Austros, cuius extremum latus | aequale monti crescit atque urbem premit | et contumacem regibus populum suis | habet sub ictu* (*Thyestes* 641–5).

aside but also in an important sense what he himself is saying is to be contrasted with Medea's control of the script. When she returns to dialogue she asks that he forget her angry words:

> et illud voce iam extrema peto,
> ne, si qua noster dubius effudit dolor,
> maneant in animo verba: melioris tibi
> memoria nostri sedeat; haec ira data
> oblitterentur. (*Medea* 553–7)

(And now lastly I make this request, that any words poured out by my distracted pain should not stay in your mind. Let the memory of my better self remain with you, and let these words that yielded to anger be *effaced*.)

Jason has unwittingly betrayed himself in his speech and Medea is determined not to follow suit. She asks that the words which her grief has uttered not remain and that her angry words be effaced or written over to leave a better recollection in his mind. Her attention to a scripted plot distinguishes her from her victim, and her comment, *bene est, tenetur* (550), is recalled in her satisfaction when the action has been completed: *bene est, peractum est* (Good, it is finished 1019). The repetition of such closural phrases is most evident in *Thyestes*. Atreus marks the completion of his crime and the tragedy[17] with the words *nunc parta vera est palma*... | ...*liberos nasci mihi* | *nunc credo, castis nunc fidem reddi toris* (now the true palm is won... Children are born to me, now I believe it; now[18] my bed is faithful and chaste 1097–9).[19] This victory and this apparent closure is paralleled earlier. When Atreus watches Thyestes complete his meal he comments *vota transcendi mea.* | *satur est* (I have surpassed my hopes. He is fed full 912–13): Atreus' knowing victory coincides with the

---

[17] The tragedy does not end with these words of Atreus and closure is deferred in its last line. Thyestes in his last speech promises vengeance to come (*Vindices aderunt dei* 1110). Atreus speaks the last line of the tragedy, *Te puniendum liberis trado tuis*. This is a torment without end (see *nefas | sine exitu* (1041–2) and *[gnatos] Reddam, et tibi illos nullus eripiet dies* (998)). Cf. the last line of T. Kyd, *The Spanish Tragedy*, 'I'll there begin their endless tragedy'—Revenge is the speaker. On closure denied in Seneca's tragedy see also *de fine poenae loqueris; ego poenam volo* (*Thyestes* 246).

[18] Fitch translates *nunc* as 'once more'—'faithful and chaste once more'.

[19] Cf. the repeated *nunc* of *Thyestes* 887 (above) and the repeated *iam* of *Medea* 982: *Iam iam recepi sceptra germanum patrem*.

unwitting and literal satisfaction of Thyestes. Earlier again Atreus concludes a vision of the banquet before his mind's eye, *bene est, abunde est* (This is good, this is ample 279), and in using these words he echoes the Fury's response to the infection of the house of Pelops by the ghost of Tantalus, *Actum est abunde* (It is done, and amply 105). In both plays the earlier statements of satisfaction and closure make the later action of the tragedy appear inevitable and to this extent the earlier statements merely anticipate later events and the pleasure of their satisfaction. Nevertheless there is a separate satisfaction, evident in Atreus' deferral of the revelation, deriving from an exclusive power of interpretation.

Atreus welcomes Thyestes to the royal palace and then excuses himself saying, *ego destinatas victimas superis dabo* (For my part I shall offer the designated victims to the gods above 545). There is a double-meaning here which can only be apprehended by Atreus, the author of a hidden plot. Even if Atreus cannot practically reveal his plan at this early stage, there is no reason but for the pleasure of an exclusive power to interpret for him to speak doubly. In the penultimate act of the tragedy Atreus anticipates Thyestes' moment of recognition and declares, *fructus hic operis mei est* (This is the fruit of my work 906), but in the final act defers that recognition to allow himself the pleasure of seeing his victim's failure to recognize the meaning of his words. He begins Act 5 with a demonstration of this superior verbal dexterity:

> Festum diem, germane, consensu pari
> celebremus: hic est, sceptra qui firmet mea
> solidamque pacis alliget certae fidem.
> *(Thyestes* 970–2)

(My brother, we must celebrate this festival day in mutual harmony. This is the day that will strengthen my sceptre, and lock up solid confidence in reliable peace.)

Atreus is lying; he is not reconciled to his brother. This continued division is marked in his words which depend for their effect on the fact that they can be read in two distinct senses—not *consensu pari* at all. It is a festal day but Thyestes has yet to discover the rite which has made his banquet possible and it will indeed strengthen Atreus' royal power and cancel the breach of *fides* which has undermined it[20] but not in the sense which Thyestes expects. Atreus delights in his superior wit and the private significance of his words.

Thyestes cannot express his horror when he discovers that he has eaten his children: *quae verba sufficient mihi?* (What speech will suffice me? 1037). Atreus, far from being satisfied with a deed which surpasses the limits of language and criminality, responds by rewriting his revenge:

> ex vulnere ipso sanguinem calidum in tua
> defundere ora debui, ut viventium
> biberes cruorem—verba sunt irae data
> dum propero.
> (*Thyestes* 1054–7)

(Straight from the wound I should have poured the hot blood into your mouth, so you could drink their lifeblood while they lived. I have cheated anger in my haste.)

He relives the murders as they were enacted and concludes:

> omnia haec melius pater
> fecisse potuit, cecidit in cassum dolor:
> scidit ore natos impio, sed nesciens,
> sed nescientes.
> (*Thyestes* 1065–8)

(all this the father could have done better. My anger was to no avail. He tore his sons in his sacrilegious mouth, but he did not know it, they did not know it.)

Medea and Atreus both desire unwilling spectators of their crimes, but here Atreus goes one stage further in demanding that Thyestes and his children participate in the drama knowingly and against their will. Elsewhere Atreus imagines the pain of Thyestes' discovery (903–7), but here he dwells only on the details of the sacrifice. Thyestes' pain is essential only as a resistance to be overcome; Atreus' pleasure in this revised version of the drama lies in no small part in his power to enforce his will. The precision of ritual observance when enforced upon an unwilling Thyestes has value as an offence against the gods but also as a mark of Atreus' power over his brother. In the revised tragedy Thyestes'

---

[20] On the breach of *fides* see 220–44 and especially *corrupta coniunx, imperi quassa est fides* (239).

Meta-Theatre and Self-Consciousness 187

every action will indicate and celebrate the *régie* of his political opponent.

It is a mark of the tyrant in Senecan tragedy and elsewhere to define himself by the unwilling obedience of his subjects. Ulysses, the representative of the Greek victors in Act 3 of *Troades*, responds to Andromache's plea for mercy on Astyanax with the words, *Exhibe natum et roga* (Produce your son then and pray, *Troades* 704). She obeys and makes Astyanax enact the formal gestures of supplication:

> Submitte manus dominique pedes
> supplice dextra stratus adora
> nec turpe puta quidquid miseros
> Fortuna iubet.   (*Troades* 708–11)

(Hold out your arms; at your master's feet bow low and do homage with suppliant hand; do not disdain whatever Fortune demands of the wretched.)

Astyanax is made to play the captive (*gere captivum* 715) and to imitate his mother's tears (*matris fletus imitare tuae* 717) while Andromache suggests a sympathetic reception of his silent performance (718–35). Ulysses' replies make it clear that this act could not but be unsuccessful:

> Matris quidem me maeror attonitae movet,
> magis Pelasgae me tamen matres movent
>   (*Troades* 736–7)

(I am certainly moved by the grief of a devastated mother, but more strongly moved by Pelasgian mothers)

> Non hoc Ulixes, sed negat Calchas tibi.   (*Troades* 749)

(Not Ulysses but Calchas refuses you this).

It serves only as a display of submission; the domination of the Greeks is evident in their ability to extort from Astyanax a performance, recognizable as such, in which he erases his ancestry and his identity:

> pone ex animo reges atavos
> magnique senis iura per omnis
> incluta terras, excidat Hector   (*Troades* 712–14)

(Put out of mind your royal ancestors and the great old man famed as a law-giver throughout the world; forget Hector).

Ulysses' motivation in demanding that Andromache ask vainly for the life of her child must be inferred, but other Senecan tyrants are more explicit. In his argument with the *satelles* Atreus defines the tyrant less perfectly realized by Lycus in *Hercules Furens*, Aegisthus in *Agamemnon*, and Creon in *Medea*:[21]

> Maximum hoc regni bonum est,
> quod facta domini cogitur populus sui
> tam ferre quam laudare.
> (*Thyestes* 205–7)

(This is the greatest value of kingship: that the people are compelled to praise as well as endure their master's actions.)

> Laus vera et humili saepe contingit viro,
> non nisi potenti falsa. quod nolunt velint.
> (*Thyestes* 211–12)

(Sincere praise often comes even to a lowly man; false praise comes only to the mighty. They must want what they do not want.)

Thyestes is a tragedy which draws attention to its Romanness, from the boundaries of its world to the imperial palace which dominates it, to the text's allusions to explicitly Roman political poems.[22] The theatricality of imperial Rome, most particularly of Nero's Rome, is so familiar and important a topic that it is difficult to discuss Atreus and not to be drawn into a discussion of the

---

[21] For Lycus see e.g. *sed ille regno pro suo, nos improba | cupidine acti? quaeritur belli exitus, | non causa. sed nunc pereat omnis memoria* (*Hercules Furens* 406–8) and *Qui morte cunctos luere supplicium iubet | nescit tyrannus esse: diversa inroga; | miserum veta perire, felicem iube* (*Hercules Furens* 511–13). For Aegisthus see e.g. ELECTRA. *Concede mortem.* AEGISTHUS. *si recusares, darem: | rudis est tyrannus morte qui poenam exigit.* | ELECTRA. *Mortem aliquid ultra est?* AEGISTHUS. *Vita, si cupias mori* (*Agamemnon* 994–6). For Creon see *Aequum atque iniquum regis imperium feras* (*Medea* 195). Creon, like Jason, is a weak character and quickly abandons (252 ff.) the pose he strikes in 195. Lycus begins by suggesting that right and wrong accommodate themselves to events. His command, *pereat omnis memoria*, hints at the force behind this accommodation, but it is not until Megara and Amphitryon refuse to change their allegiance that Lycus reaches the position from which Atreus starts that power shows itself by depriving others of self-determination; that without subjects there are no kings.

[22] On 'Romanness' in Seneca's tragedies see Steele (1922), Hadas (1939) (though his comparisons with Greek tragedy are unhelpful: Senecan tragedy is 'for entertainment only' and 'played before an audience temperamentally like a movie audience today', where Greek tragedy is played for 'an audience which was intelligently interested', 222), Walter (1975), and Tarrant (1995).

Roman actor-king.[23] In its simplest form the scholarship of imperial theatricality recognizes that art and entertainment have socio-political significance: whether public reality is represented in dramatic form, or whether a mythological tyrant on the stage is interpreted as a reference to real events, or whether theatre audiences are organized in accordance with a particular social model, the show is not an interruption in 'real life' but part of it.[24] More elusive than the integration of artistic spectacle into the broader context of Roman life is a complementary aestheticization of political life. However difficult it is—and not just in ancient literary criticism[25]—to draw distinctions between personal identity and dramatic characterization, it is clearly an article of faith that actors are not Roman citizens and Roman citizens are not actors: *il est essential que le civique et le scénique ne se mêlent pas*.[26] The historiographical and literary-critical traditions' representation of distinctions between actors and citizens, poetry and oratory, illusion and reality as blurred in Julio-Claudian Rome and beyond is commonly interpreted as a reflection of political change, particularly the concentration of power in the hands of one man. In this environment aristocratic competition for honours and power becomes mere performance and servile. Representations of Roman political life as theatrical indicate a public life debased and express the discontent of an elite which could represent itself as politically diminished.

The emperor may be implicated as an actor in this degrading substitute for public life or, more sinisterly, observe from the isolation of his power the performances of his Roman subjects. Seneca (*De Ira* 2.33.3 ff.) records an anecdote about Caligula which closely recalls the tragedy Atreus would have liked to write

---

[23] The term is a nod to Dupont (1985), *L'Acteur-roi*. The bibliography is large and would include Bartsch (1994), K. Coleman (1990), Edwards (1994), Woodman (1993), Boyle (1997) 112–37.

[24] Seneca interprets Atreus' *oderint dum metuant* as an indication that Accius was writing in Sulla's Rome (*De Ira* 1.20.4). On the political significance of the staging of Varius Rufus' *Thyestes* after Actium see Leigh (1996). Tiberius saw himself behind Atreus in Scaurus' tragedy (Dio 58.24.3–5) and Aper rightly refutes Maternus' claim to poetic isolation as inconsistent with his expressed intention and a dangerous fantasy (*Dialogus* 10.5–8). See also Beacham (1999) 58–9, 165, 235. For a survey of scholarship on the Republican *praetexta* as a vehicle of presenting Roman history see Wiseman (1998) 1–16. See Most (1992) 402, Nuttall (1996) 77, and K. Coleman (1990) on real executions, real arena deaths costumed as mythological tableaux.

[25] See Easterling (1990) 84–5.   [26] Dupont (1985) 97. See also Edwards (1994).

for Thyestes. Caligula invited Pastor to dinner on the same day that he had executed one of his sons. Pastor, who knew about the execution, was forced to drink a cup of wine: *perduravit miser non aliter quam si fili sanguinem biberet* (the poor man suffered through it just as if he were drinking his son's blood). Like Thyestes (*Thyestes* 945 ff.) Pastor wore the garlands and perfume of a party-goer, and although Thyestes was a lone diner at his banquet and Pastor was one of a hundred diners, Caligula had Pastor alone secretly watched for his reactions. In order to preserve the life of his other son Pastor masked his feelings and pretended to enjoy the evening. Seneca presents the anecdote as an example of anger controlled and is more concerned with Pastor than with Caligula, but the tyrant's theatrical expression of his power is worthy of comment. Not only does the event recall the mythological banquets of a Thyestes or a Tereus, but Pastor is made to respond to whatever provocations the tragedian-tyrant invents and his pain is to be a private spectacle for the imperial gaze. Since Pastor in fact showed no emotion the messenger speeches to which Caligula listened might appear unsatisfying, but Seneca concludes the anecdote with this justification of the father's actions: *perierat alter filius si carnifici conviva non placuisset* (the other son would have died had the banqueter not pleased the executioner *De Ira* 2.33.6). More important than the aesthetic pleasure of watching the passions of fear and grief war on a human face is Caligula's knowledge that he has made Pastor perform against his will.

In a variant of what is essentially the same anecdote Seneca recounts the story of Harpagus who, having eaten his children at a banquet and been presented with the heads, was asked by the Great King how he had enjoyed the dinner. '*Apud regem*' *inquit*, '*omnis cena iucunda est*' ('At the royal court', he said, 'every dinner is a happy occasion' *De Ira* 3.15.1–2). The story appears in a section on the deeds of the barbarous tyrants of the East, but these episodes of fantastic cruelty move via Alexander the Great to Rome:

Utinam ista saevitia intra peregrina exempla mansisset nec in Romanos mores cum aliis adventiciis vitiis etiam suppliciorum irarumque barbaria transisset! (Seneca, *De Ira* 3.18.1)

(If only that savagery had been restricted to foreign examples and that the barbarity of torture and anger had not crossed over into Roman morality together with other vices from abroad.)

Whereas Pastor saved a son by his performance, Harpagus' words spared him only from being invited to eat the leftovers (*ne ad reliquias invitaretur* (*De Ira* 3.15.2)). Seneca is far from convinced that this display of servility is valuable and suggests suicide.[27] More importantly, he says of the tyrant's table:

Sic estur apud illos, sic bibitur, sic respondetur, funeribus suis adridendum est. (*De Ira* 3.15.3)

(So one eats among them, so one drinks, so one makes reply, one must laugh at the death of one's own.)

The tyrant's pleasure derives not from any entertaining quality in the performance but from the fact that the victim performs at all, that he resigns his self-determination to the directions given by the emperor's script. In a famous counter-example, Britannicus, ordered by Nero to sing at a banquet for the amusement of the audience and his own humiliation, performed a song of exile and drew a sympathetic response from the rest of the audience.[28] Not only did Britannicus deliver a song which Nero had not planned but as a result the emperor lost power over the audience to his improvising actor. Compare the domination of Atreus, Caligula, and the king of Persia, who constitute the sole audience of their dramas. Pastor had a hundred fellow diners but without faces or reactions, no companions are mentioned for Harpagus, and Seneca's Thyestes, isolated by a tragic convention which does not allow a cast of supporting characters, dines for the audience of Atreus alone.

There is a distinction to be made between the pleasure afforded a viewer by a satisfying performance and a tyrant-director's pleasure in imposing a script on actors who resist. Caligula, Atreus, and Medea are viewers of their own dramas and their enjoyment often appears to be a blend of both pleasures.

IASON. Iam perage coeptum facinus, haut ultra precor,
  moramque saltem supplicis dona meis.

---

[27] See also his condemnation of Praexaspes, who praised Cambyses' accuracy in shooting his son, *Dii illum male perdant animo magis quam condicione manicipium* (*De Ira* 3.14.3).
[28] Tacitus, *Annals* 13.15, The song is described as a *carmen, quo evolutum*

MEDEA. Perfruere lento scelere, ne propera, dolor:
meus dies est; tempore accepto utimur.
IASON. Infesta, memet perime.
MEDEA.   Misereri iubes.—
bene est, peractum est.   (*Medea* 1014–19)
(JASON. Now finish the deed you have begun—I make no further prayers—and at least spare me this drawing-out of my punishment. MEDEA. Relish your crime in leisure, my pain, do not hurry. This day is mine, I am using the time I was granted. JASON. Kill *me*, violent woman. MEDEA. You bid me have pity.—Good, it is finished.)

Most noticeable in this short exchange is Medea's pleasure in asserting her power by acting contrary to Jason's wishes: he asks her to end the suspense so she draws it out; he asks her to have mercy so she kills the second child. At the same time she wants to enjoy the crime slowly and to make full use of her day. Medea is remarkable for her familiarity with her own myth. Not only does she speak of becoming Medea in the drama (171, 910) but shortly after the passage quoted she describes her departure in a chariot drawn by dragons as habitual: *coniugem agnoscis tuam? | sic fugere soleo* (Do you recognize your wife? This is how I always escape 1021–2).[29] For such a character her own allotted day, the day which Creon has granted her, suggests also the space of a single day which tragic convention grants for her to make her mark. Medea leaves the stage to become not an Athenian but a god: *patuit in caelum via* (A path has opened to heaven 1022).[30] It is through her achievements in this tragic day that she wins her immortality. Her need to make good use of the allotted day parallels Atreus' emphasis on the success of the event rather than its conclusion: *De fine poenae loqueris; ego poenam volo* (You talk

---

eum sede patria rebusque summis significabatur. See Bartsch (1994) 14, Beacham (1999) 199.

[29] So Boyle (1997) 59. Arguing that 'of course' M. Winterbottom is wrong to see here 'a coy allusion to Seneca's predecessors', Armstrong (1982) 239–40 is very much in the minority. On Seneca's use of *soleo* more generally see Schiesaro (1997a) 79 n. 9.

[30] Jason's closing words, *per alta vade spatia sublime aetheris, | testare nullos esse, qua veheris, deos* (1026–7) give a double meaning to Medea's *patuit in caelum via* (1022). Cf. also *nec in astra lenta veniet ut Bacchus via* (*Hercules Furens* 66) and *in alta mundi spatia sublimis ferar, | petatur aether: astra promittit pater* (*Hercules Furens* 958–9).

Meta-Theatre and Self-Consciousness 193

about punishment's conclusion: I want the punishment *Thyestes* 246). Medea does not in fact spoil her revenge by allowing her grief to run ahead of itself and cut its pleasure short, but her anxiety that she might have wasted her only opportunity is closely echoed by Atreus: *verba sunt irae data | dum propero* (I have cheated anger in my haste *Thyestes* 1056–7).[31]

Medea's pleasure in imposing her will on Jason is enhanced by the awareness that her act will be judged against other criminal performances, but more simply she luxuriates in her slow revenge. Viewing pleasure is interwoven with the pleasure of mastery, and this is nowhere better seen than in Atreus' enjoyment in the shifting colours of Thyestes' face:

> libet videre, capita natorum intuens
> quos det colores, verba qua primus dolor
> effundat aut ut spiritu expulso stupens
> corpus rigescat.
>
> (*Thyestes* 903–6)

(I long to see what colour he turns as he looks on his sons' heads, what words his first torment pours forth, how his body stiffens, breathless with shock)

Although Atreus waits to hear what Thyestes will say, he emphasizes the response of his body. The contrasting characterization here at the end of Act 4 between Thyestes as responsive, passive flesh and Atreus as controlling viewer is particularly noticeable in the final act. Thyestes' body responds to Atreus' criminal banquet before he understands what has happened, and all the while Atreus draws attention to Thyestes' lack of awareness with a series of remarks which he can only misunderstand. The unequal relationship between controlling gaze or discourse and manipulated flesh is appropriate in a tragedy where the victim is represented as a woodland beast to be trapped.[32] Not only does Atreus describe his victim as a wild animal caught in a snare (*Plagis tenetur clausa dispositis fera* (The beast is held fast in the nets I set out 491)), but Thyestes urges himself to run from the royal palace to live an unpolitical life among the animals:

[31] Cf. Medea's passing anxiety, *stulta properavi nimis: | ex paelice utinam liberos hostis meus | aliquos haberet* (*Medea* 919–21).

[32] Hippolytus, victim of Phaedra's predatory irony, is a close parallel for Thyestes. Both are likened to wild animals and both contrast the corruptions of the royal palace with the innocence of the woods and wild beasts. See Ch. 5 below.

>   Repete silvestres fugas
> saltusque densos potius et mixtam feris
> similemque vitam; clarus hic regni nitor
> fulgore non est quod oculos falso auferat.
>   (*Thyestes* 412–15)

(Better hurry back to your forest refuges, to those dense woods and your life among the beasts and comparable to theirs. There is no reason for this bright lustre of kingship to blind your eyes with its false glitter.)

Atreus ends the soliloquy which he began by representing Thyestes as an animal (491) with a description of his dishevelled appearance. Then he greets him with the words, *Fratrem iuvat videre*:

>   aspice, ut multo gravis
> squalore vultus obruat maestos coma,
> quam foeda iacet barba. praestetur fides.
> Fratrem iuvat videre.
>   (*Thyestes* 505–8)

(See how his hair is heavy with grime and shrouds his dismal face, how foul and limp his beard. But good faith must be demonstrated. I am delighted to see my brother.)

The good faith which Atreus offers is false and in this first meeting as in the final act his power over his victim is evident as Thyestes, the object of his gaze, cannot read the irony in his friendly words.

2. VIEWING, GENDER, POWER

A beast, a body without reason and discourse, is a productive figure for an innocent and a victim of irony. Visual objects are likewise productively represented as passive material lacking self-determination and these two modes of Thyestes' victimization sit easily together.[33] Commonly the relationship between controlling gaze or discourse and manipulated flesh is gendered and often also eroticized.[34] In her influential essay on the dominant male gaze

---

[33] Cf. Claudius on Ophelia, 'divided from herself and her fair judgement, | without the which we are pictures, or mere beasts' (*Hamlet* 4.v.85–6).

[34] This topic is perhaps most familiar in Latin literature in elegy. See Greene (1998) 67–92, Wyke's (1994) survey article, and Sharrock (1991) on Ovid's Pygmalion (*Met.* 10). The simple model of domination which I have sketched is one which Wyke herself rightly corrects and balances for the elegiac context. On erotic and animal pursuit see Sourvinou-Inwood (1987) and below, Ch. 5, pp. 273–4.

in cinema Mulvey distinguishes between the scopophilic and the voyeuristic.[35] The scopophilic gaze interrupts the narrative frequently to break down the object of its fascination through close-ups. The voyeuristic gaze observes its object driven though a narrative of punishment and (sometimes) controlled redemption. Hitchcock's *Vertigo* oscillates between the two modes[36] and so too does Seneca's *Thyestes*. Atreus' enjoyment of the shifting colours of Thyestes' face as he is captured in an eternal instant of punishing recognition (903-6, quoted above) is clearly scopophilic yet also the culmination of narrative of revenge. It is, I think, useful to have drawn attention to these different modes of visual victimization, but in what follows I shall use the term 'voyeurism' in a more general sense to embrace both of Mulvey's categories. Mulvey's psychoanalytic approach stresses also the subjugation of woman to a patriarchal order *and its word*.[37] Victimization not only through the gaze but through verbal irony is a prominent feature of the rape narrative which Atreus takes as his model. While this verbal irony is not a literal manifestation of subjugation to the word in the psychoanalytic sense, it is perhaps worth considering as its figurative expression.

Ovid's version of Tereus' rape of Philomela victimizes in both visual and verbal modes. In an irony apparent to narrator, reader, and Tereus, but not to Procne, Philomela, or their father Pandion, Tereus is praised for the urgency with which he pleads with Pandion to allow Philomela to visit her sister: *creditur esse pius laudemque a crimine sumit* (he is thought to be dutiful and wins praise for his crime *Met.* 6.474). Philomela herself adds her entreaties. The gulf of understanding separating the author of the crime from his victims and the pleasure of this irony is then represented in a visual context:

> spectat eam Tereus praecontrectatque videndo
> osculaque et collo circumdata bracchia cernens
> omnia pro stimulis facibusque cibo furoris
> accipit, et quotiens amplectitur illa parentem,
> esse parens vellet
>
> (*Met.* 6.478-82)

(Tereus watches her and by looking already touches her and as he sees her kisses and her arms around her father's neck takes everything as a spur,

---

[35] Mulvey (1989) 18.   [36] Mulvey (1989) 23.   [37] Mulvey (1989) 15.

food and fuel of his madness. And whenever she embraces her father he wishes that he were her father).

Tereus projects himself into scene and 'by looking handles her in advance'.[38] There is a pleasure in his fantasy which is not simply the anticipation of its realization. That night he moulds her into the form that he wishes:

> repetens faciem motusque manusque
> *qualia vult fingit quae nondum vidit* et ignes
> ipse suos nutrit cura removente soporem.
> (*Met.* 6.491–3)

(Recalling her face, her movements, and her hands he pictures as he wants what he has not yet seen and himself feeds his own fires, his desire preventing sleep.)

Immediately after the rape itself Philomela is described as a dove impaled on talons: *horret adhuc avidosque timet, quibus haeserat, ungues* (she still shudders and fears the greedy talons on which she had been impaled *Met.* 6.530). This recalls closely an earlier description of Tereus looking at Philomela:

> nusquam lumen detorquet ab illa,
> non aliter quam cum pedibus praedator obuncis
> deposuit nido leporem Iovis ales in alto;
> nulla fuga est capto, spectat sua praemia raptor.
> (*Met.* 6.515–18)

(He never turns his eye from her, just as when the predatory bird of Jupiter has from its hooked claws dropped a hare in its high nest. The captured animal has no escape, the raptor watches its prize.)

Tereus looks with anticipation as Ovid's eagle simile foreshadows the talons of the later rape, but the repetition is significant: the rape is as much paralleled by the gaze of the raptor as it is foreshadowed by it.

Philomela, raped, threatens to expose the crime. Tereus cuts out her tongue and rapes the mute body (*Met.* 6.561–2). The severed tongue murmurs without words[39] and tries to rejoin its parent

---

[38] Curran (1978) 222 notes the special importance of controlling fantasy in this rape narrative compared with others in the *Metamorphoses*.

[39] No words are reported for it or for Plisthenes' severed head in *Thyestes*: *querulum cucurrit murmure incerto caput* (729). Cf. the unsilenced lament of Orpheus' severed head and cold tongue: *Eurydicen vox ipsa et frigida lingua, | a miseram Eurydicen! anima fugiente vocabat* (Virgil, *Georgics* 4.525–6).

body. When Procne reads the rape on the tapestry she also is silenced; in sympathy with her sister's suffering her tongue seeks in vain for words:[40]

> dolor ora repressit,
> verbaque quaerenti satis indignantia linguae
> defuerunt.
> (*Met.* 6.583–5)

(grief choked her speech and her questing tongue found no words satisfactorily to express her outrage).

When Procne plans revenge she suggests, in addition to cutting out Tereus' tongue and castrating him, blinding him (Met. 6.616). The final punishment is briefly described but recalls the central qualities of Tereus' rape.[41] Tereus is deceived as were Pandion and Philomela, and like them is a victim of irony. In both scenes the irony of the situation takes a verbal form. Earlier Tereus' pleas were misinterpreted as piety and Pandion, in a disastrous choice of words given Tereus' fantasy of assuming Pandion's role, entrusts Philomela to him with the words, *per superos oro patrio ut tuearis amore* (by the gods I beg you to protect her with a father's love 499). Even more marked is the failure of Tereus, now the victim, to comprehend Procne's announcement, *intus habes quem poscis* (you have inside the child you ask for 655). He clearly assumes that this must mean 'inside the house' for he looks around the room for Itys. At the banquet Tereus is the innocent and helpless visual object, and his failure to comprehend is expressed in the same visual metaphor used earlier for Pandion: *tantaque nox animi est* (such great darkness blinded his thoughts 652) cf. *quantum mortalia pectora caecae | noctis habent* (what great blinding darkness covers mortal hearts 472–3). Procne's revenge is enacted in and of Tereus' flesh, but her failure to conceal her pleasure leaves this aspect of the punishing reversal a faint trace.

Seneca's Atreus chooses Procne's revenge as his model, but where Ovid devotes much of his narrative to the original crime

---

[40] The sympathy is perhaps pointed by verbal echo as Procne's tongue seeking (*quaerenti* 584) to speak recalls the tongue of Philomela which seeks (*quaerit* 560) to rejoin its mistress.

[41] The description of the murder of Itys recalls that of the rape of Philomela and in this repetition also the revenge on Tereus is a punishing reversal. See Larmour (1990) 134.

and passes quickly over the revenge Seneca emphasizes the banquet and sketches Thyestes' offence in a single speech (220–41). There are some clear parallels with the Odrysian banquet, for example in the description of the cooking and in Thyestes' failure to understand the host's ironic assurances that the children are close at hand,[42] but more interesting is the development of Ovid's rhetoric of victimization. Procne's intent, to punish Tereus in a manner appropriate to his crime, is fully realized in the revenge of Atreus, who enjoys the pleasures of Tereus while playing the role of Procne. If the murmuring of Plisthenes' severed head in *Thyestes* recalls the murmuring of Philomela's tongue in *Metamorphoses* 6[43] allusion points to such a blending of roles. More overt is Atreus' representation of his political rivalry and the banquet which ends it as rooted in a masculine anxiety. In his dialogue with his servant Atreus says that his hold on the throne is weak:

> pars nulla nostri tuta ab insidiis vacat,
> corrupta coniunx, imperi quassa est fides,
> domus aegra, dubius sanguis et certi nihil
> nisi frater hostis.
> (*Thyestes* 238–41)

(no part of what is mine is safe from treachery; my wife is defiled, my confidence in power shaken, my house weakened, its blood uncertain; nothing is sure—except my brother's hostility.)

He stages a revenge in which Thyestes is made the victim of irony and of the predatory gaze and in the last act becomes flesh without self-determination. Seeing Thyestes' helpless suffering Atreus finally banishes the anxiety which afflicted him in his first scene:

> nunc parta vera est palma. perdideram scelus,
> nisi sic doleres. liberos nasci mihi
> nunc credo, castis nunc fidem reddi toris.
> (*Thyestes* 1097–9)

(Now the true palm is won. I would have wasted my crime if you did not feel pain like this. Children are born to me, now I believe it; my bed is faithful and chaste once more!)

---

[42] *Thyestes* 770 and 1030–1; cf. *Met.* 6.646 and 655 respectively. For these and other parallels see Jakobi (1988) 152–67.

[43] *Thyestes* 729; cf. *Met.* 6.556. So Jakobi (1988) 162. See also n. 41 above on the parallelism in Ovid's account between the murder of Itys and the rape of Philomela.

To Atreus' mind Thyestes has been effeminized by the role he has played and therefore cannot be the threatening adulterer. The modes of Thyestes' victimization create a context in which Atreus' representation of his victory as a triumph of his masculinity seems broadly appropriate. The perfumed banqueter is a stock effeminate characterization in Roman political invective,[44] and this particular banquet, which takes Procne's rape-reversing banquet as a model, is rooted in gender conflict. From much earlier in the drama the relationship between Thyestes and his brother has a strikingly erotic mode. Speaking of Atreus' eternal hatred Thyestes says:

> amat Thyesten frater? aetherias prius
> perfundet Arctos pontus et Siculi rapax
> consistet aestus unda...
> (*Thyestes* 476–8)

(Thyestes loved by his brother? Sooner the ocean will soak the Bears of heaven, and the whirling waves of Sicily's tides will halt...)

Here and in the lines which follow (478–82) Thyestes speaks of Atreus' hatred in the *adynata* of elegiac poetry:[45] these impossibilities will come to pass before Atreus begins to love Thyestes not, as in the elegiac cliché, before the lover's devotion ends. Atreus' hatred and the eroticization of the conflict between the brothers finds its final expression in the banquet where Thyestes' body testifies to the potency of Atreus' tragedy in an ugly imitation of child-birth.[46] As Thyestes attempts to celebrate his new prosperity his body, stuffed with the flesh of his sons, rebels: *imber vultu nolente cadit, | venit in medias voces gemitus* (tear drops fall from my eyes unbidden, amidst my words there comes a groan 950–1), *subitos fundunt | oculi fletus, nec causa subest* (my eyes pour forth these sudden tears based on no cause 966–7), *nolunt manus | parere* (my hands will not obey 985–6). That Thyestes understands and controls less well than Atreus even the workings of his own body is a mark of Atreus' total domination. The groan which interrupts Thyestes' speech in line 951, like his involuntary tears, appears to be a pain which he does not

---

[44] *pingui madidus crinis amomo* (948). On the topos see Corbeill (1997) 107–10.
[45] See Tarrant (1976) 159 and Curley (1986) 149–50.
[46] So Poe (1969) 372, but he then continues, 'However, this is a comparatively minor matter' and does not pursue it (at all).

yet consciously recognize, but a few lines later Thyestes is again interrupted by a groan:

> Quis hic tumultus viscera exagitat mea?
> quid tremuit intus? sentio impatiens onus
> *meumque gemitu non meo pectus gemit.*
> adeste, nati, genitor infelix vocat,
> adeste. visis fugiet hic vobis dolor—
> unde obloquuntur?
> (*Thyestes* 999–1004)

(What is this turmoil that shakes my guts? What trembles inside me? I feel a burden beyond endurance, *and my breast groans with groaning not my own.* Come, sons, your unhappy father calls you, come! Once I see you this pain will vanish. *They interrupt—but from where?*)

Unambiguously here it is his children who interrupt him with their groaning, and they are struggling to get out:

> volvuntur intus viscera et clusum nefas
> sine exitu luctatur et quaerit fugam.
> da, frater, ensem (sanguinis multum mei
> habet ille); ferro liberis detur via
> (*Thyestes* 1041–4)

(The flesh turns within me, the imprisoned horror struggles with no way out, seeking to escape. Give me your sword, brother—it already has much of my blood: the blade must give my children a path.)

The association or deliberate confusion of stomach and womb, food and embryo is familiar.[47] *Viscera* and *alvus* are used for both stomach and womb and relatedly *satura* can mean full of either food or child.[48] Satire and invective are the most productive genres for examples of this parallelism or confusion. Particularly common are hyperbolic fantasies of masculine penetration in which the tongue or penis invades viscera of various

---

[47] This is neither a narrowly literary nor a narrowly Latin phenomenon. See Dubois (1988) 110–29 on the womb as an oven, and 125–6 on Aristotle's representation of pregnancy as the cooking of the embryo, Dean-Jones (1994) 52 on the sympathy between throat and vagina, 'Hansen notes that on several occasions in antiquity authors claim that a girl's throat expands when she has been deflowered', and Loraux (1987) 61.

[48] This confusion is the substance of a joke at Plautus, *Amphitryo* 667: *Quia Alcumenam ante aedis stare saturam intellego.* On this and parallel passages see Gowers (1993) 75.

kinds.[49] The importance of the literary tradition of masculine aggression in playing on this parallelism should not be underestimated; Thyestes, stuffed by Atreus, is no longer a rival and no threat to his paternity. Atreus' revenge is a figurative rape of a male adulterer[50] as Tereus' victimization by tongue and by eye reversed his rape of Philomela.

The extravagant effeminization of Thyestes is not equalled in any other Senecan tragedy, but gender is a significant element elsewhere in the representation of the relationship between controlling viewer and victim. As ever it is Medea who parallels Atreus most closely. Both avengers are god-like in their power to direct the tragedy acted by their victims and both crown their victory with the spectacle of their victims' impotent horror. Like Atreus Medea speaks of her power in both political and sexual terms: *regna* and *virginitas*, balanced in a single line, return simultaneously:

> Iam iam recepi sceptra germanum patrem,
> spoliumque Colchi pecudis auratae tenent;
> rediere regna, rapta virginitas redit.
> (*Medea* 982–4)

(Now in this moment I have recovered my sceptre, brother, father, and the Colchians hold the spoil of the golden ram. My realm is restored, my stolen maidenhood restored.)

This claim recalls her words to Creon:

> virgini placeat pudor
> paterque placeat: tota cum ducibus ruet
> Pelasga tellus. (*Medea* 238–40)

(Suppose the maiden should decide for modesty, decide for her father: the entire Pelasgian land will perish, following its leaders,)

By taking her revenge and setting Corinth ablaze Medea has effectively cancelled the decision she took in Colchis and so in a

[49] See e.g. Juvenal, *Satires* 9.43–4, *an facile et pronum est agere intra viscera penem | legitimum atque illic hesternae occurrere cenae?* and Martial 11.61.6–8 and 11–12, *Modo qui omnes viscerum tubos ibat | et voce certa consciaque dicebat | puer an puella matris esset in ventre. |...| nam dum tumenti mersus haeret in volva | et vagientes intus audit infantes.* Richlin (1992), who discusses the passage of Martial, has more examples *passim* and especially 11 ff. See also Walters (1997) 32–3 on Seneca, *Epistles* 95.21.

[50] On rape as a literary fantasy for the punishment of a male adulterer see Richlin (1981) 394 on Martial 2.49, 2.60, and Juvenal 10.316.

sense she has won back her virginity. *Medea* is a play full of reasoning of this kind, and it is a logic echoed in Atreus' triumph over his brother: *liberos nasci mihi | nunc credo, castis nunc fidem reddi toris* (*Thyestes* 1098–9).[51] Medea drives herself to kill her first child by arguing herself out of motherhood: if she has been displaced by Creusa then her children must be Creusa's also: *quidquid ex illo tuum est, | Creusa peperit* (all that is yours by him has Creusa for a mother 921–2). Though she refers to *liberi quondam mei* (children once mine 924) and reaffirms, *non sunt mei* (they are not mine 934), her resolve wavers in the following line: *mei sunt* (they are mine 935). Before she kills the first child she returns to the motif of birthing her own vengeance which she introduced in the prologue (25–6) and she describes herself as a mother in the final scene with Jason (1008, 1012). However inconsistent or unsuccessful Medea's argument that she has ceased to be a mother, it is an important part of her self-presentation in the final scene. Her claim to have taken back the sceptres of royal power is set against her command to Jason the parent to take back his children: *Iam iam recepi sceptra* (982); cf. *recipe iam gnatos, parens* (1024). As in the crowning ritual of revenge in *Thyestes* the domination of the tyrant-director is figured in the contrast between political (and divine) power and domestic vulnerability. In Seneca's version of the myth Jason is driven not by desire for advancement but by fear of Creon and other kings; only his children inspire in him the shadows of defiance:

> non ipse memet cogat et rex et socer.
> haec causa vitae est, hoc perusti pectoris
> curis levamen. spiritu citius queam
> carere, membris, luce.   (*Medea* 546–9)

(Not even my king and father-in-law himself could force me to endure that. This is my reason for living, this is the solace for my heart, so scorched by cares. I would sooner be deprived of my breath, of my body, of the light.)

This is the revelation upon which Medea builds her revenge. She destroys her enemies, recaptures her royal power, and exploits the parental vulnerability of a character who does not live in the world

---

[51] On the passage of Medea just quoted see Costa (1973) 158. More generally on the strange logic of Seneca's maddened protagonists see Tarrant (1985) 241.

of kings and sceptres. In Jason's mind as in Medea's, royal power threatens the private domestic world.

In Euripides' tragedy Medea's departure from the domestic world is marked by her assumption of various masculine characteristics,[52] but there is comparatively little corresponding development in the characterization of Jason. This is very much the reverse of the treatment in Seneca's *Medea*. Medea's shifting acceptance and rejection of motherhood is significant, but otherwise it is difficult to discuss reversal of gender or of domain in a heroine who is god-like from before the opening of the tragedy. Medea finds Jason's action incomprehensible not only on moral grounds but because he does not seem to remember her power:[53]

> merita contempsit mea
> qui scelere flammas viderat vinci et mare?
> adeone credit omne consumptum nefas?
> (*Medea* 120–2)

(Did he hold my services cheap, though he had seen fire and sea overpowered by my crime? Is he so confident that my evil is completely used up?)

Where Medea lives up to her billing Jason does not. Long before the final revenge he is transformed from a faithless deserter into a helpless victim. The chorus, albeit in the hyperbolic formulae of an epithalamium, ranks him in beauty above the child of the lightning who harnesses tigers to his chariot, the prescient Apollo, and Castor with his twin the boxer (*Medea* 82–9). The epithalamium as a whole is opposed to Medea's preceding monologue in which she calls on the gods to defend the rights of her marriage. The chorus closes the hymn by praying for Medea to disappear quietly into the darkness (114) and denies Medea's rights by summoning to its own cause many of the powers whom Medea had invoked as her own. Both Medea and the chorus call on Lucina (2, 61), and Hymen who oversees the marriage torches corresponds to the Furies who stood in attendance at Medea's marriage (13–17, 67). Medea is a descendant of the Sun (28–34) and Creusa's eclipsing beauty is likened to the light of the Sun

---

[52] Κορίνθιαι γυναῖκες, ἐξῆλθον δόμων (*Medea* 214) marks the beginning. See e.g. Foley (1989) 81 and relevantly also Garner (1988).

[53] In addition to the passage quoted see *vadis oblitus mei | et tot meorum facinorum? excidimus tibi? | numquam excidemus. hoc age, omnis advoca | vires et artes* (*Medea* 560–3).

(93–5) and to that of Phoebe, who shines *lumine non suo* (with light not her own 97). Lucina and the other gods cannot favour both brides and both prayers; the tragedy about to unfold promises either the conventional animal sacrifice to Lucina described by the chorus (61–2) or the more horrifying sacrifice planned by Medea (37–40).

Medea responds to the epithalamium with assertions of her power and ends her speech determined to turn Corinth to ashes and to submerge it beneath the waves (147–9). Cautioned by the Nurse she replies:

> Medea superest: hic mare et terras vides
> ferrumque et ignes et deos et fulmina.
>   (*Medea* 165–6)

(Medea remains: here you see sea and land, steel and fire and gods and thunderbolts.)

The epithets with which the chorus describes the divinities whom Jason surpasses in beauty are as formulaic as the rest of the epithalamium, but the hymn is elevated from mere conventionality by pointed opposition to Medea's preceding monologue. Jason's failure to be the divine figure suggested by the chorus is perhaps similarly pointed. The chorus sings that the child of the lightning will yield to Jason in beauty but, a few lines later, Medea in whom you see fire, gods, and lightning will not. Bacchus harnessed tigers to his chariot (85) but Medea like a maenad (382–3, 806, 849), wanders like a tigress (863–4) and cannot rein in (*frenare* 866) her anger or her love. Jason is compared to Apollo who moves the tripod (86), but it is Medea who knows the unseen destiny of the tragedy and ends it riding in the magical chariot of the Sun. Perhaps it is a mistake to look for significance in these details, but without question Medea walks with the gods as Jason does not, and her demonstration of divine power mocks the chorus's descriptions of Jason and Creusa as god-like figures.

In his first appearance Jason laments the cruel hand of fate and presents himself as caught between his obligations and certain death. He justifies his desertion of Medea not as his Euripidean counterpart does with the social benefits of the new marriage for their children[54] but with the hope of saving their lives: *quippe*

---

[54] Euripides, *Medea* 566–7.

sequeretur necem | proles parentum (437–8). Throughout the scene Jason is consistently afraid of forces which Medea then defies: nations and kings (525–8) and Fortune (518–20). In the preceding ode the chorus linked Medea with the golden fleece as a prize of the *Argo*'s voyage:

> Quod fuit huius *pretium* cursus?
> aurea pellis
> maiusque mari Medea malum,
> merces prima digna carina.   (*Medea* 361–3)

(What was the prize gained by this voyage? The Golden Fleece and Medea, an evil worse than the sea, fit merchandise for the first vessel.)

In the agon with Jason the relationship is inverted: Medea threatens to fight with Creon for Jason as the prize: *certemus sine | sit pretium Iason* (let us fight it out, and let Jason be the prize 517–18). At no point does Jason disagree with Medea's claim that the Argonauts' success was her gift, but he is consistently fearful, passive, and unhappy. He takes no pleasure in the benefits which Medea's crimes have brought: *ingrata vita est cuius acceptae pudet* (There is no gratitude for a life one is ashamed of receiving 504). She answers with the moralizing *sententia, Retinenda non est cuius acceptae pudet* (One need not hold onto a life one is ashamed of receiving 505). That a woman, stereotypically lacking in rigour,[55] rebuke a man for infirmity of purpose is a familiar rhetorical device. Oedipus the king, paralysed by fear at the opening of his tragedy, draws this response from Jocasta: *haud est virile terga Fortunae dare* (It is not manly to retreat before Fortune 86). Jocasta is more of a man than Oedipus,[56] as Medea is than Jason, who answers his failure to commit suicide as earlier he justified his unwillingness to die (436–9) by returning to his responsibility or love for his children: *Quin potius ira concitum pectus doma, | placare natis* (Instead of this, get control of your angry heart, be friends again with our sons 506–7).

---

[55] See e.g. Edwards (1993) 63–97 on *mollitia*.

[56] Töchterle (1994) 201 is taken by the importance of gender in this scene and gives a list of *loci communes* in which the rhetoric of Stoic condemnation is given added point by the fact that a man is lectured on virtuous/virile endurance by a woman. Cf. also Antigone to (again) Oedipus, *Phoen*. 188–90: *at hoc decebat roboris tanti virum, | non esse sub dolore nec victum malis | dare terga*. For a historical Roman woman of this stamp cf. the celebrated Arria Paeti in Pliny, *Epistles* 3.16.1–6 and Martial 1.13.

Euripides' parallel agon is so well known that it is difficult to read Seneca's Jason without suspecting that his every utterance is temporized sophistry. Medea accuses him of desiring royal power (529), but at no point in the entire tragedy does Jason represent himself otherwise than he does here: *alta extimesco sceptra* (I fear exalted sceptres 529). He bears a closer resemblance to Seneca's Andromache in *Troades* than to Euripides' Jason. Both are prevented from escaping the miseries of life by their children:

> Iam erepta Danais coniugem sequerer meum,
>   nisi hic teneret: hic meos animos domat
> morique prohibet
> (*Troades* 418–20)

(I would have escaped the Danaans and followed my husband by now, if this one did not hold me: he tames my spirit and prevents my death).

If we were judging Andromache and Jason we would certainly make the distinction that Jason, however passively, participated in a criminal voyage, but this does not affect the narrower issue of the role of gender in representations of power. In both *Troades* and *Medea* a clear contrast is made between the domestic world of the victim and the political power of their tormentors. Not only do Ulysses and Medea exploit their victims' attachment to their children, but they stage and observe the pain which comes from this vulnerability.

Astyanax's death is reported by a messenger (1068 ff.) and Ulysses does not observe Andromache watching her child die as Medea watches Jason. However, in the scene between Ulysses and Andromache (519–813) he realizes early the falsehood of her claim that Astyanax is already dead. As Medea interrupts her dialogue with Jason with an aside (*Sic natos amat?*... (Does he love his children so much? 549)), Ulysses interrupts his interrogation of Andromache to share with his soul and the audience his recognition that she is lying:

> scrutare matrem: maeret, illacrimat, gemit;
> sed huc et illuc anxios gressus refert
> missasque voces aure sollicita excipit:
> magis haec timet, quam maeret.
> (*Troades* 615–18)

(Observe this mother. She is grieving, weeping, groaning; yet she paces nervously up and down, and strains to catch each word spoken. She is more fearful than mournful.)

Andromache's body belies her claim and Ulysses seizes on her vulnerability:

> Intremuit: hac, hac parte quaerenda est mihi;
> matrem timor detexit; iterabo metum.
> (*Troades* 625–6)

(She trembled. This is the angle from which I must test her. Fear unmasked the mother; I shall renew her terror.)

He pretends that Astyanax is captured and again Andromache betrays herself. In this scene Ulysses' domination of Andromache is expressed in part by the representation of his victim as an object to be viewed and interpreted. She does not in turn interpret his expression and intention but reinforces his commentary with her own:

> Reliquit animus membra, quatiuntur, labant
> torpetque vinctus frigido sanguis gelu.
> (*Troades* 623–4)

(My limbs are fainting, shivering, collapsing, my blood is congealed and frozen.)

As we have already seen, Ulysses is not content with Andromache's surrender but demands a performance for the life of Astyanax.

In these three tragedies, *Thyestes*, *Medea*, and *Troades*, the domination of directing viewer over visual object and/or unwilling actor is coloured by an opposition of genders. The gendering of these relationships is in some cases no more than another mode of expressing an inequality of power. In *Troades* Andromache is uncovered (*detexit* 626) to Ulysses' gaze by her domestic vulnerability, but there is no reason to believe that his pleasure in the trembling of her body and in her performance is anything but a pleasure in the success of his scheme and in the satisfaction of his political desires. The relationship between eye and passive body has a sensual potential, but this need not be developed nor necessarily eroticized by the gendering of eye and body. The brief performances which Andromache provides in this scene for Ulysses anticipate the crowning spectacle of the tragedy, the sacrifice of Polyxena. Even here where Polyxena parades beautiful and silent before the assembled spectators before being stabbed in the throat in a fatal marriage ceremony, Seneca chooses not to exploit the potential for sexual voyeurism. In the account in the *Metamorphoses* which is the model for this episode[57] Ovid closes with Polyxena's care even as she collapses in death to prevent any immodesty: *tunc quoque cura fuit partes velare tegendas, | cum caderet, castique decus servare pudoris* (*Met.* 13.479–80).[58] In the ashes of a nation Seneca's Troades are far beyond such concerns[59] and Polyxena's last act reiterates the powerless and heroic defiance of Astyanax. Her spectators are united in their admiration for her bravery and her willingness to die (1146). Astyanax is described as a tender lion-cub who is not truly dangerous—*morsusque inanes temptat* (he tries feinting bites 1096)—and it is in this tradition that Polyxena strikes the ground angrily (*irato impetu* 1159) as if with her body to make the earth lie heavy on a ghost who earlier tore a valley apart (170 f.). In her following speech Hecuba makes no distinction between the two sacrifices: *concidit virgo et puer | bellum peractum est* (A maiden and boy have fallen: the war is finished 1166–7) and *sola mors votum meum, | infantibus, violenta, virginibus venis* (O death, my only prayer, you come with violence to infants and to girls 1171–2).

The mastery of the Greeks (including Ulysses) is apparent in their controlled staging and reinforced by an inequality of gender. A similar analysis can reasonably be offered of Medea's revenge on Jason, where the expected gender roles are reversed. Here, however, Medea's pleasure in Jason's suffering and her desire to draw it out is informed by her association of political with sexual power. The aesthetic pleasure of her revenge is in this way subtly coloured by the pleasure of erotic domination. Echoes (through

---

[57] On the importance of *Met.* 13.449 ff. for Seneca's *Troades* see Fantham (1982) 375.

[58] Cf. Euripides, *Hecuba* 568–70 and Loraux's discussion (1987) 56–65, which also includes discussion of Ovid and Seneca as readers of Euripides. For Loraux Polyxena in Ovid and Seneca dies a warrior death which is recognized as such by the observers. Polyxena in Euripides, however, asks for this death, by bearing her breasts, only to have her gesture misinterpreted: 'the Greek army saw...only a virgin unveiling her woman's breasts' (60). Cf. Mossman (1995) 157–60, who argues that the Greek army reads correctly and honours Polyxena as a warrior after her death.

[59] See Hecuba's command: *veste remissa substringe sinus | uteroque tenus pateant artus. | cui coniugio pectora velas, | captive pudor?* (*Troades* 88–91).

Ovid) of Procne's revenge for Tereus' rape[60] develop this aspect of the pleasure of the masterful gaze, but its full potential is seen not in this tragedy but in *Thyestes*. The myth of Procne and Tereus is here a more important model and erotic domination figures more prominently in Atreus' revenge than in Medea's. Atreus' extravagant effeminization of Thyestes is a reversal of his brother's adultery with Aerope in a similar way as the banquet for Tereus is an inverted restaging of the rape of Philomela. Thyestes is an object of the prolonged sadistic gaze to a degree that Jason is not, and the nature of this victimization is affected not only by the prominence of the Thracian myth but also by Atreus' visual pleasures. Where Medea's motives in wanting to draw out her revenge are as invisible as Jason's face when the last murder is committed, Atreus takes pleasure explicitly in the colours of his victim's face and in the involuntary movements of his body. He luxuriates in the visual object as no other Senecan character. In the presence of the myth of Tereus and Procne the pleasure offered by the tragedy which Atreus stages is figured in part as the pleasure of erotic violence.

3. MODELS OF AUDIENCE RESPONSE

In a discussion of poetic descriptions of anger Seneca suggests that figures like Bellona and Discordia from *Aeneid* 8 may serve a useful purpose. Just as the image of oneself in a mirror can reveal the full horror of one's anger so these poetic images can serve as a deterrent:

Quibusdam, ut ait Sextius, iratis profuit aspexisse speculum; perturbavit illos tanta mutatio sui; velut in rem praesentem adducti *non agnoverunt se.*

(*De Ira* 2.36.1)

(Some people, as Sextius says, have benefited from seeing themselves angry in the mirror; the great change in themselves shook them. As if brought to face a present reality they did not recognize themselves.)

---

[60] On the association of Medea's revenge with Procne's by Ovid (and perhaps others) see Larmour (1990) 133. When Seneca's Medea wishes for children like their parents she echoes the words of Ovid's Medea (from *Her.* 12) which in turn recur in the mouth of Ovid's Procne. The relevant passages are *liberos similes patri* (Seneca, *Medea* 24), *et nimium similes tibi sunt* (Ovid, *Her.* 12.191), and *a quam es similis patri* (Ovid, *Met.* 6.621). The presence of these allusions clarifies a passage which is otherwise 'rather obscure' (so Costa (1973) 65). See also Jakobi (1988) 51 on mater *es...cui sim vide* (*Medea* 171) and Ovid's Procne: *cui sis nupta, vide* (*Met.* 6.634) and also 59 on *Medea* 863–5 and *Met.* 6.636f.

Only some people benefit from the vision however. A few chapters earlier Seneca described the banquet in which Caligula, like Atreus, enjoyed the spectacle of Pastor drinking what tasted to him like the blood of his murdered son (*De Ira* 2.33.3-4, discussed above). An understanding of the criminality and the horror of the scene is essential to their satisfaction. People differ in their characters and Seneca is forced to admit that even the most extreme sights are therefore viewed differently:

Qui ad speculum venerat, ut se mutaret, iam mutaverat; iratis quidem nulla est formonsior effigies quam atrox et horrida, qualesque esse etiam videri volunt. (*De Ira* 2.36.3)

(The man who had come to the mirror to change himself was already changed; to angry men no image is more beautiful than the savage and the horrible, and they want to look like what they want to be.)

While those shocked by the image of their own anger did not recognize themselves it is in the severed heads and hands of his children that Thyestes recognizes Atreus (ATREUS. *natos ecquid agnoscis tuos?* THYESTES. *Agnosco fratrem* (ATREUS. I suppose you recognize your sons? THYESTES. I recognize my brother, *Thyestes*, 1005-6)) and in Medea's revenge that she looks to be recognized (*coniugem agnoscis tuam?* (Do you recognize your wife? *Medea* 1021)).

Atreus and Thyestes, Medea and Jason view the acts of revenge differently and in their difference offer opposing models for the viewing audience. Such a choice is most elegantly presented in *Thyestes* through the tragedy's dominant metaphor of consuming desire. In planning and in reflecting on his revenge Atreus insists that he and his brother are alike, and indeed they are symbolically united in the banquet where Atreus feeds on the spectacle of Thyestes eating: the brothers are satiated by one and the same episode:[61]

---

[61] See Tarrant (1985) 217-18 on the lines quoted and 242 on Atreus' perception of Thyestes as 'the mirror image of himself'. See also *Thyestes* 288-9 and Poe (1969) 362 more generally on the symbolism which unites these descendants of Tantalus. It is not only Atreus who imagines that Thyestes is like himself: the chorus asks the messenger, *auctorem indica:* | *non quaero quis sit, sed uter* (639-40). Cf. Atreus' words earlier, *dignum est Thyeste facinus et dignum Atreo,* | *quod uterque faciat* (271-2). Note also the confusion about the parentage of the children which is evident even in the structure of the drama. Atreus and his servant argue from 294 to 333—a long time in a tragedy of only 1112 lines—as to whether or not

> bene est, abunde est, iam sat est etiam mihi.
> *(Thyestes* 889)

(This is good, this is ample, this is enough now, even for me)

Compare:

> iam satis mensis datum est
> satisque Baccho. *(Thyestes* 899–900)

(Enough devotion now to the board, enough to wine)

The tyrant's appetites are commonly figured as a cannibalistic hunger[62] and here Thyestes, drawn into the royal palace against his better judgement by the *vetus regni furor* (302), is a half-hearted Atreus. Certainly Thyestes is deceived by Atreus and he does not understand the true nature of the banquet, but in the parallel earlier scene where he himself discusses the dangers of the tyrant's table he overcomes the rebellion of his body and chooses to enter the royal palace:

> animus haeret ac retro cupit
> corpus referre, moveo nolentem gradum.
> *(Thyestes* 419–20)

(my spirit falters and wants to turn my body back, my steps are forced and reluctant)

Compare:

> paternis vina libentur deis,
> tunc hauriantur—sed quid hoc? nolunt manus
> parere
> *(Thyestes* 984–6)

(The wine shall be poured out to our fathers' gods, then drained.—But what is this? My hands will not obey).

Had Atreus' and Thyestes' desires not coincided in this way there would have been no tragedy. As Tantalus before him (68 ff.), Atreus shrinks from the vision of the crime, but then he drives himself to commit it:

Agamemnon and Menelaus can be reliable conspirators in Atreus' revenge. Atreus finally decides to send them as unwitting agents (332–3). We never see them carry out their duty. Instead Thyestes is persuaded by the unwitting agency of his own son Tantalus (421–90). This surprising reassignment of the role which confuses the children of the two brothers is surely significant.

[62] Leigh (1996) collects many examples from a variety of different sources both Greek and Roman 179–85. See especially 194 n. 56 on 'eating with the eye'.

> tota iam ante oculos meos
> imago caedis errat, ingesta orbitas
> in ora patris—anime, quid rursus times
> et ante rem subsidis? audendum est, age
> (*Thyestes* 281–4)

(Now the whole picture of the slaughter hovers before my eyes—bereavement thrust into the father's face. Why take fright again, my spirit, and slacken before the event? Come you must be bold)

There is a clear parallel between the slaughter which Atreus sees before his eyes and the corpses which he will force before the face (and into the mouth)[63] of Thyestes. Atreus insisted that no crime could satiate him (*nullum relinquam facinus et nullum est satis* (I shall leave no deed undone—and none is enough 256)) and the crime which shocks him in the lines quoted above delights him later. When he murders Thyestes' children he is likened to a lion which continues to sink its teeth into its victims even when it has eaten its fill.[64] In this respect he differs from Thyestes, who cannot stomach the final revenge. Full of food and wine he asks for his children to complete his pleasure, but when their severed heads are offered he recoils in horror. Philomela ended Tereus' meal in a similar fashion by springing forth to throw the bloody head of Itys into the banqueter's face (again also mouth):

> prosiluit Ityosque caput Philomela cruentum
> misit *in ora patris*.
> (Ovid, *Met.* 6.658–9)

(Philomela sprang forward and threw the bloody head of Itys into the father's face.)

Sickened, Tereus pushed the table away (*mensas ... repellit, Met.* 6.661).

Atreus, only partially satisfied with this reworking of the Thracian crime, and Thyestes, desperate to bring the scene to a close, offer different models for an audience's response to the cannibal horror. The sacrifices which end *Medea* and *Troades* are also differently viewed by characters within the dramatic illusion and here too therefore an audience's response is not simply constructed.

---

[63] On this double meaning and the parallel *funus ingestum patri* at *Medea* 132 see Tarrant (1985) 131.

[64] *cruore rictus madidus et pulsa fame | non ponit iras: hinc et hinc tauros premens | vitulis minatur dente iam lasso inpiger* (734–6). On this passage see Poe (1969) 368.

There is more here than just a plurality of views. The spectacle is created through the words of the tragedy's speakers and therefore to some extent the audience sees now as Atreus, now as Thyestes, now as the messenger, and so on. However, an audience which has been privy to every event since the infection of the palace by Tantalus cannot hear Thyestes' unfortunate remarks with the innocence with which he utters them. The audience hears, *augere cumulus hic voluptatem potest, | si cum meis gaudere felici datur* (The final addition that could increase my pleasure would be leave to enjoy my happiness with my boys 974–5) as Atreus does, and in this objective sense is more closely aligned with one character than another. By knowing what Thyestes does not the audience and Atreus together make him a victim of irony; the audience participates in Atreus' process of victimization. Atreus achieves his victory in part by setting himself up as a viewer of Thyestes' actions[65] and in this respect also Atreus' sadistic pleasure is a more obvious and dominant model for an audience's response.

Whether literally viewed or as an ironic victim metaphorically viewed as he cannot view himself, Thyestes is circumscribed by the boundaries of the dramatic illusion and his own limited understanding. Spectators of a tragedy, if they are not for the duration of the performance simply assimilated to one of the dramatic characters, live in a larger world than those they see inasmuch as they are aware of what lies outside the dramatic illusion. In directing the play-within-the-play Atreus presents himself as external to a dramatic illusion. In addition, his desire to produce a crime which surpasses the models of the past closely parallels the desire of the tragedian, for that past is simultaneously a mythological reality and the literary works of Seneca's predecessors. Atreus is a larger figure than Thyestes in part because his thoughts have this metadramatic resonance; while Thyestes fails to master his body and his tongue Atreus' ambitions echo in more worlds than one. Knowledge of the plot and of the literary tradition from which the plot is created is a knowledge the audience shares with Atreus. Atreus' heightened knowledge, like Medea's and Tereus', is essentially predatory and the audience is constructed in accordance with this pattern.

---

[65] Note Atreus' words at 285–6: *quod est in isto scelere praecipuum nefas, | hoc ipse faciet.*

The technique of making the audience through its literary expertise participate in the destruction of the victim is used to particular effect in *Phaedra*, where Hippolytus' vulnerability and distinguishing characteristic is precisely his innocence (see Chapter 5 below). There is, however, an important difference between these two tragedies. Although Phaedra sometimes represents herself as a victim of her past, constrained to repeat the criminal loves of her ancestry, and sometimes as a knowing predator, like Oedipus she plays the victim only to a faceless destiny.[66] By contrast, at the end of *Thyestes* Atreus imagines an improved version in which his victims are knowing but nonetheless helpless (1065–8). It may be too late for Thyestes to suffer in this way, but it is a telling fantasy for the construction of a Phaedra-like audience. Poe was I think right when he saw in Atreus' sadistic pleasure 'an instinct which to some degree he himself [Seneca] shares and which he expects his audience to share',[67] but the audience is led to share Atreus' perspective by a trajectory of responses which is repeated in this and other of Seneca's tragedies: paralysed horror at the criminal spectacle is shown to give way to sadistic pleasure.

Seneca's passionate protagonists commonly experience a crisis of confidence before committing themselves fully to their crimes.[68] Atreus sees the image of the deed before his eyes and hesitates briefly (281–6). Tantalus' pride in the forthcoming drama, like Medea's, turns to horror as the crime takes more definite form. Furies intervene in both cases and driven by this hellish madness the tragedies resume their proper course.[69] These representations of the victory of tragic madness over the moral constraints which would inhibit its expression are powerful images of the creation of

[66] Briefly she blames Venus or Cupid personified (*Phaedra* 124–8, 185 ff.) but these divinities do not appear in the tragedy and Phaedra accepts the Nurse's argument (195 ff.) that the personification of *amor* is just an easy way out for those afflicted by passion.

[67] Poe (1969) 365. Seidensticker (1969) 154 talks of Seneca 'conspiring' with the audience, but the observation is not developed and no distinction is made between Atreus' sadistic use of irony in *Thyestes* (discussed 151–2) and the more impersonal irony of fate in other plays like *Phaedra*.

[68] Tarrant (1985) 131 makes this point while commenting on Atreus' brief hesitation at *Thyestes* 283–4 and offers *Phaedra* 592–9, *Medea* 895, 927–8, 988–9, and *Agamemnon* 228–9 as parallels.

[69] Tantalus' pride (*Thyestes* 18–23) disappears as the Fury anticipates the cannibal feast under his gaze (*te spectante* 66). Tantalus and Medea proceed to their task only with the violent inspiration of the Furies' whips and burning torches (*Thyestes* 96–100, *Medea* 958 ff.).

the art, but no less telling for the construction of audience response is the echoing of this victory in the eyes of those who are less intimately involved in the tragic action. Cassandra, though not a disinterested observer, plays no direct role in the murder which is the tragic action of Agamemnon and is still alive at the end of the drama. Admittedly she has not long to live, but as she suggests in the last words of the tragedy the same is true of Clytemnestra: *veniet et vobis furor* (Madness will come upon you too *Agamemnon* 1012). As a passive survivor of the tragedy Cassandra's role is closer to that of a chorus or messenger: less actor or victim than spectator.[70] Through her prophetic gift Cassandra sees the murder of Agamemnon twice, both before and as it happens. Significantly her perspective changes from that of a victim to one of enjoyment as the first vision unfolds, and the second vision is presented very differently from the first. More striking still is the change in perspective of the messenger in *Thyestes*. The messenger, a device by which what cannot be enacted is described, has no personal interest in the action of a tragedy and it is therefore remarkable that in *Thyestes* this figure traces the same trajectory as Atreus and as Cassandra in *Agamemnon*: his initial horror turns to pleasure in the visions of pain.[71] Audience response, like tragic madness, is not uniformly represented in Seneca's tragedies: the development of sadistic viewing in *Agamemnon* and *Thyestes* is, at least superficially, reversed in *Troades*, where the mixed emotions of Greeks and Trojans resolve into shared pity and sorrow at the deaths of Astyanax and Polyxena.

4. THE DEVELOPMENT OF A SADISTIC SPECTATORSHIP

Cassandra's first description of Agamemnon's murder is forced from her against her will:[72]

---

[70] Hecuba in *Troades* might be interpreted similarly: she introduces, closes, and even interprets (see her opening statement 1–6) the tragedy, but she has no special role in viewing the murders which constitute the tragic action of the drama, and in this respect she is less important as a model of audience response.

[71] Cf. the view of Tietze (1994) 65 that 'the Senecan messenger excludes himself completely from the story he tells'.

[72] Cf. the *matrona* of Lucan, *Bellum Civile* 1.674–95, and Masters (1992) 118–49 on Phemonoe, who (143) is a parallel figure. Both resist criminal inspiration, but are nevertheless driven to the ecstasy of civil war.

nunc reluctantis parat
reserare fauces, verba nunc clauso male
custodit ore maenas impatiens dei.
(*Agamemnon* 717–19)

(now she makes ready to unseal her reluctant mouth, now she tries in vain to hold in the words behind closed lips—a maenad unwilling to endure the god.)

She raves as a bacchant[73] (*cui bacchor furens?* 724) and, like Pentheus in *Bacchae* and more immediately Virgil's Dido, sees two suns (*gemino sole praefulget dies* 728).[74] This tragic inspiration controls her gaze: *quae versat oculos alia nunc facies meos?* (What different vision is directing[75] my eyes now? 737). Under its influence she sees the events leading up to the murder of Agamemnon and the event itself (738–40). In the remainder and the greater part of her speech she descends to the underworld, where among the Trojan dead and in particular the mangled forms of Hector and Deiphobus (743–9) her passive horror turns to a fierce exultation. Immediately after describing Deiphobus, so disfigured as to be unrecognizable, she says:

iuvat per ipsos ingredi Stygios lacus,
iuvat videre Tartari saevum canem
avidique regna Ditis!
(*Agamemnon* 750–2)

(What joy to embark on the very pools of Styx, what joy to see the savage hound of Tartarus and the realms of greedy Dis!)

In the following lines she prophesies her own death and that of Agamemnon; her paradoxical pleasure in seeing the underworld and its images of violent death is associated with the pleasure of revenge on Troy's conquerors. Although her descent to the underworld recalls Aeneas', her perspective has more in common with

---

[73] For a priestess of Apollo (not Bacchus) to behave in this way is not uncommon. From the Greek tradition Tarrant (1976) 306 compares Euripides, *Troades* 408 f.: εἰ μή σ'Ἀπόλλων ἐξεβάκχευεν φρένας. On Bacchus in Augustan literature see Batinski (1991).
[74] Cf. Virgil, *Aeneid* 4.469–71: *Eumenidum veluti demens videt agmina Pentheus | et solem geminum et duplices se ostendere Thebas, | aut Agamemnonius scaenis agitatus Orestes.* On this episode and tragedy in the *Aeneid* more generally see Wlosok (1976), Pöschl (1978), Hardie (1991), and Pobjoy (1998).
[75] Fitch translates 'attracting'.

Meta-Theatre and Self-Consciousness 217

that of an Atreus than that of Virgil's hero despite the apparent model:[76]

> quod si tantus amor menti, si tanta cupido est
> bis Stygios innare lacus, bis nigra videre
> Tartara, et insano iuvat indulgere labori...
> (Virgil, *Aeneid* 6.133–5)

(But if you have such great love, such great desire in your heart twice to swim the Stygian waters, twice to see black Tartarus, and you take pleasure in indulging in this mad labour...).

As it pleases Atreus to watch his vengeance unfold (*libet videre* (*Thyestes* 903)) so the reversals in the forthcoming scene will please the conquered Phrygians:

> spectate, miseri: fata se vertunt retro.
> (*Agamemnon* 758)

(Watch, you poor folk: fate is reversing itself!)

Unlike Aeneas, who escapes from the horrors of the mythological underworld to the promised order of Rome's imperial future, Cassandra is inspired by the Furies and their realm. Her painful vision was introduced by the chorus with these words: *nunc reluctantis parat | reserare fauces* (now she makes ready to unseal her reluctant mouth 717–18). In the vision itself she prays to the shades and the river Styx, reserate *paulum terga nigrantis poli* (draw back a little the covering of the dark world 756): in unbarring her throat[77] Cassandra exposes Mycenae to the gaze of the vengeful Trojans and opens the door to Hell and to the Furies:

> Instant sorores squalidae,
> anguinea iactant verbera...
> (*Agamemnon* 759–60)

(The scabrous sisters advance, they brandish snaky whips).

Like the Furies of *Hercules Furens*, *Thyestes*, and *Medea* these sisters with snaky whips and burning torches look back particularly to the demons of the *Aeneid*: Allecto and Tisiphone.[78]

---

[76] Tarrant (1976) 312 on *Agamemnon* 750 f.: 'the phrasing of the passage recalls Virg. *Aen.* 6.133 ff.)'.

[77] Note Jocelyn's observation on *Agamemnon* 717 recorded in Tarrant's note (1976: 305) that '*reserare* may invoke the metaphorical use of *fauces* for gates or doorways'.

[78] So Tarrant (1976) 315 on *Aeneid* 7.445 ff. See also Tisiphone at *Aeneid* 6.570–2.

Seneca's tragedy and the post-Virgilian epic tradition commonly find their inspiration in the anger of Juno and the infernal powers she unleashes. Here the selection of a voice of opposition and disorder from the *Aeneid* is pointed by comparison between Cassandra and Aeneas. The ghosts of mutilated Hector and Deiphobus which Cassandra sees recall their more famous and more developed predecessors in *Aeneid* 2.270 ff. and *Aeneid* 6.494 ff.[79] Both urge Aeneas to leave Troy behind him and to pursue a new and better destiny. In the meeting with Deiphobus the attractions of the Trojan past are such that the Sibyl has to intervene to break the delay. Symbolically this meeting takes place at a division in the road (*partis ubi se via findit in ambas* (*Aeneid* 6.540)). After Deiphobus turns on his heel Aeneas looks back:

> et in verbo vestigia torsit.
> Respicit Aeneas subito et sub rupe sinistra
> moenia lata videt triplici circumdata muro.
> (*Aeneid* 6.547–9)

(and as he spoke he turned his steps around. Aeneas looked back suddenly and saw under the cliff on the left broad fortifications surrounded by a triple wall)

This wall and the iron tower of Tisiphone are a threshold which the virtuous cannot touch (*Aeneid* 6.563). The Sibyl describes the infinite forms of criminality which lie beyond it and then both proceed to Elysium, Anchises, and the Roman future (6.625 ff.).

Seneca reverses the Virgilian narrative in having Cassandra respond to the apparition of Deiphobus with a prayer that Hell open to allow the Trojans to look on the destruction of Mycenae and with the apparition of figures like Tisiphone. The seal is set on the reversal with the words, *fata se vertunt retro* (*Agamemnon* 758): the fall of Troy and the murder of Priam in the past are repeated in Agamemnon's murder in this present in Mycenae.[80] The repetition of the sacrifice from the *Aeneid*'s (chronologically) first

---

[79] See Tarrant (1976) 311.

[80] Cassandra, in dialogue with Agamemnon, remarks that Mycenae is decorated for a festival as Troy was (791) and asks if they, like Priam, are to pray at the altar of Hercean Jupiter (793). To Agamemnon's, *Hic Troia non est*, Cassandra replies, *Ubi Helena est, Troiam puta* (795). On this passage see Putnam (1995) 270–2. Note also that Agamemnon even wears Priam's clothes: *et ipse picta veste sublimis iacet, | Priami superbas corpore exuvias gerens* (879–80) and see further Tarrant (1976) 338.

event[81] draws Seneca's drama back into Troy and back into Hell.[82] Cassandra is consumed by the desire for revenge and her metamorphosis from the unwilling seer of 720 ff. to the malicious viewer who delivers the second description of Agamemnon's murder (867–909) is achieved through her deviation from the model offered by Aeneas' response to Deiphobus and his Trojan ghosts. Dardanus, the author of Troy, Virgil places in Elysium (*Aeneid* 6.650), while Seneca locates him at the close of Cassandra's speech in Tartarus. Dardanus dances while Tantalus (Agamemnon's ancestor) grieves and in the background nightmares scream and a nameless body rots in a marsh (765–74). In succumbing to a desire for revenge which is represented as a madness rooted in those forces which oppose the destiny of the *Aeneid* Cassandra, hitherto a passive observer, resembles closely figures like Medea and Atreus and Juno. Not only does she begin to take a similar pleasure in scenes of horror but she is inspired by similar models.

When Cassandra delivers her second description of the murder of Agamemnon her transformation from the victim-viewer unwillingly possessed by Apollo is complete. That earlier Cassandra vainly ordered Apollo to leave her alone:

> recede, Phoebe, iam non sum tua,
> extingue flammas pectori infixas meo.
> (*Agamemnon* 722–3)

(Leave me, Phoebus: I am not yours any longer. Smother the flames you have planted in my breast.)

---

[81] So Hardie (1993) 19.
[82] On the representation of Troy as Hell in the *Aeneid* see Putnam (1965) 30–48. More recently Putnam (1995) stresses the importance of the final event of the *Aeneid*, the sacrifice of Turnus, for the troubled inspiration of Senecan tragedy. The disturbing nature of the victory of *ira* at the end of the *Aeneid* is complemented by the disturbing repetition of human sacrifice from the story's troubled beginnings. See also O'Hara (1990) 9, 19–35, 104–11 on the role of these rituals of death in questioning or qualifying optimistic prophecies which secure (directly or indirectly) the Roman future. On the threat of further repetitions and 'the dreary catalogue of vengeance killings of Roman civil war' see Hardie (1993) 21. On liberating and sterile repetitions in the *Aeneid* see also Quint (1993) 50–96. On the failure of Seneca's Trojans here and in *Troades* to break free of their Trojan past in contrast to the teleological victory of Virgil's Trojans see Schiesaro (1997a) *passim* esp. 90–1. Schiesaro (1997a) 85 marks *Agamemnon* 758 as significant, not least in the association of the reversal of destiny with a meta-literary spectatorship: poetry is constrained (or can be represented as being constrained) to reiterate its past.

This Cassandra successfully orders her soul to take the spoils of madness: *anime, consurge et cape | pretium furoris* (Rise up, my spirit, and enjoy the rewards of your madness! 868–9). *Furor* is victorious and now that Cassandra's desires coincide with it she becomes a powerful figure. That she did not herself plot the tragic crime is unimportant; revenge unfolds before her eyes as she would wish it to, and with this coincidence of her desire with the tragic spectacle she approaches the stature of an Atreus. The murder proceeds with her approval (*bene est* 870) as the crimes of *Medea* and *Thyestes* do to the satisfaction of their protagonists (*bene est, peractum est* (*Medea* 1019); cf. *bene est, abunde est* (*Thyestes* 279 and 889)). It is worth recalling that this familiar phrase, *bene est*, is used also by Medea when she hears Jason's love for his children. On this occasion Jason himself betrays his vulnerability rather than falling victim to Medea's plots, but however her dominance is achieved it is then reinforced by the aside in which she steps out of her dialogue with Jason to become a spectator of his doom: *bene est, tenetur, vulneri patuit locus* (Good, he is caught! The place to wound him is laid bare *Medea* 550). Whereas the earlier Cassandra, like the messenger in *Thyestes* and like Hercules in his tragedy,[83] finds herself adrift in a strange and horrifying world, this Cassandra gives her approval to the spectacle which her prophetic inspiration shows to her eyes. She is not detached from the murder in the sense that she is unmoved by it—far from it:

> Tam clara numquam providae mentis furor
> ostendit oculis: video et intersum et fruor;
> imago visus dubia non fallit meos:
> spectemus!
>
> (*Agamemnon* 872–5)

(My prophetic madness has never shown things to my eyes so clearly. I see the scene, I am there, I relish it; this is no hazy picture deceiving my sight. Let us watch!)

She participates in the events but as someone who is not threatened by them, someone for whose entertainment they are enacted, and as such a spectator she enjoys a powerful detachment.

---

[83] *Quaenam ista regio est?* (*Thyestes* 627); cf. *Quis hic locus, quae regio, quae mundi plaga?* (Hercules recovering from his cosmos-spanning madness, *Hercules Furens* 1138).

Cassandra's claim to see more clearly than ever before is borne out by comparison of her two speeches. The first description begins with the judgement of Paris and spans many years in a few lines. This vision is also veiled: she sees Agamemnon as a lion killed by a lioness, and the shepherd who she prophesies will destroy the palace can be interpreted as both Paris and Aegisthus.[84] By contrast, the second description is narrated as if seen with an unprophetic eye and resembles more closely the banquet scene which Atreus watches through the opened doors of his palace (*Thyestes* 901 ff.).[85] Not only is this second vision clearer, it is also more controlled. In the previous description the battle of the lions is an oblique answer to a series of terrified questions:

> Quid ista vaecors tela feminea manu
> destricta praefert? quem petit dextra virum
> Lacaena cultu, ferrum Amazonium gerens?
> quae versat oculos alia nunc facies meos?
> (*Agamemnon* 734–7)

(Why is that madwoman's hand holding an unsheathed weapon? Spartan by dress, carrying an Amazon's steel, what man does she aim to attack? What different vision is directing my eyes now?)

In a technique used to greater effect in the messenger's speech in *Thyestes* Cassandra in her second vision asks a question only to answer it with complete authority and greater horror:

> horreo atque animo tremo:
> regemne perimet exul et adulter virum?
> venere fata. sanguinem extremae dapes
> domini videbunt et cruor Baccho incidet.
> (*Agamemnon* 883–6)

(I shudder and tremble in spirit! Shall the king be murdered by an exile, the husband by an adulterer? The hour of fate has come. The feast's last course will see the master's blood—yes, blood will drop into the wine.)

Beside the detail of blood mingling with the wine and its suggestion of cannibalism a horror of regicide seems rather faint-hearted.

---

[84] *agrestis iste alumnus evertet domum* (733). See Tarrant (1976) 308.
[85] If Cassandra were seeing 'naturally' her claim to see more clearly would, as Tarrant (1976) 335–6 remarks, be rather ludicrous.

Like the regicide the decapitation of Agamemnon is a horror described only to be surpassed:

> Nondum recedunt: ille iam exanimem petit
> laceratque corpus, illa fodientem adiuvat.
> *(Agamemnon* 904–5)

(They are not yet stepping away: he attacks Agamemnon now he is dead and mutilates his body, while she assists in the stabbing.)[86]

Cassandra closes her description with two forms of amplification common in Senecan tragedy: the characters are portrayed as representatives or echoes of their criminal ancestors, and the deed committed affects Nature itself, in this case turning the sun backwards.[87] Not only does Cassandra look on these horrors clear-eyed, but she shows a degree of verbal control absent in the earlier vision. The two forms of amplification occupy two lines each, the second developing the first:

> uterque tanto scelere respondet suis:
> est hic Thyestae natus, haec Helenae soror.
> Stat ecce Titan dubius emerito die,
> suane currat an Thyestea via.
> *(Agamemnon* 906–9)

(Both show themselves true to family by such a crime: he is Thyestes' son, she is Helen's sister. But see, with the day's work ended the Titan halts in confusion: should he run his own course, or a Thyestean course?)

The *hic* ... *haec* echoes the *ille* ... *illa* of 904–5, while in the previous block of four lines Clytemnestra's aiming of her murderous hand this way and that (*huc et illuc* 900) results in a separation of Agamemnon's body on this side (*hinc* 902) from his head on the other side (*illinc* 903). Horrible or not this description is ordered in a way that the previous vision, which jerks without warning from one scene to another, is not.[88]

Cassandra speaks of her *furor* (869, 872) before beginning her description of the fatal banquet, but does not interrupt the account itself with her own reactions or those of any other observer, real or

---

[86] Literally *fodientem* means 'digging'. Cf. *fodiantur oculi* and *effossis*...*oculis* (*Oedipus* 957 and 973–4).

[87] *Agamemnon* 906–9 Cf. e.g. *Phaedra* 175–7, which combines both elements.

[88] See also Tarrant (1976) 343 on 901: 'Seneca does little in this passage to justify his reputation for indiscriminate gore. The physical precision of the brief description is matched on the stylistic level by an approximation of a golden line.'

hypothetical, except as noted at line 883. By contrast, the earlier vision is something to which she responds: she asks questions, she sees, she follows, she prays. It has been suggested that one of the distinctive features of the Senecan messenger speech is the messenger's detachment from the events described. Unfiltered by the subjective response of the messenger or an imagined audience the description is to be read as an objective, even an authorial or authoritative, reality.[89] The greater control evident in Cassandra's second speech would fit well with this analysis as the prophetess sheds her human vulnerability to become the mouthpiece of Seneca or of dramatic reality, yet she introduces the description with an assertion of her involvement and enjoyment: *video et intersum et fruor* (873). Once the description of the murder is introduced in this way the detachment of the narrator is more naturally construed as the self-possession of a spectator without pity. Although Cassandra omits her reaction to the murder she does not forget that it is a spectacle: *habet* (901) is a cry from the spectators of a gladiatorial contest.[90] Before Clytemnestra delivers the fatal blow she first traces the spot with her eyes, *designat oculis* (899).[91] Cassandra's approval of the vision is similar to the approval Medea and Atreus give to performances which they themselves stage. Here again the roles of spectator and director of the crime merge as Clytemnestra, spectator-like, anticipates the blow with her gaze and in this way offers to Cassandra and a spectator that vicarious engagement which Cassandra claimed in her introduction.

Cassandra's *furor* returns in the last line of the tragedy:

CLYTAEMNESTRA. Furiosa, morere.
CASSANDRA. Veniet et vobis furor. (*Agamemnon* 1012)

(CLYTEMNESTRA. Die in your madness. CASSANDRA. Madness will come upon you too.)

This *furor* to come is of course the vengeance of Orestes, which like that of Clytemnestra will also be the vengeance of Cassandra

---

[89] Tietze (1994) 65.
[90] See Tarrant (1976) 343 and note especially the parallel in *Aeneid* 12.296 where Messapus' sacrificial killing of Aulestes is a public gesture intended to involve the Italians in the breaking of the truce.
[91] Perhaps it is worth noting that a *designator* or *dissignator* is an official who assigns seats either at the theatre or at funerals (*OLD* 556).

and the Trojans. Electra has told Clytemnestra that Orestes is no longer in Mycenae (967), but as Clytemnestra did not see Electra handing the child to Strophius she has no way of knowing whether Electra is telling the truth. Her demand, *redde nunc natum mihi* (Restore my son to me now 967), confirms her ignorance: Orestes is now no longer in Electra's keeping.[92] So soon after the success of her own plot Clytemnestra becomes the victim of Electra's, and it is to this failing character that Cassandra says, *veniet et vobis furor*. A reference which is clear to Cassandra and to the audience must be opaque to Clytemnestra. Like other victims of irony in Senecan tragedy Clytemnestra is rendered helpless by her ignorance of the myths which have already been written. Prophetic Cassandra, like Medea who aims to become Medea and like Atreus who models his revenge on Procne's, traces a familiar path; she speaks with a private significance shared only by those who also recognize the pattern.

The promised progression of *furor* from Cassandra to Clytemnestra recalls Juno's words to herself:

> ut possit animum captus Alcides agi,
> magno furore percitus, nobis prius
> insaniendum est: Iuno, cur nondum furis?
> (*Hercules Furens* 107–9)

(So that Hercules can be hounded, deranged and enraged, you must first feel madness.—Juno, why are *you* not yet raging?)

Juno, inspired by the Furies, plots the tragedy through which her revenge will be achieved. Similarly Orestes' murder of Clytemnestra is composed first in the prophetic inspiration of Cassandra. Without doubt Juno is a more powerful figure than Cassandra. Where Juno, Hercules-like, drags the Furies up from the underworld (*Hercules Furens* 95–9), Cassandra, initially at the mercy of her visions, finds herself surrounded by horrors in the underworld (*Agamemnon* 741–74). Juno picks the day of the tragedy (*H. F. inveni diem* 114) and directs its events (*H. F. videat...redeat...iuvet...vincat...cupiat* 113–16) while Cassandra looks merely to be a messenger: *perferre prima nuntium Phrygibus meis | propero* (I am eager to reach my Phrygians first

---

[92] The similar phrase, *redde iam gnatos mihi*, recurs in the mouth of the even more helpless Thyestes (*Thyestes* 997).

with the news *Ag.* 1005–6). But despite these differences both take pleasure in overseeing the suffering of their enemies. Cassandra speaks the last line of the tragedy with the kind of irony which distinguishes Seneca's most powerful protagonists, and if the earth did not in fact roll back to allow the Trojans to watch the murder of Agamemnon[93] Cassandra will recreate Clytemnestra's act for them with the words of a messenger speech. In her progression from a victim of the tragic spectacle to a prophet who delights in its controlled narration Cassandra makes the vengeance her own. When Clytemnestra terms her *furiosa* (1012) she alludes not only to her prophetic *furor*[94] but also to the extravagant pleasure she takes in outliving Troy and thereby seeing the Greeks' sufferings: *iam, iam iuvat vixisse post Troiam, iuvat* (*Now I am happy to have outlived Troy—yes, happy!* 1011). The priestess who first recoiled from the spectacle recovers to find common cause with the avengers and to see through their eyes. She does not share Clytemnestra's desire to avenge the murder of Iphigenia or Orestes' desire to avenge the murder of Agamemnon—she has her own reasons for vengeance—but at the moment of killing she can follow the direction of Clytemnestra's gaze (see above on 899) or anticipate Orestes as her creation (1012).[95]

Cassandra is noteworthy because she has no personal engagement in the motives which drive Clytemnestra or Orestes to vengeance but she takes pleasure in making their deeds her own. As Clytemnestra strikes the fatal blow and thereby satisfies her own desire for vengeance Cassandra simultaneously fashions an artful and no less cruel narrative of the killing. Excluded from this dramatic action and distanced further by a prophetic vision shared by no other dramatic character, Cassandra takes a viewer's satisfaction in the murder. Crucially, as far as her modelling of an audience's perspective is concerned, Cassandra's pleasure develops as the tragedy unfolds: revulsion gives way to satisfaction, paralysed horror to sadism. This trajectory is repeated in the perspectives of the protagonists of other Senecan tragedies, and the parallelism can be taken further. Cassandra, like Atreus, Medea, and Juno, finds the inspiration to subdue her horror in

---

[93] This was Cassandra's hope in her first vision (756–8).
[94] The interpretation of Tarrant (1976) 361.
[95] Tarrant (1976) 361 on *Agamemnon* 1012: '*furor* is here "avenging agent"'.

the underworld and more precisely in the infernal forces of the *Aeneid*. There is a similar parallelism between viewer and actor in *Thyestes* where the messenger comes to resemble Atreus and to take vicarious pleasure in the criminal spectacle. This parallelism is all the more striking because the messenger, unlike Cassandra, has no identity or motives of his own: Cassandra assumes the role of a messenger, but the messenger in *Thyestes* is a mere formal device without personal desires or allegiances to shape his perceptions. The alignment with Atreus of a character so blank as to be little more than the act of viewing or the act of narration itself is significant as a model of audience response.

The messenger's speech in *Thyestes* together with brief interruptions from the chorus and the ode which separates this act from the next occupies the entirety of Act 4. In the final section of his speech the messenger sees Thyestes eating his children and the sun reversing its course and awaits the final revelation (776–88). The messenger does more than supply an account of the action which must be completed by the beginning of the next act (the murder and cooking of the children): the vision of Thyestes at the table and the anticipation of his discovery recurs in Atreus' first speech in Act 5. There is no difficulty in dramatic time here;[96] the same scene is simply viewed from two different perspectives. Though the perspectives are formally distinct—the messenger and Atreus are different characters—in spirit they are very similar: Atreus' determination to reveal the crime however the darkness might try to obscure it echoes a similar determination at the close of the messenger's speech: *tamen videndum est. tota patefient mala* (yet he must see. All his troubles will be revealed 788).

[96] Atreus' words, *pergam et implebo patrem | funere suorum* (890–1) are awkward because Thyestes must at this point already have eaten his children. Tarrant (1985) 217 explains the phrase, 'I shall make Thyestes realize what he has done'. There seems little credible alternative to this explanation. I would add that there is an awkwardness in discarding the most natural meaning, 'I will proceed and fill the father with his dead sons', and that this awkwardness expresses effectively Atreus' obsessive concern with the audience of an action, his belief that an event has not happened in any meaningful sense unless it has been seen to happen (cf. *Medea* 992–4). But if this line does present a problem for dramatic time it does so no less within Atreus' speech than in the continuity from the messenger's to Atreus' speeches. On difficulties with dramatic time in this play see Shelton (1975), who argues that in *Thyestes* in the most basic and literal sense time repeats itself. Cf. Owen's (1970) approach that Seneca defies realistic chronology to present the same events in different modes.

Meta-Theatre and Self-Consciousness 227

If the messenger's view of Thyestes' banquet parallels most directly Atreus' view in the following act, the defeat of the forces who would conceal the crime parallels also events in the first and second acts: Furia's victory over Tantalus and Atreus' victory over his own hesitation and over the objections of his servant. Tantalus, having heard Furia's description of the forthcoming tragedy (59–67), attempts to return to the underworld (68 ff.). The paradoxes of his speech mark the surpassing of this conventional boundary[97] of both crime and pain:

> amate poenas. quando contiget mihi
>   effugere superos?   (82–3)

(love your punishments! When shall I have the chance to escape the upper world?)

The figure of boundaries surpassed is evident also in the messenger's first words. At the end of the preceding ode the chorus had commented:

> res deus nostras celeri citatas
>   turbine versat.   (621–2)

(God keeps our lives hastening, turning in a speeding whirlwind.)

The messenger responds immediately:

> quis me per auras turbo praecipitem vehet
> atraque nube involvet, ut tantum nefas
> eripiat oculis?   (623–5)

(Will some whirlwind carry me headlong through the air and wrap me in black cloud, to wrest such an outrage from my sight?)

The horror of the acts he has witnessed is such that the chorus's expression of despair is transformed for him into a hope of deliverance.[98] The chorus asks him to recount the deed, he again wishes to be carried off by the storm,[99] but the chorus will not be denied:

> quid sit quod horres ede et auctorem indica   (639)

(Tell us the source of your horror and name the culprit.)

---

[97] On the transgression of boundaries, moral and literary, in this play see Agapitos (1998) 231–7.
[98] So Tarrant (1985) 181: 'an obvious rephrasing of the Chorus' last words... but with a radical change of attitude'.
[99] *ferte me insanae procul, | illo, procellae, ferte quo fertur dies | hinc raptus* (636–8).

Tantalus' resistance to the crime (*stabo et arcebo scelus* (I shall stand and block the crime 95)) is overcome by Furia's whip, snakes, and fire (96 ff.) and Atreus, a more willing agent, also finds in the Furies the inspiration to proceed to his revenge (250 ff.). The messenger is not the author of the crime in the sense that Tantalus or Atreus is, but merely its reporter, and when he decides to reveal the crimes he is not represented as surrendering to demonic forces. No trace of passion is evident in the description of the palace with which he begins his account. In the grove at the centre of the palace are inspirations of the forthcoming tragedy: memorials of the crimes of Atreus' ancestors and a pool fed by the Styx. Various features of his palace recall in distorted form the palace of Virgil's Latinus: both have a grove where, surrounded by the spoils won by their ancestors, the kings conduct the rites which mark the beginning of their own tenure of the throne. But where Latinus is surrounded by the images of those who fought for their fatherland and the memorials of their glorious victories Atreus is surrounded by every crime of his family. The captured chariots which Latinus shows to Aeneas were won in battle; the chariot in the Atreus' palace is a memory of Myrtilus' betrayal:

> fractique currus, spolia Myrtoi maris,
> victaeque falsis axibus pendent rotae
> et omne gentis facinus.   (660–2)[100]

(hanging up are... wrecked chariots, spoils from the Myrtoan Sea, wheels defeated because of tampered axles, and all the exploits of the clan.)

More generally the trajectory of the messenger's description reverses that of the *Aeneid* in a similar way as the trajectory of Cassandra's vision did in *Agamemnon*. Where Aeneas leaves his Trojan ghosts behind and moves to Elysium and the Roman future without setting foot on the *sceleratum limen* of Tisiphone's tower, Cassandra is overcome by an infernal passion for ven-

---

[100] The parallelism between the two palaces (*Aeneid* 7.170 f. and *Thyestes* 641 f.) is well discussed by Walter (1975) 68–74, Tarrant (1985) 183–6, and more recently by Agapitos (1998) 248–50. Up to this point I have done little more than paraphrase some of Tarrant's observations. Note also his comment 186, 'Vergil's portrait of Latinus' ancestor Picus as proto-Roman is countered by the depiction of Pelops in blatantly oriental colors (662–63).' The relationship between Atreus' palace and the aesthetics of Horace, *Odes* 1.1 I discuss above (pp. 141–8).

geance. Here the distortion of Virgil's proto-Romans is developed further by the representation of the grove as part of Hell:

> nox propria luco est, et superstitio inferum
> in luce media regnat. (678–9)

(the grove has a night all its own, and an eerie sense of the underworld reigns in broad daylight.)

The messenger's narrative unlike Cassandra's does not stretch to a vision of the underworld and the spirits of the grove do not obviously recall the creatures of Virgil's Tartarus.[101] If there is an echo of *Aeneid* 6 it is in the description of the oracle:

> hinc orantibus
> responsa dantur certa, cum ingenti sono
> laxantur adyto fata et *immugit specus*
> vocem deo solvente. (679–82)

(Here those seeking oracles are granted infallible answers; destinies are revealed amidst thunderous noise, and the hollow space booms as a god unleashes his voice.)

The oracular responses issue from a grove in the inmost part of the palace, the *penetrale regni* (652), but here for the first and only time the setting is described as a *specus*, 'a cave' (hollow space). In Seneca's text the bellowing which issues from the 'cave' picks up the triple barking mentioned a few lines above: *saepe latratu nemus | trino remugit* (675–6).

The same verb is used of the prophecy which issues from the cave of Virgil's Sibyl:

> Talibus ex adyto dictis Cumaea Sibylla
> horrendas canit ambages antroque *remugit*
> (*Aeneid* 6.98–9)

(With words such as these the Cumaean Sibyl makes her fearful labyrinthine prophecies from the shrine and bellows from the cave).

The verb is not casually chosen: this bellowing and the labyrinthine prophecies recall the minotaur and the labyrinth carved on the doors of Daedalus' temple (*Aeneid* 6.24–30) and echoed in the form of the

---

[101] See e.g. Tarrant (1985) 187 on *hinc nocte caeca gemere feralis deos | fama est, catenis lucus excussis sonat* (668–9): 'the groaning and noise of chains are reminiscent of Vergil's Tartarus, cf. *Aen.* 6.557–8 *hinc audiri gemitus et saeva sonare | verbera, tum stridor ferri tractaeque catenae.*' The parallelism rightly draws no more than a general 'cf.'

cave with a hundred entrances and a hundred voices (*Aeneid* 6.42–4). Recalling the minotaur and the hounds of Hecate[102] respectively Virgil's and Seneca's prophecies are both written as a monstrous bellowing and thus have more in common than the simple recurrence of *-mugit* would suggest.

The prophecy of Virgil's Sibyl is distinguished by her failure to break free of the past; she sees only a repetition of Troy and with good reason Aeneas responds:

> non ulla laborum,
> o virgo, nova mi facies inopinave surgit;
> omnia praecepi atque animo mecum ante peregi
> (*Aeneid* 6.103–5)

(No new or unexpected form of labours rises up to confront me, maiden. I have grasped them all before and been through them in my mind.)

The hundred voices which characterize her labyrinthine utterances recur at the close of the description of Tartarus where she confesses herself unable to capture its myriad forms of criminality with even a hundred tongues and a hundred mouths (*Aeneid* 6.625–7). Aeneas will learn the future of his race from Anchises; the monstrous bellowing of the Sibylline voice is not itself the Roman revelation or the path out of the underworld. No prophecy is sought or given in Seneca's *Thyestes*. The inspiration which Atreus finds in the oracular cave is less specific: just as the transformation of Latinus' proto-Augustan[103] palace into a monument of tyranny and crime can be interpreted as unpicking the Roman destiny which Virgil promised, so the recollection of the monstrous and hellish aspects of the Sibyl's voice can be interpreted as an invocation of the forces which threaten that same destiny. Commenting on the irrelevance of the oracle as far as the narrative is concerned, Tarrant writes, 'Seneca may have placed it here to provide a religious context for Atreus' "sacrifice"'.[104] It provides also an ancestral context as Atreus, infected by the spirit of Tantalus, begins his revenge where his ancestors found their inspiration, and a literary context: through partial reading the tragedy draws its energy from the *Aeneid*'s darker voices.

---

[102] On threefold Hecate and hell-hounds see Costa (1973) 147 on *Medea* 840–1: ter latratus | audax Hecate dedit.
[103] Servius, cross-referencing to his note on 4.410, records that the description of Latinus' palace was interpreted as alluding to the imperial palace of Augustus.
[104] Tarrant (1985) 189. See also on 687–90.

The vatic inspiration of Atreus' crime is familiar. The selective Virgilian echoes and the influence of the Furies are distinctive features of the passion of Seneca's protagonists, but to what extent is this passion present in the messenger who merely narrates the crime? There is nothing quite to parallel Cassandra's assumption of Clytemnestra's vengeance, but to a more limited degree the messenger does see through Atreus' eyes. Atreus' entrance and his decoration of the altars, the first actions in the messenger's account, are accompanied by the first reference to the narrator since the introduction to the speech over forty lines earlier: *quis queat digne eloqui?* (Who could express it adequately? 684) he asks.

The messenger's anxiety that Atreus' talent for evil exceeds his own talent to narrate it is most naturally interpreted as a 'harrowing cry of despair'.[105] Atreus had threatened to surpass human limits and the messenger's hesitation confirms that success in a similar way as the disruption in the heavens inadvertently advertises and celebrates the triumph of his evil.[106] The messenger's desire to narrate appropriately is followed by Atreus' warped concern with ritual observance and this first section of the narrative ends with Atreus' intentions:[107]

>   servatur omnis ordo, ne tantum nefas
>   non rite fiat.   (689–90)

(Every part of the ritual is kept, to ensure that such an outrage is performed by the rules.)

This paradoxical mode of expression is characteristic of Atreus' desire to transcend past limits. A distinctive feature of the early part of his dialogue with the *Satelles* is the use of the servant to express a conventional perspective which Atreus can then confound, most obviously in these lines:

SATELLES. Nefas nocere vel malo fratri puta.
ATREUS. Fas est in illo quidquid in fratre est nefas.   (219–20)

(SERVANT. Consider it wrong to harm even a wicked brother. ATREUS. All that is wrong in dealing with a brother is right in dealing with him.)

---

[105] Tarrant (1985) 189.
[106] *Nescioquid animus maius et solito amplius | supraque fines moris humani tumet* (267–8). On the failure of the heavens' attempt to supress Atreus' crime see above, Ch. 3, Sect. 2.
[107] The subjunctive *fiat*, expressing intention, is the first finite verb of the narrative (starting at line 641) which is not indicative.

Whether assisted by a foil or speaking in soliloquy Seneca's passionate protagonists herald their revenge with this kind of linguistic strain. Medea's *quidquid admissum est adhuc, | pietas vocetur* (Let any deed committed so far be called love of family *Medea* 904–5) is another example. In speaking in this style the messenger briefly mimics and thereby adopts the persona of Atreus. The effect is analogous to a phenomenon discussed by Laird as 'mimetic indirect discourse (MID)'. In MID, as opposed to ordinary indirect discourse, 'the diction does seem to be more the property of the original speaker than the narrator'.[108] The trace of the original speech (virtual or actual) may be apparent through focalization or through affinities between the style or diction of the original speaker (heard elsewhere in *oratio recta*) and that of the reported speech. Although *ne tantum nefas | non rite fiat* is not properly indirect speech it does nevertheless imply a speech: it is the justification for the elaborate preparations which Atreus might have given had he been asked, and it is written in his style.

The horrified messenger of 684 interrupts his narrative with a perspective and a style which are not his own and the chorus accentuates the effect by asking a question, *Quis manum ferro admovet?* (Who sets his hand to the knife? 690), and thereby making lines 689–90 the *sententia* which closes the section. The chorus had asked in lines 638–40 for their suspense to be ended. Fifty lines later as the messenger lingers over the details of the preparations for the sacrifice the chorus feels it has suffered enough and asks for the *coup de grâce*.[109] The messenger replies:

> *Ipse* est sacerdos, *ipse* funesta prece
> letale carmen ore violento canit.
> stat *ipse* ad aras, *ipse* devotos neci
> contrectat et componit et ferro apparat[110]
> attendit *ipse*: nulla pars sacri perit.   (691–5)

---

[108] Laird (1999) 95 for the quotation and 88, 94–6 for the discussion. See especially 96 n. 42 on *Aeneid* 7.167–78, 'There is a change in *focalization* in this sentence, from the narrator to the messenger: it is worth considering this as a marker of MID.'

[109] Cf. Jason's plea to Medea (*Medea* 1014–18).

[110] Zwierlein (1986*b*) reads *admovet* with both A and E. Fitch accepts Axelson's emendation *apparat* and translates accordingly.

(He himself is priest, he himself makes sinister prayers and sings the death-chant in a bloodthirsty voice. He stands by the altar himself, himself handles and arranges those doomed to slaughter and readies them for the knife; he himself checks details—no part of the ritual is forgotten.)

Atreus' lethal song is never heard and in fact the messenger's speech contains no voiced indirect speech. Without doubt the reference to a *carmen* and the use of the word *canit* remind one of the literary nature of Atreus' revenge,[111] but it is worth noting also that the only violent words here are the messenger's. He does not merely end the chorus's suspense by relating that Atreus wields the knife in this perverted ritual but drives the point home... five times. The chorus sets itself up to be wounded by the messenger's answer, but the messenger embraces the wounding role with some vigour.

Atreus does not rush his crime but waits to check that no part of the ritual fails. The portents which are described in the following lines are a confirmation of its potency and of divine outrage:

> Movere cunctos monstra, sed solus sibi
> immotus Atreus constat, atque ultro deos
> terret minantes.   (703–5)

(All are affected by these prodigies, but Atreus alone remains unaffected and constant; he counter-threatens the menacing gods.)

Who the other observers are is unclear,[112] but they offer an alternative perspective which by comparison underlines the inhumanity of Atreus'. However, after offering these alternatives the narrative resolves into Atreus' perspective. In the subsequent simile from the banks of the Ganges the tigress is uncertain

---

[111] The grove in *Thyestes* recalls the grove described in messenger speech by Creon in *Oedipus* 530–658. See Tarrant (1985) 184 ff. Commanded by the rites of Tiresias the earth opens up to allow passage to Furies, damned spirits, and ultimately Laius himself. Schiesaro (1997b: 93–8) discusses this representation of the poet-prophet's passionate and hellish inspiration as 'the one that reaches deepest in the reconstruction of the process of poetic creation' (97). He also compares Creon compelled to speak by Oedipus to Tantalus compelled to speak by Furia (94). Within *Thyestes* itself the unwilling messenger speech reiterates the meta-literary concerns of the prologue.

[112] The falling star would have been visible to anyone in the world of the drama, the transformation of the libation only to someone present at the sacrifice. The singers of the following ode (789–884) comment only on the celestial disruption and it seems reasonable to take them as representative of the *cunctos* of 703.

which bull to bite first: *quo primum ferat incerta morsus* (709–10). This indirect question models Atreus' view and, in the absence of any other, the view of the narrative:

> sic dirus Atreus capita devota impiae
> speculatur irae. quem prius mactet sibi
> dubitat, secunda deinde quem caede immolet.
> nec interest—sed dubitat et saevum scelus
> iuvat ordinare. (712–16)

(so dread Atreus surveys the victims consecrated to his godless anger. He hesitates: which shall he sacrifice first to himself, then which shall he offer up in the second killing? It makes no difference, yet he hesitates and takes pleasure in ordering the savage crime.)

The forthcoming murders are seen through Atreus' predatory gaze and the pleasure it affords him. As before (690 above), the chorus interrupts the messenger, who like Atreus is delaying the fatal blows, to ask for the act itself: *Quem tamen ferro occupat?* (Which one *does* he catch first with the sword? 716). Again the messenger mimics Atreus' style:

> Primus locus (ne desse pietatem putes)
> avo dicatur: Tantalus prima hostia est. (717–18)

(First place (lest you think him lacking in family feeling) is dedicated to his grandfather: Tantalus is the first victim.)

The mocking inversion of *pietas* echoes closely the earlier comment, *ne tantum nefas | non rite fiat* (689–90). However, Atreus had no audience and in speaking as he does the messenger is to be seen as appropriating Atreus' persona and adapting it to his own situation. The messenger has no crimes and no victims of his own but he does have an audience determined to have the evil revealed, whatever it is.[113] With the shift to the second person here (*ne...putes* cf. *ne...fiat*) the messenger brings the horrified audience into the narrative and mocks its moral scruples. Atreus earlier had tied a purple band around the foreheads of the victims in honour of their royal blood[114] and it would be quite consistent for him here to incorporate further mock honours into his sacrifice like giving pride of place to Tantalus. More than likely the messenger is incorporating one of Atreus' taunts into his narrative and

---

[113] *Effare et istud pande, quodcumque est, malum* (633).
[114] See Tarrant (1985) 189 on *vitta...purpurea* (686).

certainly the earlier comment, *sed dubitat et saevum scelus | iuvat ordinare* (715–16), makes it unlikely that the order of the murders was random. Nonetheless the messenger's use of the second person *putes* marks a growing identification of himself with Atreus as the chorus's sensibilities become as important a victim as the sons of Thyestes.

The chorus asks whether Tantalus died a good death. The messenger appears to reply in the affirmative, Stetit *sui securus* (He stood firm without concern for himself 720), but this Stoic resolution[115] is then undermined by the description of his lifeless body:

> educto *stetit*
> ferro cadaver, cumque dubitavisset diu
> hac parte an illa caderet, in patruum cadit. (723–5)

(When the steel was pulled out the corpse stayed upright: after long hesitation whether to fall this way or that, it fell on its uncle.)

'A mocking echo of Tantalus' resolute "stand" of a moment ago,' comments Tarrant, 'another sign of the Messenger's complete absorption of Atreus' spirit'.[116] Quite so. As the honouring of grandfather Tantalus was a gesture consistent with Atreus' persona the decision of little Tantalus to strike against Atreus even in death is appropriate behaviour for a victim: Polyxena made the same gesture in *Troades* (1158–9). Perhaps even the pitiful echo of Atreus' hesitation in the behaviour of Tantalus' corpse can be interpreted as an irony inherent in the events which the messenger witnessed, but the play on *stetit* can only be read as the narrator's construction. Atreus' sacrifice is a ritual outrage of moral sensibility and the messenger who revisits the scene increasingly shares the perspective of its author and orders the crime with similar intent.

The chorus calls the murders a *saevum scelus* (743) and the messenger's near total identification with Atreus is apparent in his response:

---

[115] Freedom from cares, at the root of *securus*, is classically an Epicurean ideal, but Tantalus' defiance of the tyrant gives a typically Stoic cast to this virtue of indifference to external threats. On mockery of Stoic resolution in the characterization of Atreus (*sed solus sibi | immotus Atreus constat* 703–4) see Agapitos (1998) 238.
[116] Tarrant (1985) 194.

NUNTIUS.   Exhorruistis? hactenus si stat nefas,
   pius est.
CHORUS.   An ultra maius aut atrocius
   natura recipit?
NUNTIUS.   Sceleris hunc finem putas?
   gradus est.
CHORUS.   Quid ultra potuit? obiecit feris
   lanianda forsan corpora atque igne arcuit?   (744–8)

(MESSENGER. You shudder? If this is where the outrage stops, he is a righteous man. CHORUS. Does nature have room for anything still greater or more atrocious? MESSENGER. You think this is the end-point of crime? It is just a step! CHORUS. What could he do beyond this? Perhaps toss the bodies to wild beasts to tear, and deny them fire?)

As in line 717 but to a greater degree the messenger recognizes the chorus as his audience in order to mock its offended scruples. The relative piety of the murders is a paradox characteristic of the expression of an Atreus. There is also some similarity between this exchange and that between Atreus and his servant in Act 2, where the servant's pallid visions of crime are dismissed as inadequate by his more accomplished master (245–8, 255–7). The messenger appears to return to sanity: he prefers the chorus's imaginings to the truth but then closes his recapitulation of its list with Atreus' reality:

$$\text{o nullo scelus}$$
   credibile in aevo quodque posteritas neget:
   erepta vivis exta pectoribus tremunt   (753–5)

(No age could believe such a crime: the future will deny it. Torn from the living chests the organs are still trembling).

Posterity will try to suppress the deed[117] but not so the messenger. No less brutally than he answered the chorus's question at 690 ff. he begins this section of the narrative with the words 'torn from the living' and the detail of the entrails still trembling.

The deliberate precision of the messenger's description reflects Atreus' own care, but as in Cassandra's second speech care must be taken to distinguish between an 'objective' vision of horror and the same events viewed by a spectator who lacks compassion.

---

[117] On the theme of failed suppression in this tragedy and its origin in one of the myths of Tantalus see Schiesaro (1994).

Meta-Theatre and Self-Consciousness 237

Nature tries to obstruct Atreus' revenge: the fire tries to jump over the meat and only reluctantly cooks it. Against such a background the character of the messenger's intrusion in 771–2 is all the more jarring:

> *invitus ardet.* strid*et in veribus iecur;*
> *nec facile dicam corpora an flammae magis*
> *gemuere.*[118]   (770–2)

(it burns grudgingly. The liver hisses on the spit; I could not easily say whether the bodies or flames groan more loudly.)

The messenger's difficulty in saying which groaned more could not be more different in spirit from the reluctance of the fire, yet consecutive lines begin superficially parallel to each other. With the first-person verb the messenger is in the midst of a crime from which Nature herself recoils and which posterity will not accept yet he feels no revulsion. Victims and witness (Nature) vie with each other in their screams and the messenger coolly declares the contest a draw.[119]

The Messenger addresses the retreating Sun:

> O Phoebe patiens, fugeris retro licet
> medioque raptum merseris caelo diem,
> sero occidisti—lancinat gnatos pater
> artusque mandit ore funesto suos   (776–9)

(O long-suffering Phoebus! Though you have fled backward, snatched the day from mid-heaven and drowned it, you set too late! The father is mangling his sons, gnawing his own limbs with entombing teeth.)

---

[118] Zwierlein (1986*b*) gives *nec facile dicas corpora an flammae gemant:* | *gemuere.* *Dicas* for *dicam* is Heinsius' emendation; *gemant* for *magis* is MS A preferred to E. The motive for choosing *gemant* over *magis* must surely be to avoid the indicative in the indirect question. Tarrant shows precedents for this (1976: 201) and the awkwardness of a rare construction is surely less than the awkwardness of meaning in the lines as A has it: *gemuere* would be an emphatic and unclear resolution to the preceding question. 'In any event there *was* groaning' seems a desperately lame conclusion. *Dicas* and *dicam* both seem reasonable to me and I am therefore reluctant to accept the emendation.

[119] Tarrant (1985) 201 suggests that 'the Messenger seems to be calling attention to the cleverness of his play on *gemere*', a word which is used for the sounds of burning wood. I find this interpretation very attractive but it is certainly less obvious than mine and to be convinced I would want a more exotic verbal stunt. In support of Tarrant's interpretation see his earlier note (1985: 201) on *flammatus latex* (766) and 'stylistic playfulness'.

This banquet described here is simultaneous with the opening of Act 5 and viewed from a similar perspective. The cruelty which the messenger has shown to the chorus is extended to the Sun: again the messenger as the source of the horror is ranked against those who are properly revolted by Atreus' deeds. It would be astonishing for Thyestes, however gluttonous, to tear his food apart as the messenger suggests. This is the behaviour of wild beasts, transposed from the chorus's fears and from Atreus' rage to characterize Thyestes' deed in such a way as to outrage the watching Sun.[120] The worst fear which the chorus could imagine was that the sons of Thyestes would lack burial and be torn apart by wild beasts (747–8, quoted above), *lanianda* dramatically first word in the line as *lancinat* is the messenger's first word of the description here.[121] The devouring frenzy eagerly anticipated in Atreus' earlier vision of the banquet and repeated in the messenger's wild beast similes for Atreus murdering (707–11 and 732–6) is an expression of Atreus' *furor* which the messenger has assumed;[122] it cannot possibly represent an 'objective' vision of Thyestes at the table. Atreus' desire in the following act (893–5) to force the fleeing gods to watch the banquet echoes the messenger's sentiment here.

The continuity between the messenger's perspective and Atreus' in Act 5 is evident also in their treatment of Thyestes. The messenger, now habitually using the second person, addresses Thyestes from a position of superior knowledge, and Atreus echoes his insistence that the horror will be revealed:

NUNTIUS.   in malis unum hoc *tuis*
   bonum est, Thyesta, quod mala ignoras *tua*.
   sed et hoc peribit.   (782–4)

(MESSENGER. In your troubles there is this one boon, Thyestes, that you are ignorant of your troubles! But this too will perish.)

---

[120] The Messenger's forceful response to the chorus in 691 ff. is comparable.
[121] *Lanio* and *lancino* may not be from the same root, but they have very similar meaning.
[122] Atreus' vision was as follows: *liberos avidus pater | gaudensque laceret* (277–8). So Tarrant (1985) 202. On projections of Atreus as wild beast onto Thyestes see also Tarrant on *madidus* which is used only of the lion's jaws (734) and Thyestes' perfumed hair (780).

Compare:

ATREUS. etiam die nolente discutiam *tibi*
  tenebras, miseriae sub quibus latitant *tuae*. (896–7)
(ATREUS. Even though the daylight is unwilling, I shall dispel for you the darkness that conceals your sorrows.)

Echoes of the messenger's speech in Atreus' vision confirm the parallelism: both see the same drunken victim (*gravisque vino* (781); cf. *vino gravatum* (910)), their superior knowledge contrasts with the victim's incapacity (*nec satis menti imperat* 919), both draw attention to the inequality between viewer and viewed by addressing Thyestes and predicting his doom in words which he cannot hear, and both insist on his belated discovery despite the attempts of natural or Olympian order to repress it. So soon after the messenger's address to the Sun his statement, *sed et hoc peribit* (784 above), cannot be read neutrally and this is confirmed in the following lines:

                verterit currus licet
    sibi ipse Titan obvium ducens iter
    tenebrisque facinus obruat taetrum novis
    nox missa ab ortu tempore alieno gravis,
    tamen videndum est. tota patefient mala. (784–8)

(Though the Titan has turned his chariot, tracing a path counter to himself, and though the foul deed is smothered in strange darkness by this oppressive night, released from the East and at an alien time, yet he must see. All his troubles will be revealed.)

Verterit currus licet (784) recalls *fugeris retro licet* (776), and the apparently dispassionate third-person narrative is invested with the malice of the earlier address. By the final line of his speech the messenger has been transformed from a figure paralysed by the murders he has seen to one who takes pleasure in watching a worse crime and who, not without malice, insists that it must be watched. The messenger is so far distanced from the dramatic action by his lack of personal interest that he is barely a character at all. In a narrative which runs past the familiar loci of tragic inspiration he metamorphoses into a second Atreus, appropriates the actions as his own, and closes his speech no less engaged than the protagonist. As well as dramatizing once again in this tragedy the power of evil to subdue moral sensibility and to find expression, the change in the messenger models a sadistic spectatorship.

5. MODELLING AN AMBIVALENT SPECTATORSHIP

Although the inscribed audience of Greeks and Trojans in Act 5 is perhaps the most natural starting point for discussion of Senecan metatheatricality in *Troades*, the messenger and the audience of his speech are significant also not least for comparison with their counterparts in *Thyestes*. As in *Thyestes* this messenger is a nameless functionary, but more strikingly so here where a named messenger, Talthybius (who announced the deaths of Astyanax and Polyxena in Euripides' *Troades* and *Hecuba*) appeared earlier in the tragedy to deliver the account of Achilles' ghostly apparition.[123] Recent commentators have interpreted Seneca's nameless messenger as neutral and objective in a way that the Greek Talthybius could not be. For Fantham the messenger's neutrality is a guarantee of the narrative's moral truth.[124] There is much to recommend such an interpretation—it is indeed difficult to imagine Talthybius presenting the events as a *scelus* (1057)—but as the messenger of *Thyestes* illustrates, anonymity is not necessarily a mark of moral authority. Boyle notes also the artistry of the messenger's speech and observes grief contained and controlled by poetic order. Again there is nothing objectionable in this interpretation but that it need not be so: both the messenger of *Thyestes* and Cassandra in *Agamemnon* overcome their own horror to subjugate their victims with their rhetorical art. The anonymous and faceless messenger is a device to focus attention on the narrative of tragic crime, but the model it offers need not be uniform, static, or morally authoritative.

The messenger of *Troades* is closely associated with Andromache and the ambivalence of their perspective here to some extent echoes the ambivalent pleasure she took earlier in the lamentation

---

[123] See Fantham (1982) 366.
[124] Fantham (1982) 367. See also Boyle (1994) 225, who argues that the messenger's anonymity indicates Seneca's 'desire to focus on the messenger's narrative as narrative' and that this narrative offers verbal resolution to the play's pain.

which Ulysses permitted her. Where Astyanax makes a premature departure from the Greek ritual Andromache and the messenger remain to dwell on the horror of his ruined body. The inscribed audience of Greeks (and less importantly Trojans) offers a different perspective again. The familiar savagery of the victimizing gaze, complete with selective reminiscences of the *Aeneid* and a Fury's inspiration, gives way to the tragic emotions of pity and fear. Certainly the Greeks are moved by the doomed youth of Astyanax and Polyxena, but one may still ask to what extent these tragic sensibilities are a mere aesthetic gloss on Achilles' thirst for vengeance and to what extent they represent a serious alternative to the criminal ritual and a different tragic voice. *Troades*, I will argue, differs from *Thyestes* and *Agamemnon* partly in that it does not so simply or so powerfully represent tragic madness growing from a narrative of horrors, frenzy inspired in the narrator from the telling or the vision of crime. This element is present but only as one image of reception among many and in this respect it resembles more closely the polyphonic self-consciousness of *Hercules Furens*.

Like the messenger of *Thyestes*, *Troades'* messenger is called to speak by his audience: *ede et enarra omnia* (Speak out, recount everything *Troades* 1067); compare *quid sit quod horres ede et auctorem indica* (Tell us the source of your horror and name the culprit *Thyestes* 639). Perhaps the theatrical connotations of *ede* remind an audience to hear the following speeches as performances,[125] but even before the *ekphrasis topou* which begins both speeches the relationship between *editor*, audience, and events and hence the nature of the performance has been differently constructed. *Thyestes'* messenger recovers from a private terror to reveal to an anxious chorus deeds of which Atreus is the only other witness. He narrates the crime as carefully as Atreus enacted it and his audience receives the recreated horror when and how the messenger represents it. This inequality of roles is avoided in *Troades*. In two lines prior to his long speech the messenger confirms that the sacrifices have been committed and offers a consolation:

> Mactata virgo est, missus e muris puer;
> sed uterque letum mente generosa tulit.
> (*Troades* 1063–4)

---

[125] So Boyle (1994) 224, who compares also the use of the verb at *Oedipus* 222.

(The maiden is sacrificed, the boy thrown from the walls; but each bore death with a noble heart)

From the start the audience and speaker share knowledge of the events to be told. The preceding ode (1009–55) closed with a vision of the smoke of Troy blackening the sky and the words, *Troes hoc signo patriam videbunt* (By this sign Trojans will see their land 1055). The forthcoming killings are described against this setting and in the context of the memories of the past ten years (1057–8). In this respect the final act of the tragedy recalls its opening, which Hecuba began by calling the audience (or more precisely those who trust in their power and prosperity) to look on her and the smoke of the burning city.[126] Talthybius entered after an ode reviewing the sorrows of the past ten years (67–163) and then described the still unsatisfied anger of Achilles (164–202). By defining her audience as the powerful and the prosperous Hecuba asks the audience to see itself in another world empire, now ruined.[127] The audience at the beginning of the tragedy is aligned with the Trojans and the sympathies of the nameless messenger are equally clear in the first words of the final act:

> O dura fata, saeva *miseranda* horrida!
> quod tam ferum, tam triste bis quinis scelus
> Mars vidit annis? quid prius *referens gemam*,
> tuosne potius, an tuos luctus, anus?   (1056–9)

(O cruel deaths, harsh and *pitiable* and horrible! What crime as grim and savage has Mars beheld in these twice five years? What shall I first *tell with tears*: your griefs [*to Andromache*] or yours, old woman?)

This messenger's narrative is a lament of pitiable deaths and Andromache identifies him even more closely with herself:

> Expone seriem caedis, et duplex nefas
> persequere: gaudet magnus aerumnas dolor
> tractare totas. ede et enarra omnia.   (1065–7)

---

[126] *me videat et te, Troia* (4); *diripitur ardens Troia, nec caelum patet | undante fumo: nube ceu densa obsitus | ater favilla squalet Iliaca dies* (19–21).

[127] See Fantham (1982) 208 and Boyle (1994) 134–7 on the extent of Troy's power and Roman aspects of its characterization. Allusions to the *Aeneid* are important: the catalogue of Trojan allies (*Troades* 8–14) recalls the scenes on Dido's temple (*Aeneid* 1.46 ff.) and Seneca's description of the sack of Troy recalls Virgil's (see Boyle (1994) 136–7 on *Troades* 15–20).

(Describe the sequence of killing, detail the double crime; great pain enjoys dwelling on its sorrow in full. Speak out, recount everything.)

Most obviously it is Andromache who will take pleasure in the narrative of her sorrows, but the verb *tractare* more naturally suggests a narrator rather than an audience.[128] The preceding ode opened with a similarly provocative conjunction of pleasure and pain (*dulce maerenti populus dolentum, | dulce lamentis resonare gentes* (Sweet to one grieving is a host of mourners, sweet that whole peoples are loud with laments 1009–10)). This consolation of a community of suffering is to be set against the consolation of a merciful extinction: the world of the drama makes trial of the different arguments. In the same way Andromache's claim that grief finds consolation in its expression is not an authoritative view but one of which trial will be made in the course of the messenger's speech. Just as a carelessness for one's own life may indicate Stoic contempt for the morally indifferent or raging passion so the paradoxical *gaudet...dolor*, taken in isolation, is potentially indicative of madness or a transforming resolution.

The description of the smoke of Troy (1053–5) with which the chorus closed the preceding ode recalls a description of the soul dissolved at death as the smoke rising from funeral fires (392–6).[129] The consolation that evils cannot pursue one beyond the grave is no consolation for Andromache: in the first speech following this second ode she complains that Astyanax keeps her from death and its freedom from cares (418–23). Astyanax obstructs the closure which would otherwise be hers as is seen very clearly in the scene where he is surrendered to Ulysses. Andromache asks for a brief delay in which to say farewell to her son and Ulysses agrees:

ANDROMACHE. Brevem moram largire, dum officium parens
   nato supremum reddo et amplexu ultimo
   avidos dolores satio.
ULYSSES. Misereri tui
   utinam liceret. quod tamen solum licet,
   tempus moramque dabimus. arbitrio tuo
   implere lacrimis: fletus aerumnas levat.

(*Troades* 760–5)

---

[128] The verb can be used for dramatic performance, e.g. *cum tractaretur Atreus* (Cicero, *De Officiis* 3.106), but it is more common in a non-theatrical context for other forms of interpretation or discussion. See *OLD* (1982) 1955.

[129] So Fantham (1982) 365.

(ANDROMACHE. Grant me a brief delay, while I pay my son a mother's final service, and satisfy my yearning grief with a last embrace. ULYSSES. I wish I were allowed to show you pity. But I shall give the only thing that is allowed, a respite of time. Take your fill of tears without constraint; weeping eases troubles.)

Twenty lines later Ulysses interrupts Andromache as she is advertising in characteristically Senecan fashion a crime worse than any seen before:

ANDROMACHE. flebilius aliquid Hectoris magni nece
  muri videbunt.
ULYSSES. Rumpe iam fletus, parens:
  magnus sibi ipse non facit finem dolor.
                    (*Troades* 784–6)

(ANDROMACHE. The walls will see something more pitiful than the killing of great Hector. ULYSSES. Break off your weeping now, mother; great grief sets itself no limit.)

This great pain does not find consolation or resolution—it makes no end for itself—and the pattern is immediately repeated: Andromache laments for twenty lines (792–812) until interrupted by Ulysses:

          Nullus est flendi modus:
  abripite propere classis Argolicae moram.
                    (*Troades* 812–13)

(There is no limit to weeping: [*to soldiers*] quickly, carry off this delay to the Argive fleet.)

The fleet cannot leave until Astyanax is sacrificed and certainly he delays the Greeks by continuing to live, but Ulysses justifies his termination of the *mora* here because Andromache's lamentation has no limit. She was granted a delay in which to satisfy her pain (762) and lighten her sorrow with weeping (765) but to no avail: the pain burns ever more fiercely as it is allowed to express itself. The first lament on the future which Astyanax will now not enjoy culminates in a description of an ecstatic dance and the advertisement of the forthcoming crime as surpassing established limits. After Hector's death and mutilation Andromache was *torpens malis* (numbed by adversity) and endured everything *sine sensu* (without feeling 417), but here she finds some even more lamentable spectacle (*flebilius* 784) and a form of doom sadder than dreadful death: *o morte dira tristius leti genus!* (783). It is strange to imagine a Trojan prince actually participating in the frenzied rites of oriental eunuchs,[130] but the function of the description is to provide an appropriately frenzied introduction to the excessive pain referred to in the following lines. Ulysses interrupts the lament not simply because it has not come to an end in the space of twenty lines but because her grief is growing with the telling rather than subsiding. He interrupts again to close the second lament in part perhaps Andromache has started repeating herself,[131] but most obviously to curtail a passion which knows no restraint. The description of Andromache seeking out grains of Hector's dust with her lips (*si quid hic cineris latet,* | *scrutabor ore* (If any of his dust lurks here, my lips will discover it 811–12)) has drawn comparisons with the self-destructive madness of Medea and of Oedipus.[132] 'Seneca *knows no bounds* in describing macabre physical details': as Fantham on Seneca so Ulysses on Andromache, *nullus est flendi modus* (812).[133] Andromache's statement to the messenger, *gaudet magnus aerumnas dolor* | *tractare totas* (great pain enjoys dwelling on its sorrow in full 1066–7), must be coloured by her previous behaviour.[134]

The messenger's account, though framed in this way by the ambivalence of Andromache's sympathy, is concerned at first to contrast the hostile Greek audience with the object of their gaze, Astyanax. The messenger begins with Troy's single surviving

[130] So Fantham (1982) 318. Boyle (1994) 200 makes the point that the priesthood of the cult in Rome had recently been opened to Roman citizens by the emperor Claudius, but this is rather different from immediate participation in the frenzied dance described here: *non inter aras mobili velox pede,* | *reboante flexo concitos cornu modos,* | *barbarica prisco templa saltatu coles* (780–2). Any similarity between this dance and that of the Roman *Salii* (see Boyle) is surely rejected by the pointed reference to *barbarica ... templa.*

[131] So Fantham (1982) 322 on 806 ff. as an expansion and repetition of 799–800.

[132] *Medea* 1012–13, *in matre si quod pignus etiamnunc latet* | *scrutabor ense viscera* and *Oedipus* 965 *scrutatur avidus manibus uncis lumina.* See Fantham (1982) 323 and Boyle (1994) 201–2 on these passages and Seneca's use of *scrutari.* On *Oedipus* 372 and 965 as paradigmatic of a vision of criminal horror see above, pp. 175–7.

[133] Fantham (1982) 323, my emphasis. The parallelism between authors and audiences is surely implicit in Fantham's choice of words, but I felt constrained to spell it out.

[134] Cf. also Helen's words: *ratione quamvis careat et flecti neget* | *magnus dolor...* (903–4).

tower which is not only the scene of Astyanax's death but a symbol of this last Trojan prince.[135] Similarly the surrounding landscape in which the crowd gathers is more than just a setting: the very wood trembles with the people hanging in suspense: *et tota populo silva suspenso tremit* (the whole woodland trembled with people hanging in it 1083).[136] Once the tower was a safe place where Priam embraced his grandson (*turre in hac blando sinu | fovens nepotem* (On this tower he would gently fold his grandchild in his arms 1071–2)) and looked out over the battle. As the positions are reversed and the Greek army becomes the audience the tower is transformed: *haec nota quondam turris et muri decus, | nunc saeva cautes* (This once famous tower and glory of the wall, now a grim crag 1075–6). Although the reversal of fortune and the pathos of little Astyanax have their origins in the tower of Priam's palace in *Aeneid* 2.453 ff., Seneca's association of the Trojan defeat with a reversal of the roles of viewer and viewed is his own development. Once Priam watched from the battlements when Hector drove the Greeks in flight (1072–3), now the victorious Greek sits on the memorial of Hector's defeat to view the tower:

> atque aliquis (nefas)
> tumulo ferus spectator Hectoreo sedet.
> (*Troades* 1086–7)

(and—an outrage—one callous spectator took his seat on Hector's tomb.)

The *ferus spectator*, a paradigmatic figure,[137] blends together elements from within and without the dramatic illusion. The Roman colouring of plebis*que turba cingitur* (1077) encourages the natural identification of the real (or virtual) audience of the play with the audience inscribed,[138] but there are reminiscences

---

[135] *Est una magna turris e Troia super* (1068). For the symbolism see Boyle (1994) 225.

[136] See Fantham (1982) 370 and Boyle (1994) 225.

[137] So Boyle (1997) 120.

[138] See also Caviglia (1981) 300, who recalls Horace's use of *coibat* for theatre crowds: *quo populus numerabilis, utpote parvus, | et frugi castusque verecundusque coibat* (*Ars Poetica* 206–7); cf. *totum coit | ratibus relictis vulgus* (*Troades* 1077–8). Shelton (2000) 101–6 argues that the Romans would naturally identify with the victorious Greeks in this scene and certainly Hecuba in her first lines offers the tragedy as a lesson for the proud rather than the defeated. As descendants of Aeneas' Trojans the Romans would also identify with the victims, however, and the reversal of roles which Fortune threatens is in some sense achieved by these contradictory identifications.

Meta-Theatre and Self-Consciousness 247

also of the first messenger speech which describes the appearance of Achilles' vengeful ghost (168 ff.). There too the trembling which shakes the human frame is echoed and amplified in the landscape:

> pavet animus, artus horridus quassat tremor
> (*Troades* 168)

(My mind feels fear, a shuddering tremor shakes my body.)

Compare:

> nec terra solum tremuit: et pontus suum
> adesse Achillem sensit ac stravit vada.
> (*Troades* 176–7)

(Not only the earth trembled: the sea too sensed its own Achilles near, and prostrated its waters.)[139]

Achilles rises up from Erebus, lifts up his tomb (*tumulum levat* 180), and demands the death of Polyxena which will close the tragedy. The supernatural manner in which Achilles shakes the landscape has a more mundane parallel in the trees which tremble with the weight of the Greek spectators.[140] Achilles' easy lifting of the tomb as he rises from the dead contrasts with the impotence of Hector and Troy, both trapped under the mundane weight of the Greek audience. For Fantham *pressit* (1086) is a poor choice of word for a description of a Greek merely standing on the buildings,[141] but the symbolism is clear enough. The sacrifices of Astyanax and Polyxena, the culminating acts of the drama, are inspired by chthonic anger.[142] In identifying with the *ferus spectator* and watching from the grave the reader/audience takes as paradigmatic the familiar perspective of a Fury (and indeed the familiar selective reading of the *Aeneid*). At the same time, however, the audience is encouraged to identify with the Troades, the dramatic audience of the speech: the messenger interrupts his

---

[139] Fitch reads *volvit* for *stravit* and translates accordingly.
[140] On the supernatural as an element of the tragedy which mirrors events represented more realistically see Owen (1970) 122–3 on Achilles' ghost and the subsequent agon between Pyrrhus and Agamemnon.
[141] Fantham (1982) 370.
[142] Strictly speaking Achilles asks only for Polyxena, but the two sacrifices are presented as parallel and brought closer together through allusion to Ovid as Astyanax is represented as Polyxena. On *Troades* 1092–3 and 1098–1100 and Ovid, *Met.* 13.474 ff. see Jakobi (1988) 39.

own description to call the sacrifice of Astyanax a *nefas*. The parenthetic commentary, though a brief and futile voice of dissent, prevents a resolution into a single audience, a single perspective.

The fearless bearing of Astyanax, the *parvus tenerque fetus* (tender little cub 1094), shocks the Greek audience from its criminality, but as in *Medea*[143] the momentum of the sacrificial ritual and the savagery of its presiding divinities overcomes pity:

> moverat vulgum ac duces
> ipsumque Ulixem. non flet e turba omnium
> qui fletur; ac, dum verba fatidici et preces
> concipit Ulixes vatis et saevos ciet
> ad sacra superos, sponte desiluit sua
> in media Priami regna.
> (*Troades* 1098–1103)

(He moved the people and their leaders and Ulysses himself. Of the whole crowd, he did not weep who was wept for. And while Ulysses pronounced the words and prayers of the fate-telling prophet and summoned the cruel gods to the ritual, he leapt down of his own accord, into the midst of Priam's kingdom.)

By jumping down of his own accord Astyanax shows his self-determination even at the moment of death and also curtails the ritual. Whatever its religious significance one effect of this premature suicide is that there is no expression of Hellish anger; neither Ulysses nor the savage gods are allowed to savour a moment of calculated cruelty. The poem itself is stranded part-way through a line. Andromache rescues the stumbling scene with a paroxysm of grief appropriate to a more successful performance:

> Quis Colchus hoc, quis sedis incertae Scytha
> commisit . . .
> (*Troades* 1104–5)

(What Colchian, what nomad Scythian perpetrated this?)

In the following lines she distinguishes it as crime surpassing other boundaries also—even Busiris and Diomedes did not kill children (1106–9)—before concluding, *quis tuos artus teget | tumu-*

---

[143] Medea's last long monologue (893–977) is a conflict between anger and pity. The conflict is resolved with her anger personified as her *antiqua Erinys* (953). The other Furies gather (958 ff.) and the murder is offered as a propitiatory sacrifice to the hostile shade of her brother: *victima manes tuos | placamus ista* (970–1).

loque tradet? (Who will cover your body and consign it to the tomb 1109–10). As Thyestes' and Jason's extravagant expressions of pain finally reassure Atreus and Medea that their crimes have been successful so here Andromache's amplified grief revives a faltering ritual.[144] Her final question, like the chorus's questions of the messenger in *Thyestes* 743 ff., sets up a response which exceeds expectation: *Quos enim praeceps locus | reliquit artus?* (What body did that steep place leave? 1110–11). Ulysses had earlier found Andromache's limitless lamentation quite the opposite of a resolution of pain and here again her paradoxical role in producing horror is apparent.

It would be senseless to argue that the messenger had always intended to describe the fate of Astyanax's body. Whether or not there are tragic parallels,[145] as it is presented the description of the brain bursting from the boy's shattered skull, the deformation of his body, springs from and outdoes Andromache's excesses. Her response to his closing words, *iacet | deforme corpus* (He lies a shapeless corpse 1116–17), is troubling again: *Sic quoque est similis patri* (Even in this he is like his father 1117). That a boy resemble his father is typically a cause for celebration and as Boyle comments of this inversion of the figure, 'In other contexts her remarks would simply be witty'.[146] The graphic outrage of Astyanax's body is framed by boundary-breaking lamentation and wit which seems inhuman because it appears in the midst of horror. If, as Fantham argues, Andromache's epitaph on Astyanax is a mark of her devotion to Hector, it is a mark of an obsessive passion no less disturbing than the inhuman wit it would otherwise suggest.[147] The savagery of the gods finds expression through Andromache's lament and the messenger's description and this savagery is apparent not only in the 'objective facts' of the murder but also in the manner of the telling. Criminal horror has its own distinctive rhetoric. The impropriety of Andromache's wittiness and of the messenger who outdoes even her extravagant grief

---

[144] Cf. *Perdideram scelus | nisi sic doleres* (*Thyestes* 1097–8), *derat hoc unum mihi, | spectator ipse. nil adhuc facti reor: | quidquid sine isto fecimus sceleris perit* (*Medea* 992–4).

[145] Compare with Caviglia (1981) 302 Sophocles, *Trachiniae* 780 ff.

[146] Boyle (1994) 228.

[147] Fantham (1982) 375. For Andromache's devotion to dead Hector at the expense of living Astyanax see her refusal to allow Hector's tomb to be razed (*Troades* 705 ff.) and her farewell to Astyanax (792–812).

suggests an uncomfortable collusion between this victim-audience and the directors of the sacrifice. The contrast between Astyanax who curtails the criminal rite and Andromache and the messenger who give suitable poetic expression to its savagery encourages us to question the joy which grief takes in the detailed narration of suffering and in the pursuit of crime (*Troades* 1065–7).

The central question of *Troades* is the morality of surviving one's world. In its closing act this question appears in overtly theatrical form: by premature suicide Astyanax refuses to be a docile actor in the Greek ritual while Andromache, Hecuba, and the other Trojan women survive as slaves, chorus, and audience. The ode which precedes the final act begins with paradoxical pleasure in a community of suffering.[148] In theatrical terms the Greeks, represented by the figure of the *ferus spectator*, are not the only audience, yet the wrongness of Andromache's response to the death of her son and the ambivalence of her joy in the telling suggest that the integrity of this audience's grief is fragile indeed.

Polyxena dies on cue and the rite is not threatened as it is by Astyanax's premature suicide; there is no need to rouse the tragedy's savage energy. The play ends as it began with Hecuba's nightmare life-in-death and the wrongness of her survival is evident as she speaks of herself as of an unburied body: *non ignis meos | absumpsit artus* (no fire consumed my body 1176–7). As at the end of *Oedipus*, the protagonist survives the closural *peractum est* to face further pain:[149]

> concidit virgo ac puer;
> bellum peractum est. quo meas lacrimas feram?
> ubi hanc anilis expuam leti moram?
> (*Troades* 1167–9)

(A maiden and boy have fallen: the war is finished. Where shall I take my tears? Where shall I spew out this obstacle to an old woman's death?)

If there is nothing in her words to echo the ambivalent pleasure of Andromache the same is not perhaps true of the messenger. He ends his account of the death of Polyxena with the groans of the crowd and the closural phrase *hic ordo sacri* (Such was the order of the ritual 1162) and then adds the detail that the tomb drank her

---

[148] *Dulce maerenti populus dolentum | dulce lamentis resonare gentes* (1009–10).
[149] *Oedipus* 998. Oedipus thinks he has escaped the world through blindness only for Jocasta's voice to fall on his ears.

blood: *obduxit statim | saevusque totum sanguinem tumulus bibit* (immediately the tomb swallowed and savagely drank down all the blood 1163–4). We are reminded of the ghost of Achilles, of the Achilles-like spectator sitting on Hector's tomb,[150] but also of Andromache's amplification from a sacrifice to a banquet on human flesh: *nec parva gregibus membra Diomedes suis | epulanda posuit* (Diomedes did not set out young limbs for his animals to feed on 1108–9). A comparison which seemed more appropriate to *Thyestes* finds its relevance in the second sacrifice.[151] Though the blood-drinking itself can be explained as an unexpected event which is narrated by the messenger objectively and in strict chronological order, he uses his art to create a shock conclusion. The closural tone of *hic ordo sacri* encourages a reader/audience to leave the scene with a memory of ritual murder transformed, of Greeks and Trojans reconciled in shared pity (1160–1). The bloodthirsty Fury beneath the earth shatters this comforting illusion all the more rudely because he is unexpected and for this the messenger's art must take some credit. If he is still some way from the cruelty of his counterpart in *Thyestes* he is further from using his art to contain or assuage pain.

The primary difference between the final act of *Troades* and the fourth act of *Thyestes* is the inscribed audience of Greeks and Trojans. Andromache and the messenger are to be contrasted not only with Astyanax but also with the other spectators. The black wit of Andromache's *Sic quoque est similis patri* (Even in this he is like his father 1117) is pointed by its contrast with the earlier simile of the lion-cub (1093–8) where the spectators saw in Astyanax an image, if not of Hector specifically, of an adult warrior and were moved to tears of pity. The pathos of this scene has a very different tone from that of the following exchange where Astyanax fulfils his inheritance in more brutal fashion. As surprising as the close relationship between Andromache's extravagant grief and the ritual of savage gods is the transformation of the Greek spectators. Astyanax's brave show brings the entire audience to tears (1098–1110) and Polyxena's more explicitly erases the distinctions between the spectators: *terror attonitos tenet | utrosque populos* (Both peoples were held paralysed by dread 1136–7); *stupet omne*

---
[150] On spectating and devouring see n. 62 with text.
[151] For Thyestean allusion here see Fantham (1982) 373.

vulgus (The whole crowd was awestruck 1143); *movet animus omnis* (all were moved 1146); *tam fortis animus omnium mentes ferit* (So brave a spirit struck everyone's mind 1153); *uterque flevit coetus* (Each group wept 1160). Elsewhere the Greeks rejoice at their victory (1126–8) as the Trojans tremble at their final destruction (1129–31), but here the audience sees as one. The lustre of Polyxena's cheeks is likened to the light of the setting sun (1138 ff.) and it is this image of doomed beauty which unites the audience. Even if the *sententia: et fere cuncti magis | peritura laudant* (and all tend to praise more highly what is about to be lost 1143–4) is spurious, the sentiment is implicit in the generalizing conclusion:

> hos movet formae decus,
> hos mollis aetas, hos vagae rerum vices.
> (*Troades* 1144–5)

(Some were moved by her beauty, some by her tender years, some by life's shifting changes)

That Polyxena in this play within a play[152] should exemplify the alternating rhythm of the universe is significant in a tragedy which begins with Hecuba asking the audience to reflect on the transience of Fortune. Polyxena's ritual murder at the hands of Pyrrhus in the final act echoes that of Priam in the first.[153] But before adopting the inscribed tragedy as an image of its frame we should note the differences between the two. Most obviously, Hecuba, Priam, and Troy itself move no one, as Astyanax and Polyxena do, with the delicacy of their vulnerability; the adjectives *tener* and *mollis* are nowhere to be found in Act 1. Troy itself was once a mighty, imperial city, the killing of its king was a sacrilegious murder (*execrandum nefas* 44), and its destruction is an ugly blot on the day: *ater favilla squalet Iliaca dies* (the daylight is befouled with Ilium's ash 21). Hecuba and the other survivors, covering their hair in its ashes, mirror its ugliness (*Troiae pulvere turpes* (filthy with the...dust of Troy 86)). Where Act 1, lit by the smoky flames of the dead city, dwells on the ugliness of the surviving ruins, Act 5, illuminated by the rays of the setting sun, lingers on the beauty of the youth condemned to untimely death.

---

[152] Note especially *theatri more* (1125) and Boyle (1994) 228–9 ad loc.

[153] On verbal reminiscences and a shared literary model in Virgil's death of Priam (*Aeneid* 2.552 ff.) see Boyle (1994) 232.

Parallel to this aesthetic contrast is a moral distinction. Hecuba portrays herself as a victim of the fickle gods (*leves...deos* 2) whereas the *vagae rerum vices* (life's shifting changes) suggests an order in the world: 'what is implied by the word is the rightness and inevitability of such sequences'.[154]

One may argue, cynically, that this strikes a deliberately jarring note. Proud Troy was sacked in scenes of anger (*ira*), darkness (*tenebrae*), pain (*dolor*), raging madness (*furor*), and insane lust (*vecors libido*) (279–85). These are the forces which Agamemnon promised to restrain by prohibiting the sacrifice of Polyxena. The Greeks rationalize the sacrifices as obedience to destiny or divine will (351–2, 358–9) but the true character of the murders is evident in the bloodthirstiness of their presiding deity. Achilles rose from Erebus in defiance of the order of the celestial bodies to reverse day's victory over night.[155] There is no moral order in the world of Seneca's *Troades*. Polyxena's physical beauty is as fleeting and fragile as the suggestion of any moral beauty in her death; the tragedy's true face is to be seen in Hecuba's *rupta cicatrix* (burst-open scar 123) or in Astyanax's *deforme corpus* (shapeless corpse 1117). As for the wonder and pity which overwhelm the Greek spectators, these are the responses of a crowd as fickle, as morally incoherent as the gods themselves:

> Quicumque regno fidit et magna potens
> dominatur aula nec *leves* metuit *deos*
>
> . . . .
>
> me videat et te, Troia
>
> (*Troades* 1–2, 4)

(Anyone who trusts in royal power, anyone who rules supreme in a great palace without fear of the *fickle gods*... should look upon me, and upon you, Troy.)

Compare:

> magna pars *vulgi levis*
> odit scelus spectatque (*Troades* 1128–9)

(most of the *shallow mob* detested the crime—and gazed).

[154] Fantham (1982) 379.
[155] Talthybius' messenger speech begins at dawn: *vicerat noctem dies* (170b). Achilles brings darkness with him. Whether he banished (*dimisit*) the day or interrupted it (*divisit*) the challenge to celestial order is clear. On the different manuscript readings for line 197 see Fantham (1982) 238. Compare the banishment of the day in *Thyestes* and the onset of the madness which Juno summoned *ab imo Tartari fundo* (*Hercules Furens* 86): *medium diem | cinxere tenebrae* (939–40).

The audience weeps for the evil of Astyanax's murder and immediately turns to another crime and to the site and symbol of Achilles' desire for vengeance:

> Praeceps ut altis cecidit e muris puer
> flevitque Achivum turba quod fecit nefas,
> idem ille populus aliud ad facinus redit
> tumulumque Achillis.
> (*Troades* 1118–21)

(After the boy fell headlong from the high walls and the Achaean crowd wept for the outrage it had done, that same host turned back to another crime and to Achilles' burial-mound.)

The theatre crowd wipes the tears for one crime from its eyes only to view the next more clearly. There is no tragic mystery here, no paradox. The aesthetic rightness of a beautiful performance simply masks the moral triviality of an audience which is only superficially troubled by the shedding of innocent blood. Human suffering is not so much transfigured in the tragic spectacle as disguised by it.

Yet to argue that this rite is murder, comfortingly aestheticized, sits awkwardly with the drama's contrast between the felicity of the dead and the misery of those still trapped in Troy. The noble deaths of Astyanax and Polyxena cannot be dismissed as affecting performances for a morally trivial audience without undermining the play's criticism of the servile lives of the Trojan women. Polyxena is walking the road to freedom and her beauty is no illusion but a true echo of her moral choice.[156] She and Astyanax may perform affectingly for their theatre audience, but this audience's superficiality does not diminish the morally more significant heroism which another audience might observe. Boyle is rightly reminded of the many gladiators who model Stoic defiance in Seneca's prose works by choosing suicide over a degrading performance.[157] In one passage Fortune, *quae ludos sibi facit* (who stages games for her amusement), explains that the gladiator who holds life in contempt lives longer and dies faster.[158] This

---

[156] She is no victim because she does not surrender: *nec tamen moriens adhuc | deponit animos* (1157–8). On the difference between following and being dragged by fate see *SVF* 1.527 (Cleanthes) and *SVF* 2.975 (Zeno and Chrysippus).
[157] Boyle (1997) 120.
[158] *At tu et vives diutius et morieris expeditius* (*De Tranq.* 11.5).

abbreviation of humiliation is the central point of the figure: in *Epistles* 70 three gladiators are praised who take their own lives so as not to have to perform at all (*Ep.* 70.20–1, 22–3, 26–7). They are the image of the Spartan boy in the other great suicide letter, *Epistles* 77, who the first time he was ordered to act the slave smashed his head open against the wall.[159] Astyanax in jumping prematurely and Polyxena in not retreating but facing the blow are of the same stamp. The young Trojans do all that can be expected of them but the audience is morally more problematic.

Leigh discusses a distinction Seneca makes between Jupiter's observation of Cato's defiance in the ruins of the Republic and a crowd's observation of a young man killing a lion (*De Providentia* 2.7–10). While there is nothing more beautiful than Cato's resistance, the lion-killing is dismissed as *puerilia et humanae oblectamenta levitatis* (childish, pleasure for human triviality).[160] As in *Troades* this theatrical audience is marked by its *levitas*. Certainly Cato is more magnificent than the lion-killer because he walks on a grander stage and has phrased his challenge in more philosophical terms:

Ecce spectaculum dignum ad quod respiciat intentus operi suo deus, ecce par deo dignum, vir fortis cum fortuna mala compositus, utique si provocavit. (*De Prov.* 2.9)

(Look, a spectacle worthy for a god intent on his work to look at; look, a pair worthy of a god, a brave man set against ill fortune as if he challenged it.)

But if one had to pin down the triviality of the theatrical audience one would point surely to the description of Cato's performance as 'more beautiful' (*pulchrius* 2.9): the word is chosen precisely because an older man, often defeated and standing in the ruins, is not *superficially* as beautiful as a young man hunting. The first of the gladiators in *Epistles* 70 dies by choking himself with a toilet-brush,[161] which shows that the dirtiest death is to be preferred

---

[159] *Ep.* 77.14–15 *ut primum iussus est servili fungi et contumelioso ministerio, adferre enim vas obscenum iubebatur, inlisum parieti caput rupit*.

[160] This opposition between moral exemplarity and theatrical entertainment Leigh argues is fragile and deconstructed by the narrator of Lucan's *Bellum Civile*. See Leigh (1997) 95–6 and also 259–64 on the suicide of Vulteius and his men in book 4.

[161] *Ibi lignum id, quod ad emundanda obscena adhaerente spongia positum est, totum in gulam farsit* (*Ep.* 70.20).

to the cleanest slavery (*praeferendam esse spurcissimam mortem servituti mundissimae*, *Ep.* 70.21). Seneca continues unrepentant, *Quoniam coepi sordidis exemplis uti, perseverabo* (Because I have begun by using ugly examples I will continue, *Ep.* 70.22). The Spartan boy of *Epistles* 77 commits suicide when ordered to fetch a chamber-pot. Chamber-pots and sponges on sticks are no more the expected props of a noble death than gladiators its usual icons: Seneca has deliberately selected anecdotes which combine steadfastness of spirit with a contempt for the decorum and the trappings of this world.[162]

Hoc fuit morti contumeliam facere. Ita prorsus, parum munde et parum decenter: quid est stultius quam fastidiose mori? (*Ep.* 70.20–1)
(This was to insult death. So it was, it was not a very elegant or becoming way to die: what is more foolish than to be over-nice about dying?)

Tragedy speaks in a different register from the moral epistle and one cannot expect to find similar breaches of decorum in representations of death in *Troades*. However, there is perhaps a parallel in the contrasting descriptions of Astyanax first as a young lion and then as a welter of blood and bone. I suggested above that the exchange between the messenger and Andromache colludes awkwardly with the bloodthirstiness of Achilles' spirit and the *ferus spectator*, and that the savagery of Andromache's grief is pointed particularly by comparison with the tearful admiration of the Greek audience. Despite its role in exposing the limitations of Andromache's pain this theatrical audience is not itself beyond reproach. Can a crowd whose sensibilities are so shallow that it turns immediately from one crime to another, be trusted to respond to the moral beauty of the victims' strength of will rather than to the pathos of the beautiful cut down before their time?[163]

---

[162] Seneca is not of course the first Roman writer to use gladiators implicitly or explicitly as moral exemplars, but commonly the argument (as in this letter of Seneca) runs, 'If even gladiators... how much the more should we/you freeborn Romans...'. See the survey of Leigh (1997) 234–43.

[163] There is a taste for such scenes: Dewar (1991) xxxiv–xxxvii on the Parthenopaeus episode in Statius, *Thebaid* 9.570–907 speaks of a 'mawkish sensibility which is particularly Roman and which increased in prominence in the first century' (xxxv). Though the death-scenes of Astyanax and Polyxena accord with this sensibility, the triviality of the inscribed audience suggests perhaps a cliché, something superficial about the deaths of the beautiful.

Aristotle's tragic emotions of pity, fear, and wonder appear in lines 1147–8 (*omnium mentes tremunt | mirantur ac miserantur*)[164] and one may reasonably assume that Astyanax, parallel in other respects to Polyxena, is to be received in the same way. These classic tragic sensibilities respond to the beauty of Polyxena as the (amphi)theatrical pleasures of the audience in *De Providentia* 2.7 respond to the beauty of the young hunter. One may contrast not only Cato's divine audience (in the same work) but Hecuba's correction of the Trojan women in Act 1 of this tragedy. Hecuba and the chorus lament Priam, unburied while his city burns (54–6), discarded and mutilated on the Sigean shore (141), only to end the act with the refrain *Felix Priamus* (145, 156, 161). Priam, in a conspicuous deviation from his Ovidian predecessor, is lucky not in his simultaneous departure from life and kingdom but because he takes his kingdom with him: secum *excedens sua regna* tulit (in departing he has taken his kingdom with him, 157).[165] The words are repeated in the act's last lines:

> felix quisquis bello moriens
> omnia *secum* consumpta *tulit*.   (*Troades* 162–3)

(blest is anyone who, dying in war, has taken with him his whole destroyed world.)

The ruined city and the ruined body are nothing; consolation lies in the recognition that at death nothing is left behind. There is, it seems to me, a significant difference between the austerity of the drama's first act, as interpreted and directed by Hecuba,[166] and the pathos of the tragic scenes inscribed in the final act.

My intention in this discussion of the theatrical self-consciousness of *Troades* is not to isolate a particular tone as this tragedy's

---

[164] So Fantham (1982) 381 and Boyle (1994) 231. See also Fantham (1982) 380–1 on why Zwierlein is wrong to delete line 1147, which Caviglia (1981) and Boyle (1994) also accept.

[165] On Ovid, *Met.* 13.522, *vitam pariter regnumque reliquit* cf. Fantham (1982) 231 and Boyle (1994) 157, who find the reminiscence uninteresting: 'Seneca adds nothing to Ovid's thought' (Fantham). Jakobi (1988) quotes Ovid and also an identical (in sentiment) statement of Priam's felicity from Dio 58.23. Seneca's line that Priam took his kingdom with him rather than leaving his life and kingdom behind him is the exception.

[166] Not only does she introduce it as a spectacle (*me videat et te, Troia* 4) but she directs its chorus 63 ff. Delrius (1593) in his preface quotes Epictetus to the effect that tragedy is the *speculum eorum qui a fortuna dependent* and argues that examples may be drawn from it to encourage people to bear the blows of fate with fortitude.

characteristic voice, or to argue that its first and last acts are offered respectively as models of serious and trivial theatre, but to contrast the variety of its representation of the theatrical experience with the monolithic power of *Thyestes*. There are common elements. Andromache's frenzied grief, in contrast to Astyanax's premature exit, is a satisfying affirmation of the rite of the savage gods, very much as Thyestes' extravagant pain restores Atreus' pleasure in his revenge. Although neither the messenger nor Andromache approaches the astonishing transformation of the messenger in *Thyestes*, both are arguably infected with the horror which they describe and threaten briefly to mimic the cruelty of a *ferus spectator*. There is one clearly contrasting element, namely the pity of the Greek audience, which develops in the course of the description and which opposes Achilles' desire for vengeance and the momentum of the criminal ritual. Where *Thyestes* offers a single trajectory of tragic response, as tragic passion defies repression, *Troades* offers rival responses. More significantly, *Troades'* final act is built on the genuinely ambivalent pleasures of Andromache and the messenger and the genuinely ambivalent tragic sensibilities of the inscribed audience. Where the messenger speech which occupies almost all the fourth act of *Thyestes* confirms and reiterates the genesis of the tragedy as described in the opening act, the messenger speech which occupies almost all the final act of *Troades* complicates the vision which Hecuba offered in the first act. Like Hector and Priam, Astyanax and Polyxena depart into the sanctuary of death, but if the moral value of their act is clear the experience of viewing it is contrastingly represented as complex and unresolved.

5
Phaedra: Intertextuality and Innocence

JASON and Thyestes are the ironic victims of their more knowing persecutors. Atreus' claim to walk the equal of the stars and above everyone (*Thyestes* 885) is a figurative truth in a tragedy where Thyestes' agony is scripted by his brother and performed for his pleasure. The dramatic illusion barely contains Medea and Atreus as they search the mythological and literary past for material to imitate and surpass. Common to both characters is a concern that their revenge should afford them a satisfying spectacle, and in this respect their heightened awareness reflects their dramatic context.[1] Phaedra's awareness, like Atreus' or Medea's, threatens the integrity of the dramatic illusion in so far as it suggests an awareness of a literary tradition. She ends her opening lament thus:

> stirpem perosa Solis invisi Venus
> per nos catenas vindicat Martis sui
> suasque, probris omne Phoebeum genus
> onerat nefandis: nulla Minois levi
> defuncta amore est, iungitur semper nefas
> (*Phaedra* 124–8)

(Venus hates the offspring of her enemy the Sun; she is avenging the chains that bound her dear Mars and herself, burdening the whole tribe of Phoebus with unspeakable scandals. No daughter of Minos has got through a love-affair lightly; always it is linked to infamy.)

She is concluding a speech which, in its descriptions of Pasiphaë and the minotaur, Daedalus and the labyrinth, recalls very closely the laments of Ovid's Phaedra from *Heroides* 4 and Iphis from *Metamorphoses* 9.[2] The chains of Venus and the crushing weight of Phaedra's heritage figures here the weight of literary tradition; in a very real sense Phaedra is fated to suffer the experience of other

---
[1] See above, Ch. 4, Sect. 1. *derat hoc unum mihi | spectator iste. nil adhuc facti reor* (*Medea* 992–3) testifies to the importance of theatre in Medea's revenge.
[2] See Segal (1986) 35 n. 10, Zwierlein (1987) 8–10, Jakobi (1988) 65–7.

Cretan princesses.[3] However, unlike Atreus or Medea, Phaedra is no surrogate-tragedian staging and viewing Hippolytus' death from within the play; theatrical metaphor does not inform interpretation of Phaedra's awareness and Hippolytus' innocence in this way.

In this chapter I approach Senecan tragedy more as text than as theatre (whether real or virtual) and discuss the importance of intertextual irony in the characterization of Hippolytus as an innocent, primarily in the opening song (1–84). That Seneca's art is embedded by imitation and allusion in the non-theatrical Roman literary tradition in this way is, I think, a point worth reiterating in the face of continued insistence that Greek tragedy is an immediate and dominant influence.[4] If 'the ghost of Euripides haunts every line'[5] of this play it is as one ghost among many. That said, Euripides' second Hippolytus play is a highly significant predecessor of Seneca's *Phaedra* for its treatment of both imitation and the difficulty of interpretation. Ultimately, if not immediately, it is Euripides' treatment of the myth which makes Seneca's *Phaedra* so attractive a vehicle for the exploration of intertextual irony and misrepresentation.

Fatal misrepresentation, uncertain interpretation are features of the basic myth: Theseus misreads the signs of Phaedra and of Hippolytus with tragic consequences. Euripides develops uncertain communication into a major theme of his tragedy: after Aphrodite has revealed to the audience her motives and her responsibility for Phaedra's desire and what the final result will be, the chorus spends a scene misinterpreting the queen's behaviour. Later she and the audience cannot properly hear her desire when it is expressed to Hippolytus by the nurse behind closed doors. Hippolytus is not persuaded, so Phaedra commits suicide and leaves in place of her living word a duplicitous written text.[6]

---

[3] On 'fate' as 'what has been said' see Boyle (1994) 119 on *Troades* 360. In *Phaedra* the body of the text has, for obvious reasons, been a more popular metaliterary figure than chains or weight. See Segal (1986) 215–26, Most (1992), and, on text as body in Lucan, Quint (1993) 140 ff. For recent surveys on intertextuality in Latin literature see e.g. Farrell (1991) 3–25 and Hinds (1998).
[4] On Seneca and Greek tragedy see Ch. 1 above.
[5] Segal (1986) 203.
[6] This presentation betrays certain sympathies. See Segal (1992) on signs and language in this play. For a Derridean perspective see especially Goff (1990) 95–104. For opposition to this methodology (and in particular the difference between lying and communicating in a medium in which significance is endlessly deferred) see Clark and Csapo (1991).

Hippolytus points to his life of devotion to Artemis, but Theseus believes the tablet, dismisses Hippolytus' life as a façade, and condemns him to death. Artemis appears, fleetingly, to undermine Hippolytus' perception of their companionship and to mark the distance between Hippolytus and the guiding principle of his life. As for imitation, in a few lines of greater importance to Roman elegy than to Euripides' tragedy[7] Phaedra famously desires to be the image of her love:

> πέμπετέ μ᾽ εἰς ὄρος· εἶμι πρὸς ὕλαν
> καὶ παρὰ πεύκας, ἵνα θηροφόνοι
> στείβουσι κύνες
> βαλιαῖς ἐλάφοις ἐγχριμπτόμεναι.
> πρὸς θεῶν· ἔραμαι κυσὶ θωΰξαι
> καὶ παρὰ χαίταν ξανθὰν ῥῖψαι
> Θεσσαλὸν ὄρπακ᾽, ἐπίλογχον ἔχουσ᾽
> ἐν χειρὶ βέλος
> (Euripides, *Hippolytus* 215–22)

(Take me to the mountains. I will go to the wood and among the pines where the deadly hounds stalk and pursue the spotted stags. By the gods, I desire to set on the dogs and to throw a Thessalian spear from beside my golden hair, holding the barbed javelin in my hand.)

This imitation of Hippolytus is of course an expression not of Phaedra's shared devotion to Artemis, but of her possession by the opposing divinity, Aphrodite. In this way Phaedra's imitation is a disfiguring echo: it corrupts the gestures and language with which Hippolytus fashions his self-identity.

In Seneca's tragedy the failures of interpretation and of understanding are concentrated more narrowly on Hippolytus[8] at least as long as he lives, for Seneca's Hippolytus, unlike Euripides', is dead for the final act. There are no gods in this play and the range of irony is reduced accordingly. Phaedra comments on her own behaviour, questions it for no more than a line (112), and then informs nurse and chorus:

> fatale miserae matris *agnosco* malum
> peccare noster *novit* in silvis amor
> (*Phaedra* 113–14)[9]

---

[7] See Conte (1986) 115 ff.   [8] See further Motto and Clark (1972) 71–2.
[9] Cf. the awareness of Oedipus, whose prologue is an admission of guilt: *fecimus caelum nocens* (*Oedipus* 36).

(I recognize my poor mother's fateful evil; our love is experienced at sinning in the forests.)

Hippolytus, however, remains completely unaware. The nurse tries to persuade him obliquely through a discussion of the natural behaviour of young men and of the role of Venus in nature. He rejects any kind of sexuality in an account of the virtues of the Golden Age, but does not of course understand what argument is taking place. Phaedra tries to persuade him more directly. Finally he understands, and flees to the woods for sanctuary, never to speak again. Theseus dismisses his devotion to Diana as a façade and condemns him to death *in absentia*: Hippolytus thus does not represent himself at all and has no role in the agon of the life and character of Hippolytus. As a result, when he is finally destroyed by the sea-monster which Theseus summons he has no idea what forces are at work. If, as Segal argues, the sea's monstrous birth recalls Phaedra's Cretan heritage and her sexualizing of the rhetoric of the sea earlier in the play, then Hippolytus is doubly oblivious of the mechanisms of his destruction.[10]

When Phaedra tries to persuade Hippolytus he remains innocent of her meaning for eighty lines (591–671). *Ambigua voce verba perplexa iacis:* | *effare aperte* (639–40), he demands, and then completely misinterprets her love: *Amore nempe Thesei casto furis?* (645). When he discovers the truth he is appalled that he has unintentionally appeared easy material for adultery:

> sum nocens, merui mori:
> placui novercae. dignus en stupris ego?
> scelerique tanto visus ego solus tibi
> materia facilis? hoc meus meruit rigor?
> (*Phaedra* 683–6)

(I am guilty, I deserve to die: I have attracted my stepmother. Look, am I suited to adulteries? Did I of all men seem to you easy material for such a crime? Did my sternness earn this?)

What surprises him surprises no other reader inside or outside the text. Theseus rewrites Hippolytus' Amazonian heritage as a perversion rather than a rejection of Venus, while Phaedra and the

---

[10] See Segal (1986) 38–43 and, on Hippolytus' confrontation with the bull from the sea, 'Hippolytus encounters him [Theseus] only through the monstrous shapes that Phaedra's language in the play causes to surface from the subterranean places of earth or sea' (177).

nurse have both articulated the plot against him through the inversion and erotic contamination of the rhetoric of the hunt: Phaedra plays a huntress and an Amazon in whose erotic pursuit the virgin hunter becomes prey. The nurse reminds Hippolytus' patron of her liaison with Endymion and enlists her aid as a conspirator. Even the chorus compares Hippolytus to Hesperus (Venus) and redraws his virginal idyll, through Ovid, as a 'landscape of *deluded* innocence, of purity about to be lost to sexual violence in the background'.[11] Whether a scholar recognizes Hippolytus' landscape subversively reworked through an Ovidian topos or a dramatic character finds different significance in his chaste utterances,[12] Hippolytus is everyone's ironic victim.

Hippolytus' vulnerability to erotic contamination is achieved in part through memories of less innocent intertexts both specific and generic. Although it would be inappropriate to offer any single intertextual effect as canonical, one may, by analogy with Don Fowler's discussion of focalization,[13] reasonably speak of 'deviant intertextuality'. As 'deviant focalization' is 'seeing with the wrong eyes' so 'deviant intertextuality' is 'writing with the wrong voice'. When Phaedra describes Hippolytus' beauty at 651 ff. she reworks the words of Ovid's Phaedra at *Heroides* 4.72 ff. She speaks with another's voice, but this is as harmonious and 'right' an intertextual effect as one could hope to find. More interesting and productive an effect is created when one text does not reinforce the other so neatly. When, for example, Theseus' words to Hippolytus at 1250–1 repeat Pyramus' words to Thisbe from Ovid, *Metamorphoses* 4.110, the relationship between father and son is re-voiced.[14] Phaedra's first speech recalls the words of Virgil's Dido and Ovid's Iphis[15] and these voices again are different but hardly deviant. When, however, Hippolytus is describing a sexless Golden Age with lines from Ovid's *Amores* he is invoking a voice deviant inasmuch as it runs directly counter to his intentions. *Non*

---

[11] Segal (1986) 68. On Hesperus as Venus see P. J. Davis (1983) 116.
[12] See e.g. Hippolytus' unfortunate words to Phaedra, *En locus ab omni liber arbitrio vacat* (601) and *ac tibi parentis ipse supplebo locum* (633).
[13] D. P. Fowler (1990).
[14] Cf. Catullus 72.3–4.
[15] Seneca, *Phaedra* 104–8; cf. Virgil, *Aeneid* 4.74–89. See also Fantham (1975) 6 and *passim*. *Phaedra* 112–23; cf. Ovid, *Met.* 9.724f. See Jakobi (1988) 65 and more generally Zwierlein (1987) 8–11.

264 Phaedra: *Intertextuality and Innocence*

arma saeva miles aptabat manu (533) is rewritten slightly from *et miles saevas aptat ad arma manus* (*Amores* 1.13.14), where Ovid chronicles the end of his *erotic* idyll. In this passage the order of elements which mark out the end of the Golden Age (527–38) is modelled on *Amores* 3.8.41–8.[16] Here Ovid, like Hippolytus, shocked at the decline of sexual morals, complains that the rich soldier can buy up all the poor poet's loves now that the Golden Age has ended. This is not the Golden Age which Hippolytus remembers nor the persona he is trying to present.[17] Deviant intertextuality very much of this kind happens throughout the play, even in the opening song where Hippolytus assumes the role of protagonist and speaks for himself.

The memories which Hippolytus evoked in his description of the Golden Age are deviant because erotic, deviant because elegiac. Generic opposition is an important dynamic in this tragedy not least because of the influence of Ovid's *Heroides*.[18] These tragic monologues in elegiac form play on generic tension. Here I paraphrase from the first three pages of Casali's article on *Heroides* 4 (1995). Phaedra writes an elegiac letter to Hippolytus and asks, *Quid epistula lecta nocebit?* (*Heroides* 4.3). Readers of the tragedy know what harm there is in reading a letter and through this allusion a tension is created between the tragic denouement and the elegiac goal which Phaedra pursues with her letter here. Her representation of herself as a *Cressa puella* in line 2, when she is not easily a *puella*, is a deliberately elegiac construction. She 'tries to activate the erotic nuances of Hippolytus' *vigor*'[19] but her

---

[16] Coffey and Mayer (1990) 139 comment that this passage is a conflation of both *Amores* 3.8 and *Metamorphoses* 1.94 ff. I do not disagree, but it should be noted (as it is by Coffey and Mayer) that the very first detail, the boundary markers, appears only in *Amores* 3.8, not in *Metamorphoses* 1. If we accept multiple allusion then Hippolytus' words are modelled on one 'deviant' version of the Fall and one 'straight' version. Seneca's Hippolytus inherits rather than fashions the opposition, but I don't think this is an important difference here. For multiple allusion in Senecan tragedy cf. Jakobi (1988) on Agamemnon 656–8; Ovid, *Met.* 13.409 ff.; Virgil, *Aen.* 2.501 ff.; and *Georgics* 3.492.

[17] The deviant persona which threatens Hippolytus is Ovidian but also more generally elegiac. Cf. Tibullus 1.10 for a similar lament on the end of the Golden Age.

[18] Ovid commonly opposes tragedy to elegy outside the *Heroides*. In addition to *Amores* 2.11 and the programmatic 3.1 see Morrison (1992) on *Amores* 1.7. The violence which the lover does to his mistress is paralleled by the poet's violence to his Muse as, inspired by tragic madness, he shakes off elegiac *servitium*.

[19] Casali (1995) 2.

elegiac fantasy is doomed to failure by a tragic future already written. As ever, Seneca follows in Ovid's footsteps: Phaedra offers herself to Hippolytus in elegiac mode as a servant willing to endure any slavery, walk over snow and fire (611 ff.). Though primarily here I am concerned with the representation not of Phaedra but of Hippolytus, *Heroides* 4 is nonetheless important as writing Phaedra's desire as the product of a particular genre. The corruption of Hippolytus is achieved in part through elegiac contamination of his speech. As Ovid writes elsewhere, though tragedy surpasses all other genres in weight and seriousness it too contains the *materia amoris*:

> omne genus scripti gravitate tragoedia vincit:
> haec quoque materiam semper amoris habet.
> num quid in Hippolyto, nisi caecae flamma novercae?
> (Ovid, *Tristia* 2.381–3)

(Tragedy surpasses every genre of writing in seriousness: this also always has the material of love. For what is there in *Hippolytus* but the fiery passion of a blind stepmother?)

As we have seen, Seneca's Hippolytus is astonished to learn that his moral *rigor* has been misread but Phaedra easily eroticizes and subverts it in her vision:[20]

> scelerique tanto visus ego solus tibi
> materia facilis? hoc meus meruit rigor?
> (Seneca, *Phaedra* 685–6)

(Did I of all men seem to you easy material for such a crime? Did my sternness earn this?)

Compare:

> in ore Graio Scythicus apparet rigor.
> si cum parente Creticum intrasses fretum,
> tibi fila potius nostra nevisset soror.
> (*Phaedra* 660–2)

(in your Greek face a Scythian sternness is evident. If you had entered Cretan seas with your father, my sister would rather have spun the thread for you.)

Hippolytus' austerity and innocence is expressed through his devotion to Diana and, in a sentiment which distinguished him from

---

[20] On *rigor* here see Boyle (1987) 175 and 177.

his Euripidean predecessor, an attachment to the woods and a hatred of the city. To represent Hippolytus' innocence Seneca has created him in generic terms less of the heaviness of tragedy than of the vulnerability of pastoral. In his agon with the nurse, and to a lesser extent in his opening song, Hippolytus shows his attachment to the innocence of a pastoral idyll and his suspicion of urban sophistication. The failure of innocence and the pleasurable tensions created by the juxtaposition of sophistication and simplicity is central in the *Idylls* and *Eclogues* of Theocritus and Virgil. The practitioner in Seneca's time was Calpurnius Siculus and in his *Eclogues* the fragility which Virgil gave the genre becomes more acute. Famously in *Eclogues* 7 Corydon returns to a pastoral idyll from Nero's amphitheatre, which he sees as a superior and more sophisticated form of the rustic grove. Now the innocent pleasures of the rustic grove are lost. Taking his lead from the programme of Virgil's *Eclogues* 1, Calpurnius has exposed the vulnerability of the pastoral landscape to a political irruption. Leach's reading of the fragility of pastoral landscapes as a vulnerability to 'the world of power'[21] can be developed by allowing a variety of powerful worlds. The damaging contamination of Gallus' elegy in Virgil's tenth *Eclogue* can be read as the same figure as is presented in a different, political form in his first *Eclogue*, and differently again in Theocritus' eleventh Idyll, where the pain of the Cyclops' desire is expressed through his awkwardness beside Galatea's seascape. For all three pastoral poets, contamination by an alien world and by an alien genre are related figures. To illustrate from Theocritus: the intertextual irony which mocks Polyphemus' eager anticipation of a stranger's arrival valorizes the gulf between his and Galatea's worlds, and equally, the elusive grace of the sea-nymph figures a literary sophistication which the reader but not Polyphemus possesses.[22] Whether in the formal genre of pastoral or merely in a pastoral interlude in another genre the rustic *locus amoenus* is a mode of writing political, sexual, and literary innocence and their vulnerability.

[21] Leach (1975) 223. Her article on Neronian pastoral closes with a discussion of Seneca's *Phaedra*.

[22] On Polyphemus and the mysterious stranger see Spofford (1969) 34. My sketch of the *Idyll*, ignoring the frame, is over-simplified: the boundaries of sophistication and rusticity in this Idyll are more subtle than I have suggested—see Spofford (1969) 29–31. On innocence and experience both literary and sexual see also Zeitlin (1990c) 438 on Longus, *Daphnis and Chloe*.

Hippolytus sketches his pastoral world in his agon with the nurse and in his opening hunting song.[23] The hunting song has been criticized for being dramatically weak because it does not appear to perform the duties of a prologue nor does it introduce the following speech of Phaedra which does perform them.[24] One expects that a prologue will establish the crisis whose unfolding is the tragedy, and in no conventional sense does this happen here. Sympathetic readers of Seneca have tended to argue that it must be read against Phaedra's speech. Heldmann discusses it through the structural model of opposed outer and inner prologues, Henry and Walker stress the opposition of idyll and nightmare, and Segal the distance between the respective psychological landscapes.[25] Most clearly of the three, Segal states that this distance between the landscapes 'contains the underlying structure of the work':[26] Hippolytus' idyll and Phaedra's sea and palace are the landscapes of their souls and in their juxtaposition the nature of the ensuing tragedy is anticipated. Certainly a progression may be traced from the virtual agon of these opening landscapes to the oblique agon with the nurse to the final confrontation with Phaedra. Parallel to the growing immediacy of confrontation in such a progression is a developing instability and vulnerability in Hippolytus' self-presentation: 'darker touches' develop into fatal flaws. The sterility of Ilissus' stream in the hunting song looks forward to the forthright and unqualified rejection of sexuality in the agon with the nurse and ultimately to Hippolytus' response to Phaedra's revelation. Similarly the contradictions in Hippolytus' conception of the Golden Age, perhaps already visible in the hunting song, are

[23] For the attribution to Hippolytus see Coffey and Mayer (1990) 88–9. Grimal (1965) 7 and Boyle (1987) 18–19, 134–5 assume without discussion that the huntsman is Hippolytus. On his pastoral world see Leach (1975) 224 'H's answering speech... is virtually a pastoral poem'.
[24] Coffey and Mayer (1990) 88; Zwierlein (1987) 104–5. On the duties of the opening of a tragedy see also Aristotle, *Poetics* 1450^b.
[25] Heldmann (1974) 74, Henry and Walker (1966) 228–32, Segal (1986) 29 ff. See also Motto and Clark (1972) 74 and Cattin (1960) 67. Cf. Zwierlein (1987) 26, for whom the awkward prologue is a sign of Seneca bewitched by a Greek precursor. Barrett (1964) 35 is confident that the hunting song is a Senecan innovation. See also Leeman (1976) 203.
[26] Segal (1986) 37. Cf. A. Fowler (1982) 88–9: 'The generic markers that cluster at the beginning of the work have a strategic role in guiding the reader. They help to establish, as soon as possible, an appropriate mental "set" that allows the work's generic codes to be read' (88). On inversion of generic codes see also Cairns (1972) 129–30.

exposed in the agon with the nurse, notably the 'special pleading' by which the deception, toil, and bloodshed of hunting are admitted into the age of the world's innocence.[27] But it should be emphasized that these and other problematic elements in the hunting song become problematic retrospectively from later developments: at the moment of its utterance the hunting song is innocent of its many disfiguring echoes later in the tragedy. It is in fact the only occasion on which Hippolytus is allowed to speak first. Later he responds to the nurse and to Phaedra and finally has no voice at all to oppose Theseus, but here at the beginning of the play he speaks apparently from and for himself. The world of forests and beasts is not yet more ambiguous and complex than he thinks;[28] the erotic crises of the play, the crises of duplicitous language, have not yet developed. In the solo lyrics of Hippolytus' opening song we still have a univocal language of single-spirited intentions:[29] hunting-speak is still virginal.

Or at least it would be if it had never been written before. As it is, erotic hunting is so familiar that there can be little material which admits desire more easily. There is of course a useful distinction to be made between a text's or landscape's potential and the realization of that potential: 'Hippolytus the hunter' is a vulnerable figure wounded by Phaedra's assumption of the role. But dramatic characters are not the only interpreters. When Hippolytus first sets foot on the page, the reader's knowledge of the myth brings Phaedra's desire into the play before she has spoken,[30] and the accommodating material of hunting and pastoral idylls in Latin literature gives that desire form. No Aphrodite threatens Hippolytus at the opening of the tragedy—indeed the nurse insists that such divinities are mere constructs (195–7)—but

[27] On this see Segal (1986) 84–5.
[28] Boyle (1997) 64, 'The world of "forests" and "beasts" to which the young prince flees at 718 is more ambiguous and complex than he thinks'.
[29] Segal (1986) 154, 'the erotic crises of the play develop as crises of duplicitous language and problematical communication. Only in the solo lyrics of Hippolytus' opening song do we have a univocal language of single-spirited intentions.' Heath (1987) 93 comments on the importance of Euripides' Hippolytus appearing before Phaedra does to make his formal rejection of Aphrodite. Where Euripides' hero takes a clear stand against a known power Seneca's does not see the danger and therefore does not engage in the determined self-definition which one expects of a tragic hero.
[30] See Pfister (1992) 41–4.

Desire, as a principle not of nature but of literature,[31] speaks her destructive intent as clearly as if she were personified. She is present in specific erotic intertexts, generic vulnerabilities and ambiguities. The song does not happen impersonally—Hippolytus speaks it—and a gulf opens between the self-consciousness of the text and its experienced readers, and the self-consciousness of its speaker. These two levels of consciousness can be interpreted through the model of conscious and subconscious meaning: by this model Hippolytus imperfectly represses his sexual desire, allowing two dissonant voices to speak simultaneously.[32] I have preferred an innocent Hippolytus destroyed by the readings of others; his alienation from his own words is a mode of his victimization. The contrast between his innocence and Phaedra's understanding is akin to the contrast between the heightened even metaliterary consciousness of an Atreus or a Medea and the victims of their irony. In drama, where no words happen but that a character speaks them, literary self-consciousness is an aspect of characterization.

1. HIPPOLYTUS' HUNTING SONG

Hippolytus' intention in the opening song is to direct his hunters over the landscape and later to praise Diana. Only later (483–564) will he explain how this world is opposed to Venus. However, the role of the huntsman is traditionally a marginal one, and devotion to Diana is at odds with and remote from both civic values and respect for Venus.[33] More narrowly any reader of this tragedy would anticipate the corruption from the royal palace, the heart of the city, which will infect Hippolytus' countryside. Seemingly deprived of a dramatic Venus or Phaedra to initiate the tragedy, Seneca's audience reads things into Hippolytus' innocent words.[34]

[31] For Venus as Nature see P. J. Davis (1983) and Boyle (1997) 63. See also Segal (1986) 71 on literary artifice and Seneca's reconception of the Euripidean gods. Cf. also Casali (1995) 5 on *Heroides* 4.7 ff., for whom *Amor* is an 'elegiac transposition' of the Euripidean Aphrodite.

[32] So Segal (1986).

[33] See Vidal-Naquet (1986) 106–28 esp. 117–20, Goldhill (1986) 117–25, Sourvinou-Inwood (1987) 145 and 152–3 on reversal of the accepted pattern and the consequent fate of Melanion and Atalanta.

[34] Reading things into these words has been made much easier by Stähli-Peter (1974) and De Meo (1978), who have both written commentaries on this song. Jakobi (1988) and Gahan (1988) both discuss literary imitation in this tragedy.

1.1.

> Ite, umbrosas cingite silvas   (*Phaedra* 1)
> (Go, surround the shady forests)

The use of *cingo* for hunting is surprisingly rare, and is related to a more familiar use of the verb in a military context.[35] Before Seneca it is only used twice for the activities of a huntsman: Virgil, *Aeneid* 4.121, *dum trepidant alae saltusque indagine cingunt* (while the beaters hurry about and surround the glades with nets), and Ovid, *Metamorphoses* 7.766, *venimus et latos indagine cinximus agros* (we arrived and surrounded the broad fields with nets). Ovid follows Virgil in constructing the verb with *indagine*, and these two passages are related. In *Aeneid* 4 Juno plans a hunt for Dido and Aeneas so that they may take shelter together in the same cave. Though Dido and Aeneas will believe themselves to be predators on the hunt, they will in fact be victims of Juno's and Venus' plot to obstruct Aeneas' journey to the promised land. Juno's use of a word for surrounding people for surrounding animals works well in the tragedy of book 4,[36] where the human hunters are themselves the prey of higher beings. The figure has been prepared earlier in the text, where love-stricken Dido is likened to a wounded Cretan deer (4.69–73), a simile which itself looks back to the description of Aeneas hunting deer (1.180–93). Outside the text, erotic pursuit as hunting and the *militia amoris* are both familiar topoi. Virgil's Dido, the Cretan deer, will be important later in Seneca's tragedy as a model for Cretan Phaedra[37] and perhaps one can take this early allusion as programmatic in that sense. In the song itself Diana will hunt Cretan deer,[38] feminine like Virgil's: *tua Gaetulos dextra leones | tua Creteas sequitur cervas* (60–1). Hippolytus' quarry is less explicit. Apart from the boar of Phyle (27–30) nothing more definite than a *fera* is given (36, 47, 51, 75), though the manner of hunting in

---

[35] See Stähli-Peter (1974) 76, though she might have added *Sauromatae cingunt, fera gens, Bessique, Getaeque* (Ovid, *Tristia* 13.10.5), where the contexts are creatively merged.

[36] On the tragic colouring of this book of the *Aeneid* see Pobjoy (1998) and his bibliography 58 n. 2.

[37] See Fantham (1975), Segal (1986) 34, 35, 38.

[38] See Stähli-Peter (1974) 165–6.

39–47 recalls the usual method of hunting deer.[39] Whether or not Phaedra intrudes through Virgil's Dido, Venus certainly does, personified through Virgil's plotting divinities (and the ghost of Euripides' Aphrodite-prologue), and impersonally as erotic and elegiac topoi. The key element in Virgil's text for Seneca's opening line is the conjunction of irony and eros: Aeneas and Dido are innocent; gods and readers are not. The erotic contamination of the hunt is the site and the form of the irony, and this is the figure which Seneca borrows. Hippolytus knows neither Venus nor Virgil and is the victim of both.

Ovid's use of *cingo* for a hunter's activity comes in the story of Cephalus and Procris. Cephalus, a huntsman loved by the Dawn,[40] is a major figure for Hippolytus. Homer places Phaedra and Procris together (*Odyssey* 11.321), Euripides classes Cephalus with Semele as a victim of divine desire and in this spirit presents him as a model for Hippolytus (*Hippolytus* 453–8). Ovid's Phaedra also makes Cephalus a model for Hippolytus as her first example of a hunter who loved (*Heroides* 4.93). In the *Metamorphoses* Cephalus is again an object of Aurora's desire (7.704 ff.),[41] but here she is rejected. In revenge she tells Cephalus that Procris, his wife, is unfaithful. He disguises himself, seduces her, and then accuses her of infidelity. Procris, annoyed, takes to the mountains and to Diana to express her hatred of all men: *offensaque mei genus omne perosa virorum | montibus errabat, studiis operata Dianae* (7.745–6). The two are finally reconciled. To mark this Procris gave Cephalus a spear and a dog which, together with a fearsome beast, was turned into a statue in the course of a hunt. The relationship was then disrupted again by someone telling Procris

---

[39] This passage closely parallels the elements of a deer hunt outlined in Virgil, *Georgics* 3.371–2. See also *Aeneid* 12.749–51. De Meo (1978) 60–1 suggests further that the preparatory stages of Virgil's hunt, cut short by Juno's storm, are recalled in Hippolytus' hunting song: *Alius* raras *cervice gravi portare* plagas, | *alius teretes properet laqueos* |...*tu grave dextra laevaque | simul robur* lato *derige* ferro (Seneca, *Phaedra* 44–5, 49–50); cf. *retia* rara, plagae, lato *venabula* ferro (Virgil, *Aeneid* 4.131). However, *lato ferro* is conventional in descriptions of hunting (see e.g. the hunt of the Calydonian boar in Ovid, *Met.* 8.342) and although it appears both in Aeneas' hunt in *Aeneid* 1.313 and in Phaedra's description of Hippolytus in Ovid, *Heroides* 4.83, the community of language is not, I think, significant in the way that the repetition of the unusual use of *cingo* is.
[40] See Hesiod, *Theogony* 986.
[41] Cf. also Cephalus in *Amores* 1.13.39–40.

that Cephalus loved a nymph. The evidence for this was that when Cephalus was tired from the hunt he used to take shelter in the cool forests and give heartfelt thanks to *aura*, the breeze. Procris came to investigate, made a noise in the undergrowth, and was killed by Cephalus, who thought she was a wild animal. The structure of this story is a repeated pattern: mutual love is disrupted by a rumour (first Aurora then Aura), and each half ends with an encounter with a real or suspected wild beast.

Some elements in Cephalus' story appear also in Hippolytus': the first mover of events is a divine being whose erotic delights are spurned by a huntsman; running around the mountains as a devotee of Diana is a gesture of chastity; the final tragedy, the killing of the 'prey', is brought about by a false rumour that the huntsman has an adulterous love. Cephalus' story is long and involved, but at the point of the allusion, line 766, he is hunting with the new dog Procris has given him. This dog, Laelaps, is as fast as an arrow from a Gortynian bow.[42] What elsewhere might be no more than a cliché[43] is here a significant detail: in the usual story of Cephalus and Procris King Minos of Crete seduced Procris with a dog and a spear, presents which she passed on to Cephalus. To suggest that there is anything Gortynian (Cretan) about the dog is 'an Ovidian slip, in which the truth is unintentionally revealed'.[44] At the beginning of Ovid's narrative (7.490) Cephalus has just triumphed over his rival Minos for an alliance with Aegina: the two alliances, political and personal, are clearly parallel. Cretan adultery connects Procris to Phaedra and to Dido. More important than any identification of characters in which Hippolytus is modelled on Cephalus or Phaedra on Procris is the disguise and suspicion which recur throughout Cephalus' complicated narrative. Procris' desire to run around the mountains is offered explicitly as a gesture of chastity, but its effect is to make Cephalus burn more violently with desire: *tum mihi deserto violentior ignis ad ossa | pervenit* (7.747–8). Add to this that Procris makes the gesture because she is annoyed at having been seduced, that

---

[42] *Met.* 7.776–8 *non ocior illo | hasta nec exutae contorto verbere glandes, | nec Gortyniaco calamus levus exit ab arcu.*

[43] Cf. e.g. Virgil's African with a Spartan dog and a Cretan quiver (*Georgics* 3.344–5).

[44] See Ahl (1989) 19. In Ahl's discussion Cephalus, the narrator, and Ovid are very closely aligned: Cephalus' *naïveté* is only apparent.

the gesture is an intermission in an erotic relationship, and finally that when she returns she brings the rewards of adultery with her. At one level the gesture is part of an erotic game or narrative, but at another level it is a statement of chastity.

In the second part of the story Cephalus says that it was his custom to go hunting at first light: *Sole fere radiis feriente cacumina primis* (7.804). This is no more than conventional except that he has been abducted by Aurora and therefore the dawn is suspect. Also, this line follows immediately and provocatively from:

> nec Iovis illa meo thalamos praeferret amori,
> nec, me quae caperet, non si Venus ipsa veniret,
> ulla erat.
> (*Met.* 7.801–3)

(She would not prefer marriage with Jupiter to my love, nor was there any woman who could win me, not if Venus herself were to come.)

Cephalus' speech to *aura* is obviously erotic:[45]

> 'Aura,' recordor enim, 'venias,' cantare solebam,
> 'meque iuves, intresque sinus, gratissima, nostros;
> utque facis, relevare velis, quibus urimur, aestus.'
> Forsitan addiderim—sic me mea fata trahebant—
> blanditias plures et 'tu mihi magna voluptas,'
> dicere sim solitus 'tu me reficisque fovesque:
> tu facis ut silvas ut amem loca sola; meoque
> spiritus iste tuus semper captatur ab ore.'
> (*Met.*, 7.813–20)

('Aura,' I used to cry—for I remember—'come and help me, enter my embrace, dearest, and, as you do, please relieve the heat with which I burn.' Perhaps, for so my fate drew me on, I might add more soft words and I used to say, 'You are my great pleasure, you revive and warm me, you make it that I love the woods and lonely places. My lips always long for that breath of yours.')

Someone (*Nescio quis* 822), deceived by words which even Cephalus admits are ambiguous (*vocibus ambiguis* 821), tells Procris and she investigates. This time, now that the suspicion exists in more than the reader's mind, he sets off not at first light but at dawn, *postera depulerant Aurorae lumina noctem* (835). At midday he hears a noise and, mistaking an erotic situation for a hunting

---

[45] See Bömer (1976) 396–7 on these lines.

274   Phaedra: *Intertextuality and Innocence*

situation, kills the woman who mistook a hunting situation for an erotic situation. The point of the story, its repeated figure, its 'hypogrammatic sentence',[46] is that the (rhetoric of the) chaste hunter is corrupted by the (rhetoric of the) erotic. Ahl, noting that both Cephalus and Procris have winds in their family history, comments, 'Small wonder, then, that their lives seem affected by the breezes and that the boundaries between physical love and love of the breezes or love of hunting are indistinct'.[47] It is possible to relate episodes in this story to episodes in Seneca's tragedy: one can compare Procris' desire to run to the wilds with Phaedra's similar desire, and/or with Hippolytus' escape to the woods and to chastity,[48] but this more systematic reading is not supported by a systematic pattern of verbal reminiscences even though Cephalus is marked in the tradition of Hippolytus' myth as a useful figure of comparison. When Seneca writes *cingite silvas* he nods briefly towards Ovid's single-minded essay on the vulnerability of hunting-speak, who in turn looks back to the erotic hunt in Roman literature's master text.[49] The significant inheritance for Seneca from Ovid is not a model for one of his characters but a more general literary phenomenon: the erotic contamination of hunting.

1.2.
summaque montis *iuga* Cecropii   (*Phaedra* 2)
(and the *high* mountain *ridges* of Cecrops' land)

Summa iuga is an Ovidian phrase[50] which Ovid's Phaedra uses at *Heroides* 4.42 when describing her intention to imitate Hippolytus by going hunting: *in nemus ire libet pressisque in retia cervis | hortari celeris per* iuga summa *canes* (I wish to go into the woods and when the deer are caught in the nets to drive the dogs over the mountain

[46] The terms 'hypogram' and 'hypogrammatic sentence' are taken from Riffaterre (1980) 11–13, 46.
[47] The winds are Boreas for Procris and Aeolus for Cephalus. See Ahl (1989) 20.
[48] See Euripides, *Hippolytus* 208–31; Seneca, *Phaedra* 110–12, 717.
[49] Comparable to the Cephalus and Procris story is the myth of Actaeon and Diana in *Met.* 3.138–52 where both hunters alternately take up and relinquish the role within the context of erotic violence. On Actaeon see below, Sect. 1.6. See also Apollo and Cupid at *Met.* 1.452–73 discussed below, Sect. 1.5, and Callimachus, *Aetia* 70.
[50] *Summo iugo* appears in *Ex Ponto* 4.7.24 and *summa iuga* in the Ps.-Ovidian *Consolatio ad Liviam* 390. In addition, from the *Appendix Virgiliana*, *montis iuga summa* appears in the pastoral context of *Culex* 46 and *summo iugo* at *Aetna* 340. Perhaps strangely, no other author before Seneca seems to have used these words together.

tops 41–2). Sexual desire gives her this intention and she soon compares herself to Bacchants (47–50) who rush around the mountains and are suspected of erotic frenzy.[51] Phaedra imitates Hippolytus in both Euripides' and Seneca's tragedies, but the imitation becomes an emphatic inversion in Seneca's play: Phaedra casts herself as a hunter and Hippolytus as her prey. He runs to the refuge of forests and beasts (717–18), is torn apart, tracked down by his own dogs, and finally brought back as a carcass to the palace (1105–14). Phaedra's imitation is predatory in this tragedy. Phaedra recognizes her woodland hunting as traditional (110–28) and sets her learning against obdurate and feral Hippolytus: *Ferus est; amore didicimus vinci feros* (240) (He is wild; I have learnt that wild things are overcome by love). She consciously chooses her models:

NUTRIX. Patris memento.
PHAEDRA. Meminimus matris simul (242)

(NURSE. Remember your father. PHAEDRA. I remember my mother as well).

Through Pasiphaë she adapts Hippolytus, assumes and alters his role to suit her purpose. Her imitation is deliberate.[52] By contrast, only the reader remembers Ovid's Phaedra in Hippolytus' *summa iuga*: far from reshaping his model Hippolytus does not know that he has one. He innocently recalls himself already imitated, contaminated, and denatured. This is significant when one considers that this hunting song is generally accepted as the place where Hippolytus is still intact. Dramatic structure grants Hippolytus the right to speak first; deviant intertexts steal the power away.

Hippolytus' hunting song is divided into two parts: commands to his hunters (1–53) and an invocation of Diana (54 ff.). The invocation, the second beginning, opens:

Ades en comiti, diva virago,
cuius regno pars terrarum
secreta vacat
(*Phaedra* 54–6)

---

[51] So Euripides, *Bacchae* 221–5. Note also the *sparagmos* of Pentheus, *Bacchae* 1125 ff. and of Orpheus in Virgil, *Georgics* 4.520–2.
[52] The irony unseen even to Phaedra that Hippolytus will finally be killed by a bull is present also in Ovid, *Heroides* 4.166. So Casali (1995) 10–11.

(Come to your comrade here, virile goddess, you for whose rule the secluded parts of the earth are open.)

Diana's privacy is a conventional element, but as Jakobi notes[53] these words recall the prayer of Ovid's Phaedra:

sic tibi *secretis* agilis dea saltibus *adsit*
(Ovid, *Heroides* 4.169)

(So may the nimble goddess come to you in the secluded woods).

Phaedra prays that Diana may be there for him as he is not there for her. By the parallelism she eroticizes his relationship with Diana and develops the idea further by wondering whether nymphs to assuage his thirst will in fact please him because they are *puellae* (173-4).[54] It is appropriate that Phaedra sees Hippolytus' devotion to Diana in these terms, but significant that Hippolytus unknowingly inherits this view from her. Later in the tragedy the eroticization of Hippolytus' prayer and his world will become more direct: the nurse will echo his invocation in her prayer to Diana that Hippolytus return to the laws of Venus (417), and the chorus at 736 ff. will present Diana corrupted and him as vulnerable to the predations of *Naiades improbae* (780) and the *lascivae nemorum deae* (783).[55] This early passage anticipates the later destruction of Hippolytus by eros, but significant also is the manner of this anticipation. Hippolytus the character cannot see the vulnerability which the reader sees; more precisely he cannot see that his free self-definition is an imitation of Phaedra's elegiac fantasies.

Similar (but not identical) effects are created from *Heroides* 4 later in the tragedy. Hippolytus, in his agon with the nurse (435-579), which is in many ways a development of his hunting song, says: *regios luxus procul est impetus fugisse* ('His impulse is to flee from royal luxury', Seneca, *Phaedra* 517-18). Henry and Walker note that this recalls the desire of Ovid's Phaedra: *est mihi per saevas impetus ire feras* ('My impulse is to go among the savage beasts', Ovid, *Heroides* 4.38). I do not find productive their distinction between the 'strongly positive feeling' of *impetus est ire* and

---

[53] Jakobi (1988) 64. See Stähli-Peter (1974) 159 for a fuller list.
[54] Not only are the nymphs rendered elegiac as *puellae*, but, Casali (1995) 12 argues, *quamvis odisse puellas* (173) recalls Propertius, *castas odisse puellas* (1.5). This 'is something irremediably different from Hippolytus' misogyny'.
[55] See e.g. Segal (1986) 66-70.

the 'negativing *fugisse*'.⁵⁶ To my mind the important point is that we can hear Phaedra in the background pursuing wild beasts, but Hippolytus can't. We have known since line 233 ff. that she views Hippolytus as a wild beast to be hunted, and he has yet to discover it. Her predatory intent informs the intertextual effect. The allusion to an external text reminds the reader that Hippolytus lives in a larger world than he knows. Without the awareness of a Medea he does not transcend the boundaries of the dramatic illusion; his stature, relative to the reader's, is diminished as he becomes an ironic victim.

When Hippolytus finally does understand Phaedra's intentions he says:

> dignus en stupris ego?
> scelerique tanto visus ego solus tibi
> materia facilis?
> . . . . . .
> o maius ausa matre monstrifera malum
> genetrice peior! illa se tantum stupro
> contaminavit
> (Seneca, *Phaedra* 684–6, 688–90)

(Look, am I suited to adulteries? Did I of all men seem to you ready material for such a crime?...You have dared a mightier evil than your monster-bearing mother, you are worse than your parent! She defiled only herself with adultery).

If the manuscript tradition is correct, Ovid's Phaedra says to Hippolytus:

> tu modo duritiam silvis depone iugosis;
> non sum materia digna perire tua.
> (Ovid, *Heroides* 4.85–6)⁵⁷

(You now leave your hardness in the hills and woods; I do not deserve to be killed by your nature.)

Seneca's Hippolytus, horrified to discover that his *materia* has been found receptive to Phaedra's desires, says, *dignus...ego?*, echoing Ovid's Phaedra's *non sum...digna*. Ovid's Phaedra demands that Hippolytus abandon *duritia* in his characteristic

---

⁵⁶ Henry and Walker (1966) 234.
⁵⁷ All the major MSS (E, F, G, L, V) give this reading, but many editors have not been convinced, and most of those who emended the line changed the word *materia*. See Dörrie (1971) 77. I accept the line.

278   Phaedra: *Intertextuality and Innocence*

context, the *silvis iugosis*, and, invoking Cephalus as a model, constructs a new, softer idyll (93 ff.). One may usefully note *silvis* in the previous line and compare Du Quesnay's discussion of a Hellenistic convention in Virgil, *Eclogue* 4.3, *silvae sint consule dignae*.[58] *Silvae* is there not only a marker of bucolic poetry but, through ὕλη, literary material. *Materia*, Latin's ὕλη, points to a similar meta-literary play on Ovid's *silvis*: Phaedra does not want to die by Hippolytus' wood/nature/rhetoric and asks him to leave his hardness behind in the woods. So, at the same time as Seneca's Hippolytus is expressing his astonishment that he has somehow been misread, he is echoing Phaedra, in another text, seeing his world as text and rewriting it. The mismatch between Hippolytus' innocent outrage and the literary sophistication of both Ovid's Phaedra and Seneca's reader is striking. Hippolytus complains that Phaedra is worse than her mother because Pasiphaë only contaminated herself. *Contaminavit*, first word in the line like *materia*, also has meta-literary currency.[59] Soon Hippolytus will threaten to stab Phaedra with his sword only to find that she sees erotic potential in this also (704–12).[60] The episodes are parallel: speech and act recoil against him. In desperation he throws away the sword and has no speech to defend himself against the subsequent accusations of Phaedra and Theseus.

In these three places (*Phaedra* 2, 517–18, 684–6) Seneca erotically contaminates Hippolytus' words in the most direct way by having him echo the words of Ovid's Phaedra. Traditionally, desire drives Phaedra to imitate Hippolytus. Here, developing Phaedra's inversion of Hippolytus' characteristic activity in the tragedy as she becomes the hunter and he the prey, Seneca reverses the roles of model and imitator: through the chronology of the two poets, (Seneca's) Hippolytus can imitate (Ovid's) Phaedra. Whereas Phaedra imitates Hippolytus intentionally, he involuntarily imitates her: he innocently defines himself with tainted words and expresses sincere astonishment when he sees how she has interpreted him. With this all-important difference Phaedra's

[58] Du Quesnay (1977) 52–4. The single Hellenistic text which serves as Virgil's primary model is Theocritus, *Idyll* 17. See also Hinds (1998) 11–13 on *Aeneid* 6.179–82.
[59] For *contaminatio* as a metaphor for the influence of one text on another see Terence, *Heautontimorumenos*, *Prol.* 17.
[60] Segal (1986) 132–5.

Phaedra: *Intertextuality and Innocence* 279

imitation of Hippolytus within the dramatic illusion is paralleled by his imitation of her without. In this way Seneca renews a familiar element of the myth, Phaedra's imitation of Hippolytus, by relating it to the intertextual irony which is central to his tragedy. A densely allusive art is characteristically Hellenistic and Roman, and Seneca's treatment of imitation in the Hippolytus myth marks his tragedy as Roman and shows its close affiliations with non-dramatic literature.

1.3.

HIPPOLYTUS. Committe curas auribus, mater, meis.
PHAEDRA.   Matris superbum est nomen et nimium potens:
  nostros humilius nomen affectus decet;
  me vel sororem, Hippolyte, vel famulam voca,
  famulamque potius: omne servitium feram.
  non me per altas ire si iubeas nives
  pigeat gelatis ingredi Pindi iugis;
  non, si per ignes ire et infesta agmina,
  cuncter paratis ensibus pectus dare.

(*Phaedra* 608–16)

(HIPPOLYTUS. Entrust your cares to my ears, mother. PHAEDRA. The name of mother is too grand and mighty. A humbler name suits my feelings: call me sister, Hippolytus, or servant—yes, servant is better: I will bear any servitude. If you bade me go through deep snows, I would not object to travelling on Pindus' frozen heights; if you bade me go through fire and enemy ranks, I would not hesitate to breast drawn swords.)

In the first stages of her meeting with Hippolytus, Phaedra tries to set a suitable scene for her persuasion. The relationship of mother to son clearly has to change, and slave to master is her preferred alternative. She follows the redefinition of their relationship with a different perspective on his landscape. For Hippolytus running over icy mountains was an expression of his devotion to Diana, but Phaedra's willingness to do the same is both an imitation of Hippolytus and a stock element in the elegiac lover's *servitium amoris*.[61] Procris' decision to devote herself to Diana's hunt, simultaneously a gesture of chastity and an episode in an erotic game,

---

[61] See Conte (1986) 115–19 on an elegiac, erotic devotion to Diana and her landscape in Virgil, *Eclogues* 10, Propertius 1.1, 2.19, and Tibullus 4.3. See also Segal (1986) 50 n. 35 with references to Henry and Walker (1966) and Paratore (1957).

confused the distinction between hunting and sexual desire. Similarly here Phaedra's offer echoes two opposing originals and thereby compromises the landscape Hippolytus thought his own. The conventionality of her gesture is underlined by a certain awkwardness as she speaks the words of a male elegiac lover. Warfare, like hunting, can be opposed to the erotic relationship or inform it as the *militia amoris*, but in either case the soldier parallels the male lover.[62] It is incongruous that Phaedra should imagine herself, however hypothetically, as facing hostile armies and swords. Hippolytus ignores this part of her speech and responds to the question of Theseus' return. The reader, prompted by the awkwardness of Phaedra speaking as the (male) elegiac lover, sees the contamination of Hippolytus' landscape by the erotic as a seduction of which he is unaware, for he fails to respond appropriately.

Phaedra's seduction does not depend on a single text but on the familiar conventions of another genre. Her male voice,[63] apparently awkward, reinforces her assumption of Hippolytus' role and the reversal by which she becomes the hunter and he the prey. The persona she inherits from the foreign genre reinforces the persona she wishes to present in the drama, and her description of the landscape is part of her construction of the persona. Hippolytus' description of his landscape in his opening song is similarly an act of self-definition. Phaedra's later imitation of his landscape is a predatory, erotic rewriting of it, but there is an unstable plurality in his description even before she speaks. This derives both from the different meanings of the many landscapes which are his models, and from contradictory elements within his own description. The violent, icy mountains and the softer idylls are both part of his landscape, but clearly opposed to each other. Further, the pastoral idylls are familiar locations for a fragile innocence: they carry with them the expectation of invasion and destruction. In this sense they are doomed by a literary convention, of which Hippolytus, who takes them as his own, is innocent.

> Ite, umbrosas cingite silvas
> summaque montis iuga Cecropii!

---

[62] Cf. Tibullus 1.3, 1.10; Ovid, *Amores* 1.9.
[63] She does argue that her voice is characteristically feminine in its renunciation of power (619), but this ignoble passivity is of course a familiar elegiac posture.

Phaedra: Intertextuality and Innocence

> celeri planta lustrate vagi
> quae saxoso loca Parnetho
>   subiecta iacent,
> quae Thriasiis vallibus amnis
> rapida currens verberat unda;
> scandite colles semper canos
>   nive Riphaea.
> Hac, hac alii qua nemus alta
> texitur alno, qua prata patent
> quae rorifera mulcens aura
> Zephyrus vernas evocat herbas,
> ubi per graciles levis Ilisos
> labitur agros piger et steriles
> amne maligno radit harenas.
> Vos qua Marathon tramite laevo
>   saltus aperit,
> qua comitatae gregibus parvis
> nocturna petunt pabula fetae;
> vos qua tepidis subditus austris
> frigora mollit durus Acharneus.
> Alius rupem dulcis Hymetti,
> parvas alius calcet Aphidnas;
> pars illa diu vacat immunis,
> qua curvati litora ponti
>   Sunion urget.   (*Phaedra* 1–26)

(Go, surround the shady forests and the high mountain ridges of Cecrops' land! Roam widely on swift feet, and range the lands that lie below the crags of Mt Parnethus and the lands that the river in Thria's vale buffets as it rushes with its whirling current; climb the hills always white with Riphaean snow. Other men, go here where lofty alders weave a grove, where meadows lie caressed by the Zephyr's dewy breeze inviting the growth of springtime grasses, and where through thin-soiled fields the slight Ilisos glides sluggishly, and scrapes the barren sands with its grudging stream. You men, go by the left-hand path where Marathon opens its glades, where in the company of their small brood dams seek out forage at night; you, where exposure to warm south winds softens the frosts for the rugged Acharnian. Let one man tread the crags of sweet Hymettus, another the plain of Aphidnae. That region has long been lying untouched where Sunion pushes back the edge of the curving sea.)

The hunting song opens with swift movement through a savage environment. The huntsmen are to range *celeri planta* through the places which lie cast down beneath (*subiecta iacent*) Mt Parnes, and through places beaten by fast-running water. The mountain ridges are always white with Riphaean snow. Every place named in this landscape is Attic except for the Riphaean snow, which comes from the edges of the world.[64] Geographical boundaries in Latin literature are used to express other limits: the messenger in Seneca's *Thyestes* sees Atreus' crime and begins his report by asking '*quaenam ista regio est?*' (627). So unnatural a deed cannot have been committed in Argos, Sparta, or Corinth, so this place must be the Danube, the Hyrcanian land, or Scythia. Perpetual snow can mark simply the end of civilization, but snow and ice are also easily opposed to the heat of desire. When Orpheus wished to distance himself from Venus after losing Eurydice for the second time:

> solus Hyperboreas glacies Tanaimque nivalem
> arvaque Riphaeis numquam viduata pruinis
> lustrabat.
> (Virgil, *Georgics* 4.517–19)

(Alone he wandered Hyperborean ice, snowy Tanais and the fields never free of Riphaean frost.)

The unmelting Riphaean snow in Hippolytus' violent landscape indicates the harshness of his character and his barbarian ancestry.[65] More narrowly it also foreshadows his rejection of Phaedra and all other women: *detestor omnis, horreo fugio execror* (566). But, as Procris' flight from cultivated land[66] to Diana was revealed as a gesture in an erotic game, so a cold, unyielding landscape is for elegists, erotic practitioners, an interruption or a trial in their *amores*.[67] Hippolytus' world and persona have been destabilized in the first two lines and this snowy landscape too has the potential of becoming an episode in an erotic narrative.

The Latin poem which above all others establishes a mode of writing the vulnerability of a pastoral landscape to erotic contamination is Virgil, *Eclogues* 10. Its model is Theocritus, *Idylls* 1, on the sufferings and death of Daphnis. Aphrodite, angered by the chastity of Daphnis, infects the shepherd-hunter with desire. He

---

[64] Coffey and Mayer (1990) 91. See Virgil, *Georgics* 1.240, 3.382, 4.518.
[65] Cf. 580–2 and see 658–60 and 906–17 for Hippolytus' maternal ancestry. Cold mountains are also sterile in Catullus 63.69–73.
[66] For the association between cultivated land and *amor* see e.g. Tibullus 1.1, 1.2.99–100, 1.4, 1.7.29 ff., 2.1.37 ff.
[67] See e.g. Propertius 1.8.2, 1.18.27. Cf. Catullus 63.69–73.

dies rather than act upon it. Virgil replaces Daphnis with the elegist Gallus and phrases the irruption of destructive desire into a pastoral sanctuary as the collision of elegiac and Theocritean bucolic. From the invocation of Arethusa in its first line *Eclogues* 10 constantly reminds the reader of its literary status: carmina *sunt dicenda; neget quis* carmina *Gallo?* (3). Although pastoral elements cannot perhaps be distinguished from elegiac elements as sharply as Conte would wish,[68] the collision of genres is nevertheless central to an interpretation of the poem: Gallus adapts material he wrote in the style of the elegist Euphorion to Theocritean pastoral[69] and cuts his *amores* into the delicate pastoral fabric to grow as the trees grow (53–4).[70]

Elegiac love is ultimately victorious (*omnia vincit Amor* 69) and the generic fusion unstable. In the section which most directly recalls Theocritus, the appearance of the divinities, Apollo tells Gallus, '*tua cura Lycoris | perque nives alium perque horrida castra secuta est*' (Your love Lycoris has followed another through the snows and horrid camps 22–3). This is a brutal revelation because the soldier, though a familiar rival of the elegiac lover, has no place in the pastoral setting which Virgil offers as sanctuary. Gallus tries to escape from the grim truth into a pastoral world clearly marked (by a string of subjunctive verbs)[71] as unreal. The memories of elegy make pastoral sanctuary impossible. Even Gallus' attempt to wander Mt Maenalus with the Nymphs or to hunt braving the *frigora* of the Parthenian glades is an imitation and memorial of Lycoris braving the *frigora* of the Rhine (55–7; cf. 46–9). When he finally surrenders to love, admits the victory of elegy and the defeat of pastoral, the cold returns unequivocally as an elegiac *adynaton*:

---

[68] See Martindale (1997*b*) 113–14 and Halperin (1983) as commentary on Conte (1986).

[69] These figures are indicated by the place-names *Chalcidico* (50) and *Siculi* (51). See Quintilian 10.1.56 and R. Coleman (1977) 289. On this poem more generally see Coleiro (1979) for a survey of pre-1979 scholars of whom the most rewarding in my opinion is Putnam (1970) esp. 352–67. Post-1979 on generic contamination see Conte (1986) 100–30.

[70] *tenerisque meos incidere amores | arboribus* (*Eclogues* 10.53–4). On this detail see Conte (1986) 122, and R. Coleman (1977) 290, 'It is probably another indication of Gallus' imperfect conversion to Arcady'. See also n. 58 above on *materia* and Martindale (1997*b*) 109 on *silva* as a bucolic marker.

[71] 33–43. The end of the daydream is signalled by *nunc* in line 45.

> iam neque Hamadryades rursus nec carmina nobis
> ipsa placent; ipsae rursus concedite silvae.
> non illum nostri possunt mutare labores,
> nec si frigoribus mediis Hebrumque bibamus
> (Virgil, *Eclogues* 10.62–5)

(And now again neither the Hamadryads nor the poetry itself gives me pleasure. Again, woods yourselves yield. Our efforts cannot change him not if we were to drink the Hebrus in midwinter.)

Ultimately Gallus' pastoral escape fails because he himself brings the memory of his *amores* to the idyll and so causes the *medicina* to fail.

Eclogues 10 as a whole is concerned with generic contamination. Gallus' icy landscape (55 ff.), presented as a cure for sexual desire, recalls through imitation the landscape of Lycoris, her soldier-lover, and the Rhine: the non-pastoral elements are invoked even as they are escaped. Gallus' memories of Lycoris turn an act of chastity, hunting in the icy mountains, into an episode in an erotic narrative. Because of these external, elegiac memories the Arcadian world is for him never more than a fragile fantasy. Gallus assumes a posture of innocence, but his literary experience will not allow him to forget the erotic connotations of firing arrows (*libet Partho torquere Cydonia cornu | spicula—tamquam haec sit nostri medicina furoris* 59–60) and he ends his section of the poem as a victim of sexual desire but not of irony. For a Roman elegist hunting simply cannot be a remedy for desire. Elegy typically appropriates what it playfully represents as outside its boundaries[72] and here in *Eclogues* 10 *Amor* shows its power to infect and exhaust any landscape (62–9).

The relevance of this poem to Hippolytus' hunting song is primarily generic rather than specific: *Eclogues* 10 shows an influential mode of pastoral vulnerability. However, it is possible to argue for a closer relationship. Gallus' desire to go hunting (*Eclogues* 10.55–60) is modelled, directly or indirectly, on the similar desire of Euripides' Phaedra (*Hippolytus* 215–21).[73] Seneca then remixes the material by having his Hippolytus recall Gallus: *planta* (Seneca, *Phaedra* 3) looks back to *plantas* (Virgil,

---

[72] See G. Davis (1983) 12–13 on the *militia amoris*.
[73] See Conte (1986) for Virgil's imitation of Theocritus (104, 107, and *passim*) and Euripides (120). See also 121 n. 22 on Greek tragedy and Latin love poetry. See also the erotic female hunter Arethusa in Propertius 4.3.

Eclogue 10.49); *lustrate* (3) to *lustrabo* (55); *Parnetho*[74] (4) to *Parthenios* (57). Gallus also surrounds woods (*circumdare saltus* (Virgil, 57) cf. *cingite silvas* (Seneca, 1)) and wanders with the nymphs of Diana (55, 62). Arguably the very first line, *ite umbrosas cingite silvas* looks back to the darkness which falls on the pastoral world at the end of *Eclogues* 10:[75]

> surgamus: solet esse gravis cantantibus umbra,
> iuniperi gravis umbra; nocent et frugibus umbrae.
> ite domum saturae, venit Hesperus, ite capellae.
>
> (*Eclogues* 10.75–7)

(Let us arise. shade is always heavy on singers, heavy is the shade of juniper; and shade harms the fruit. Go home satisfied, Hesperus is coming, go, goats.)

Whether *Eclogues* 10 is present in Seneca's *Phaedra* with the immediacy of a specific intertext or more distantly as a study in erotic and elegiac contamination of the pastoral, Gallus is a useful point of comparison for Hippolytus. Where the elegist brings fatal memories to his idyll, Hippolytus and his pastoral world are vulnerable to the experience of others and to elegy's ability to assimilate unwilling material.

1.4.

I have argued consistently that Hippolytus' doom comes on him from outside; the desire which destroys him is Phaedra's, a construct of Venus or of literary history but not his own. He is not, however, a simple figure. Looking at him Phaedra sees a blend of softness and savagery (*in ore Graio Scythicus apparet rigor* 660) which is apparent also in his landscape. This, and in particular his devotion to hunting in idylls, problematizes his construction as a pastoral character. It is certainly significant that Hippolytus, hunted by Phaedra, is destroyed by a dissonant aspect of his own character and one easily eroticized. Though I am more inclined to stress the common corruption by external forces of hunting as a gesture of chastity and of the idyll as a locus of innocence, there is an element of self-conflict in Hippolytus. The violence which

---

[74] On the MSS and the reading of *Parnetho* for the unsatisfactory *carpaneto* see Stähli-Peter (1974) 26–9.
[75] I am grateful to Ken Dowden for this suggestion.

destroys him, though eroticized and denatured, is to some degree internal.

In Hippolytus' narrative the violent landscape is interrupted and opposed by parallel idylls[76] which begin at line 9. Although both are elements of Hippolytus' landscape, there is an obvious contrast between the harshness of the mountains and rivers and the softness of the intervening spaces. This internal contradiction in Hippolytus' self-definition is ultimately expressive of an instability in his persona. The features of the idylls are familiar from a variety of texts which present a *locus amoenus*.[77] In a passage in the *Georgics* which closely parallels lines 11–12 Virgil sets just such a summer idyll in temporal opposition to the winter's cold and in spatial opposition to the intemperate zones of the earth.[78] The idyll is bounded further by the rising of Lucifer (324) and the appearance of Vesper (336), the stars which the Romans knew were the planet Venus.[79] In this narrow perfection she is a gentle goddess providing dew and tender grass for the animals which have survived the winter. She is very different here from a few lines earlier where she maddened animals, people, and the poet himself,[80] sending them raging over mountains and rivers (*Georgics* 3.242–85). And this difference is an important characteristic of many idylls: they are as vulnerable to sexual Venus as they are to snow, ice, and burning heat. Virgil's bees, the *Georgics*' ideal, asexual animals, exist in a similar idyll and are restored to life in the epyllion of book 4 only by Aristaeus expiating his attempted rape of Eurydice.[81]

The sexuality or asexuality of Hippolytus' idyll is the subject of the agon between the nurse and Hippolytus in Seneca's tragedy. The nurse argues that there is a single principle of Venus by which mortal creatures are replaced, and that he cannot consistently delight in the fish of the sea, the beasts of the woods, and the

---

[76] On the structure of the first 30 lines of the song see Stähli-Peter (1974) 71–3.
[77] See De Meo (1978) 44–5 and Stähli-Peter (1974) 88–92.
[78] *Georgics* 3.322–38. Note especially *vocantibus* (Georgics 3.322), *evocat* (Phaedra 12); *Zephyris* (322), *Zephyrus* (12); *ros* (326), *rorifera* (11).
[79] See e.g. Cicero, *De Natura Deorum* 2.20.53. Seneca, by comparing Hippolytus to Hesperus and Lucifer in *Phaedra* 743 ff., contaminates him with Venus. On this see P. J. Davis (1983) 116.
[80] *Sed fugit interea, fugit inreparabile tempus, | singula dum capti circumvectamur amore* (*Georgics* 3.284–5).
[81] Virgil, *Georgics* 4.197–201, 453–9, 531–58.

birds of the air and yet remain chaste himself (466–82). He does not answer her question directly, but praises the Golden Age and condemns the vices which accompanied the development of technology. In the Golden Age the earth was unploughed and produced crops by itself:

> iussa nec dominum pati
> iuncto ferebat terra servitium bove:
> sed arva per se feta poscentes nihil
> pavere gentes   (*Phaedra* 535–8)

(nor was the earth, bidden to suffer a master, enduring servitude beneath teams of oxen. Rather the fields, fruitful of themselves, fed the peoples who made no demands).

This idyll is broken by luxury, warfare, and lust (540–2) and Hippolytus ends his speech with an attack on stepmothers and other women and an unqualified rejection of Venus. The virginal nature of the land in the Golden Age is conventional[82] and the myth is a suitable vehicle for Hippolytus' self-characterization. Hippolytus' account of the Golden Age in his agon with the nurse looks back to Ovid's account in *Metamorphoses* 1, which also ends with an attack on stepmothers.[83] Ovid described the idyll of world's innocence as follows:

> ver erat aeternum, placidique tepentibus auris
> mulcebant Zephyri natos sine semine flores;
> mox etiam fruges tellus inarata ferebat.
>   (*Met.* 1.107–9)

(It was eternal spring and with warm breezes the gentle Zephyrs softened flowers born without any seed. Soon also the unploughed earth brought forth crops.)

There is a similarity between this virginal environment and Seneca's first idyll in the hunting song:

> qua prata iacent
> quae rorifera mulcens aura
> Zephyrus vernas evocat herbas
> (Seneca, *Phaedra* 10–12)

---

[82] But in particular Seneca's *poscentes nihil* recalls Virgil's *ipsaque tellus | omnia liberius nullo poscente ferebat* (*Georgics* 1.127–8).
[83] Ovid, *Met.* 1.147 cf. Seneca, *Phaedra* 558. On the comparison between *Met.* 1 and Seneca's description see Coffey and Mayer (1990) 139 and n. 16 above.

(... where meadows lie caressed by the Zephyr's dewy breeze inviting the growth of springtime grasses).

The Zephyr is the bringer of spring or summer since Homer,[84] and its appearance in a description of the world's springtime[85] is to be expected: the Zephyr and the softening breeze are not peculiar to descriptions of the Golden Age. When Hippolytus later characterizes his landscape as a Golden Age idyll he is not making explicit what a well-read audience would already have noted, but selecting a form for a more general *locus amoenus*. Ovid describes the Golden Age as eternal spring, but this eternity is ultimately no more than a season in the world's existence: perpetual virginity is not permitted and, as far as its narratives are concerned, the Golden Age is always *the time before* the ploughing and 'the Fall'. This fragility is a particular form of a more general fragility of all idylls and untouched meadows.[86]

The detail of the softening breeze can be found elsewhere. Catullus uses it in the context of a wedding song for the brief and fragile idyll of a virginal flower: *quem mulcent aurae* (which the breezes soften, Catullus 62.41). A slightly different kind of vulnerability can be seen in the idyll of Ovid, *Amores* 2.16.[87] Here Ovid, like Virgil's Gallus, is trying unsuccessfully to take refuge from his desire in a rustic idyll. He says that if his mistress were with him he would dare to walk the world's extreme environments: the Alps, Libya, and even Charybdis (19–26). Although trees and rivers surround him, *frigidaque arboreas mulceat aura comas* (36), he feels that he lives at the edges of the world in Scythia, Cilicia, Britain, and (perhaps) the Caucasus (37–40). The characteristic intemperance of sexual desire, evident in his willingness to range across the harshest landscape, has infected his idyll and deformed it to reflect his imbalance. Unlike Hippolytus or Catullus' virgin flower Ovid himself brings the sexual desire which dooms the idyll, but the point of the parallel is that the same detail of the softening breeze is used to characterize a fragile landscape which will be destroyed by the wildness of sexual desire.

[84] So Stähli-Peter (1974) 92. [85] Cf. Mynors (1990) 124–5.
[86] Cf. Barrett (1964) 170–5 on Euripides, *Hippolytus* 73–81 and the 'transparent symbolism' of the virgin meadow.
[87] All three passages (Catullus 62.41; Ovid, *Amores* 2.16.36, and *Metamorphoses* 1.107 ff.) are noted by Stähli-Peter (1974) 90.

The second idyll in Hippolytus' song lies near Acharnae:

> qua comitatae gregibus parvis
> nocturna petunt pabula fetae;
> vos qua tepidis subditus austris
> frigora mollit durus Acharneus.
> (Seneca, *Phaedra* 18–21)

(where in the company of their small brood dams seek out forage at night; you, where exposure to warm south winds softens the frosts for the rugged Acharnian.)

Again, the contrast between the softness of the idyll and the harsh coldness of its surroundings marks its vulnerability. In such an idyll the animals are suitably fragile: mothers with their small young. It seems reasonable to presume that these creatures are not simply descriptive details but the object of the hunt which Hippolytus is beginning. In this case the vulnerability of the idylls, set against the violence of the snow and mountains, is exploited as they are selected for invasion by hunters. In the next lines the hunters are to pass through sweet Hymettus and little Aphidnae:

> alius rupem dulcis Hymetti,
> parvas[88] alius calcet Aphidnas;   (*Phaedra* 22–3)

(Let one man tread the crags of sweet Hymettus, another the plain of Aphidnae.)

The word for their passing, *calcet*, frequently has the connotation of trampling underfoot, a reading encouraged by the following line, *pars illa diu vacat immunis* (That region has long been lying untouched 24). The idylls in Hippolytus' song, whether strictly virginal or merely free from the wild violence which is the mark of sexualized Venus, are vulnerable to the invasion of Hippolytus and his hunters. When Phaedra describes Hippolytus in a passage which recalls this opening song, she associates him with the snow and rock, not with the *loci amoeni*:[89]

---

[88] Zwierlein (1986*b*) 166 is suspicious of *parvas*, but Coffey and Mayer (1990) 92 argue convincingly that this epithet 'is clearly a maid of all work'. To my eyes there is a deliberate connection between the hunting of little animals (*gregibus parvis*, 19) and the trampling of little Aphidnae (*parvas...Aphidnas*, 23).

[89] On the parallelism between these passages see De Meo (1978) 51.

hunc in nivosi collis haerentem iugis,
et aspera agili saxa calcantem pede
sequi per alta nemora, per montes placet.
(*Phaedra* 233–5)

(Though he lingers on the ridges of snowy hills and treads jagged rocks with nimble feet, I intend to follow him across deep forests, across mountains.)

As the nurse warns her, he will not be softened:[90]

resistet ille seque mulcendum dabit
castosque ritus Venere non casta exuet?
(*Phaedra* 236–7).

(Will he stop and allow himself to be caressed, and throw off his chaste ways for an unchaste love-affair?)

Until the second chorus (see especially 764 ff.), which follows the nurse's false representation of Hippolytus, it will be Phaedra who corresponds more closely to the softer environment of the idylls:

lacrimae cadunt per ora et assiduo genae
rore irrigantur, qualiter Tauri iugis
tepido madescunt imbre percussae nives.
(*Phaedra* 381–3)

(Tears fall across her face, her eyes are flooded with constant moisture, as on the ridges of Taurus the snows melt when struck by warm rain-showers.)

Hippolytus' self-dramatization through his landscape is contradictory and unstable. Much of the confusion derives from the shifting meaning of hunting and the inversion of his role. As a hunter Hippolytus invades the idylls of a life-giving Venus, but as a pastoral innocent he is vulnerable to Phaedra's erotic form of hunting. This confusion, as Segal has noted, is underlined as a contradiction in Hippolytus' character. In his agon with the nurse Hippolytus characterizes his sylvan life in the impossible image of a Golden Age which includes hunting. Hunting, unnecessary when Nature provides food and shelter, is one of the many skills which mark human development from the Golden Age.[91]

---

[90] Cf. Phaedra's hope in Ovid, *Heroides* 4.85–6.
[91] See Segal (1986) 60 ff. and 77 ff., Segal (1983) 244–7, P. J. Davis (1983) 126. Of Latin descriptions of the Golden Age, Ovid, *Met.* 15.96–103 characterizes most clearly hunting as a kind of deception.

Phaedra: *Intertextuality and Innocence* 291

Hippolytus sees nothing but perversion in this development and attacks the luxury and lusts which civilization has won. However, his own description of hunting concedes a similarity between the destructive deception of hunting and the duplicitous behaviour of the rich and powerful:

> sed rure vacuo potitur et aperto aethere
> innocuus errat. callidas tantum feris
> struxisse fraudes novit
>   (*Phaedra* 501–3)

(But he is lord of the empty countryside, and wanders guiltless under the open sky. The cunning snares he knows how to devise are against beasts only.)

His description of the end of the Golden Age also recalls hunting:[92]

> venit imperii sitis
> cruenta, factus praeda maiori minor   (*Phaedra* 542–3)

(There followed the bloody thirst for power; the weaker fell prey to the stronger).

The nurse had argued that Hippolytus' rejection of Venus, taken to its logical conclusion, would result in a world empty of life:

> orbis iacebit squalido turpis situ
> vacuum sine ullis piscibus stabit mare
>   (*Phaedra* 471–2)

(the world will lie rank in squalid neglect, the seas will stand empty of fish).

Hippolytus' choice of words in 501 is therefore unfortunate: 'he has power over an empty countryside'. Diana and Venus are diametrically opposed and Hippolytus' hunting, his devotion to Diana, accelerates the exhaustion of life which follows from his passive rejection of Venus. Diana, in this play is a goddess of death.[93] Apart from these ominous words, the environment which Hippolytus sets against the corruption of royal palaces is not the emptiness which the nurse foresaw but an idyll (501 ff.) with new flowers and the sweet sound of cool water. This description is very much in keeping with the idylls of his opening song

---

[92] Cf. the end of Diana's hunt: *fertur plaustro praeda gementi* (*Phaedra* 77).
[93] Boyle (1997) 60–2 and (1985) 1282.

which were vulnerable to the invasion of the hunters. The inhabitant of this idyll survives not on animals but on the fruit which an uncultivated Nature supplies:

> excussa silvis poma compescunt famem
> et fraga parvis vulsa dumetis cibos
> faciles ministrant.
> (*Phaedra* 515–17)

(Fruits shaken from trees check his hunger, and wild strawberries plucked from little bushes provide easy food.)

Hippolytus' opposition to civilization is undermined: the violent art of hunting here and elsewhere has more in common with the world he rejects than with the delicate innocence of the Golden Age which he prefers. Hippolytus' unqualified hatred of Venus is ultimately the reason for this instability: his violence is directed against her every manifestation. That he makes no distinction between the life-giving principle by which the natural world is renewed and the intemperate sexuality which is the subject of the first chorus (274 ff.) ultimately condemns his idylls to extinction. Further, it allows a paradoxical association between the violence which he intends 'as a defense against sexuality'[94] and the violent eroticism which is a traditional destroyer of idylls and which will finally destroy him when he seeks sanctuary there:

> Quid deserta petis? tutior aviis
> non est forma locis: te nemore abdito
> cum Titan medium constituit diem,
> cingent, turba licens, Naiades improbae,
> formosos *solitae* claudere fontibus,
> et somnis facient insidias tuis
>   lasciviae nemorum deae
>   montivagive Panes.
> (*Phaedra* 777–84)

(Why seek the wilds? Beauty is no safer in pathless places. In the woods' seclusion, when the Titan has brought midday, a brazen throng will surround you, the shameless Naiads, apt to catch handsome boys in springs; and an ambush will be set for your siesta by the wanton woodland goddesses or mountain-roving Pans.)

---

[94] Segal (1986) 60. The thought is developed in the following pages: 60–3 and 81 ff.

Phaedra: *Intertextuality and Innocence* 293

As this chorus knows, the pastoral idyll is a habitual site for rape.[95] Hippolytus is attacked here in three different ways: first, by simple inversion as the hunter who ordered his comrades to surround the woods (*cingite silvas*, 1) is in turn surrounded by predatory Naiads; second, by a predatory literary tradition which has always made his sanctuary, the pastoral idyll, vulnerable; and third, by the parallelism between his chaste invasions and others' erotic invasions of idylls. In no sense does Hippolytus intend his hunting to be erotic, but he does help to compromise his austere devotion to Diana by associating himself both with pastoral idylls and with their aggressors, both with the virginal Golden Age and with its Fall.

1.5.

Hippolytus' characteristic activity and environment are changed in the course of the drama: hunting is a gesture whose meaning shifts. These shifts in meaning are shifts in a balance of power. Hippolytus, when he finds that he has unknowingly become material for Phaedra's desires, cannot respond except by flight. In his opening song Hippolytus introduces Diana as a figure of power: she is a victor (52) whose worshipper returns from the hunt in triumph (80); her hunt is not confined to Attica but extends to the limits of the known world. This world-domination is challenged by the first chorus (274–357) addressed to Venus who, through her son, controls earth, sea, sky, and even heaven: *vindicat omnes | natura sibi, nihil immune est* (352–3). This chorus is clearly set in opposition to Hippolytus' song to Diana.[96] Not only are both songs of world-domination, but Cupid like Diana (and indeed Hercules 317) uses a bow but in a different sense. To underline the challenge Diana is made one of Cupid's victims: *arsit obscuri dea clara mundi | nocte deserta* (309–10). The victory of Cupid is a victory of the use of the bow in its erotic sense. In this respect Seneca's presentation is very similar to Ovid's conflict between Cupid and Diana's brother in *Metamorphoses* 1.452 ff. Apollo, proud in his recent victory over the Python, rebukes Cupid for carrying the bow which befits only hunters and warriors: *nec laudes adsere nostras* (462). In response:

[95] See Parry (1964) esp. 272–5, and also Segal (1969) and Goff (1990) 58–61.
[96] See Davis (1993) 95–6, Boyle (1997) 63, and Davis (1984) more generally on the relationship between this ode and the rest of the tragedy.

filius huic Veneris 'figat tuus omnia, Phoebe,
te meus arcus' ait; 'quantoque animalia cedunt
cuncta deo, tanto minor est tua gloria nostra.'
(Ovid, *Met.* 1.463–5)

(To him the son of Venus said, 'though your bow pierces everything, Phoebus, my bow will pierce you. As all animals are less than a god, so your glory is less than mine.)

Cupid then shoots Apollo and Daphne. She takes to the woods as a devotee of Diana and as prey for Apollo's first experience of an erotic hunt. In this hunt the arts in which Apollo excels—prophecy, shooting, and medicine—fail or are powerless to help him (491, 519–24), but he succeeds through the art of Cupid: *utque monebat | ipse Amor* (531–2), *qui tamen insequitur pennis adiutus Amoris, | ocior est* (540–1). Apollo complained that Cupid had appropriated his weapons for trivial purposes; Cupid wins the victory by making Apollo represent or imitate his form of hunting. The metamorphosis of Daphne into a tree is preceded by the metamorphosis of hunting itself as the erotic hunt becomes the pattern to which Apollo conforms rather than vice versa. When Apollo styles himself as the model and Cupid as the trivial imitator, Cupid responds by reversing the roles, by making Apollo imitate him.

The struggle between Hippolytus and Phaedra is also expressed through imitation. Phaedra imitates Hippolytus to different effect and the success of her construction of hunting is assured by the literary tradition which has already written the end of their story[97] and by Hippolytus' innocent imitation of her words. Whereas the structure of the drama appears to allow him to make his own beginning, this effect is negated by the echoes of texts past: Hippolytus' construction of hunting loses its status as the original and the model. The relationship between Hippolytus' song to Diana and the chorus's ode to Venus is analogous. Hippolytus' presentation of Diana, hunting, and the bow precedes the chorus's rival presentation of Venus and Cupid: its ode is a challenge to a

---

[97] Cf. Goff (1990) 81 on cultural paradigms in Euripides, *Hippolytus*: 'it begins to seem that there is a limited number of available narratives, and that "new stories"... can only be generated by the imitation of old. Phaedra is fated to act out and repeat in her own story that of the young girl before the mirror who becomes the adulteress, and to become exactly what Hippolytos claims she is.' Cf. also Zintzen (1972) 164 on Hercules as a captive of his own heroic labours.

Phaedra: *Intertextuality and Innocence* 295

construction already established. However, in the chronology of the dramatic world, the chorus is referring to the past: Hercules has already dressed as a woman, Diana has loved Endymion, and other Olympians have in the past left heaven to live on earth in false form (*vultibus falsis habitare terras* 295). The various myths to which the chorus refers support the conclusion not only that Venus' power extends to the limits of the world but that it has always done so. Cupid in the *Metamorphoses* implied that beside him Apollo was no more than an animal. Similarly here Jupiter, under Cupid's influence, takes on lesser forms (*formas...minores* 299) like that of a swan or a bull. As in *Heroides* 4.55 we discover that in fact Pasiphaë was not the first, that the woes of Phaedra's house and the recurrent figure of the bull can be traced back to the king of the gods.[98] Here the leader of heaven (*ipse qui caelum nebulasque ducit* (300), is driven to an unseemly parody of the irresistible power which defines him:

> perque fraternos, nova regna, fluctus
> ungula lentos imitante remos
> pectore adverso domuit profundum
> (*Phaedra* 305–7)

(and through a new realm, his brother's waves, as his hooves played the role of pliant oars, he breasted and overcame the deep).

The Olympians are degraded by their ridiculous lesser forms but also by the fact that they have become imitators rather than the powers which define the universe. Cupid's use of the bow appears a distorted echo of Diana's or Apollo's but when Hippolytus sings his song to Diana it is an imitation already familiar from the mythological and literary traditions which are his world's past: it is an echo heard *before* his song.[99] This chorus serves not so much to change Hippolytus' song as to remind the reader of the metamorphoses which have already been written.

---

[98] See Casali (1995) 10.

[99] 'The reference to gods transformed for love is bound to recall Ovid's *Metamorphoses*', Coffey and Mayer (1990) 119, but as their notes show (119–21) there are many more authors and texts (starting with the *Iliad* in line 300) recalled here. This sequence of literary metamorphoses provokes Coffey and Mayer into general discussion of Classical and Senecan views on imitation (120 and 121). On Hercules' metamorphosis see especially Ovid, *Heroides* 9 and *Ars Amatoria* 2.215–21 (cf. *Ars Amatoria* 1.689–704) and Warden (1982) on Hercules' transformation in Propertius 4.9 as a metamorphosis of genre.

296   Phaedra: *Intertextuality and Innocence*

1.6.

At the end of the tragedy Hippolytus is destroyed by the bull from the sea in a scene which echoes and inverts his own descriptions of hunting in the opening song. The dogs which once hunted with Hippolytus and wore the blood of his triumphs now track the bloody trail of their master's corpse (77–80; cf. 1105–8). This inversion is underscored by a series of verbal reminiscences which several commentators on the tragedy have recorded.[100] The dewy breeze (*rorifera aura* 11) from Hippolytus' idyll and the dewy earth (*roscida tellus* 42) of the dawn hunt are recalled by the salt spray which announces the monster's arrival (*summum cacumen rorat expulso sale* 1027). The noose (*laqueus* 46, *laqueum* 76) which Hippolytus uses against wild animals figures the reins which entangle him (*laqueo tenaci* 1086) when the monster spooks his horses. Finally, the wandering huntsmen (*vagi* 3) of the opening song become their master's broken body still wandering at the end of the play (*corporis partes vagas* 1278). Taken in isolation this grim foreshadowing is, at the moment of utterance, as invisible to the reader as it is to Hippolytus. But just as with the eroticization of Hippolytus' chaste world, the simpler inversion by which the hunter Hippolytus becomes the prey takes place through deviant intertexts before Phaedra has ever spoken. The hunting song began with an echo of Juno's trapping of Dido and Aeneas, the innocent hunters of *Aeneid* 4. It ends as follows:

>En, diva, fave! signum arguti
>misere canes: vocor in silvas
>*hac, hac* pergam qua *via* longum
>   compensat iter.   (*Phaedra* 81–4)

(Ah! Favour me, goddess: the clear-voiced hounds have sent the sign; I am called to the woods. I shall go this way, where a path shortens the lengthy journey.)

---

[100] In his discussion 72–3 Segal (1986) refers to Henry and Walker (1966) 232 and P. J. Davis (1983) 114f. In addition to the elements I have listed above, Segal notes on 73 that 'the "shade" with which he opened the play (*umbrosas silvas*) is now tinged with the underworld "shades" that weigh heavily on the last scene'. Cf. Theodorakopoulos (1997) 162–4 on the *umbra* which closes the *Aeneid*.

Before Phaedra speaks Hippolytus runs to the sanctuary of the woods. His last words are a fatal imitation of Ovid's metaphorical use of *compendium* in *Metamorphoses* 3.234:[101]

> ea turba cupidine praedae
> per rupes scopulosque adituque carentia saxa
> *qua*que est difficilis, *qua*que est nulla *via*, sequuntur.
> Ille fugit per quae fuerat loca saepe secutus.
> Heu, famulos fugit ipse suos! clamare libebat
> 'Actaeon ego sum, dominum cognoscite vestrum!'
> Verba animo desunt. Resonat latratibus aether.
> Prima Melanchaetes in tergo vulnera fecit,
> proxima Theridamas; Oresitrophus haesit in armo.
> Tardius exierant, sed per *compendia* montis
> anticipata *via* est.
> (*Met.* 3.225–35)

(that pack with desire for prey pursue over crags and cliffs and trackless rocks where the path is difficult and where there is no path. He flees through those places where he had often pursued. Alas he flees his own servants. He wanted to cry, 'I am Actaeon, recognize your master!' The words he intends fail him; the air echoes with barking. First Melanchaetes made a wound in his back, next Theridamas; Oresitrophos fastened to his shoulder. They had set out later but through a short-cut across the mountain had got ahead of their course.'

The relevance of the Ovidian model goes beyond its hunting context. Where he once hunted, Actaeon is pursued by his followers and, in a few lines, torn apart by his dogs: *undique circumstant, mersisque in corpore rostris | dilacerant falsi dominum sub imagine cervi* (They surround him on all sides, and with their muzzles buried in his body tear apart their master concealed by the false form of a deer 249–50). Hippolytus' death and its manner is thus already written. Diana transformed Actaeon so that he could never tell that he had seen her naked. It is therefore ironic that Hippolytus should preface his echo of Actaeon with the words, *En, diva, fave! signum arguti | misere canes* (Ah! Favour me, goddess: the clear-voiced

---

[101] Jakobi (1988) 64–5 writes, 'Eine elegante Imitation: die ovidische Bedeutungserweiterung von *compendium* als *abbreviatio viae* führt Seneca in einem inhaltlich gleichen Kontext einer Jagdszene analog für das Verbum *compensare* ein.' See also Stähli-Peter (1974) 195.

hounds have sent the sign 81–2). The context which he innocently recalls is not different but exactly counter to his intention.

Ovid's Actaeon is a fine role for Seneca's Hippolytus to play. Actaeon came upon Diana and her nymphs by accident (*sic illum fata ferebant*, *Met*. 3.176) after a successful hunt (146–54). The myth is introduced with a statement of Actaeon's innocence: *at bene si quaeras fortunae crimen in illo | non scelus invenies* (but if you look rightly you will find chance to blame and no crime in him 141–2). The punishment for his unintentional erotic invasion is the transformation of his body and the loss of his voice:

> 'Me miserum' dicturus erat, vox nulla secuta est:
> ingemuit, vox illa fuit; lacrimaeque per ora
> non sua fluxerunt. mens tantum pristina mansit.
> (*Met*. 3.201–3)

('Woe is me' he wanted to say, but no voice came. He groaned, that was his voice. tears flowed down a face not his own. Only his mind remained untouched.)

Hippolytus similarly remains innocent to the end though he loses power over his appearance, his words, his acts, and his ancestry. Though he finally understands Phaedra's intentions he does not hear Theseus' condemnation or recognize the monster which destroys him. Most importantly he does not show any awareness of the texts, the narratives, and the figures which make him 'easy material'.

1.7.

Seneca uses the Golden Age in both *Medea* and *Phaedra* to characterize a literary innocence. Similar treatments of the Golden Age in the two plays are pointed by references to Medea in *Phaedra*: Hippolytus ends his long agon with the nurse and his description of the end of the Golden Age with Medea:

> sileant aliae: sola coniunx Aegei,
> Medea, reddet feminas dirum genus.
> (*Phaedra* 563–4)

(To say nothing of others, Aegeus' wife Medea alone will reveal women as a monstrous tribe.)

Phaedra: Intertextuality and Innocence

This agon anticipates the scene of Phaedra's revelation to Hippolytus. When he has finally understood her he again concludes his condemnation with Medea:

> Colchide noverca maius hoc, maius malum est.
> (*Phaedra* 697)
> (this is an evil worse, worse than your Colchian stepmother).

In this play, as in her own, Medea marks the end of the Golden Age.[102] In *Medea* she is the prize of the first voyage:

> Quod fuit huius pretium cursus?
> aurea pellis
> maiusque mari Medea malum,
> merces prima digna carina.   (*Medea* 361–3)

(What was the prize gained by this voyage? The Golden Fleece and Medea, an evil worse than the sea, fit merchandise for the first vessel.)

Here she is the archetype of woman, the *dux malorum* (the leader in evil) and the *scelerum artifex* (artificer of crimes, *Phaedra* 559). The description of wickedness and warfare which follows these epithets is clearly intended to parallel the preceding description of the end of the Golden Age (540 f.). In *Medea* this age is no more than a choral memory. Medea, with her world-shaping magic and her unparalleled freedom from the dramatic illusion, revels in the loss of her innocence:

> levia memoravi nimis:
> haec virgo feci; gravior exurgat dolor:
> maiora iam me scelera post partus decent.
> (*Medea* 48–50)

(But these things I talk of are too slight; I did all this as a girl. My bitterness must grow more weighty: greater crimes become me now, after giving birth.)

The chorus which in two great odes looks back to the Golden Age is protected from Medea by dramatic convention: even Seneca does not allow his heroine to destroy the chorus. In *Phaedra*, however, there is a character determined to recall the Golden Age and to arrest the development of the fatal arts. Hippolytus' failure to resist Phaedra is inevitable: the Golden Age has ended for everyone else and his innocence has no defence

---

[102] Segal (1986) 88–9 notes the similarity between Phaedra 697 and Medea 362.

against the texts and arts familiar to Phaedra, the nurse and his readers.

Although Hippolytus and Medea are directly opposed across the line marking the end of the Golden Age, his destroyer differs from Medea and Atreus. Whereas these figures insisted, with varying degrees of success, on surpassing the models of their past and dominating their own tragedies, Phaedra sees only a choice between criminal repetition and simple extinction. Either she will conform to the pattern of her heritage or she will die. In this respect she has more in common with the *Troades* who drag out a servile existence in the emblems of the past and of a dead city or die. Although Hippolytus judges her a greater evil than Medea (697 above), the nurse confirms Phaedra's verdict: *natura totiens legibus cedet suis, | quotiens amabit Cressa?* ('shall Nature always abandon her laws, when a Cretan woman loves?' *Phaedra* 176–7).[103] What for characters is a biological repetition is a textual phenomenon for the reader. There is no hugely powerful protagonist in this tragedy, no Medea or Atreus. Hippolytus is destroyed by means of Phaedra by a biological force of Nature (or Venus or Cupid) which in its textual aspect is the literary tradition. Schiesaro, in a discussion primarily of *Troades*, *Agamemnon*, and *Oedipus*, has argued that the criminal repetition in Senecan tragedy, as poetic form, is to be read with and through Ovid's *Metamorphoses* against the irresistible movement of Virgil's epic towards its *telos*.[104] The confrontation with Virgil works particularly well in *Troades*, partly of course because the *Aeneid* is *Troades*' past in a very immediate sense, but also because the Trojans and their past occupy most of the drama. Phaedra is set as much against Hippolytus as she is against her own past. The weight of tradition in this tragedy is felt by the reader in two opposite senses. While a competent reader can share Phaedra's perspective of a dominant, constricting past, he/she cannot share Hippolytus' innocence. To read Hippolytus competently is to make him a victim not so much of situational irony but of verbal

---

[103] Cf. Theseus' response to Hippolytus' guilt: *redit ad auctores genus | stirpemque primam degener sanguis refert* (907–8).
[104] Schiesaro (1997a) 77–85 on *Troades*. For the reversal of Nature as a figure of repetition in Senecan tragedy see 86–8.

and literary irony.[105] Hippolytus is diminished not by his failure to master events but by his failure to master language and literature, for this failure is only apparent through the arts which he lacks. There is power and pleasure in seeing Hippolytus destroyed and the innocent as artless. This, the perspective of Nature, balances the despairing passivity of Phaedra.

Post-Augustan poetry, particularly when described as Silver, is constantly threatened by and at war with its Golden parents. Whether exceeding, reversing, denying or being crushed by its classic predecessors, Silver Latin poetry is frequently characterized as being in a state of conflict with its past. While Seneca's recurrent negation of the *Aeneid*, through inversion or partial reading, suggests such a relationship, it is not the only relationship with his predecessors which he offers. While the paralysis of Seneca's Phaedra, like the determination of Medea and Atreus to surpass everything that has been done before, suggests an agonistic relationship of this kind, the experience of reading Hippolytus does not. Familiar texts, familiar topoi, familiar generic tensions are recalled to the mind of a reader who luxuriates in a continuous literary tradition to which Hippolytus, with his ostentatious rejection of city sophistication, is blind.

---

[105] I have taken the distinction between situational and verbal irony from Muecke (1969) 42 ff.

References

ABEL, L. (1963), *Metatheatre: A New View of Dramatic Form* (New York).
AGAPITOS, P. A. (1998), 'Seneca's Thyestes and the Poetics of Multiple Transgression', *Hellenika* 48: 231–53.
AGGELER, G. D. (1970), 'Stoicism and Revenge in Marston', *English Studies* 51: 507–17.
AHL, F. (1976), *Lucan: An Introduction* (London).
——(1989), 'Homer, Vergil, and Complex Narrative Structures in Latin Epic: An Essay', *Illinois Classical Studies* 14: 1–31.
ALTHUSSER, L. (1976), *Essays on Ideology* (London).
ARMSTRONG, D. (1982), 'Senecan *soleo*: *Hercules Oetaeus* 1767', *Classical Quarterly* 32: 239–40.
ASMIS, E. (1990), 'Seneca's *On the Happy Life* and Stoic Individualism', in M. C. Nussbaum, *The Poetics of Therapy* (Edmonton), 219–55.
ASTIN, A. E. (1978), *Cato the Censor* (Oxford).
BARRETT, W. S. (1964), *Euripides, Hippolytos* (Oxford).
BARTON, C. (1993), *The Sorrows of the Ancient Romans: The Gladiator and the Monster* (Princeton).
BARTSCH, S. (1994), *Actors in the Audience: Theatricality and Doublespeak from Nero to Hadrian* (Harvard).
——(1997), *Ideology in Cold Blood. A Reading of Lucan's Civil War* (Harvard).
BATINSKI, E. E. (1991), 'Horace's Rehabilitation of Bacchus', *Classical World* 84: 361–78.
BEACHAM, R. (1999), *Spectacle Entertainments of Early Imperial Rome* (New Haven).
BELFIORE, E. (1992), *Tragic Pleasures: Aristotle on Plot and Emotion* (Princeton).
BENJAMIN, W. (1977), *The Origin of German Tragic Drama*, tr. J. Osborne (London).
BERGER, H. (1989), *Imaginary Audition: Shakespeare on Stage and Page* (Berkeley).
BIONDI, G. G. (1984), *Il Nefas Argonautico: Mythos e Logos nella Medea di Seneca* (Bologna).
BISHOP, J. D. (1985), *Seneca's Daggered Stylus* (Meisenheim).
BLOOM, H. (1973), *The Anxiety of Influence* (Oxford).
BÖMER, F. (1969–76), *P. Ovidius Naso, Metamorphosen* (Heidelberg).
BOYLE, A. J. (1983) (ed.), *Seneca Tragicus* (Berwick).

BOYLE, A. J. (1985), 'In Nature's Bonds: A Study of Seneca's Phaedra', *Aufstieg und Niedergang der römischen Welt* II.32.2. 1284–347.
—— (1987), *Seneca's Phaedra* (Leeds).
—— (1988), *The Imperial Muse: Ramus Essays on Roman Literature of the Empire*, i. *To Juvenal through Ovid* (Berwick).
—— (1994), *Seneca's Troades* (Leeds).
—— (1997), *Tragic Seneca: An Essay in the Theatrical Tradition* (London).
BRADEN, G. (1970), 'The Rhetoric and Psychology of Power in the Dramas of Seneca', *Arion* 9: 5–41.
BRAMBLE, J. C. (1970), 'Structure and Ambiguity in Catullus LXIV', *Proceedings of the Cambridge Philological Society* 16: 22–41.
BRAUN, L. (1983), 'Sind Senecas Tragödien Bühnestücke oder Rezitationsdrame?', *Res Publica Litterarum* 5: 43–52.
BRAUND, S. M. and GILL, C. (1997) (edd.), *The Passions in Roman Thought and Literature* (Cambridge).
BRECHT, B. (1964), *Brecht on Theatre: The Development of an Aesthetic*, tr. J. Willett, (London).
BURNETT, A. (1998), *Revenge in Attic and Later Tragedy* (Berkeley).
CAIRNS, F. (1972), *Generic Composition in Greek and Roman Poetry* (Edinburgh).
CALDER, W. M. (1976), 'Seneca: Tragedian of Imperial Rome', *Classical Journal* 72: 1–11.
—— (1983), 'Secreti Loquimur: An Interpretation of Seneca's Thyestes', in Boyle (1983), 184–98.
CASALI, S. (1995), 'Strategies of Tension (Ovid *Heroides* 4)', *Proceedings of the Cambridge Philological Society* 41: 1–15.
CATTIN, A. (1960), 'Le Prologue de la Phèdre de Sénèque', *Revue des études latines* 38: 67.
CAVIGLIA, F. (1981), *L. Anneo Seneca Le Troiane* (Rome).
CLARK, M., and CSAPO, E. (1991), 'Deconstruction, Ideology and Goldhill's *Oresteia*', *Phoenix* 45: 95–125.
COFFEY, M. (1963), Review of Zintzen (1960), *Gnomon* 35: 310–11.
—— and MAYER, R. (1990), *Seneca, Phaedra* (Cambridge).
COLEIRO, E. (1979), *An Introduction to Virgil's Bucolics with a Critical Edition of the Text* (Amsterdam).
COLEMAN, K. (1990), 'Fatal Charades: Roman Executions Staged as Mythological Enactments', *Journal of Roman Studies* 80: 44–73.
COLEMAN, R. (1977), *Vergil, Eclogues* (Cambridge).
CONTE, G. B. (1986), *The Rhetoric of Imitation: Genre and Poetic Memory in Virgil and Other Latin Poets*, tr. C. Segal (New York).
CORBEILL, A. (1997), 'Dining Deviants in Roman Political Invective', in Hallett and Skinner (1997), 99–128.

COSTA, C. D. N. (1973), *Seneca, Medea* (Oxford).
CSAPO, E., and SLATER, W. J. (1995), *The Context of Ancient Drama* (Ann Arbor).
CURLEY, T. (1986), *The Nature of Senecan Drama* (Rome).
CURRAN, L. C. (1978), 'Rape and Rape Victims in the Metamorphoses', *Arethusa* 11: 213–41.
DAVIS, G. (1983), *The Death of Procris: 'Amor' and the Hunt in Ovid's Metamorphoses* (Rome).
DAVIS, P. J. (1983), 'vindicat omnes Natura sibi: A Reading of Seneca's *Phaedra*', in Boyle (1983), 114–27.
——(1984), 'The First Chorus of Seneca's Phaedra', *Latomus* 43: 396–401.
——(1993), *Shifting Song: The Chorus in Seneca's Tragedies* (Hildesheim).
DEAN-JONES, L. (1994), *Women's Bodies in Classical Greek Science* (Oxford).
DE LACY, P. (1948), 'Stoic Views of Poetry', *American Journal of Philology* 69: 241–71.
DELRIUS, M. (1593), *Syntagma tragoediae latinae* (Antwerp).
DE MEO, C. (1978), *Il prologo della 'Phaedra' di Seneca* (Bologna).
DE ROMILLY, J. (1975), *Magic and Rhetoric in Ancient Greece* (London).
DEWAR, M. (1991), *Statius Thebaid IX* (Oxford).
DIGGLE, J. (1970), *Euripides Phaethon* (Cambridge).
DINGEL, J. (1974), *Seneca und die Dichtung* (Heidelberg).
DOLLIMORE, J. (1984), *Radical Tragedy: Religion, Ideology and Power in the Drama of Shakespeare and his Contemporaries* (London).
DÖRRIE, H. (1971), *P. Ovidii Nasonis Epistulae Heroidum* (Berlin).
DUBOIS, P. (1988), *Psychoanalysis and Ancient Representations of Women* (Chicago).
DUPONT, F. (1985), *L'Acteur-roi* (Paris).
DU QUESNAY, I. M. (1977), 'Vergil's Fourth Eclogue', in F. Cairns (ed.), *Papers of the Liverpool Latin Seminar* (Liverpool), 25–99.
EASTERLING, P. (1990), 'Constructing Character in Greek Tragedy', in C. Pelling (ed.), *Characterization and Individuality in Greek Tragedy* (Oxford), 83–99.
EDWARDS, C. (1993), *The Politics of Immorality in Ancient Rome* (Cambridge).
——(1994), 'Beware of Imitations: Theatre and the Subversion of Imperial Identity', in Elsner and Masters (1994), 83–97.
EITREM, S. (1941), 'La Magie comme motif littéraire chez les Grecs et les Romains', *Symbolae Osloenses* 21: 39–83.

References

ELIOT, T. S. (1927), Introduction to T. Newton (tr.), *Seneca his tenne tragedies* (London).
——(1964), 'Shakespeare and the Stoicism of Seneca', in *Elizabethan Essays* (New York), 33–54.
ELSNER, J., and MASTERS, J. (1994) (edd.), *Reflections of Nero: Culture, History and Representation* (London).
ERSKINE, A. (1990), *The Hellenistic Stoa: Political Thought and Action* (London).
FANTHAM, E. (1975), 'Virgil's Dido and Seneca's Tragic Heroines', *Greece and Rome* 22: 1–10.
——(1978), 'Imitation and Decline: Rhetorical Theory and Practice in the First Century after Christ', *Classical Philology* 73: 102–16.
——(1982), *Seneca's Troades* (Princeton).
——(1983), 'Nihil iam iura naturae valent: Incest and Fratricide in Seneca's Phoenissae', in Boyle (1983), 61–76.
FARRELL, J. (1991), *Vergil's Georgics and the Traditions of Ancient Epic* (Oxford).
FEENEY, D. C. (1991), *The Gods in Epic* (Oxford).
FERRUCCI, F. (1980), *The Poetics of Disguise: The Autobiography of the Work in Homer, Dante and Shakespeare*, tr. A. Dunnigan (New York).
FIORE, R. L. (1975), *Drama and Ethos. Natural Law Ethics in Spanish Golden Age Theatre* (Lexington).
FITCH, J. G. (1981), 'Sense-Pauses and Relative Dating in Seneca, Sophocles and Shakespeare', *American Journal of Philology* 102: 289–307.
——(1987), *Seneca's Hercules Furens* (New York).
——(2000), 'Playing Seneca', in Harrison (2000), 1–12.
——(forthcoming), Loeb edition of Seneca's Tragedies.
——and MCELDUFF, S. (2002), 'Construction of the Self in Senecan Drama', *Mnemosyne* 55: 18–40.
FOLEY, H. (1989), 'Medea's Divided Self', *Classical Antiquity* 8: 61–85.
FOWLER, A. (1982), *Kinds of Literature: An Introduction to the Theory of Genres and Modes* (Oxford).
FOWLER, D. P. (1990), 'Deviant Focalization in Virgil's *Aeneid*', *Proceedings of the Cambridge Philological Society* 36: 42–63.
——(1995), 'Horace and the Aesthetics of Politics', in S. J. Harrison (ed.), *Homage to Horace* (Oxford), 248–66.
FREARS, J. R. (1974), 'The Stoic View of the Career and Character of Alexander the Great', *Philologus* 118: 113–30.
FRIEDRICH, W. (1972), 'Sprache und Stil des Hercules Oetaeus', in Lefèvre (1972), 500–44.

FYFE, H. (1983), 'An Analysis of Seneca's Medea', in Boyle (1983), 77–93.
GAHAN, J. T. (1988), 'Imitation in Seneca "Phaedra"' 1000–1115', *Hermes* 116: 122–4.
GALE, M. (2000), *Virgil on the Nature of Things* (Cambridge).
GALINSKY, G. K. (1972), *The Heracles Theme* (Oxford).
GARNER, R. (1988), 'Death and Victory in Euripides' *Alcestis*', *Classical Antiquity* 7: 58–71.
GEORGE, D. B. (1991), 'Lucan's Cato and Stoic Attitudes to the Republic', *Classical Antiquity* 10: 237–58.
GIGON, O. (1938), 'Bemerkungen zu Senecas Thyestes', *Philologus* 93: 176–83.
GILL, C. (1997), 'Passion as Madness in Roman Poetry', in Braund and Gill (1997), 213–41.
GOFF, B. (1990), *The Noose of Words: Readings of Desire, Violence and Language in Euripides' Hippolytos* (Cambridge).
GOLDBERG, S. M. (2000), 'Going for Baroque: Seneca and the English', in Harrison (2000), 209–31.
GOLDHILL, S. (1986), *Reading Greek Tragedy* (Cambridge).
GOWERS, E. (1993), *The Loaded Table* (Oxford).
GREENE, E. (1998), *The Erotics of Domination: Male Desire and the Mistress in Latin Love Poetry* (Baltimore).
GRIFFIN, J. (1985), *Latin Poets and Roman Life* (London).
GRIFFIN, M. T. (1976), *Seneca: A Philosopher in Politics* (Oxford).
——(1989), 'Philosophy, Politics and Politicians at Rome', in M. Griffin and J. Barnes (edd.), *Philosophia Togata, i: Essays on Philosophy and Philosophers at Rome* (Oxford), 1–37.
GRIMAL, P. (1965), *L. Annaei Senecae Phaedra* (Paris).
GRISWOLD, C. L. (1986), *Self-Knowledge in Plato's Phaedrus* (New Haven).
HADAS, M. (1939), 'The Roman Stamp of Seneca's Tragedies', *American Journal of Philology* 60: 220–31.
HALLETT, J. P., and SKINNER, M. B. (1997) (edd.), *Roman Sexualities* (Princeton).
HALLIWELL, S. (1986), *Aristotle's Poetics* (London).
HALPERIN, D. (1983), *Before Pastoral: Theocritus and the Ancient Tradition of Bucolic Poetry* (London).
HAMON, P. (1977), 'Texte littéraire et métalangage', *Poétique* 31: 261–84.
HARDIE, P. (1986), *Virgil's Aeneid: Cosmos and Imperium* (Oxford).
——(1991), 'The Aeneid and the Oresteia', *Proceedings of the Virgil Society* 20: 29–45.

References

——(1993), *The Epic Successors of Virgil* (Cambridge).
——(1997), 'Closure in Latin Epic', in D. H. Roberts, F. M. Dunn, and D. P. Fowler (edd.), *Classical Closure: Reading the End in Greek and Latin Literature* (Princeton), 139–62.
HARRISON, G. (2000) (ed.), *Seneca in Performance* (London).
HEATH, M. (1987), *The Poetics of Greek Tragedy* (London).
HELDMANN, K. (1974), *Untersuchungen zu den Tragödien Senecas* (Wiesbaden).
HENDERSON, J. (1983), 'Poetic Technique and Rhetorical Amplification: Seneca Medea 579–669', in Boyle (1983), 94–113.
——(1988), 'Lucan / The Word at War', in Boyle (1988), 122–64.
——(1991), 'Statius' Thebaid / Form Premade', *Proceedings of the Cambridge Philological Society* 37: 30–80.
HENRY, D., and WALKER, B. (1966), 'Phantasmagoria and Idyll: An Element of Seneca's Phaedra', *Greece and Rome* 13: 223–39.
————(1967), 'Loss of Identity: *Medea Superest?*', *Classical Philology* 62: 169–81.
————(1983), 'The Oedipus of Seneca: An Imperial Tragedy', in Boyle (1983), 128–39.
HERINGTON, C. J. (1966), 'Senecan Tragedy', *Arion* 5: 422–71.
HERSHKOWITZ, D. (1998), *The Madness of Epic: Reading Insanity from Homer to Statius* (Oxford).
HEXTER, R., and SELDEN, D. (1992) (edd.), *Innovations of Antiquity* (New York).
HINDS, S. (1998), *Allusion and Intertext: Dynamics of Appropriation in Roman Poetry* (Cambridge).
HINE, H. (1981), 'The Structure of Seneca's *Thyestes*', in F. Cairns (ed.), *Papers of the Liverpool Latin Seminar* (Liverpool), 259–75.
HOOLEY, D. M. (1997), *The Knotted Thong: Structures of Mimesis in Persius* (Ann Arbor).
HORNBLOWER, S. (1991), *A Commentary on Thucydides, vol. i* (Oxford).
JAKOBI, R. (1988), *Der Einfluß Ovids auf den Tragiker Seneca* (Berlin).
JOCELYN, H. (1967), *The Tragedies of Ennius* (Cambridge).
JOHNSON, W. R. (1976), *Darkness Visible* (Berkeley).
——(1987), *Momentary Monsters* (New York).
KAPNUKAJAS, C. K. (1930), *Die Nachahmungstechnik Senecas in den Chorliedern des Hercules Furens und der Medea* (diss. Leipzig).
KELLY, H. A. (1979), 'Tragedy and the Performance of Tragedy in Late Roman Antiquity', *Traditio* 35: 21–44.
KENNEY, E. J. (1971), *Lucretius, De Rerum Natura Book III* (Cambridge).
KERFERD, G. B. (1978), 'What Does the Wise Man Know?', in J. M. Rist (ed.), *The Stoics* (London), 125–36.

KNOCHE, U. (1941), 'Senecas Atreus. Ein Beispiel', *Das Antike* 17: 60–76.
KNOX, B. M. W. (1964), *The Heroic Temper: Studies in Sophoclean Tragedy* (Berkeley).
LADA, I. (1993), ' "Empathic Understanding": Emotion and Cognition in Classical Dramatic Audience-Response', *Proceedings of the Cambridge Philological Society* 39: 94–140.
LAIRD, A. (1999), *Powers of Expression, Expressions of Power: Speech Presentation in Latin Literature* (Oxford).
LAPIDGE, M. (1979), 'Lucan's Imagery of Cosmic Dissolution', *Hermes* 107: 344–70.
LARMOUR, D. H. J. (1990), 'Tragic *Contaminatio* in Ovid's *Metamorphoses*: Procne and Medea; Philomela and Iphigeneia (6.424–674); Scylla and Phaedra (8.19–51)', *Illinois Classical Studies* 15: 131–41.
LAWALL, G. (1979), 'Seneca's Medea: The Elusive Triumph of Civilization', in M. Bowersock, W. Burkert, and M. Putnam (edd.), *Arktouros: Hellenic Studies presented to B. M. W. Knox* (New York), 419–26.
—— (1982), 'Death and Perspective in Seneca's *Troades*', *Classical Journal* 77: 244–52.
—— (1983), Virtus and Pietas in Seneca's Hercules Furens', in Boyle (1983), 6–26.
LEACH, E. W. (1975), 'Neronian Pastoral and the World of Power', *Ramus* 4: 204–30.
LEEMAN, A. D. (1976), 'Seneca's Phaedra as Stoic Tragedy', in J. M. Bremer, S. L. Radt, and C. J. Ruigh (edd.), *Miscellanea Tragica in Honorem J. C. Kamerbeek* (Amsterdam), 199–212.
LEFÈVRE, E. (1972) (ed.), *Senecas Tragödien* (Darmstadt).
LEIGH, M. (1996), 'Varius Rufus, Thyestes and the Appetites of Antony', *Proceedings of the Cambridge Philological Society* 42: 171–97.
—— (1997), *Lucan: Spectacle and Engagement* (Oxford).
LIEBERMANN, W. (1974), *Studien zu Senecas Tragödien* (Meisenheim).
LITTLEWOOD, C. A. J. (1995), Review of P. J. Davis (1993), *Journal of Roman Studies* 85: 327–8.
LLOYD, G. E. R. (1979), *Magic, Reason and Experience* (Cambridge).
LONG, A. A. (1974), *Hellenistic Philosophy* (London).
LORAUX, N. (1987), *Tragic Ways of Killing a Woman*, tr. A. Forster (London).
LYNE, R. O. A. M. (1987), *Further Voices in Vergil's Aeneid* (Oxford).
—— (1989), *Words and the Poet: Characteristic Techniques of Style in Vergil's Aeneid* (Oxford).
MAGUINNESS, W. S. (1956), 'Seneca and the Poets', *Hermathena* 88: 81–98.

MANNING, C. E. (1981), *On Seneca's 'Ad Marciam'* (Leiden).
MARTI, B. (1945), 'Seneca's Tragedies: A New Interpretation', *Transactions and Proceedings of the American Philological Association* 76: 216–45.
MARTINDALE, C. (1997a), *The Cambridge Companion to Virgil* (Cambridge).
—— (1997b) 'Green Politics: The Eclogues', in Martindale (1997a), 107–24.
MASTERS, J. (1992), *Poetry and Civil War in Lucan's Bellum Civile* (Cambridge).
MAZZOLI, G. (1991), 'Seneca e la Poesia', *Fondation Hardt Entretiens* 36: 177–209.
MELTZER, G. (1988), 'Dark Wit and Black Humour in Seneca's "Thyestes"', *Transactions and Proceedings of the American Philological Association* 118: 309–30.
MICHEL, A. (1969), 'Rhétorique, tragédie, philosophie, Sénèque et le sublime', *Giornale italiano di filologia* 21: 245–57.
MORGAN, L. (1999), *Patterns of Redemption: Virgil's Georgics* (Cambridge).
MORRISON, J. V. (1992), 'Literary Reference and Generic Transgression in Ovid *Amores* 1.7: Love, Poet and Furor', *Latomus* 51: 571–89.
MOSSMANN, J. (1995), *Wild Justice: A Study of Euripides' Hecuba* (Oxford).
MOST, G. W. (1992), '*disiecti membra poetae*: The Rhetoric of Dismemberment in Neronian Poetry', in Hexter and Selden (1992), 391–419.
MOTTO, A. L., and CLARK, J. R. (1972), 'Senecan Tragedy: Patterns of Irony and Art', *Classical Bulletin* 48: 69–76.
—— (1988), *Senecan Tragedy* (Amsterdam).
MUECKE, D. C. (1969), *The Compass of Irony* (London).
MULVEY, L. (1989), 'Visual Pleasure and Narrative Cinema' (1976), repr. in *Visual and Other Pleasures* (London), 14–26.
MYNORS, R. A. B. (1990), *Virgil* Georgics, (Oxford).
NEWMAN, J. K. (1967), *Augustus and the New Poetry* (Brussels).
NISBET, R. (1987), 'The Oak and the Axe: Symbolism in Seneca's Hercules Oetaeus 1618 f.', in M. Whitby, P. Hardie, and M. Whitby (edd.), *Homo Viator* (Bristol), 243–51.
—— and HUBBARD, M. (1970), *A Commentary on Horace: Odes Book 1* (Oxford).
NUSSBAUM, M. C. (1982), '"This Story isn't True": Poetry, Goodness and Understanding in Plato's *Phaedrus*', in J. Moravcsik and P. Temko (edd.), *Plato on Beauty, Wisdom and the Arts* (London), 79–124.
—— (1993), 'Poetry and the Passions: Two Stoic Views', in J. Brunschwig and M. C. Nussbaum (edd.), *Passions and Perceptions: Studies in*

Hellenistic Philosophy of Mind; Proceedings of the Fifth Symposium Hellenisticum (Cambridge), 97–149.

—— (1994), 'Serpents in the Soul: A Reading of Seneca's *Medea*', in *The Therapy of Desire: Theory and Practice in Hellenistic Ethics* (Princeton), 439–83.

NUTTALL, A. D. (1996), *Why does Tragedy give Pleasure?* (Oxford).

O'HARA, J. J. (1990), *Death and the Optimistic Prophecy in Vergil's Aeneid* (Princeton).

O'HIGGINS, D. (1988), 'Lucan as Vates', *Classical Antiquity* 7: 208–26.

ORLANDO, F. (1978), *Toward a Freudian Theory of Literature*, tr. C. Lee (London).

OWEN, W. H. (1970), 'Time and Event in Seneca's *Troades*', *Wiener Studien* 4: 118–37.

PADEL, R. (1992), *In and Out of the Mind. Greek Images of the Tragic Self* (Princeton).

PARATORE, E. (1957), 'Originalità del teatro di Seneca', *Dionisio* 20: 53–74.

PARRY, H. (1964), 'Ovid's Metamorphoses: Violence in a Pastoral Landscape', *Transactions and Proceedings of the American Philological Association* 95: 268–82.

PETRONE, G. (1988), 'Nomen/omen: Poetice e funzione dei nomi (Plauto, Seneca, Petronio)', *Materiali e discussioni per l'analisi dei testi classici* 20: 33–70.

PFISTER, M. (1992), *The Theory and Analysis of Drama*, tr. J. Halliday (Cambridge).

POBJOY, M. (1998), 'Dido on the Tragic Stage: An Invitation to the Theatre of Carthage', in M. Burden, (ed.), *A Woman Scorned: Responses to the Dido Myth* (London), 41–64.

POE, J. P. (1969), 'An Analysis of Seneca's Thyestes', *Transactions and Proceedings of the American Philological Association* 100: 355–76.

—— (1983), 'The Sinful Nature of the Protagonist of Seneca's Oedipus', in Boyle (1983), 140–58.

PÖSCHL, V. (1978), 'Virgile et la Tragédie', in R. Chévallier (ed.) *Présence de Virgile: Actes du Colloque des 9, 11 et 12 Décembre 1976* (Paris), 73–9.

POUND, E. (1960), *Literary Essays* (London).

PRATT, N. T. (1948), 'The Stoic Base of Senecan Drama', *Transactions and Proceedings of the American Philological Association* 79: 1–11.

—— (1963), 'Major Systems of Figurative Language in Senecan Melodrama', *Transactions and Proceedings of the American Philological Association* 94: 199–234.

PUTNAM, M. (1965), *The Poetry of the Aeneid: Four Studies in Imaginative Unity* (London).

—— (1970), *Virgil's Pastoral Art* (Princeton).
—— (1979), *Virgil's Poem of the Earth: Studies in the Georgics* (Princeton).
—— (1995), 'Virgil's Tragic Future: Senecan Drama and the Aeneid', in *Vergil's Aeneid: Interpretation and Influence* (London), 246–85.
QUINT, D. (1993), *Epic and Empire: Politics and Generic Form from Virgil to Milton* (Princeton).
REGENBOGEN, O. (1961), 'Schmerz und Tod in den Tragödien Senecas', in *Kleine Schriften*, ed. F. Dirlmeier (Munich), 409–62.
REINHARDT, K. (1926), *Kosmos und Sympathie* (Munich).
RICHARDSON, L. (1977), *Propertius Elegies 1–4* (Norman).
RICHLIN, A. (1981), 'Approaches to the Sources on Adultery at Rome', in H. Foley (ed.), *Reflections of Women in Antiquity* (New York), 379–404.
—— (1992), *The Garden of Priapus* (New York).
RIFFATERRE, M. (1966), 'Describing Poetic Structures: Two Approaches to Baudelaire's *les Chats*', *Yale French Studies* 36–7: 200–42.
—— (1980), *The Semiotics of Poetry* (Bloomington).
RIST, J. M. (1969), *Stoic Philosophy* (Cambridge).
ROSE, A. J. (1979–80), 'Seneca's *HF*: A Politico-Didactic Reading', *Classical Journal* 75: 135–42.
ROSENMEYER, T. G. (1989), *Senecan Drama and Stoic Cosmology* (Berkeley).
ROSS, D. A. (1987), *Virgil's Elements: Physics and Poetry in the Georgics* (Princeton).
ROZELAAR, M. (1985), 'Neue Studien zur Tragödie Hercules Oetaeus', *Aufstieg und Niedergang der römischen Welt* II.32.2: 1348–1419.
RUDICH, V. (1993), *Political Dissidence under Nero* (New York).
RUSSELL, D. A. (1964), *'Longinus' On the Sublime* (Oxford).
—— (1979a), 'De Imitatione', in D. West and A. J. Woodman (edd.), *Creative Imitation and Latin Literature* (Cambridge), 1–16.
—— (1979b), 'Rhetors at the Wedding', *Proceedings of the Cambridge Philological Society* 25: 104–17.
—— (1981), 'Longinus Revisited', *Mnemosyne* 34: 72–86.
SAMBURSKY, S. (1959), *Physics of the Stoics* (London).
SCHETTER, W. (1972), 'Senecas Oedipus-Tragödie', in Lefèvre (1972), 402–49.
SCHIESARO, A. (1994), 'Seneca's Thyestes and the Morality of Tragic *furor*', in Elsner and Masters (1994), 196–210.
—— (1997a), 'L'intertestualità e i suoi disagi', *Materiali e discussioni per l'analisi dei testi classici* 39: 75–109.

—— (1997b), 'Passion, Reason and Knowledge in Seneca', in Braund and Gill (1997), 89–111.
SEGAL, C. (1969), *Landscape in Ovid's Metamorphoses*, Hermes supplement 23 (Wiesbaden).
—— (1982), *Dionysiac Poetics and Euripides' Bacchae* (Princeton).
—— (1983), 'Dissonant Sympathy: Song, Orpheus and the Golden Age in Seneca's Tragedies', in Boyle (1983), 229–51.
—— (1986), *Language and Desire in Seneca's Phaedra* (Princeton).
—— (1992), 'Signs, Magic and Letters in Euripides' *Hippolytus*', in Hexter and Seldon (1992), 420–56.
SEIDENSTICKER, B. (1969), *Die Gesprächsverdichtung in den Tragödien Senecas* (Heidelberg).
—— (1985), 'Maius solito. Senecas Thyestes und die tragoedia rhetorica', *Antike und Abendland* 31: 116–36.
SHARROCK, A. (1991), 'Womanufacture', *Journal of Roman Studies* 81: 36–49.
SHELTON, J. A. (1975), 'Problems of Time in Seneca's Hercules Furens and Thyestes', *Classical Antiquity* 8: 257–69.
—— (1978), *Seneca's Hercules Furens: Theme, Structure and Style* (Göttingen).
—— (2000), 'The Spectacle of Death in Seneca's *Troades*', in Harrison (2000), 87–118.
SKOVGAARD-HANSEN, M. (1968), 'The Fall of Phaethon: Meaning in Seneca's "Hippolytus"', *Classica et Medievalia* 29: 92–123.
SMITH, K. F. (1913), *Tibullus, The Elegies* (New York).
SOURVINOU-INWOOD, C. (1987), 'Erotic Pursuits: Images and Meanings', *Journal of Hellenic Studies* 107: 131–53.
SPOFFORD, A. (1969), 'Theocritus and Polyphemus', *American Journal of Philology* 90: 22–35.
STÄHLI-PETER, M. (1974), *Die Arie des Hippolytus: Kommentar zu Eingangsmonodie in der Phaedra des Seneca* (Zurich).
STEELE, R. B. (1922), 'Roman Elements in the Tragedies of Seneca', *American Journal of Philology* 43: 1–32.
STEINER, G. (1975), *After Babel* (London).
SULLIVAN, J. P. (1985), *Literature and Politics in the Age of Nero* (New York).
SUTTON, D. F. (1986), *Seneca on the Stage* (Leiden).
TANNER, R. G. (1985), 'Stoic Philosophy and Roman Tradition in Senecan Tragedy', *Aufstieg und Niedergang der römischen Welt* II.32.2: 1100–33.
TARRANT, R. J. (1976), *Seneca: Agamemnon* (Cambridge).
—— (1978), 'Senecan Drama and its Antecedents', *Harvard Studies in Classical Philology* 82: 213–63.

—— (1985), *Seneca's Thyestes* (Atlanta).
—— (1995), 'Greek and Roman in Seneca's Tragedies', *Harvard Studies in Classical Philology* 97: 215–30.
THEODORAKOPOULOS, E. (1997), 'Closure: The Book of Virgil', in Martindale (1997a), 155–65.
TIETZE, V. (1988), 'Seneca's Tragic Description: A "point of view"', *Classical Views* 32: 23–49.
—— (1991), 'The *Hercules Oetaeus* and the Picture of the *Sapiens* in Senecan Prose', *Phoenix* 45: 39–49.
—— (1994), *The Role of Description in Senecan Tragedy* (Frankfurt).
TÖCHTERLE, K. (1994), *Oedipus / Lucius Annaeus Seneca* (Heidelberg).
USHER, S. (1969), *The Historians of Greece and Rome* (Bristol).
VIARRE, S. (1982), 'Caton en Libye: L'Histoire et la métaphore (Lucain, Pharsale, IX.294–949)', in J. M. Croisille, and P. M. Fauchère (edd.), *Neronia 1977* (Clermont-Ferrand), 103–10.
VIDAL-NAQUET, P. (1986), *The Black Hunter: Forms of Thought and Forms of Society in the Greek World*, tr. A. Szegedy-Maszak (Baltimore).
VITSE, M. (1988), *Elements pour une théorie du théâtre espagnol du XVIIième siècle* (Toulouse).
VON ARNIM, H. F. H. (1903–24), *Stoicorum Vetera Fragmenta* (Leipzig).
WALKER, B. (1969), Review of Zwierlein (1966), *Classical Philology* 64: 183–7.
WALSH, G. B. (1984), *The Vanities of Enchantment: Early Greek Views of the Nature and Function of Poetry* (Chapel Hill).
WALTER, S. (1975), *Interpretationen zum römischen in den Tragödien Senecas* (Zurich).
WALTERS, J. (1997), 'Invading the Roman Body: Manliness and Impenetrability in Roman Thought', in Hallett and Skinner (1997), 29–46.
WANKE, C. (1964), *Seneca Lucan Corneille: Studien zum Manierismus der römischen Kaiserzeit und der französischen Klassik* (Heidleberg).
WARDEN, J. (1982), 'Epic into Elegy: Propertius 4.9.70 f.', *Hermes* 110: 228–42.
WEST, D. (1969), *The Imagery and Poetry of Lucretius* (Edinburgh).
WIGODSKY, M. (1972), *Vergil and Early Latin Poetry* (Wiesbaden).
WILKINSON, L. P. (1969), *The Georgics of Virgil* (Cambridge).
WILLIAMS, G. (1978), *Change and Decline: Roman Literature in the Early Empire* (Berkeley).
WILSON, A. M. (1985), 'The Prologue to Manilius 1', *Papers of the Liverpool Latin Seminar* 5: 283–98.

WILSON, M. (1983), 'The Tragic Mode of Seneca's Troades', in Boyle (1983), 27–60.
WINKLER, J. J., and ZEITLIN, F. (1990) (edd.), *Nothing to do with Dionysos? Athenian Drama in its Social Context* (Princeton).
WISEMAN, T. P. (1998), *Roman Drama and Roman History* (Exeter).
WLOSOK, A. (1976), 'Vergils Didotragödie: Ein Beitrag zum Problem des Tragischen in der Aeneis', in H. Görgemanns and E. A. Schmidt (edd.), *Studien zum antiken Epos* (Meisenheim), 228–50.
WOODMAN, A. J. (1993), 'Amateur Dramatics at the Court of Nero (*Annals* 15.48–74)', in T. J. Luce and A. J. Woodman (edd), *Tacitus and the Tacitean Tradition* (Princeton), 104–28.
WYKE, M. (1994), 'Taking the Woman's Part: Engendering Roman Love Elegy', *Ramus* 23: 110–28.
ZEITLIN, F. (1990a), 'Playing the Other: Theater, Theatricality and the Feminine in Greek Drama', in Winkler and Zeitlin (1990), 63–96.
——(1990b) 'Thebes: Theater of Self and Society in Athenian Drama', in Winkler and Zeitlin (1990), 130–67.
——(1990c), 'The Poetics of Eros: Nature, Art and Imitation in Longus' Daphnis and Chloe', in D. Halperin, J. Winkler, and F. Zeitlin (edd.), *Before Sexuality: The Construction of the Erotic Experience in the Ancient Greek World* (Princeton), 417–64.
ZINTZEN, C. (1960), *Analytisches Hypomnema zu Senecas* Phaedra (Meisenheim).
——(1972), 'Alte virtus animosa cadit: Gedanken zur Darstellung des Tragischen in Senecas "Hercules Furens"', in Lefèvre (1972), 149–209.
ZWIERLEIN, O. (1966), *Die Rezitationsdramen Senecas* (Meisenheim).
——(1986a), *Kritischer Kommentar zu den Tragödien Senecas* (Mainz).
——(1986b), *L. Annaei Senecae Tragoediae* (Oxford).
——(1987), *Seneca's Phaedra und ihre Vorbilder* (Mainz).

Index of Passages

Aristotle
Poetica
1460a18   95 n. 177

Catullus
62. 41   288

Cicero
De Officiis
3. 106   243 n.
De Oratore
2. 193   95 n. 177g
Tusculanae Disputationes
1. 30. 73   64 n. 111

Cleanthes
SVF 1.537   18

Corneille
Médée
320–1   46

Diogenes Laertius
7. 32–3   19

Euripides
Hippolytus
215–22   261
Medea
214   203 n. 52
Troades
408   216 n. 73

Horace
Ars Poetica
206–7   246 n. 138
Carmina
1. 1. 3–8   141–2

1. 1. 29–36   141–3
1. 1. 31   146
2. 2. 19–21   49 n. 77

Juvenal
9. 43–4   201 n. 49

Livy
3. 10. 10   95 n. 177

Longinus
8. 2–4   121
9. 7–8   121–2
13. 2   127
15. 1–6   122–4
35. 4–36. 2   124–5

Lucan
1. 2   26
2. 284–8   28
7. 261–3   27
7. 457   28 n. 40
7. 501–2   28 n. 39
9. 564–5   25
9. 572   25

Lucretius
3. 998   78

Manilius
1. 1–5   158
1. 21–2   159
1. 75–8   159
1. 91–4   159
1. 96–7   160 n. 134

Martial
11. 61. 6–12   201 n. 49

Ovid
Amores

1. 13. 14	264
2. 16. 36	288

Heroides

4. 3	264
4. 38	276
4. 85–6	277
4. 169	276
4. 173	276 n. 54
12. 191	209 n.

Metamorphoses

1.107–9	287
1. 149–50	109 n. 19
1. 166	112
1. 190	120 n. 41
1. 285	109 n. 17
1. 463–5	294
1. 531–2	294
1. 540–1	294
2. 114–5	107 n. 11
2. 202	109 n. 17
2. 229–30	113
2. 255	130 n. 68
2. 296–9	133
2. 326–7	109
3. 201–3	298
3. 225–35	297
6. 472–3	197
6. 474	195
6. 478–82	195
6. 491–3	196
6. 499	197
6. 515–18	196
6. 530	196
6. 561–2	196
6. 583–5	197
6. 601–2	128 n. 62
6. 652	197
6. 621	209 n.
6. 634	209 n.
6. 655	197
6. 658–61	212
7. 745–8	271–2
7. 776–8	272 n. 42
7. 801–4	273
7. 813–22	273
7. 835	273
13. 479–80	208
13. 522	257 n. 165

Tristia

2. 381–3	265
13. 10. 5	270

Plautus
Amphitryo

667	200 n. 48

Propertius

1. 5	276 n. 54

Seneca
Agamemnon

44	64
131–44	63
160–1	64
252–3	92
303	92
357–8	92
360	91
529–30	67
537–40	66
545–6	66
552–6	67
717–19	216
722–3	219
724	216
728	216
733–7	221
737	216
750–2	216
758–60	217
795	218 n. 80
868–70	220
872–5	220
879–80	218 n. 80

Index of Passages

883–6	221	75–6	116
895–6	65	79–83	118
904–9	222	84–99	115–16
967	224	95–6	73
994–6	32 n. 44, 188 n. 21	98	79 n. 139
1005–6	224	105	117 n. 34
1011	225	107–9	116, 224
1012	15 n. 1, 215, 223	113–16	224

De Constantia

3.2	49	123–8	74
		128	107

Epistulae

7. 8	20	134–5	74
7. 11	20 n. 8	137–8	111
9. 14–17	20 n. 7	192–7	108
9. 16	18	201	110 n. 21
9. 18–19	19	247	32
13. 2–4	21–2	251–3	32
25. 3	85 n. 149	269–74	32
48. 11	25 n. 29, 28 n. 40	291–3	161
70. 20–2	256	306–8	161
70. 20	255 n. 161	338–41	31
76. 31–2	96	353	31
77. 14–15	255 n. 159	394–7	34
77. 15–20	53–4	406–10	31
78. 2	20 n. 7	407–8	17
79. 4–5	125–6	423	33
79. 12	126	431–3	34
80. 7–8	96	437	34
85. 11	55	444–5	35
85. 24–7	49	459–60	35
88. 28	25 n. 28	489	33
		500	34

Hercules Furens

		511–13	31 n. 44, 188 n. 21
1–5	114	569–75	162
5	73	577	160
15	73	590–1	160
33–6	115	886–90	161–2
35–40	107–8	926–7	112
45–7	115	930–7	111
60–1	118	937–9	117
64–5	107	944–7	113
66	192 n. 30	953–4	78 n. 137
67–8	73	957	112
68–74	119	958–9	192 n. 30

960	79	49–50	151, 299
965–8	35	55	154
968–70	79	61–2	72
1138	220 n.	89–90	72
1139–42	113	97	204
1142	162	120–2	203
1207–10	78	129–30	154
1219–21	79	132	212 n. 63
1262–3	79	157–76	44–5
1265–7	79	159	47, 49
1297–8	117 n. 35	166–7	15, 50, 204
1319–29	80	168	38

Hercules Oetaeus

265–70	61	170	39 n. 61
284–6	62	171	50, 209 n.
297–8	61 n. 107	173	48 n. 75
351–2	62	175–6	47
417–22	68	178	39
474	61	181	154–5
806–7	61 n. 109	189–90	39
1396–8	17, 69	190–91	164
1404–7	62	195–6	39, 188 n. 21
1638	61	203–6	39

De Ira

		219–20	39
1. 1. 1–2	37 n. 59, 53	228–9	162
1. 2. 5	173	229	157, 164
2. 2. 6	173	238–40	201
2. 15. 3	56 n. 93	245–6	154
2. 33. 3–6	190	252	40
2. 36. 1–3	209–10	263–6	40 n. 62
3. 14. 3	191 n. 27	290	155
3. 15. 1–3	190–1	320	151, 159
3. 18. 1	190	329–30	155

Ad Marciam

		335–9	165
10. 1	96	335	55 n. 91, 151

Medea

		346–9	163
		346–7	156 n. 124
1–4	148	355–60	163–4
8–10	47 n. 72	361–4	153, 205, 299
11–12	149	363–4	155 n. 121
23–8	149–50	364–79	166–8
24	209 n.	397–8	154
37–41	149–50	411–14	151
44–7	180	424–5	157

Index of Passages

437–8	205	1024	202
444	37	1025	157
479	165	1026–7	15, 139, 164 n.
490–4	38		146, 192 n. 30
504–5	205	*Naturales Quaestiones*	
505	38	3. 26. 7–	
506–7	205	3. 27. 7	169–71
516–18	155	3. 27. 15	170 n. 159
516	22 n. 20	3. 30. 3	171
518–20	23, 38, 40	3. 30. 8	170 n. 158
525–6	22 n. 20	*Oedipus*	
529	22 n. 20	11	82 n. 144
540–1	38, 48	27	176 n.
546–9	202	30–6	24
549–50	183–4, 206, 220	36	82, 261 n. 9
553–7	184	53–5	24 n. 23
560–3	203	48–9	24 n. 24
597	149	62–3	83
599–606	156	70–8	82–3
606	151	78–81	88
613	166 n. 149	82–6	24, 82, 205
614–15	151, 155, 165	160–3	24 n. 25
617	149	197–8	82
665–6	59	180–1	82
666–7	155	203–7	83
757–9	165	371–80	176
840–1	230 n. 102	868	84 n. 148
881–2	168 n. 156	879–81	84, 86
904–5	23 n. 21, 232	915–19	84
911–14	90 n. 160	942–5	84 n. 149, 86
915	154 n. 119	949–51	85
919–21	193 n. 31	965–9	176
921–4	202	965	245 n. 132
934–5	202	970	84
953	23 n. 22, 248 n.	975–7	85
967–71	154, 248 n.	980–2	87
982–4	38, 201–2	983–4	177 n. 8
992–4	181, 249 n. 144, 259 n. 1	995–7	89
		998	85 n. 151, 89
1012–13	150, 245 n. 132	999–1001	87
1014–19	191–2	1007–8	87
1019	184, 220	1014–15	86
1021–2	22 n. 16, 192, 210	1032–3	88

Index of Passages

1038–9	88	683–6	262, 277
1046	86	685–6	265
1058	88	688–90	277
1061	89	697	299
Phaedra		777–84	292
1–26	280–1	780	276
1	270, 285	783	276
2	274	875–82	42
10–12	287	881	50 n. 78
11	296	907–8	300
18–23	289	1027	296
42	296	1066–7	70
44–5	271 n. 39	1086	296
49–50	271 n. 39	1278	296
54–6	275	*Phoenissae*	
60–1	270	40–4	177
77	291 n. 92	67–73	179
81–4	296–7	77–9	179
113–14	261	188–90	205 n. 56
124–8	259	249–53	178
174	78 n. 138	347–8	178
176–7	60 n. 104, 300	358–62	178–9
195–7	52	542–53	179
233–7	290	579–80	180
240–3	52, 275	625–6	180
295	295	632	180
299–30	295	*De Providentia*	
305–7	295	2. 9	235
381–3	290	5. 10–11	110
471–2	291	*Thyestes*	
501–3	291	18–20	23 n. 21
515–17	292	19–22	132
517–18	276	21–3	29, 78
533	263–4	30	15 n. 1
535–8	287	48–51	129
542–3	291	56–7	128 n. 62
563–4	298	62–6	131
566	282	82–3	227
608–16	279	86–7	61 n. 108, 128, 253 n.
639–40	262		
645	262	91–3	131
660–2	265	95	228
660	285	98–101	129

Index of Passages

103–4	128 n. 62	545	185
119	130 n. 68	621–2	227
120–1	132	623–5	227
122–3	138	627	220 n., 282
130–3	138	633	234 n. 113
140	138	635–8	134–5, 227 n. 99
155–6	130 n. 68	639–40	210 n., 227, 241
158–62	131 n.	641–5	183 n.
192–7	182	643	30 n. 42
205–7	28, 188	648–52	144
211–12	17, 29, 47 n. 73, 188	651–2	146
		659–62	146, 228
218–20	23, 29, 85, 231	668–9	229 n.
237	29–30	678–82	145, 145 n. 94, 229
238–41	198		
239	186 n. 20	684	231
246	192	686	234 n. 114
247–8	32 n. 44	689–92	145
249–52	128 n. 60	689–95	231–2
258–9	61 n. 108, 143 n. 89	703–5	233, 235 n. 115
267–8	231 n. 106	712–18	234–5
271–2	210 n.	723–5	235
272–4	182 n.	729	196 n. 39
275–6	128	734–6	212
277–8	238	744–8	236
279	185, 220	753–5	236
281–4	134, 212	770–2	237
285–6	213	776–9	237, 239
302	22, 29	781–8	135, 238–9
342–3	142	802–4	136
365–6	142	885–7	15, 30, 133, 142, 183
391–3	30		
400	144 n. 90	889–91	29 n. 41, 135, 211, 220, 226 n.
406–7	139		
409–12	139, 141	892	29
412–15	22 n. 18, 194	893–5	182
419–20	211	896–7	239
442–3	12 n. 19, 43	903–6	185, 193
476–8	199	910	239
486–9	131 n.	912–13	184
489	23, 133	919	239
491	193	939–40	253 n. 155
505–8	194	948	199 n. 44

Index of Passages

950–1	199	264–9	100
966–7	199	285	253
970–2	185	327–36	41
974–5	213	371–2	94
978–9	36	404–5	95
985–6	199, 211	417	98, 244
997	224 n.	418–20	206
999–1004	200	450	97
1005–6	210	464–5	97
1006–7	84 n. 148	553–5	101
1021–3	84 n. 147	615–18	206
1035–6	22 n. 17	623–6	207
1037	186	646–7	97
1041–4	200	683–5	93
1051	22 n. 17	708–17	187
1054–7	186, 193	736–7	187
1065–8	186	749	187
1068–71	137	750	155 n. 121
1081–5	136	760–5	243
1096–8	137	780–2	245
1097–9	140, 181, 184, 198, 202, 249 n. 144	783–6	244–5
		791	98
1110–11	15 n. 1	811–13	244–5
De Tranquillitate Animi		888–9	98
11. 5	254 n. 158	900–2	99
17. 11	121	903–4	245 n. 134
Troades		946	98
1–4	39 n. 61, 4, 253, 257 n. 166	949–50	98
		1009–10	243, 250 n. 148
19–21	242	1055–9	242
21	252	1063–7	241–2, 245
44	252	1067	241
67–9	90	1068	246 n. 135
82	90	1071–2	246
86	252	1075–7	246
88–91	208 n. 59	1077–8	246 n. 138
123	253	1083	99, 246
156–7	98, 257	1086–7	246
162–3	257	1090	99
168	247	1096	208
170b	253 n. 155	1098–1105	248
176–7	247	1098–1100	99
180	247	1102	99

Index of Passages

1108–9	251	4. 131	271 n. 39
1109–11	248–9	4. 166	152 n. 109
1116–7	249	4. 469–71	216 n. 74
1117	97, 251, 253	6. 98–9	229
1118–21	254	6. 103–5	230
1125	252 n. 152	6. 133–5	217
1128–9	253	6. 547–9	218
1136–7	251	6. 557–8	229 n.
1143–6	99, 252	7. 338	117
1147–8	257	7. 312	177 n. 9
1147	99	7. 345	117 n. 34
1153	252	7. 586	65
1157–8	254 n. 156	9. 189	74
1159	208	12. 830–1	118 n. 37
1160	252	12. 948–9	152 n. 112
1162–4	250–1	*Eclogae*	
1165	100 n.	1. 6–7	21 n. 12
1166–7	208	1. 61–3	167
1167–9	250	4. 3	278
1169–71	100	4. 24–5	112
1171–2	208	10. 3	283
1176–7	250	10. 22–3	283
		10. 53–4	283 n. 70
Statius		10. 57	285
Thebais		10. 59–60	284
11. 338–42	88 n.	10. 62–5	284
		10. 69	283
Tacitus		10. 75–7	285
Annales		*Georgica*	
13. 15	192 n. 28	1. 127–8	287 n. 82
		2. 412	111
Virgil		3. 284–5	286 n. 80
Aeneis		4. 114	111
1. 125–7	67 n. 119	4. 517–19	282
1. 283–7	167–8	4. 525–6	196

General Index

Absyrtus 154, 165
Acastus 38
Acharnae 289
Achilles (ghost) 76, 91–2, 94–5, 101, 242, 247, 251, 253–4, 258
Actaeon 297–8
actors 96–7, 99; *see also* theatre
Aegisthus 188, 221
Aeneas 65, 68, 152, 216–19, 228, 230, 270–1, 296
Aerope 209
Aeschylus 37, 123–4, 153, 160 n. 133
Aetna 125–6
Agamemnon 41–2, 64–5, 76, 91–2, 100, 215–16, 221–2, 225, 253
Agave 175
Ajax son of Oileus 17, 65–8
Alcmena 17, 62, 69
Alcyone 65
Alexander the Great 26, 190
Allecto 117, 217
allusion 65, 67–8, 74, 81, 97, 104–14, 116–17, 119–20, 128–34, 140–7, 152–4, 156–8, 162, 164, 167–9, 170, 175, 182, 195–9, 208–9, 212–13, 216–19, 226, 228–31, 241, 242 n. 127, 246, 259–301; *see also by author esp.* Horace, Ovid, Virgil
Alpheus 76, 138
Althaea 165
Amazon 262
Amphitryon 32–5, 77, 79–81, 94, 111, 161

Andromache 90, 93–5, 97–9, 101, 173–4, 187, 206–7, 240, 242–5, 249–51, 256, 258
Antigone 178
Aphidnae 289
Aphrodite 260–1, 268, 271, 282
Apollo 35, 73, 110, 203–4, 219, 283, 293–6
Arabs 167
Arcadia 284; *see also* pastoral
Argo 59, 148, 163, 166, 168
Argonauts 58–9, 149, 151, 153–4, 156–7, 159, 163, 165, 168, 205
Argos 44, 57, 75–7, 139, 282
Aristaeus 162, 286
Aristotle 23, 40, 49, 173, 257
Artemis 261
Astyanax 16, 90, 97–101, 172–4, 187–8, 206–8, 215, 240–1, 243–58
Atreus 15, 17, 22–3, 25, 27, 29–32, 34, 36, 40, 46, 56, 58, 76, 84, 86, 105, 128–9, 131–47, 150, 166, 174, 181–6, 188, 190–5, 197–9, 201–2, 209–14, 216, 219–21, 223–8, 230–9, 241, 258–60, 269, 282, 300–1
Aurora 271–3
Augustus 20, 230; *see also* Rome

Bacchus 35, 75, 204
Bellona 209
Bloom, Harold 105–6, 120
body, Stoic disdain for 20–2, 49, 69, 84, 86, 255–6
Brecht, Bertolt 50–1, 173

Briseis 92
Britannicus 191
Busiris 248

Cadmus 34, 74
Caesar, Julius 26–8, 31, 59
Calchas 76, 91
Caligula 53, 190–1, 210
Callimachus 143–4
Calpurnius Siculus 266
Cassandra 215, 217–26, 228, 240
Castor 203
cataclysm, *see* flood
Cato Uticensis 21, 24–8, 59, 255, 257
Catullus 288
Cephalus 271–4, 278
Cerberus 73, 75, 115, 118, 216
chariots 104, 107–110, 112–14, 120–4, 126–34, 136–42, 144, 148, 156–7, 163, 172, 228, 239
Cicero 16, 20
Cithaeron 75, 124, 179
Clymene 108
Clytemnestra 63–5, 68, 215, 222–5, 231
Colchis 50, 201, 248, 299
cold imagery 282–4, 286, 289–90
confusion
  of physical order 15–16, 23–4, 118, 129–30, 133, 136–7, 145–6, 148, 151, 156, 159–60, 165, 222, 231
  of divine order 15, 29, 34–5, 73, 107–8, 114–15, 133, 136–7, 141, 149, 182–3, 233
  of rhetoric of vice and virtue 16–17, 23, 26–40, 43–9, 52–6, 59, 63, 67–8, 71, 85–90, 98–9, 115–18, 144–6, 227, 231–2, 235–6

Corinth 23, 40, 58, 76, 151–2, 180–1, 201, 204, 282
Corydon 266
Creon 36–41, 46–7, 154–5, 164, 188, 192, 201
Crete 51, 260, 262, 264, 270, 272, 300
Creusa 58, 72, 150, 156–7, 168, 202–3
Cupid 293–5, 300

Daedalus 229, 259
Danaids 34
Daphne 294
Daphnis 282
Dardanus 219
declamation 16, 19, 41–2
Deianira 17, 60–2, 68–71
Deiphobus 216, 218–19
Demetrius Poliorcetes 19
Diana 74, 204, 262, 265, 269–72, 275, 279, 282, 291, 293–4, 297–8
Dido 106, 152, 168, 216, 263, 270–2, 296
Diomedes 248, 251
Dionysus, *see* Bacchus
Dis 73, 116, 216
Discordia 209

eating, as image of viewing 210–11
ekpyrosis 18
Electra 224
elegy 194 n. 34, 199, 264–6, 271, 276, 279–80, 282–5
Empedocles 159
Endymion 263, 295
Epicurus 20, 23, 77, 95, 98, 102, 235 n. 115
Ethiopia 108, 120
Euphorion 283

General Index

Euripides 33, 104, 107–9, 111, 120, 122–4, 126, 130, 151, 175, 203–6, 208 n. 58, 240, 260–1, 266, 271, 275, 284
Eurydice 157, 161, 163, 282, 286

Fate 66, 83, 91, 150, 175, 248
　as prescripted narrative 46, 51–2, 95–7, 101–2, 259–60, 294–5, 300
　Stoic presentation of 23, 86–7, 129, 150, 254 n. 156
fire imagery 17–18, 59–64, 66–70, 151, 169
flood 18, 109, 112, 155, 169–71
fortune 16–17, 21–2, 38–9, 45, 49, 53, 57, 84, 96–7, 102, 252, 254
Freud, Sigmund 55, 177 n. 9
Furia 75, 77, 91, 104, 117, 128–39, 146–8, 152, 185
Furies 16, 33–4, 37, 47, 73, 104–6, 116–17, 122–3, 145, 148–9, 151–3, 160, 166, 203, 214, 217, 224, 227–8, 231, 247, 251

Galatea 266
Gallus 283–4, 288
ghosts, see Achilles (ghost), Hector (ghost), Tantalus (ghost), Thyestes (ghost)
giants 29, 35, 112, 118–20, 125, 129, 136
gladiators 116 n. 31, 173, 223, 254–7
gods
　divine soul of Stoic *sapiens* 25, 28
　see also confusion of divine order, Olympian

Golden Age 104–5, 109–112, 114, 119–20, 126–9, 148, 154–5, 159, 167–8, 172, 262–4, 267, 287–8, 290–3, 298–300

Hamlet 51
Harpagus 190–1
Hecate 72
Hector (ghost) 90, 93–5, 97–8, 216, 218, 244–7, 249, 251, 258
Hecuba 39, 90, 99–100, 102, 208, 242, 250, 252–3, 257
Hercules 17, 32–6, 47, 60–2, 68–71, 73–4, 76–81, 84, 93–4, 104, 107–8, 110–20, 126–7, 131, 140, 152–3, 160–3, 220
Hesperus 263, 286
Hippolytus 44, 60, 69–71, 104, 214, 260–72, 274–80, 282, 284–301
Hitchcock, Alfred 195
Homer 65, 92, 121, 271, 288
Horace 81, 141–6
humour, *see* wit
Hyginus 109
Hylas 157
Hymen 203

Ida 35
imagery 17–18; *see also* chariots, cold imagery, eating as image of viewing, fire imagery, water imagery, storm
India 167
Iole 68
Iphigenia 64, 92, 95, 101
Iphis 259, 263
isolationism, Stoic 16–17, 19–21, 42–3, 53–5
Ister 167, 282
Itys 197, 212

General Index

Jason 16, 22–3, 27, 37–41, 56, 104, 139, 148, 150, 154–5, 180–4, 192–3, 202–6, 208, 210, 220, 249, 259
Jocasta 23–4, 82, 86, 179–80, 205
Juno 33, 36, 61, 66–8, 72–81, 84, 106–8, 112, 114–20, 126–7, 131–2, 140, 150, 152–3, 161, 218–19, 224–5, 270
Jupiter 18–19, 33, 35, 69, 72–3, 78, 106–7, 109–12, 114, 118–19, 133, 136, 152–3, 167, 255

king, *see* tyrants

Laius 177
landscape, description of 15, 17–18, 24, 29, 57–71, 78–81, 98, 144–6, 178–9, 246, 263, 266–7, 280–93
Latinus 66, 228, 230
Libya 24–5, 84, 288
limits of criminality surpassed 23, 47, 67, 84, 86, 132, 150–1, 155–7, 166, 182, 186, 227, 231–2, 236, 244–5, 248
Longinus 121–7
Lucan 20–1, 24–8, 41, 59
Lucilius 21, 125
Lucina 72, 203–4
Lucretius 77–8, 94
Lycoris 284
Lycus 16, 31–5, 107, 162, 188

Macbeth 51
madness as hallucination 77–9, 83–4, 93–4
mad rationality 84–90; *see also* confusion of rhetoric of vice and virtue
Maenalus 283

magic 105, 148, 153, 157–60, 165, 169, 299
Manilius 158–60
Manto 176
martyrdom 16, 27, 39, 86, 98–9, 254–6
Medea 15–17, 22–3, 25, 27, 34, 36–41, 44–8, 55–6, 59–60, 68, 72, 84, 103–6, 139, 148–57, 160, 162–5, 168–70, 174, 180–4, 186, 191–3, 201–6, 208–10, 213–14, 219–20, 223–5, 232, 245, 259–60, 269, 277, 298–301
Megara 32–4, 47, 79, 160–2
Meleager 165
Messana 169
metadrama 46, 50–1, 57, 95, 101–2, 157–69, 172–258
Minerva, *see* Pallas
Minos 78, 272
Mycenae 217–18
Myrtilus 137–8, 228

Naiads 293
Nature 105, 151, 155–6, 159–60, 163–5, 169–71, 222, 237, 262, 290, 292, 300–1
    Stoic presentation of 57, 59, 62, 86–7, 169–71
Neptune 67
Nero 20, 188, 191, 266; *see also* Rome
Nessus 61, 69–70
Nietzsche, Friedrich 55

Odysseus 65, 90; *see also* Ulysses
Oedipus 17, 23–4, 81–90, 167, 175–80, 205, 214, 245
Oenomaus 137
Oeta 74, 117

General Index

Olympus, Olympian 33, 35, 37, 47, 67, 73, 79, 118–19, 125–6, 130–1, 133–4, 136–7, 146–7, 152, 162, 239, 295
Olympic games 137–9, 141–2, 144, 147
order, *see* confusion
Orestes 225
Orpheus 156–8, 160–3, 166, 168–9, 282
Ovid 41, 65, 104–5, 107–10, 112–14, 117, 119–20, 128–30, 132–4, 154, 156–7, 162, 164–5, 170, 175, 182, 195–9, 208–9, 212, 257, 259, 263–5, 270–8, 287–8, 293, 297–8, 300

Pallas 65, 67–8, 149
Panaetius 20
Pandion 195, 197
paradoxes, Stoic 16–17, 19, 24–6, 30, 33, 36, 38, 43, 54, 141–2, 243
Paris 221
Parnes, Parnethian 281, 285
Parthenius 283, 285
Parthians 167
Pasiphae 60, 259, 275, 295
Pastor 190–1, 210
pastoral 266–68, 282–5, 293
Pelias 59, 155, 157
Pelops 15, 131, 137, 139, 142, 144, 185
Pentheus 75, 124, 175, 216
Persius 20
Phaedra 42–4, 51–2, 60, 69–71, 214, 259–65, 267–72, 274–80, 282, 284–5, 289–90, 293–301
Phaethon 104–10, 112–14, 119, 121–34, 137–8, 147–8, 156–7, 161, 164, 166, 168–9, 172
phantasia 122–4
Pharsalus 27
Philomela 195–8, 201, 212
Phoebe, *see* Diana
Plato 121, 123–4, 126, 173
Plisthenes 198
politics, *see* Rome
Polynices 179–80
Polyphemus 266
Polyxena 16, 98–101, 72–4, 207–8, 215, 235, 240–1, 247, 250–5, 257–8
Posidonius 20
Priam 42, 44, 92, 98, 218, 246, 252, 257–8
Procne 105, 128, 130, 175, 182, 195, 197–200, 209, 224
Procris 271–4, 279, 282
providence 16, 18
Proserpina 149
Pyramus 263
Pyrrhus 41–2, 44, 76, 91–3, 99–100, 252

Quintilian 20

repetition 64, 86–8, 90–3, 97, 100–2, 140, 152, 154, 196–7, 259–60, 300
repression 128–9, 131–7, 214–15, 218, 230, 236–9
Ripaean 282
Rome 20–1, 26, 188–90
 political colouring of Senecan tragedy 108, 126, 142–3, 246
 political colouring of Seneca's engagement with Virgil's *Aeneid*, 106, 152–3, 167–9, 217–18, 228–30, 242 n. 127, 301
royal power, *see* tyrants

General Index

sacrifice 36, 41, 64, 72, 92, 95, 98, 107, 147, 150, 154, 165, 176, 186, 204, 207–8, 212, 218, 230–7, 241, 244–58
sage, *see sapiens*
sapiens 16–28, 30–40, 43–9, 52–7, 68, 71, 86–90, 110, 129, 141–4, 235
Scaeva 26
Scylla 163–4
Scythia 248, 282, 285, 288
Semele 271
sententiae 16, 41, 49, 232
Shakespeare 51, 194 n. 33
Sibyl 218, 229–30
Siren 157–8, 163–6
Sisyphus 78
slavery 16, 19, 32, 34, 49, 53–4, 56, 98, 254–6, 265
smoke imagery 98
snow, *see* cold
Sophocles 175 n. 7, 249 n. 145
Sparta 54, 255–6, 282
Stilbo 19, 23
Stoicism 16–26, *see also* body, confusion of rhetoric of vice and virtue, fate, fortune, gods, isolationism, martyrdom, paradoxes, providence, *sapiens*, *sententiae*, slavery, suicide, sympathy (cosmic), tyrants
storm 17, 63, 65–8, 100, 227
stage, *see* theatre
Styx 24, 75, 145, 228
suicide 20, 43, 48, 53–4, 80, 88, 191, 205, 248, 250, 255–6, 260
sympathy, cosmic 58, 62
Symplegades 78, 168

Talthybius 240, 242

Tantalus (ghost) 29, 37, 76–7, 104, 128–40, 152, 182, 185, 211, 213–14, 219, 227–8, 230, 235
Tantalus son of Thyestes 43, 234–5
Tereus 128, 175, 182, 195–199, 201, 209, 212–13
theatre, as moralist's metaphor 18, 53–4, 95–7
Thebes 24–5, 32–4, 57, 74, 81, 83, 145, 167, 179–80
Theocritus 266, 282–3
Theseus 42–4, 70, 77, 161, 260–3, 268, 298
Thisbe 263
Thyestes 22–3, 29, 36, 40, 44, 46, 84, 85, 104, 136, 139–41, 144, 150, 181–6, 190–1, 193–5, 198–201, 209–10, 211–14, 226–7, 235, 238, 249, 259
Thyestes (ghost) 64
Tiphys 149, 159, 163, 165
Tiresias 176
Tisiphone 217–18, 228
Tityrus 167
Troy 90, 94, 98, 100–1, 216, 218–19, 225, 230, 242–3, 245, 247, 252–3
tyrants 16–19, 22, 25–41, 44, 47–8, 52–6, 71, 107, 111–12, 141–6, 187–91, 202, 211, 230, 235 n. 115

Ulysses 100–1, 187, 206–7, 241, 243–5, 248–9

Venus 259, 262, 269–71, 276, 286–7, 289–94, 300
Virgil 34, 65–7, 74, 106, 110–12, 116–18, 120, 128, 152–3,

158, 162, 167–9, 209, 216–19, 226, 228–31, 241, 242 n. 127, 246, 263, 266, 270–2, 278, 282–6, 288, 296, 300–1; *see also* Rome

virtue, *see* confusion of rhetoric of vice and virtue

water imagery 17–18, 59–60, 63–8, 151, 169
wit 28, 52, 84, 88, 155, 185–6, 234–5, 237, 249, 251
witch, *see* magic

Zeno 19, 44
Zephyr 287–8